WASHOE COUNTY LIBRARY
3 1235 03232 5503

P9-BJY-151

HO CHI MINH

Ho Chi Minh is one of the towering figures of the twentieth century, considered an icon and father of the nation by many Vietnamese. Pierre Brocheux's biography of Ho Chi Minh is a brilliant feat of historical engineering. In a concise and highly readable account, he negotiates the many twists and turns of Ho Chi Minh's life and his multiple identities, from impoverished beginnings as a communist revolutionary to his founding of the Indochina Communist Party and the League for the Independence of Vietnam, and ultimately to his leadership of the Democratic Republic of Vietnam and his death in 1969. Biographical events are adroitly placed within the broader historical canvas of colonization, decolonization, communism, war, and nation building. Brocheux's vivid and convincing portrait of Ho Chi Minh goes further than any previous biography in explaining both the myth and the man, as well as the times in which he was situated.

Pierre Brocheux is retired Professor of History at Université de Paris VII – Denis-Diderot. His previous publications include *The Mekong Delta: Ecology, Economy and Revolution, 1860–1960* (1995).

Ho Chi Minh

A BIOGRAPHY

Pierre Brocheux
Université de Paris VII – Denis-Diderot

Translated by
Claire Duiker

CAMBRIDGE
UNIVERSITY PRESS

CAMBRIDGE UNIVERSITY PRESS
Cambridge, New York, Melbourne, Madrid, Cape Town, Singapore, São Paulo

Cambridge University Press
32 Avenue of the Americas, New York, NY 10013-2473, USA

www.cambridge.org
Information on this title: www.cambridge.org/9780521850629

Originally published in French as *Hô Chi Minh: Du révolutionnaire à l'icône* by Éditions Payot & Rivages, 2003, and © Éditions Payot & Rivages 2003. First published in English by Cambridge University Press as *Ho Chi Minh: A Biography*, 2007. English translation © Cambridge University Press 2007

Printed in the United States of America

A catalog record for this publication is available from the British Library.

Library of Congress Cataloging in Publication Data

Brocheux, Pierre.
[Hô Chi Minh. English.]
Ho Chi Minh: A biography / Pierre Brocheux; translated by Claire Duiker.
p. cm.
Translation from French.
Includes bibliographical references and index.
ISBN-13: 978-0-521-85062-9 (hardback)
1. Hồ, Chí Minh, 1890–1969. 2. Vietnam – History – 20th century.
3. Presidents – Vietnam (Democratic Republic) – Biography. I. Title.
DS560.72.H6B8313 2007
959.704′092–dc22 2006024898

ISBN 978-0-521-85062-9 hardback

Ouvrage publié avec le concours du Ministére français chargé de la Culture – Centre national du livre.

This book is dedicated to the idealists of the world,
for whom history always ends in disappointment.

Contents

Maps

Foreword

By any measure, Ho Chi Minh was one of the most influential figures of his era. As a prominent member of the international communist movement, he helped to shape the strategy and tactics of the socialist community for nearly five decades. As the founder and leader of the Vietnamese Communist Party, he created a revolutionary organization that first brought an end to three-quarters of a century of French rule in Indochina and then was able to fight the powerful armed forces of the United States to a standstill, leading in 1975 to the unification of his country under communist rule. The process that he set in motion eventually changed the course of the Cold War and had a dramatic impact on American society as well. There are few people of the twentieth century whose life experience is more indelibly printed on his era.

Yet for all his worldwide notoriety, Ho Chi Minh has remained a figure of mystery and controversy. During his lifetime, adversaries and other observers of international politics debated interminably over his true character and intentions. Critics charged that he was a doctrinaire communist who sought to impose a Stalinist gulag on his compatriots. Sympathizers countered that he was a patriot dedicated above all to the reunification of his country and the creation of a society based on self-determination and social justice. At his death in 1969, he was one of the most revered figures in the world, and one of the most reviled.

Ho Chi Minh contributed to such controversy by his own behavior. During a revolutionary career that lasted nearly half a century, he adopted a number of pseudonyms designed to disguise his movements and his real identity from hostile authorities. After becoming president of the Democratic Republic of Vietnam in the fall of 1945 (under the new pseudonym of Ho Chi Minh), he took an obvious delight in covering up his background as a career revolutionary, even from his own people. As a result, today there are still significant gaps that hinder the ability of biographers to trace his life trajectory with any degree of confidence.

Ho Chi Minh was equally adept at disguising his true ideological convictions. Having begun his political career as a fervent Vietnamese patriot, he embraced communism shortly after settling in Paris at the end of World War I. From the outset, however, he was viewed in Moscow as a maverick, arguing that in colonial countries in Asia, national liberation from colonial rule had to take precedence over revolutionary transformation. Ho Chi Minh's dual allegiance to nationalism and social revolution is undoubtedly behind the slippery maneuverings to be all things to all people that he engaged in throughout his adult life. That he was not always successful in his efforts is demonstrated by the persistent charges – from both sides of the ideological spectrum – that he was an opportunist and a hypocrite. Among those who doubted his ideological conviction were no less than his fellow revolutionaries Joseph Stalin and Mao Zedong. It is the daunting and often thankless task of the biographer to penetrate the mask and find the real man inside.

With *Ho Chi Minh: Du révolutionnaire à l'icône*, published by Éditions Payot & Rivages in Paris in 2003, Pierre Brocheux has become the most recent biographer seeking to untangle the complex threads of Ho Chi Minh's life. A respected historian well versed in the modern history of Vietnam, he is supremely qualified to undertake the task. Faced, like his many predecessors, with closed archives in Moscow, Beijing, and Hanoi, as well as Ho Chi Minh's own chronic reticence about personal matters, Brocheux has sensibly refrained from engaging in the kind of psychohistorical speculation that has characterized so many other political biographies in recent years. He is not averse, however, to offering informed judgments on some of the key issues that have provoked debate among students of the Vietnam War. On the central issue of Ho Chi Minh's core political beliefs, for example, he rejects the simplistic extremes of doctrinaire Marxism and simple patriotism, offering instead a balanced portrait of an astute mind capable of weaving together the strands of nationalism and social revolution into a complex political strategy.

Brocheux is equally persuasive in tracing the course of Ho Chi Minh's intellectual development. While conceding that as an adolescent Ho had initially been impressed with the humanistic tradition of the European Enlightenment, he suggests that it was his childhood exposure to Confucian moral and political philosophy – with its emphasis on communal responsibility and the perfectibility of Man – that led him, in the disillusioned years following World War I, to the siren call of Marxism-Leninism. In Ho Chi Minh's eyes, Karl Marx represented the realization of Confucian ideals in a modern historical context. As the author has pointed out, however, the failure in his later years to grasp the pitfalls in Marx's utopian vision was not only a serious blemish on Ho Chi Minh's character but also a tragic event in the modern history of the Vietnamese nation.

In this sensitive and often elegant biography, author Pierre Brocheux manages to bring into sharp relief some of the personal and ideological characteristics that have made Ho Chi Minh one of the most important and influential figures of the twentieth century.

William J. Duiker
The Pennsylvania State University

Preface

This is not the first biography of Ho Chi Minh; others have been published in French, English, and Russian.[1] The American historian Alexander Woodside has thus questioned the validity of and interest in writing another biography while certain periods of the subject's life are still obscure and questions remain about the man even today.[2] Moreover, when the crimes of Stalin and Mao Zedong were brought to light, Ho Chi Minh suffered by association, and he was relegated by some to the ranks of the murderous red tyrants of the twentieth century.

Difficult to categorize, Ho Chi Minh has not been granted the intellectual depth of a political thinker, the creative genius of a writer, or the skill of a military strategist, and so one may question the importance of this "frail Annamite" who rose up to become leader of his people and head of state. What gave rise to the aura that surrounded him from a young age? In what way was he a symbol, deserving a place among the gallery of great men? It is especially hard to answer these questions now, because the man of flesh and blood has become a "man of marble." There are statues of Ho not only in his own country but also in Moscow, where his sculpted figure stands in one of the city squares, as well as in Antananarivo, the capital of Madagascar. And in Thailand, Vietnamese nationals have erected a shrine in his honor in Nachok, near Nakhon-Phanom, which was listed as a national monument by the local authorities in 2003. In his native land, Ho has become an object of veneration, literally, in temples dedicated to village spirits, national heroes, bodhisattvas, and even the Cao Dai.[3]

In addition to the images, rites, and teachings that celebrate and spread his memory, his embalmed body is on display for respectful pilgrims and curious tourists. It is laid out in an oppressive mausoleum that Ho himself had rejected in his Testament. He had wanted his ashes put into urns, to be placed at the four cardinal points of the country.[4] Obviously, then, Communist leaders and his most devout admirers made use of his mortal remains and memorialized him for their own purposes, to serve the state or factional interests.

In Ho Chi Minh's case, the cult of personality – because it truly is a cult – had little or nothing to do with his own wishes but was the work of his entourage. The cult has today been institutionalized, and "Ho Chi Minh thought" has been taught officially in schools since 1997. It was meant to replace the Marxist-Leninist doctrine that fell out of favor after the disintegration of the socialist camp, since communist ideology has now become "localized" or has simply given way to a pragmatism in search of a new doctrinal reference point.

For the last seven years or so, a whole host of works dedicated to Ho Chi Minh – more like monuments than documents – have appeared in Vietnam, complicating the biographer's task even further. The recently opened Soviet archives, specifically those dealing with the Third International (the Comintern), did not provide as much information as historians had hoped. And the crucial documents from the Chinese archives, released only in that language and relatively unknown in Europe, were used by the Chinese to glorify their own role in bringing victory to the Vietnamese Communists in their struggle for national liberation.

We historians dream of a day in the not-too-distant future when we will have free access to the Kremlin archives and the former Soviet security apparatus (the GPU) in Moscow, as well as to the archives in the Ho Chi Minh Institute and the Ho Chi Minh Museum in Hanoi. But for the time being these sources remain closed, or consultation is permitted only after careful screening. Moreover, some aspects of the life of the "Great National Hero" are still off-limits. For example, a few years ago the official state publishing house in Hanoi wanted to publish a translation of the biography by the American historian William Duiker, but only on condition that they delete certain episodes that did not conform to official dogma. The same criticism was leveled at this biography two years later when a translation in Vietnamese was halted because of certain references to Ho's personal life. Both authors refused to comply with the demands for censorship.

ANY HISTORIAN WHO WISHES TO FOLLOW THE TRACKS OF HO CHI MINH IS often frustrated, because the places where he lived and worked have changed and are still changing at a vertiginous pace. In Paris, the Impasse Compoint in the 20th arrondissement was razed to the ground in the 1980s to make room for an apartment complex, and in Moscow, the building that held the famed Stalin School closed its doors long ago. Only the Chinese have preserved the past: There are memorials for the headquarters of the Revolutionary Youth League (Thanh Nien) in Canton and for the liaison office of the 8th Route Army in Nanning, and the museums of Guilin and Nanning have collections tracing the Vietnamese presence in Guangxi province. However, will the city planners of Kunming respect the "Indochina" tea house, home to the Vietnamese Communists where Ho met with the American lieutenant Charles Fenn in March 1945? And along the route from Pac Bo to Liuzhou, where Ho and his comrades set up their revolutionary network of camps and meeting places, the market villages have barely changed over the years, but for how much longer?[5]

This book does not necessarily provide new answers to questions raised by the life of Ho Chi Minh, nor does it defend a reputation that has been darkened by the crimes of Stalinism and Maoism, which tarnished all those fighting for the communist ideal. It is, rather, an attempt to situate the evolution of a man in the twentieth century. Ho Chi Minh had his virtues, illusions, weaknesses, and faults like everyone else; as he once said to his friends, "I am a normal man."

Ho Chi Minh lived in a century that saw not only the confrontation among nations but also the clash and interaction among the world's great civilizations. Thus, from East to West and back again, it is worth following Ho throughout his century. After all, millions of people were making the same journey.

I WOULD LIKE TO THANK EVERYONE WHO SHARED THEIR INFORMATION WITH me: Dao Hung (Hanoi), Do Quang Hung (Hanoi), D. Foulon (Lyon), C. Goscha (Montreal), D. Hémery (Paris), J. Kleinen (Amsterdam), Ngo Manh Lan (Paris), Nguyen Ngoc Giao (Paris), and A. Sokolov (Moscow). Many thanks also to Professors Philippe Devillers (Paris) and Dinh Xuan Lam (Hanoi) who rightly pointed out some errors.

I am grateful to Nicolas Offenstadt and Sophie Bajart (Paris) for having stimulated and encouraged my interest in Ho Chi Minh's life, and to Marie-Martine Serrano (Paris), Marigold Acland, and Isabelle Dambricourt (Cambridge), without whom this English version would not exist. I must not forget Phyllis Berk, who polished up the text during the final phase of this edition. If I have forgotten anybody in this acknowledgment, I beg her or his pardon.

And last but not least, I appreciate very much the careful work of translation by Claire Duiker and the critical attention of William Duiker, as well as his friendly foreword.

Translator's Note

To simplify the difficulties of rendering the tones of the Vietnamese language into English, accents and diacritical marks have been dropped. Vietnamese names are listed in the index by the family name (i.e., Vo Nguyen Giap is under Vo, Ho Chi Minh under Ho).

Many of the works cited from the Vietnamese have not been translated into either French or English. If no translated source is given, the Vietnamese was translated into French by the author, and then rendered into English by the translator. Where translations are available, I have included them in the Bibliography, leaving the original language text and page numbers in the Notes.

Every effort has been made to secure permissions to reproduce copyright material in this work, though in some cases it has proved impossible to trace copyright holders. If any omissions are brought to our notice, we will be happy to include appropriate acknowledgments in reprints or future editions.

As always, I thank my father for his continued help and patience. I am also grateful to my cousin, Kevin Phillips, for his editorial assistance. Uncle Ho has now truly become a part of the family.

Abbreviations

ACRONYMS

AGAS Air Ground Aid Services

ATK An Toan Khu – the "zone of total security"

CAOM Centre des Archives d'Outre-Mer, in Aix-en-Provence, France

CEFEO Corps Expéditionnaire Français en Extrême-Orient

CCP Chinese Communist Party

CGT Confédération Générale du Travail (major French confederation of trade unions)

CLI "Light Intervention Corps"

CPSU Communist Party of the Soviet Union

ICP Indochinese Communist Party

DRV Democratic Republic of Vietnam

EDC European Defense Community

FCP French Communist Party

FSP French Socialist Party

GBT (acronym for L. L. Gordon, Harry Bernard, and Frank Tan)

GPU *Gosudartsvenoïe politicheskoie upravlenic* (Political Police in the Soviet Union, 1922–34)

ICC International Control Commission (set up to supervise the application of the Geneva Accords in Indochina after 1954)

KUTV (Russian acronym for the University of the Toilers of the East [the Stalin School])

MRP People's Republican Movement (or French Christian Democracy)

NEP New Economic Policy

NKVD *Narodnyï Komissariat vnoutrennykh del*, People's Commissariat of Internal Affairs (successor to GPU from 1934 to 1946)

NLF National Front for the Liberation of South Vietnam

OSS Office of Strategic Services

PAVN People's Army of Vietnam

POUM (Spanish) Workers' Party of Marxist Unification

PRC People's Republic of China

ROSTA (Soviet News Agency)

SEAC Southeast Asia Command

SFIC French Section of the Communist International

SFIO French Section of the Workers' International

VCP Vietnamese Communist Party

VNQDD Viet Nam Quoc Dan Dang (National-Democratic Party of Vietnam)

VWP Vietnamese Workers' Party

LITERARY SOURCES

APP Archives de la Préfecture de Police de Paris

BEFEO Bulletin de l'École française d'Extrême-orient

BNTS *Bien nien tieu su*, chronology of Ho Chi Minh's activities

CAOM, Agence FOM Agence de la France d'Outre-mer

CAOM, GGI, CM Gouvernement general de l'Indochine, Commission militaire

CAOM, HCI Haut commissariat en Indochine

CAOM, Indo NF nouveau fonds Indochine

CAOM, RST Résidence Supérieure du Tonkin

CAOM, SLOTFOM Service de Liaison des Originaires des Territoires d'Outre-Mer

CAOM, SPCE Service de Protection du Corps Expéditionnaire

ÉLÉ Éditions en Langues Étrangères, in Hanoi

FLP Foreign Languages Press

MEP Missions étrangères de Paris

NXB Nha Xuat Ban (Publishing House)

NXB CTQG Nha xuat ban chinh tri quoc gia (State Political Publishing House)

QDNZ Quân Dôi Nhân Zân (People's Army, refering to NXB QDNZ: People's Army's Publishing House)

RFHOM, Revue française d'Histoire d'Outre-mer

RHMC Revue d'Histoire Moderne et Contemporaine

RHSGM Revue d'Histoire de la Seconde Guerre Mondiale

SHAT Services Historiques de l'Armée de Terre at Vincennes

ONE

In Search of a Future

One's character is based largely on that of the people with whom one lives. . . . Knowledge opens the mind. . . . Travel also greatly expands the mind; we leave the circle of our nation's prejudices, and are hardly in a position to take on those of another.

– Montesquieu

THE LOST HOMELAND (*MAT NUOC*)

The myth of Ho Chi Minh is multifaceted. One aspect, added long after the man himself had become myth, concerns his family and native region. Funerary monuments have been dedicated to his ancestors, their houses have been restored, his father's family temple has been maintained, and all of these sites have been listed as national memorials.[1] His family saga represents the edifying history of the men and women who symbolized traditional Vietnam. They were faithful to their nation's cultural values and passed them on from generation to generation by transcribing their language and teaching the fundamental Confucian texts.

Both the regional and family backgrounds of Ho Chi Minh suggest a certain geographical and sociological determinism, as well as individual destiny. Nghe An province is known as the forge of great men, from the conventional to the rebellious, and as the theater of historical events that gave birth to a tradition of heroism and sacrifice for the common good.

Ho Chi Minh came from Hoang Tru, which together with six other hamlets comprises the village of Kim Lien. According to a popular saying (*ca dao*), it is

A most pleasant place
Its landscapes immortal. Its inhabitants happy.[2]

And yet, nature has not been kind to the inhabitants of Nghe An. They suffer from an alternating cycle of drought and flooding, as the dry winds rush down from the Annamite mountains (*Truong Son*) or typhoons rise up from monsoons, leading to food shortages and sometimes outright famine. From birth, the men and women of the province are subjected to the dangerous caprices of nature, and so they learn to be frugal.

The area is caught between the sea and the mountains, and the flatness of the landscape is punctuated by hills that once were the stronghold of the resistance against Chinese and French invasions. The ghost of Nguyen Hue (under his royal name, Quang Trung), victorious over the armies of the Manchu Dynasty in the eighteenth century, hovered over these skies, but the villagers of Kim Lien were more attuned to contemporary exploits from their homeland. They remembered the scholar-official Phan Dinh Phung, who resisted the French until his tragic death in 1895. For the parents and grandparents of Ho Chi Minh, he was not just a memory but a real presence to those who looked to the foothills of Truong Son. Some of the villagers had even participated in Phung's "Save the King" movement (*Can Vuong*), which spread throughout northern Annam and Tonkin at the end of the nineteenth century.[3]

Ho Chi Minh was born in 1890 into troubled times.[4] His given name was Nguyen Sinh Cung, but he took the name Nguyen Tat Thanh at age ten, in keeping with Vietnamese custom. The French invaders, faced with stubborn resistance, had just barely managed to conquer the northern provinces of the Kingdom of Vietnam. They had completely taken over the southern part of the nation in 1872 and had established their protectorate over the kingdom of Cambodia in 1863. Then, moving progressively northward along the peninsula, they took control of the rest of Vietnam in the last two decades of the nineteenth century and proceeded to "protect" the Lao principalities that had recently been pried away from Siamese domination.

Nguyen Tat Thanh was fed at his mother's breast and lulled to sleep in a hammock by the songs she hummed while weaving silk. At first he lived in his grandparents' home, then moved nearby with his parents when they acquired a separate house, a modest straw structure with rudimentary furniture. Both sides of his peasant family combined had about 2,500 to 3,000 square meters of land (just over half an acre), which they cultivated for their own subsistence. When Ho returned to his native village in 1957 as President of Vietnam, he pointed out where the jackfruit tree used to be, and the guava, the orange tree, and the areca palm: Their shape, their perfume, and the taste of their fruits retained a hold on his memory.

Official history presents Kim Lien as a haven of community spirit, harmony, and solidarity among families who shared common bonds, many through marriage.[5] Ho's father, Nguyen Sinh Sac (Nguyen Sinh Huy), an orphan, had been adopted and then chosen as son-in-law by a scholar of the village. He began his studies there and then prepared for the civil service examinations required for entry into the imperial bureaucracy. To earn money for his family, Sac taught the children of the village, but it was his wife who put food on the table by working in the fields and weaving silks. She also wove cotton fabrics that she sold in the market or used to clothe her family at the New Year.

Sac's perseverance eventually paid off, and he successfully passed the examinations given in the imperial capital, graduating with the title of *pho bang*, "doctorate, second class" (literally "subordinate list," it was second only to the *tien si* who had passed the palace examinations). He set up a placard in his home bearing the maxim "Good studies will lift you out of poverty" – which he must have looked upon with some satisfaction, if also a bit of frustration. Sac was then thirty-nine years old, and Thanh Thai, the scandalously immoral emperor, had just been deposed.[6]

Nguyen Sinh Sac is a perfect illustration of the possibilities that existed at the time for a humble Vietnamese of rural background to gain access to the official Confucian bureaucracy, sometimes at even the highest level, via the civil service examinations. Traditionally, new graduates would then pursue a career in the bureaucracy, but they could also return to their villages to teach or become writers. The latter option offered a way of maintaining a certain distance from the established power; in the early twentieth century that meant refusing to serve a monarchy under French domination. Sac chose to return to his village. Although inspired by the spirit of resistance, in 1906 he nonetheless accepted the imperial court's invitation to take a government job as subaltern to the Minister of Rites.[7] Was this an act of submission, or did he think that by entering the government he would be able to work for the good of the people without bending to the will of new masters? It is interesting to note that Sac was a close friend of the scholar and nationalist revolutionary Phan Boi Chau, who was also from Nghe An province.[8] In 1905, Chau had wanted Sac to send his youngest son, Thanh, to Japan to train as a freedom fighter, but Sac refused or at least did not follow up on the invitation.

In May 1909, Sac was sent to Binh Dinh province as proctor of the examinations and, while there, was nominated vice magistrate of Binh Khe district, which had just been created. This newly cleared mountainous zone became the subject of land disputes, which sometimes turned to confrontation, leading Sac to remark: "Our country is shipwrecked, but 'they' fight each other for the layout of the low embankments in our rice fields."[9] As vice magistrate, Sac became known as a defender of the lowly and poor against the high and "wicked" – whether indigenous landlords or Catholic missionaries in collusion with French officials – and he soon found himself in low standing with his superiors. Although one report stated that "he is a good employee," others accused him of repeated absences from his office or of freeing prisoners who had protested against the tax system. This revolt of the political center – popularly called the "Revolt of the Short-Hairs" because the demonstrators had cut off the traditional chignon – was part of a larger, nationwide movement (*Duy tan*/modernization, *Minh tan*/enlightenment) that wanted to reform traditional institutions and modernize the country, following the example of Meiji Japan. Sac expressed his support for the demonstrators, and his son, then a student at the Quoc Hoc (National Academy) in Hué, did the same (some even say that Thanh served as interpreter between the demonstrators and the French Résident Supérieur).[10]

Nguyen Sinh Sac's luck ran out in 1910, when his temper got him into serious trouble. He already had a reputation for being quick-tempered, but one day he unleashed his anger against a "tyrannical" landlord, who then appealed directly to the French resident administrator of Quy Nhon in an effort to bypass Sac. Sac then ordered the landlord to be beaten with a wicker switch, and the man died two months later. In May 1910, Sac received a harsh sentence: one hundred lashes with a switch, a demotion of four ranks, and dismissal. Fortunately for him, the punishment was reduced four months later due to his lack of administrative experience and especially because the delay between the beating and the man's death had made Sac's direct responsibility difficult to establish.

After his release from prison, Nguyen Sinh Sac neither requested readmission into the administration nor returned to Kim Lien. Evidently, he could not bear the judgment of the townspeople who, according to custom, had given him a triumphal welcome after he passed his exams. He instead went to South Vietnam where he took a variety of odd jobs, from plantation supervisor to "doctor" to public scribe. Some also said that he fell prey to periodic bouts of mysticism. When someone asked him where he lived, he responded with bitterness, "when the country is lost, how can you have a home?"[11] He died at age 63 on 27 November 1929, in Cao Lanh in the Mekong delta, where he had found shelter and comfort with a family of scholars. The local organization of the Communist Party erected a mausoleum at his burial site in 1977.

Ho Chi Minh's father belonged to a world of scholars and officials who were consumed with dismay and bitterness at the realization that French domination of the Vietnamese monarchy would endure and become even stronger in the early twentieth century. French administrators selected and deposed the Vietnamese monarchs, who were reduced to nothing more than civil servants. They also directed the imperial administration, with the French Résident Supérieur presiding over the Privy Council, and French Résidents stood in for the local mandarin and the magistrates on the provincial level, as Sac knew from personal experience. They also reorganized the educational system, a fundamental pillar of the nation since it nurtured the next generation of mandarin officials.[12] The French restructured the system in such a way that a knowledge of Chinese characters and the Confucian classics was rendered both obsolete and useless. The last examinations were held in 1915, four years before they were definitively abolished. As a result, the old educational system gave way to a Franco-Annamite one that relied on the romanized transcription of the Vietnamese language, called *quoc ngu*.[13]

By the time misfortune struck Sac, he had already lost his wife – who died in 1901 at the age of thirty-three – and his son Nguyen Sinh Xin. Out of gratitude to his mother-in-law, who had sold a portion of her rice field to help him through his doctoral exams, Sac turned down an offer by a mandarin family to wed their young daughter. The family now began to disperse. Sac's daughter, Nguyen Thi Thanh, went back to live in Kim Lien and was soon joined by her older brother. Only Cung, who had taken the name Nguyen Tat Thanh in 1905, went down to Binh Dinh, where he entered boarding school in Quy Nhon. This separation was not uncommon; temporary or permanent migration is common among the Vietnamese, but they still keep an emotional attachment to their homes and families. On the other hand, Nguyen Thi Thanh had testified to the police about her father's irascibility and brutality that she attributed to his penchant for "the bottle" – which might explain the incident at Binh Khe. In the end, when Nguyen Tat Thanh went to visit his father in Binh Khe before leaving for Saigon, Sac greeted him with the words: "Why did you come to see me? When you've lost your country, searching for your father doesn't matter." These words from a father to his son (some say he was the favorite) resonate like those of a desperate man in the throes of *mat nuoc* syndrome. Extreme behavior can often be the expression of pain in heart and soul.

As for the son's perspective, Thanh later wrote two autobiographical accounts, only one of which mentioned his family's past, and that only briefly.[14] Was this his way of suppressing a painful or shameful period in his life?

WHEN NGUYEN TAT THANH HEADED TO SAIGON HE HAD JUST TURNED eighteen. He stopped at Phan Thiet, an area of Annam famous for its fishing and pickling (such as for *nuoc mam* sauce). For several months he worked as a teacher's assistant in a school founded by the reformist scholar Phan Chu Trinh (1872–26), who had graduated as a *pho bang* in the same class as Nguyen Sinh Sac. It was no chance encounter, since Trinh backed the reformation of the monarchy and the mandarinate under the leadership of republican France. Trinh was also a supporter of the "Journey to the West" (*Tay Du*), which drew young Vietnamese away from the "Journey to the East" (*Dong Du*). The latter was supported and organized by Phan Boi Chau, who called out to the younger generation to come and join him in Japan. The young Thanh thought logically. He did not join up with the *Dong Du*, but turned toward the *Tay Du* to learn about the outside world so as not to end up confined within the Asian universe.

Thanh already had a basic understanding of the key concepts of Chinese culture. His father and others had taught him Chinese characters and Confucian morality, but Sac had also wanted his son to receive the rudiments of French culture and so sent him to Franco-Annamite schools in Vinh, Hué, and Quy Nhon, for elementary, middle, and high school education. At one point, Thanh attended the Quoc Hoc (1907–9), the National Academy that trained the sons of mandarins, the court, and other officials. It was at this time that he supposedly became involved in the Revolt of the Short-Hairs against the French regime.

Although he was sometimes mocked by his fellow students, Thanh earned the respect of several teachers for his tireless curiosity, quick wit, maturity, and talent for writing. One of his French teachers, Mr. Queinnec, returned a paper with this glowing praise: "Thanh wrote his paper on the writing of verse; he is an intelligent and very distinguished student."[15] As a teenager he enjoyed the history lessons of a Mr. Griffon, who gave fascinating lectures glorifying the French Revolution.

Thanh especially admired two of his teachers, the scholar Hoang Thong, who later ran into trouble with the authorities, and the artist Le Van Mien. Thong helped him with his Chinese characters and introduced him to the "New Writing" of the Chinese and Vietnamese modernist scholars, as well as Chinese translations of the works of Jean-Jacques Rousseau and Montesquieu. Mien spoke to him of Paris where, as a scholarship student at the École Coloniale (Colonial School), he had arranged to continue his studies at the École Supérieure des Beaux-Arts. He described a nation of people who were different from the French in Indochina, a society that had its humble and poor, where at nightfall old men rummaged through garbage cans and young women prostituted themselves to survive. Mien explained that both commoner and elite looked down on disreputable Vietnamese, but admired and respected those who were dignified, educated, or talented, and added that racial discrimination among the French was rare. He described the museums in Paris, which were rich in classical antiquities and works of art, as well as the libraries where books about revolution and the birth of nations were neither limited nor prohibited.[16] In France, the words "Liberty, Equality, Fraternity" had real meaning.

It is fair to say, then, that before embarking on a ship to France in 1911, Nguyen Tat Thanh was mentally prepared. He had a plan for the future but was not locked into it, and was determined to discover the world and make his own destiny. In 1946, he told the American journalist David Schoenbrun, "Do we know what it means to be a man? Do we really know ourselves? Our parents give us a name and tell us about where we come from. That doesn't matter. What really matters is where we are going."[17] Undoubtedly, Nguyen Tat Thanh was sensitive to the currents of change in Asian culture, and he had a strong will. As a young man he fell in love with his landlord's daughter in Saigon and faced a dilemma: Should he choose his individual destiny over the fate of the collective, or vice versa? Should he satisfy the desires of the heart, raise a family, and put down roots in his homeland? Or should he leave in order to train himself and then return to help his country? He made his choice.

LOOKING FOR ANSWERS: 1911–1917

> Born in somber times, from my earliest childhood, I lost my homeland.
> Before the sky and the earth I was ashamed of living among slaves.
> My heart is sickened to feel my still fragile wings, but boldly I took flight.
>
> – Phan Boi Chau

Whether he was beginning a voyage of initiation or just running away, Nguyen Tat Thanh was neither the first nor the last to board a ship to see the world. Before the West had begun its conquest of the world, seventeenth- and eighteenth-century travelers from China, Japan, Vietnam, and Siam had gone to Europe on diplomatic and other missions.[18] By the nineteenth century, imperialist expansion was in full swing, and then the world was forever changed by the opening of the Suez Canal, the invention of the steamship, and the laying of underground telegraphic cables that encircled the globe as if completing Magellan's voyage.

Countries around the world were opening up to outside influences, leading to economic, political, and cultural change and an unprecedented migration of peoples. In Asia a wave of contractual laborers (mainly Indian and Chinese) flowed to Europe to replace the African slave trade, but others had to yield to imperial power, beaten but not broken. Many Japanese, Chinese, Vietnamese, Javanese, and Indians headed to Europe and the United States to discover the secret of Western superiority.[19]

The Journey to the West (*Tay Du*) gave birth to other groups that encouraged learning, like those that had flourished in China since the end of the nineteenth century, and many young people left to study and/or work abroad. Some left alone, but most went in groups; if they were poor they would seek employment on ships or stow away with the help of fellow countrymen working on board.

At the time of Thanh's departure in 1911, Saigon was the terminus of two French shipping lines with regular service between Europe and the Far East: Messageries Maritimes and Chargeurs Réunis. This modern port was growing fast. The city of 1910 was not yet the "Pearl of the Far East," which grew out of the urban and architectural development of the 1920s, but it was still a European-style city clustered around an impressive center of monumental buildings (the palace of the Governor-General and the Governor of Cochinchina, the cathedral, City Hall, the Hall of Justice, the Customs House, the military barracks). And it looked nothing like the small towns familiar to Thanh, like Vinh, Quy Nhon, and Phan Thiet. In 1907, the city of Saigon, combined with the Chinese section of Cholon, had some 250,000 inhabitants, including 7,000 French nationals. Even Hué, with its "palaces that look like tombs and tombs that look like palaces" – in the words of the journalist Andrée Viollis, author of *Indochine S.O.S.* (1935) – had shown nothing new to the young man from Nghe An.

In Saigon, Nguyen Tat Thanh took his first steps in a westernized setting. He discovered the electric light and ice cream, but also noted that a civilization known for its scientific and technological advancement also forced others to bend under its power. He would go down to the port looking for a ship bound for France, and one day had the nerve to walk aboard the *Amiral Latouche-Tréville* of the Chargeurs Réunis company and ask if they had a job for him. The captain was skeptical at the sight of this young man with the intelligent face and frail body, but took him on as chef's assistant. On the morning of 5 June 1911, the ship cast off, carrying with it the man who now called himself Van Ba.

The crossing was rough due to monsoons in the Indian Ocean, but Ba managed it well, working hard during the day carrying buckets of coal, peeling vegetables, washing dishes, and scrubbing the kitchen. He learned to eat bread, beef, and potatoes and how to use a spoon and fork instead of chopsticks. Later, he remembered conversations on board with the engineer Bui Quang Chieu, who had known his father, Nguyen Sinh Sac, and was traveling in first class with his own son. But more than this, Ba recalled the friendships he made with two French colonial soldiers who had been demobilized and were returning to France. They loaned him books and helped him with his French, a language he was far from mastering, while he slipped them cups of coffee. He confided to the Vietnamese chef: "Some Frenchmen are okay, eh, brother Mai?"[20]

Ba disembarked in Marseilles with ten francs in his pocket and discovered some wondrous things. There were pleasant surprises, like riding on the tramway ("the house that moves electrically") and being addressed as "monsieur" in a café. But occasionally he was scandalized, taking offense when prostitutes came on board to ply their trade. These mixed images led him to form a more positive opinion of the French on the Continent, who did not behave like those in the colonies. And yet, since they had their own loose women and hoodlums, he wondered: "Why don't the French civilize their own people instead of trying to civilize us?" This mention of civilization shows that Thanh was already imbued with a notion of cardinal importance in Sino-Vietnamese wisdom. At the same time, he seemed to grant a superiority to European civilization.

After Marseilles he went to Le Havre, where he worked briefly as an assistant gardener for a rich bourgeois family with a Vietnamese valet among their household staff. Ba improved his French with the help of a "young and pretty" servant girl and befriended the chef, who was temperamental but "a good person." The chef sometimes made him the same dishes that he cooked for their boss, and Ba greatly appreciated their friendship. But he did not settle in for long. As soon as his boss told him about a cargo ship ready to sail, he hurried to find work as cabin steward and waiter in the officers' wardroom.

Before leaving Marseilles, however, he sent a letter to the President of the Republic of France seeking admission to the École Coloniale. Primarily a school for training future administrators of the colonies, it also accepted a contingent of students from the colonies on scholarships. The latter, in exchange, had to serve the colonial administration. When news of this letter came to light years later, many people saw it as proof that in 1911 the young Thanh had not yet sketched out the path he was later to follow. To some, he was taking advantage of the resources offered by the French Republic in order to penetrate the "enemy" fortress, while to others, he was hoping to become a colonial official in order to rehabilitate his father. None of these opinions, however, take into account the influence of Thanh's former teacher, Le Van Mien, whose experience surely had an impact on Thanh's decisions.[21]

Ba spent another two years at sea before making a long stop in England. During this time, from late 1911 to 1913, he visited Dunkirk, made a brief stop back in Saigon, then continued on to Bordeaux, Lisbon, Tunis, Dakar, the ports of East Africa, Reunion Island, and as far as the Congo, observing the life of the people in every port. From there he went to North America, but did not record precise details on the length of his stay nor on his activities while in the United States. He completed his journey in England after having seen the Antilles, Mexico, and South America.

Nguyen Tat Thanh's observations during those two years of wandering reinforced what he knew about colonial regimes, as he witnessed the oppression suffered by Arabs, Africans, and the blacks of the United States. It was in the United States, in fact, that he noticed the most flagrant contradiction between great idealistic principles and the actual condition of people of color, who were subjected to segregation, denied civil rights, and lived under the constant threat of lynching. He saw how England, the largest colonial empire in the world, harshly suppressed Ireland's quest for independence. Here was a people who would take up arms in 1916 (right in the middle of World War I) yet were fair-skinned. He wrote that he cried upon learning of the death of the Mayor of Cork, McSwiney, who had been condemned by the British to two years in prison and who languished in agony for seventy-four days during a hunger strike. Thanh saw clearly the stark difference between theory and practice, and especially how even the most liberal democracies tolerated both racism and colonialism. These experiences led him later to relativize the "dictatorship of the proletariat" and, by consequence, the Stalinist regime.

Thanh demonstrated a deep sympathy for the "obscure, the underlings," for the oppressed, the humiliated, and, of course, resistance fighters. His travels showed him misery and oppression throughout the world, not just in Vietnam. Internationalism – even proletarian – was neither new nor strange to one who had read Confucius: "All men are brothers across the four oceans." He had also read Christ's teaching on the brotherhood of man and knew of the Buddha's call for human compassion. While working as a busboy in the restaurant of the Carlton Hotel in London, Thanh came to the attention of Auguste Escoffier when he gave leftover food to the poor instead of throwing it away. He won the esteem of this famous French chef, who promoted him to chef's assistant with a higher salary. According to Thanh's account, Escoffier even suggested that he "drop [his] revolutionary ideas" to learn the art of cooking.

It is true that these travel accounts come almost exclusively from Thanh's own autobiographical writings, but they reveal something of his moral character.[22] He was thirsty for knowledge, and spent all of his free time on board ship reading, writing, working on his French, and learning English, while his friends spent their time sleeping, playing cards, or getting drunk. Not content with simply being cultivated, he wanted to educate others, starting with his own Vietnamese acquaintances. Many of them were illiterate and unschooled, and so Thanh taught them to read and write *quoc ngu* and urged them to behave so as not to tarnish the image of Vietnam and the reputation of its people. A certain cook who usually spent his salary on games of chance and loose women, for example, thanked Thanh for teaching him, for helping him save money, behave with dignity, and rid his speech of foul language.

One should not see these accounts as mere products of an iconography, as edifying inventions, inasmuch as Ho Chi Minh later behaved in exactly the same manner. His conduct was the same as communist leader and as President of the Democratic Republic of Vietnam, with his own people or with foreigners, and with his followers as with his adversaries. In any case, while some followed his example, others did not, a sign that maybe he placed the bar a bit too high.

RADICALIZATION: 1917–1923

In late 1917 (some say 1919), Nguyen Tat Thanh crossed the English Channel and settled in Paris, where he found the scholar Phan Chu Trinh, as well as his friend and mentor Phan Van Truong, who was practicing law there.[23] The three worked together until Thanh left for Moscow in 1923. The correspondence between Thanh and Trinh from 1913 to 1917, while the former was still in London, shows that they monitored "news from home" but also the global situation. When war was declared in 1914, Thanh had written to Trinh:

> Gunfire rings out through the air and corpses cover the ground. Five great powers are engaged in battle. Nine countries are at war. . . . I think that in the next three or four months the destiny of Asia will change dramatically. Too bad for those who are fighting and struggling. We just have to remain calm.[24]

Thanh could see that Old Europe would exhaust its strength in the conflict. Later, he understood that he had to go to France in order to take the pulse of the world and of his country.

Indeed, between 1915 and 1919, there were 49,180 Indochinese workers, 42,922 Indochinese infantrymen, and an equal number of Chinese workers and student workers present in Europe, studying or working at the front lines in northern France. Then in February 1917, the Russian Revolution erupted, overthrowing the absolute monarchy and opening a breach that allowed the Bolsheviks to take power in October, while the West was crippled by workers' strikes and revolts. Meanwhile, two events in Indochina greatly worried the French: In 1916, Emperor Duy Tan, whom the French had placed on the throne of Annam in place of Thanh Thai, agreed to lead an uprising in the central provinces; and in 1917, inmates at the Thai Nguyen prison, in collusion with the wardens and the Garde Indigène, rebelled and took over the city. Both revolts came to nothing, but they were a sign that the pacification was fragile and that the spirit of resistance was just below the surface.[25]

These two close calls posed no risk to the French, but victory over Germany and the Austro-Hungarian Empire in World War I had left France badly drained: 1,310,000 dead and missing and 388,000 wounded, sapping a nation whose low population was already striking compared to that of its European neighbors. The greatest material losses were felt in the industrial centers, but also in the agricultural regions in northern and eastern France. In those regions, three million hectares (7.4 million acres) of land had become contaminated due to the bombings. Recovery seemed an impossible task. "Germany will pay!" Clemenceau announced, but French leaders undoubtedly thought of their resources in the colonial empire, and must have been happy to know they were there.

Expatriates from Asia (especially the Indochinese) offered fertile soil for political dialogue. Ho Chi Minh later said that this was his primary reason for going to France, but there was undoubtedly another reason for waiting until 1917 to cross the English Channel: In 1914, Phan Chu

Trinh and Phan Van Truong, who had founded a Vietnamese friendship group, were incarcerated in Santé Prison in Paris on suspicion of preparing an uprising, in collusion with Germany, against France's domination in Indochina. They were liberated in 1915 through the intervention of friends, including Commander Jules Roux and Marius Moutet, as well as the League of Human Rights.[26] But Trinh prudently abstained from any political demonstrations until the end of the war, and because the government stopped paying him an allotment when he was arrested, he found work retouching photographs, a skill he later passed on to Thanh.

After the Great War was over, the three men returned to their anticolonialist activities. Their most audacious act came in June 1919 when Thanh presented a petition to the Allied leaders at the Versailles conference, entitled *Demands of the Annamite People*.[27] Drafted by Thanh with the help of Phan Chu Trinh and written down by Phan Van Truong, the petition asked for autonomy, equal rights, and political freedom for the Vietnamese. The document was signed Nguyen Ai Quoc – Nguyen the Patriot – the name adopted by Nguyen Tat Thanh, who had it changed officially in the record books. Thus began a new stage in his life.

In July 1920, in an effort to facilitate their meetings as well as save money, Nguyen Ai Quoc moved in with Phan Van Truong at number 6, Villa des Gobelins, in the 13th arrondissement of Paris.[28] By then, the police had made the connection between Nguyen Tat Thanh and Nguyen Ai Quoc and had him "tailed" by the informers "Jean," "Édouard," and "Marcel," three Vietnamese who had moved into his entourage. Thanks to them, we have complete reports of Quoc's activities down to the last detail, sometimes hour by hour.

From the moment he set foot on French soil, Quoc was involved in political debate. In fact, he repeatedly claimed that his almost exclusive goal was the liberation of peoples subjected to colonialism of any sort. In his tireless pursuit of the anticolonialist struggle, he moved progressively toward more radical positions, finally adhering to the communist revolutionary venture proposed by the Russian Bolsheviks. The turning point in this evolution came around 1920, but some reports go back a year earlier. According to a report by agent Édouard (dated 20 December 1919), Nguyen Tat Thanh believed that the reforms of colonial institutions proposed by Albert Sarraut, Governor-General of Indochina, were weak and limited, that they would have no effect on the living conditions of the Vietnamese people, and that colonized peoples lived in scorn and humiliation. This situation would not change so long as the colonial regime and all French personnel in the colonies continued to dominate the indigenous peoples.[29]

Shortly after his arrival in France, Quoc founded a Vietnamese network, the Association of Annamite Patriots, with Phan Chu Trinh and Phan Van Truong. He also worked with Koreans who were fighting against the Japanese colonial regime, and he established relations with the Irish. He became a member of the French Socialist Party, which he considered the embodiment of the ideals of the French Revolution, and which, after the immediate postwar crisis, saw its numbers increase dramatically. The values of Liberté, Égalité, Fraternité continued to nourish his hopes; perhaps he was credulous enough to take the words literally, or else some naïveté led him to believe in the immediate application of great philosophic principles and moral values. In a way, he was like the student protestors of the 1960s who wanted "everything, right now."

Nguyen Ai Quoc was quickly disenchanted. He realized that the colonial question was neither a priority nor very important for the socialists, who were more preoccupied with the struggle between socialism and capitalism. For example, it was in the early 1920s that the workers' unions (especially the railway workers) began their large-scale strikes. What is more, the socialists did not agree on colonial policy. Some still held to the ideas of Paul Louis put forth in his pamphlet *Le Colonialisme* (1905), but Louis was not a moderate like Jean Jaurès. More similar to Rosa Luxembourg and the leftists of social-democratic Germany, Louis presented an analysis of colonialism that resembled that of Marx. (As it happens, Quoc was a member of the Ninth Section of the SFIO – the French Section of the Workers' International, the Second International – in Paris at the same time as Paul Louis and the Russian émigré Boris Souvarine.) Most socialists, however, envisaged a humanist type of colonialism that would usher in modern civilization and progress. When Quoc asked his "friend Jean Longuet"[30] to explain Marxist doctrine to him, he was told, "Read *Das Kapital*." Quoc hurried to the library in the 13th arrondissement and borrowed the book. He later admitted that he used it as a pillow.

DURING THE WAR, FRANCE'S COLONIAL EMPIRE HAD "GIVEN" ITS SONS to the motherland – like the famous "Black Force" of Senegal – as well as its resources in the form of raw materials and foodstuffs. Between 1914 and 1918, some 267,000 North African soldiers and 211,359 Senegalese infantrymen went to fight on French soil.[31] On 7 July 1921, a sports competition in honor of the Senegalese troops was organized in the Tuileries

Garden to remind France of the debt it owed them, but also to show the loyalty of the colonized toward the "Great Motherland."

These events undoubtedly created "the imperial illusion": "Great France" bestowing the benefits of civilization on all of her sons, thereby compensating for the crimes of her conquest and domination. In fact, what the historian Raoul Girardet calls "the colonial conscience" had penetrated the minds of the French people in the 1920s, sparking either approval of or opposition to colonialism. After the end of World War I, the growth and intensification of economic and cultural relations between France and its colonies (like Citroën's "Yellow Cruise") raised public interest in the nations of the empire. Certain events ushered in this colonial conscience, like the first exhibition of "Negro art" in Paris in 1919, the creation of a Literary Prize for Colonial Literature, and the awarding of the Goncourt Prize in 1921 to an Antillean writer, René Maran.

Indeed, the Colonial and Maritime League was born this same year to popularize "greater France." At the same time, the League of Human Rights opened a colonial section to handle "colonial abuses" – the term itself revealing a fundamental acceptance of the status quo. Then in 1925, high schools and universities began to teach colonial history and geography, and a group of surrealist writers and artists spoke out against colonialism. These events culminated with the Exposition coloniale internationale, inaugurated in 1930 in the Vincennes park. The Orient, in the widest sense of the term, had always held an attraction for European intellectuals who deplored the spiritual void of Western civilization and felt that they could rediscover their spirituality in India or China. So far as these facts enhanced the influence of imperialism, they exemplified what Raoul Girardet called "a gradual process of integration of colonialist ideology into the national psyche."[32]

In step with the new trend in colonial affairs and growing interest in the empire, Albert Sarraut, formerly Governor-General of Indochina on two occasions (1911–14 and 1916–19), was appointed Minister of Colonies by the government of Prime Minister Aristide Briand, which took office in January 1921. Sarraut envisaged a wide-ranging economic development project for the colonies, and to gain support from Parliament and the public, he published an essay in 1923, entitled "La Mise en valeur des colonies françaises" (The development of the French colonies). He hoped to carry out this project while continuing his policy of close association with indigenous peoples working for France, for he wanted to stress the moral and humanitarian dimension of colonial conquest over the "primitive act of force." His project was advanced by Louis Arnoux, an official in charge of the surveillance of colonial émigrés in France, who set up a meeting between Sarraut, the apostle of empire, and the new symbol of Vietnamese patriotism: Nguyen Ai Quoc accepted the invitation to meet with the minister face-to-face, and spoke frankly about his feelings and his goal – the liberation of his country – showing a quiet audacity, which he would display again on future occasions.

Later, Quoc complained to a compatriot (identified as one of the three "close" informers) that the Vietnamese did not come to his meetings on revolution, and added:

> You accuse me of being violent but what have you done, any of you, that was even moderate in the last five years? No one knows that Annam exists. We need something messy, maybe even some silly mistakes [provocations], so people learn who I am [to draw the attention of the public and the authorities]. If somebody asks me where the revolutionaries are, I will tell them that they are the twenty million people over there who cry out every day but who have been completely silenced. Anyway, what can they do about me? Put me in prison, deport me, cut off my head, I don't care.[33]

He then announced that he was writing a book on colonial oppression. Published in 1925, it was called *Le Procès de la Colonisation Française* (French colonialism on trial).

Quoc showed the same conviction and belligerence with a senior official at the Ministry of Colonies (notably Pierre Pasquier, later Governor-General of Indochina), who had called him in to lecture him. But Quoc was just as categorical in his discussions with Phan Chu Trinh, who told him to trust the French Republic to reform their "Annamite" institutions and modernize their country. Later, when Quoc began to speak at the Congress of the FSP in Tours, the Socialist deputy Jean Longuet interrupted him and said that he, too, had spoken on behalf of the natives. Quoc, with calm self-assurance, cut him off with "Silence, the Parliamentarians!"

Quoc, who had joined the FSP in 1919, was soon impatient and angry at the way colonial oppression was underestimated, or even downright ignored – intentionally by some.[34] These contradictions were exacerbated by other debates, which divided the Socialists, especially the FSP's adherence to the Third International, recently established by Lenin in Moscow. Quoc leaned toward those within the party who were fighting for adherence to the new International, like Marcel Cachin and Paul Vaillant-Couturier.

The Bolsheviks had taken power in Russia in November 1917 (October of the Julian calendar). In 1919, with Lenin at their head, they founded the Third International, denouncing the ineffectiveness of social democracy against the "imperialist war" and the "failure of the Second International." They labeled their organization "communist" to distinguish it from the previous socialist entity, and presented it as the force for world social revolution in the twentieth century. The founding congress opened on 2 March 1919 in Moscow, while "soviet" movements were being crushed in Eastern Europe. The social revolution remained active, however, maintaining its strength even as the Soviet nation was beset by civil war and the intervention of allied troops. The Communist International (Comintern) was both a political and symbolic gesture, created to organize the forces of global social revolution and to take advantage of the store of sympathy for the Russian Revolution. The historian François Furet called this "the universal charm of October," which was a palpable force in the world at that time.[35] Social-democratic parties were already divided on the question of war and peace, and were now further split into factions, some of which called for adherence to the new International.

Although Nguyen Ai Quoc could not get through Marx's *Das Kapital*, he now discovered Lenin's "Theses on the National and Colonial Questions," presented in June 1920 at the Second Congress of the Comintern. Lenin stated that the colonial and national question was one of the principal stakes in Bolshevik revolutionary strategy, and that the revolutionary path could lead to global liberation. Quoc hoped that revolution would be an alternative to the slow and legal path of reforms, and to dependence on the great powers to decide the fate of the world, often against the will of the people involved. Lenin stressed the failure of Woodrow Wilson's "Fourteen Points," specifically the one affirming a people's right to self-determination. This must have reminded Quoc of his bitter experience at the Versailles peace conference, which he had left empty-handed, and of his contact with the French government, who had turned a deaf ear to him. It was at Versailles that Quoc had gotten his first lesson in realpolitik, and realized that the "powerful" were redesigning the map of the world and deciding the fate of other nations. Even in the Far East, Korea was still a Japanese colony, and Japan controlled the German settlement and interests in Qingdao, against the will of the Chinese.

In December 1920, the Eighteenth Congress of the FSP was held in Tours, and Nguyen Ai Quoc made a solemn appeal to French Socialists "of the left and of the right," that "the Socialist Party must act effectively in favor of the oppressed natives." He hoped to see in the "Party's joining the Third International the promise that from now on it will attach to the colonial questions the importance they deserve."[36] Quoc, the "delegate from Indochina" (though he had no mandate from any socialist organization), voted for adherence to the Third International because it placed the liberation of colonized peoples on the agenda:

> I didn't understand what you said about strategy, proletarian tactics, and other points. But there is one thing that I understood clearly: The Third International is interested in the problem of liberating the colonies. . . . As for the Second International, it is not concerned about the colonial question.[37]

This majority vote led to the founding of the French Communist Party, or the French Section of the Communist International. Socialism in France had set a new course, and with it, the Vietnamese Nguyen Ai Quoc sailed on to new horizons. In a burst of proselytizing, Quoc initiated five Chinese student workers into the new FCP.[38]

FROM 1921 TO 1923, NGUYEN AI QUOC DEVOTED HIMSELF TO THE liberation of his country, but he also wanted to help other nations in their struggle against French domination. He was asked to participate in the FCP's colonial commission, and in the spring of 1921 created the Intercolonial Union, an organization outside of the FCP that he established with other foreign nationals. In April 1922, they began publishing a weekly journal, *Le Paria*, and Quoc was one of its main contributors, with twenty-one articles to his credit. He also became the illustrator, providing drawings and caricatures for the journal, and was one its most active distributors. A number of his comrades from those days went on to make a name for themselves in the political sphere.[39]

An interesting group of people collaborated on *Le Paria*; they were representatives of a political generation following a similar course. The journal was published as a joint effort by the League for French Citizenship Rights for Madagascar Natives (1920) and the Association of Annamite Patriots. Jean Ralaimongo (1884–1943), a young Malagasy slave who was liberated by the French and became a teacher, saw colonialism as an evolutionary process and fought for "mass naturalization." He volunteered for the army in 1917 and helped found the Communist Party of Madagascar. His compatriot Samuel Stéphany (1890–1939), a teacher and then a lawyer (1922–32), enlisted in 1916 as a volunteer on the eastern front and survived a gas attack in Serbia. He was a Socialist but joined the majority of the party that founded the FCP at the Tours Congress, and was cofounder of the Intercolonial Union and managing director of *Le Paria*. Henri Charles Sarrotte, from Martinique, was a veteran of World War I and originally a Socialist who then founded the FCP's Commission for

Colonial Studies with Stéphany. There he met Max Clainville Bloncourt, a lawyer from Guadeloupe (whose brother, the teacher Élie Bloncourt, was blinded at the Aisne front during the war and became a Socialist deputy), who was also a cofounder of the Intercolonial Union and member of the FCP.[40]

These men from the colonial empire believed in the ideals of the French Revolution and aspired to full French citizenship within the Republic; some were driven by anticolonialist convictions and gravitated toward the communism of the Third International. This circle of some 150 men undoubtedly inspired strong feelings of solidarity and brotherhood in Quoc. They were all transplants whose common denominator was the struggle against the colonial regime and for whom *Le Paria* was their converging point and their forum. Several years later, when Ho Chi Minh learned of Ralaimongo's death, he was "very moved, with tears in his eyes. And his voice tremble[d]." He explained: "Ralaimongo was a model of courage and optimism for me.... It was Ralaimongo who animated the group and when we were dying of hunger, Ralaimongo worked as a porter at Les Halles to buy us bread. Since then I have never forgotten him."[41]

DURING THE GREAT WAR, THE FRENCH HAD BEGUN TO EXPLOIT THE resources of their colonial empire, and the postwar period saw a notable rise in economic development, giving Nguyen Ai Quoc ample fodder for denouncing colonialism. Indeed, Indochina had been used for its human "cannon fodder," as well as for its manual labor during the war. The French government's wartime loans surpassed 167 million francs between 1915 and 1920, and the sale of war bonds came to 13,816,117 francs. The colony had to ensure the wages, pensions, and family benefits for the Indochinese who had been mobilized, as well as pay the expenses of the Indochinese Military Hospital, adding up to 4,040,000 francs sent to France in 1917 and 1918.[42]

Shortly afterwards, in 1919, Albert Sarraut left his post as Governor-General of Indochina and promised the Indochinese some participation in the affairs of their country, but not political freedom.[43] This led Nguyen Ai Quoc not only to denounce the colonial system but also to criticize Sarraut and call Khai Dinh, the "protected" sovereign, an "ignoramus" in an issue of *Le Paria* (1 August 1922). He took one step further and made fun of the Emperor of Annam in a play, *The Bamboo Dragon*, which was performed at a festival sponsored by the newspaper *L'Humanité* in Garches in 1922. He submitted the text to the leftist writer and journalist Léo Poldès (alias of Léopold Seszler), who appreciated its qualities: "Hardly Molière, *n'est-ce pas*, yet carefully crafted, animated by a certain Aristophanic verve and not lacking in scenic qualities."[44]

Thus, Nguyen Ai Quoc began an intense period of writing and attending conferences. It was all propaganda, of course, but it revealed his desire to instruct and convince others to follow him, to express himself simply and clearly so as to reach as many people as possible. As a writer, he sometimes targeted his adversaries directly – the Colonial Deputy of Cochinchina Max Outrey, the writer Alexandre de Pouvourville, Minister of Colonies Albert Sarraut; at other times he addressed the French, both communists and others, in *Le Journal du peuple*, *La Vie ouvrière*, *L'Humanité*, *La Revue communiste*. He often appealed to other colonized citizens, especially in *Le Paria*.[45] During this period, he developed some of those characteristics for which he would later become famous.

Among the characteristics was his lack of dogmatism, his refusal to wipe the cultural slate clean, and his desire to bridge the gap between past and present by finding elements in the former that he could reappropriate in the latter. His article in *La Revue communiste* of 15 May 1921 reveals this intellectual and political approach:

> Asians – although considered backward by Westerners – understand better, however, the need for total reform of the present society. And here is why.... The great Confucius (551 B.C.) advocated internationalism and preached the equality of wealth. He says that world peace comes only with a universal Republic. One should not be afraid of having little, but of not having equally. Equality cancels out poverty.... His disciple Mencius continued his doctrine and sketched out a detailed plan for the organization of production and consumption. Nothing was forgotten in his plan: the protection and development of a healthy childhood, education and mandatory work for adults, the severe condemnation of parasitism, and rest for the elderly. Happiness and well-being should be equally accessible to all, not only to a majority – this was the economic policy of the Wise One. Responding to a question by the king, he frankly replied that "the interests of the people come first, those of the nation come second, and those of the king are of no importance."[46]

For Quoc, equality had already become a key aspiration.

Evidently, Nguyen Ai Quoc had some cultural baggage that would neither be pushed aside nor erased by the teachings of the gospel of Stalinism, the *Dia-Mat* (the theory of dialectical materialism attributed to Stalin that was adopted as the official philosophy of the party and the Soviet state). Meanwhile, he continued his cultural education, spending long hours in the library at Sainte-Geneviève and the Bibliothèque Nationale, where Longuet had obtained a library card for him. He traveled within France, but also visited Switzerland and Italy with a popular tour company. He went to theater performances, art exhibitions, and salons, like the one on aeronautics at Le Bourget. It seems that he clearly remembered the teachings of Le Van Mien, who had inspired him with dreams of Paris as a teenager.

Quoc often participated in the debates at the Club du Faubourg, which had been founded in 1922 by Léo Poldès, a member of the FSP until the Tour Congress. The club welcomed speakers from all philosophical and political persuasions, and Quoc was known to have attended lectures on subjects as eclectic as reincarnation, the method of Doctor Coué, and the occult in order to perfect his French and gain self-confidence. In an interview years later with Stanley Karnow, Poldès sketched a vivid portrait of him:

> It was at one of our weekly meetings that I noticed this thin, almost anemic indigene in the rear. He had a Chaplinesque aura about him – simultaneously sad and comic, *vous savez*. I was instantly struck by his piercing dark eyes. He posed a provocative question; it eludes me now. I encouraged him to return. He did, and I grew more and more affectionate toward him. He was *très sympathique* – reserved but not shy, intense but not fanatical, and extremely clever. I especially liked his ironic way of deprecating everything while, at the same time, deprecating himself.[47]

In a different context, Karnow related an amusing anecdote regarding an article that Quoc (under the pseudonym Guy N'Qua) wrote for the magazine *Cinégraph* in 1922. The French boxer Georges Carpentier had just defeated the British champion Ted Lewis, "but Ho scarcely mentioned the bout in his piece. Instead he denounced the Paris sportswriters at ringside for contaminating their dispatches with such Franglais as 'le manager,' 'le round,' and 'le knock-out.' He further implored Premier Raymond Poincaré to outlaw foreign phrases from the French press."

As for his personal life, Quoc was not immune to the charms of the Parisian women, like the dressmaker Marie Brière – with whom, the police alleged, Quoc had a steady relationship – or Miss Boudon, whose photograph he had retouched and whose beauty moved him to ask her out twice for a date. Those who knew Quoc in the 1920s recall his humor, sensitivity, and sentimentality, traits that charmed those around him. And these traits reappeared later in his political maneuvers, in diplomatic negotiations, and in his public statements, which some saw as posturing designed only to fool his interlocutors and adversaries.

Certainly, Nguyen Ai Quoc was already a tactician, but he also had a spontaneous side, as revealed in two stories related by Jacques Sternel and Michele Zecchini. Sternel was a union organizer who edited a small journal, and one day he took the side of the Annamite workers in France. Quoc went to thank him and seemed "as frail as a sparrow, but he burned with the zeal of a Crusader."[48] Sternel added: "He asked permission to kiss me on both cheeks. And it was certainly not an exceptional gesture on his part. There were only three of us there: him, my wife, and I. That's just the kind of emotional impulses he always had."[49] Zecchini, who was a typographer for *L'Humanité* but remained a member of the Socialist Party, confirms that "Ho had a spirit of tolerance and respect for freedom that was rare among Marxist-Leninists, and had a sense of generosity and friendship that I have not seen since."[50]

Be that as it may, four days of debates at a party congress are not enough to change the way people think, and in the end, the SFIC gave barely more priority to the colonial question than the FSP had. Quoc realized this, and it was undoubtedly one of the reasons he was determined to leave for Moscow, moving progressively closer to his home and hoping to work more effectively toward throwing off the yoke of colonialism. He had already experienced the disappointment of the Versailles Conference, which showed him that he would get nothing from the world powers. They continued to remake the world, blind to the aspirations of other peoples and nations, and not even taking them into account. This was one more reason for him to turn his eyes from the horizon that had drawn him on thus far.

In so doing, he followed the advice of Phan Chu Trinh, from whom he had distanced himself in the previous two years but who approved of his political approach, even though it was opposed to his own. Trinh was living in Marseilles at the time, and wrote to Quoc that he now realized that the French Republic was not going to extend its political ideals to its colonial possessions. Like his young compatriot, he had given up his hopes and illusions, and wrote to Quoc that he should not stay abroad any longer, for there was no one capable of affecting the course of events. He suggested that his friend return home:

> If you turn in circles over here, how will you make use of your skills? For this reason I sincerely and eagerly advise you to completely change your methods and aim for greater things. I wish you success and hope that we will see each other again in our country.[51]

In June 1923, Quoc slipped away from the police surveillance and surreptitiously made his way to Berlin by train, destination Petrograd.[52]

TWO

A Missionary of Revolution

"THE GREAT SOCIALIST FAMILY"

Ho Chi Minh gave two reasons for his journey to Moscow in 1923 – he strongly wanted to meet Lenin and he wanted to move closer to his country – but his departure was so carefully prepared in advance that there had to be something else at work. In all likelihood, Dmitri Manuilsky, "the eye of Moscow" for the Communist Parties of Europe and particularly the FCP, had noticed Nguyen Ai Quoc in October 1922 at its Second Party Congress. It was there that Quoc had criticized the FCP for underestimating the colonial question and for not taking action. Manuilsky summoned him to Moscow because he needed a collaborator from one of the colonies.[1]

The voyage was well organized. On 13 June, to elude police surveillance, Quoc took a bus out to the suburbs of Paris and then returned almost immediately to the Gare du Nord, where he picked up a passport in the name of a Chinese national, Chen Vang (Tran Vuong in Vietnamese), and a first-class ticket for Berlin – as befitted a businessman. He was dressed like a bourgeois gentleman, most likely in the first of many outfits he used to pass unnoticed or evade police surveillance. A psychologist might read something deeper into this, but in reality these disguises were a necessary part of clandestine operations and war.

From then on, other Vietnamese nationals leaving for Moscow received Chinese passports and train or boat tickets, as well as sums of money.[2] In Berlin, the Russian plenipotentiary representative issued Quoc a safe-conduct pass dated 16 June for the Russian Soviet Socialist Federal Republic. "Chen Vang" then embarked on the *Karl Liebknecht* in Hamburg and arrived in Petrograd on 30 June. From there he made his way to Moscow.

FROM JUNE 1923 TO EARLY 1924, NGUYEN AI QUOC STAYED IN THE capital of the young Soviet Republic, the meeting place for those who had come from around the globe to make a clean break with the past. The first thing he wanted to do was meet Lenin in person, but the Soviet leader was very ill and in fact died in January 1924. Quoc learned of the news "with great pain," since for him, "Lenin was our father, our teacher, our comrade, our representative. Now, he is a shining star showing us the way to Socialism."[3] He attended the funeral in −30°C temperatures, his hands retaining frostbite scars for several weeks afterward.[4]

Quoc arrived in Russia as the New Economic Policy (NEP) was beginning to reap benefits, putting an end to wartime communism with its requisitions, bad harvests, famine, and mass deaths. Material conditions had greatly improved, especially in the capital. The Chinese Communist Peng Shuzhi was enrolled in the Stalin School during this harsh period, and wrote a vivid description of it in his memoirs.[5] From the start, Quoc was busy with meetings, visits, discussions, and article writing. He attended the Fifth Congress of the Third International, the Second Congress of the Peasant International (Crestintern),[6] the Fourth Congress of the Youth International, the Third Congress of the Women's International, the Third Congress of the Red Labor International, and the First Congress of International Red Aid.

He spoke three times during the important Comintern meeting, to "drive home" the colonial question:

> You must excuse my frankness, but I cannot help but observe that the speeches by comrades from the mother countries give me the impression that they wish to kill a snake by stepping on its tail. You all know that today the poison and the life energy of the capitalist snake is concentrated more in the colonies than in the mother countries.[7]

He then added that the destiny of the international proletariat was dependent on that of the colonies, the latter providing the basic materials for factories and the military rank-and-file for imperialist countries. Therefore, if they wanted to defeat the imperialists they had to take away their colonies. Quoc's notion of the community of interests and of the indispensable solidarity between the proletariat of imperialist nations and colonized peoples was basically a restatement of Lenin's idea about the "weakest link in the imperialist chain." Later, Mao Zedong would use another image, that of the "soft underbelly of imperialism." When Quoc went to the podium for the second time, he made some critical remarks about the FCP, which he then addressed in a letter to their Central Committee. He was still a member of the FCP, of course, and judging by his correspondence, he wanted to retain contact with them. After all, he had been one of its founding members.

In his letter to the FCP, Quoc wrote that the Comintern's decisions regarding the colonies in the First Congress "have served, so far, only to decorate the paper they were written on." It is true that the FCP had set up a committee for colonial studies and added a column on colonialism in *L'Humanité*, but unfortunately, the committee had gotten bogged down and the newspaper column had been cancelled.[8] Quoc soon realized that the International was also underestimating the importance of the colonial question. On two occasions, one month apart, he asked for a meeting with Gregory Zinoviev, President of the Comintern, but the latter was not an expert on colonial problems and did not even reply to Quoc's request.[9] Quoc then wrote a letter to the organization's Executive Committee to remind them of their commitment to colonial peoples. He did not agree with Stalin and the other Communists who maintained that the revolution had to triumph in imperialist countries and even in China before it could focus on the liberation of colonies; on the contrary, he was quite skeptical and even openly ironic.[10] He was convinced that the revolution had to begin there immediately and that a Bolshevik-style revolutionary party needed to be created in Vietnam. It was with this goal in mind that he kept pressure on the Comintern to send him on a mission to China. It was not an easy task, as we see in a letter he wrote to Albert Treint, a French member of the Executive Committee of the Comintern.[11] When he finally received the green light from the Executive Committee, he went to see Manuilsky, who told him that he understood his friend's impatience to take action.

In Moscow, Quoc was considered the specialist on colonial affairs and also on Asia, about which he published articles in *L'Humanité*, *Le Paria*, and *Inprecor*, the journal of the Comintern. He put the finishing touches on the book he had written in French, *Le Procès de la Colonisation Française* (French colonialism on trial), which was published in 1925. In it, he explained how the "exploitation" of French Indochina had begun in the early 1920s, as investments of French capital flooded in after the closing of the Russian and Turkish markets, and it was accompanied by the exploitation of labor on the plantations and the newly opened work sites, with all imaginable excesses. The rise of the colonial economy had led to social inequality and greater oppression, while the Minister of Colonies, Albert Sarraut, and French politicians talked about the "politics of association" and the humanist values of France. Quoc was in a perfect position to show the disparity between word and deed, and how France's actions often contradicted the promises made to its colonies.

It is widely believed that Nguyen Ai Quoc studied at the University of the Toilers of the East (Russian acronym: KUTV), or the Stalin School, which functioned from 1921 to 1938, training communist cadres and helping to initiate revolutionary movements in Asia. Most of the students were from Central Asia, with only a few Chinese students arriving later (including Xiao Sen, whom Quoc had recruited to the FCP). The first five Vietnamese students were admitted in 1925, and by 1931 they numbered fourteen.[12] We know that Quoc attended meetings and organized conferences, but it is not clear whether he was a student, as the Indian M. N. Roy claims.[13] The chronological listing of Ho's activities (*Bien nien Tieu su*) refers to the school, but not in much detail ("towards the end of 1924," for example). Peng Shuzhi makes no mention of him in his memoirs, and the only Vietnamese biography based on Soviet documents merely takes note of Quoc's interest in the school and his frequent visits there.[14] What's more, the Russian Vietnam specialist Anatoli Sokolov has searched the archives of the Comintern and found no trace of Quoc's enrollment.[15]

Quoc himself provided only a rather basic description of the Stalin School and its functions, as if solely for informational purposes, and so we turn to the Chinese student Peng Shuzhi for a description of the training given there:

> What do they teach us? Five subjects: political economics, dialectical materialism, revolution and development of the workers' movement in the West, social movements in Russia since the early nineteenth century, and the history of Russian communism from the creation of the Social-Democratic Party to the October Revolution. Current events, naturally, are always a popular topic in our classrooms.... Those at the Stalin School do their best to instill in our group of hand-picked foreigners... some of the basic techniques of clandestine work, like writing in code, for example.... The training is not very refined. It is often done too quickly and is oversimplified.... But it is also a very solid training, systematic, bearing the stamp of Leninism in the best sense of the term. [And] in the end I found, and I will say this again and again, that for us young Chinese, who initially had only a very limited notion of Marxism and didn't really know anything about the history of world revolutions, the training that we receive at *Dongfang daxue* [University of the East] is of inestimable value; it is even indispensable.[16]

A Vietnamese trained in Moscow in the 1920s would certainly have understood Peng's sentiments.

Not only did the school teach courses on theory but it also provided practical training, like the "Communist Sundays" when students performed works for the public good; did gardening or military exercises; visited rural communities (later called kolkhozes), factories, schools, or Pioneer camps; or went to the rest camps on the Black Sea.

In Moscow, Nguyen Ai Quoc must have felt at home within what he called "the great Socialist family." He was finally free of the police presence that had shadowed him in France, where he could be arrested at any moment, and free of endless worry about his next step. More than this, the strategy put forth by the International matched his own revolutionary aspirations. In France, Quoc had attacked every aspect of the French colonial regime, while in Moscow, where the International was still quite Eurocentric in its vision of world revolution and in its recruitment of cadres, he set himself apart by highlighting the specifics of the Asian world, a position he had already established with his 1921 text on Confucius (cited in the preceding chapter).

Shortly before leaving for Canton (now Guangzhou), Quoc wrote a report that clearly revealed his vision of the world and of revolution, but it was not given the attention it deserved. He began by placing Marxist doctrine at a distance, in particular the question of the class struggle and its emergence as the engine of history only within an analysis of European societies. Quoc wrote, however, that "Europe is not all of humanity."[17] He anticipated the changes in the social sciences during the second half of the century, for in his view, they needed to "revise Marxism, down to its historical foundations, by strengthening it with Oriental ethnology."

Nguyen Ai Quoc did not explicitly identify capitalism with colonialism, nor the colonized peoples with the proletariat, but he affirmed nonetheless that the primary objective of the revolution in the colonies was the liberation of preindustrial societies, which were as open to revolution as the advanced capitalist nations – "nationalism is our country's greatest resource." Two years later, he wrote to a student that the mandarins and landlords – the higher strata of society – were as much victims of colonialism as the peasants and workers, and so the ranks of the revolution should be open to them as well.[18]

He repeatedly told the Comintern, and then the Crestintern, that the peasantry was a source of potential revolutionary force, and he reminded the poet Osip Mandelstam that Confucius had conceived of an egalitarian society.[19] He also wrote to Fedorivitch Petrov, General Secretary of the Far Eastern Bureau of the Comintern, asking him to stop dividing the Asian communists by country of origin, particularly at the Stalin School. Instead, they should be introduced to one another and brought together to create an Asian group, because "in a general sense, Oriental people are very sentimental; for them, one [real-life] example is worth more than one hundred propaganda speeches."[20]

Quoc prioritized human relations while showing apparent indifference to – or at least a distance from – theory, from notions of class and the class struggle, and from the great debates regarding political strategy. As far as we know, he did not get involved in the discussion between Lenin and M. N. Roy as to whether communists should ally themselves with nationalists or fight alone. However, his unflagging support for national emancipation above all else and his later activities clearly show that his position was similar to Lenin's. On many occasions in the years to come, he reiterated that national liberation was a prerequisite to social emancipation.

Similarly, we do not know what stance he took on the China question, which sparked debate within the Comintern from 1924 to 1927. Should the Chinese Communists merge with the Kuomintang, risking their political commitments and their lives? And when Chiang Kai-shek began to turn against his allies, should the Communists break with him and arm the "working class" in the cities, or launch guerrilla warfare by mobilizing the peasants? While the debate about "the China question" raged among Roy, Borodin, Stalin, Trotsky, and Hans Maring (pseudonym of the Dutchman Hendrikus Sneevliet), the Comintern's delegate in China, Nguyen Ai Quoc, remained silent – at least on paper.

This first trip to Moscow was a milestone in Quoc's early revolutionary career, and the notoriety he had acquired by bringing the *Demands of the Annamite People* before the Versailles Conference began to grow. He was seen in Red Square in the company of Zinoviev and Voroshilov, and his portrait was sketched by a Soviet artist at the International Congress and later by a Swedish Communist artist, Eric Johansson.[21] In addition, Mandelstam interviewed him for the journal *Ogoniok* and called him a *Cominternchik*, a title not given lightly. More importantly, the poet was visibly won over by Quoc's personality and wrote: "Nguyen Ai Quoc's face exudes innate tact and delicacy.... Nguyen Ai Quoc is a man of culture. Not European culture, of course. But it could very well be the culture of the future."[22]

The French historian Paul Mus best captured the extent to which the Moscow visit broadened Quoc's political scope:

> Modern emulator of the great Buddhist pilgrim Hiuan-Tsang, he awaited the revelation at the end of this new voyage to the West – beyond Buddhism and beyond India. Thus, between 1924 and 1938 in the capital of world communism, we find our little country boy from Nghe Tinh transported to the dimensions of a new world. He is the first of his countrymen to have

> reached "the summit": full citizenship within this modern universe under the title of Marxist, without the reduced status automatically implied from our side – even had he been an "emperor" – in the enslavement to the protectorate. The Union of Soviet Socialist Republics deliberately exalted national entities, within the scope of the Party and according to its own themes. In terms of his career and for the prestige he gained before his own people, this meant more to this leader of men than many of us would be willing to admit.[23]

PREPARING FOR THE REVOLUTION IN INDOCHINA

In August and September 1924, Nguyen Ai Quoc spent about two weeks in a rest home on the Crimea where he discovered new vistas – those of Yalta, Sotchi, and Batchisarai – and saw the faces of Tartars, which would have seemed familiar to him. These new sights must certainly have strengthened his conviction that the global Federation of Soviet Socialist Republics was not just a pure utopia.

From Moscow to Canton

In October 1924, the train journey from Moscow to Canton took several weeks and added Siberian landscapes to Quoc's vision of Russia's European and southern regions. The train made frequent stops, since the Trans-Siberian railway had not been completely restored and, undoubtedly, anti-Russian or anti-Bolshevik bandits still disrupted their journey. After all, the defeat of Admiral Koltchak and the White Army had taken place in 1920, the escapade of the crazy Baron Ungern von Sternberg had ended only in 1921, and the Japanese army had not abandoned Vladivostok until October 1922. This Far Eastern capital of the Soviet Republic was a nerve center within the global workings of the Third International and was the USSR's window onto the Pacific. Memories of foreign intervention were still fresh, from the Japanese to the Americans to the French (the French government had sent a contingent of Annamite infantry, though Quoc himself had opposed sending his compatriots to the front in France as well as in Syria). No doubt Quoc felt that he was fighting the good fight against imperialism. Along the way he passed Korea, which was a Japanese colony at the time, and the large seaports of China, where Westerners had assumed the right of establishing settlements, disembarking in Canton in November 1924. He must have felt as though he had moved up to the front lines.

In one sense, literally, it was true: On 19 June 1924 in the Franco-British settlement at Shamen (an island in the Pearl River), the young Vietnamese Pham Hong Thai had thrown a bomb at a banquet in honor of the Governor-General of Indochina, Martial Merlin, who was stopping in Canton. Merlin miraculously escaped, but five people died and a number were injured. "Terrifying, simply terrifying!" wrote the *South China Morning Post*.[24] Ever since 1911, China had become the theater of both civil war and powerful movements against foreign imperialists – both Westerners and Japanese – including the May 4th Movement, named for the large student demonstrations that took place in Beijing on 4 May 1919. First, the forces of General Yuan Shikai seized control of the republican revolution; then came a period of anarchy controlled by "warlords" (*dujun*, or military commanders and provincial governors). The imperialists leaned in favor of the government of Yuan Shikai, then of the generals who took power in Beijing and in the provinces. So Sun Yat-sen and his Democratic Nationalist Party (the Kuomintang) launched a second revolution to unify China under the republican regime. After the bitter experience of having been manipulated by Chen Jiongming, the *dujun* of Canton, Sun created his own army and ousted the latter in 1923.[25]

To consolidate Canton's revolutionary base before launching his "great expedition to punish the North," Sun sought a reliable ally in the Soviet Union. In 1923, he sent Chiang Kai-shek to Moscow to form a relationship with the Bolsheviks and to study on-site the workings of the Red Army and the regime. Then he himself signed the "Sun-Joffé Declaration," which sealed the alliance between the two governments. The cooperation that resulted from these exchanges and negotiations arose out of their common interests and strategies. On one side, Lenin had lost hope of seeing the triumph of revolution in Europe after the failure of the Red Army outside of Warsaw (1919), the fall of the Budapest Commune (1919), and especially the crushing of the Spartakus movement and the Bavarian "soviets" (1919), as well as the failed "October 1923" revolution in Germany. The Bolsheviks and the Comintern thus turned their eyes toward the Far East.[26] Sun Yat-sen, on the other hand, was tired of being dependent on warlords and mercenary armies in his quest to restore a united republic, but had to contend with the foreign imperialists. Accordingly, he responded to the advances of the Soviet Union and invited a mission of political, military, and economic advisors to Canton under the leadership of Borodin, who arrived in October 1923 to reorganize the Kuomintang along the model of the Bolshevik Party.

From then on, power was held by a limited Executive Committee, discipline was strict, the party was endowed with an advanced social program, and Sun accepted an alliance with the Chinese Communist Party. Several dozen military advisors under the successive commands of General P. A. Pavlov and General V. K. Blücher stayed at the Whampoa Military Academy to train the officers of the Nationalist army. The academy was on Whampoa Island (Huangpu), twenty-five kilometers downriver from Canton, and was placed under the command of Chiang Kai-shek, who would later become the Communists' most bitter enemy. The Soviet generals trained an army that was different from private or mercenary armies, although there was not as much emphasis on political education as they would have liked.[27]

Canton also seemed like the front lines because of the Kuomintang government's fragile hold on power. In 1925, the authority of Sun's government was tested yet again as he had to face insurrections, like that of the "merchant militia" between September and December, which forced the government to flee Canton and take shelter on Whampoa Island, under the protection of the cadets from the academy. On 20 March 1925, Chiang Kai-shek began to apply intimidation tactics, notably directed at Soviet advisors, which foreshadowed his move to the right in 1927. Factional groups from Hunan and Yunnan began to resist Kuomintang leadership. In the countryside, tension was increasing between peasants and their landlords, and conflict plagued even the workers' movement of Canton, pitting unions against guilds and unions against one another along political lines. The class struggle further intensified these clashes between political and provincial factions, leading Chiang Kai-shek to turn against the Communists. By the time Nguyen Ai Quoc arrived in November 1924, he found an atmosphere rife with conflict and thus with the unexpected: "Canton is a quagmire of intrigue, treason, and blackmail."[28]

On 11 November of that year, Quoc was driven to the eastern hills, to the neighborhood of Douchan where the rich bourgeoisie and Chiang himself lived. The Soviet mission was headquartered there in a comfortable villa surrounded by a flower garden, which the Chinese called the "Borodin Residence." He met with Borodin as soon as he arrived, then decided to cover his tracks and change his name to Ly Thuy (Ly being a common Chinese surname but also evoking several Vietnamese heroes, such as Ly Thuong Kiet, who drove out the Chinese in the eleventh century). He began signing his articles and reports as Vuong Son Nhi, and to his compatriots he was "comrade" or "Mister Vuong."

The interpreter Vera Vichniakova-Akimova described him thus:

> Slim in appearance with baggy clothes, a worried look, both passionate and sad. . . . He spoke French very well, as well as English and Cantonese, and he also knew a lot of Russian. . . . [H]is name was Ly Thuy but we usually called him Ly An-Nam [for his Vietnamese homeland]. . . . He behaved very well with everyone but he was rather discreet and very serious. . . . Later, Borodin's wife informed me that he was none other than Nguyen Ai Quoc.[29]

Ly Thuy slept on the ground floor of the residence, next to an old acquaintance from Moscow, the Chinese Zhang Tailei. Zhang had studied at the Stalin School and was appointed as Borodin's assistant and interpreter by the CCP. Ly and Zhang had become friends in Moscow and traveled together from Vladivostok to Canton. Ly also met up with men he had known in Paris, such as Li Fuchun, Zhou Enlai, and Chen Yannian, all of whom became leaders of the CCP.[30]

Ly Thuy wore several hats. His position as press correspondent for the Soviet agency ROSTA gave him a legal façade, or at least an official one. He asked Borodin to introduce him as one of the interpreters of his mission. And most importantly, he was a delegate of the Comintern and Crestintern, sent to work with the newly born CCP (1923) to found an Indochinese revolutionary organization. His activities fell into three main categories: writing for *Inprecor*, *Le Paria*, and occasionally other Communist journals like *L'Ouvrier de Bakou* (The Bakou Worker); training Indochinese revolutionary cadres; and creating an organization ready to take action on the Indochinese peninsula. The last two were the real reasons for his presence in Canton and comprised the bulk of his activity, for this was the Comintern's highest priority.[31]

At the same time, he participated in the activities of the CCP, which he considered hands-on practice. He gave lectures at the party's Peasant Institute, which had been set up by the Kuomintang, and attended and spoke at congresses and demonstrations held by the CCP and workers' and farmers' unions, like the one described by Akimova in her memoirs:

> Drums had been beating since morning; thousands of bare feet or wooden sandals slapped on the sidewalk while rows of demonstrators armed with beating drums and bristling with flags gathered in the square behind Borodin's residence. Flags from the farmers' unions and workers' organizations fluttered by the dozen, above hundreds of red banners bearing slogans. I was afraid it would end in a gigantic stampede, but there was nothing of the sort: each row of marchers went calmly to take its place between the metal and bamboo podiums. . . .

> I stayed on Borodin's rooftop terrace, and from there I had a very good view over the whole square and the sea of yellow braided hats.... All of a sudden there was silence: the orators were about to speak. I have always been struck by the strict discipline of the mass gatherings in Canton....
>
> Borodin was speaking on one of the podiums and Zhang Tailei translated.... I was grabbed by enthusiastic hands and hoisted onto another podium so that I could tell the assembly about the liberation of Soviet women. I don't know if the farmers around me understood what I was saying since I spoke with a Beijing accent, but in any case I was deafened by their applause.... Afterwards there was a *tableau vivant* that was a huge success: the advisor Naoumov had a granddaughter, who must have been about thirteen at the time, who climbed onto a podium hand in hand with a little Chinese girl of the same age, and they kissed each other on both cheeks. This moving symbol of Sino-Soviet friendship unleashed joyous laughter from everyone and wild applause.[32]

Ly Thuy usually spoke in French, except at the workers' or peoples' meetings when he addressed the audience in Chinese, which he spoke fluently "with a Cantonese accent." This was the case during the great strike-boycott that paralyzed the British colony of Hong Kong in June 1925, where he spoke at the Chinese rallies. During this time in Canton, which some called the Moscow of the Far East, Ly Thuy also founded and participated in the League of Oppressed Nations, which brought together Vietnamese, Chinese, Koreans, Indonesians, Filipinos, and Burmese, but it seems to have played only a symbolic role.

The Founding of the Revolutionary Youth League and Its Activities

Ly Thuy had gone to Canton mainly to organize his country's revolutionary movement. He was in the right place at the right time, since the second Chinese revolution was based in the southern province of Guangdong, which, along with Guangxi and Yunnan, is on the border with Tonkin (see Map 1). Guangdong was already a sanctuary for Vietnamese exiles who had led abortive uprisings against the French in the first decades of the twentieth century. Moreover, the key leader of this resistance movement, the scholar Phan Boi Chau, had been declared persona non grata in Japan and had settled into semiretirement in China by 1912. A vast area began to take shape, from the southern provinces of China to Laos, Siam (now Thailand), and the northern provinces in colonial Tonkin, making a geopolitical sphere where Vietnamese resistants could come and go, lead their anticolonialist activities, and prepare a fallback position.

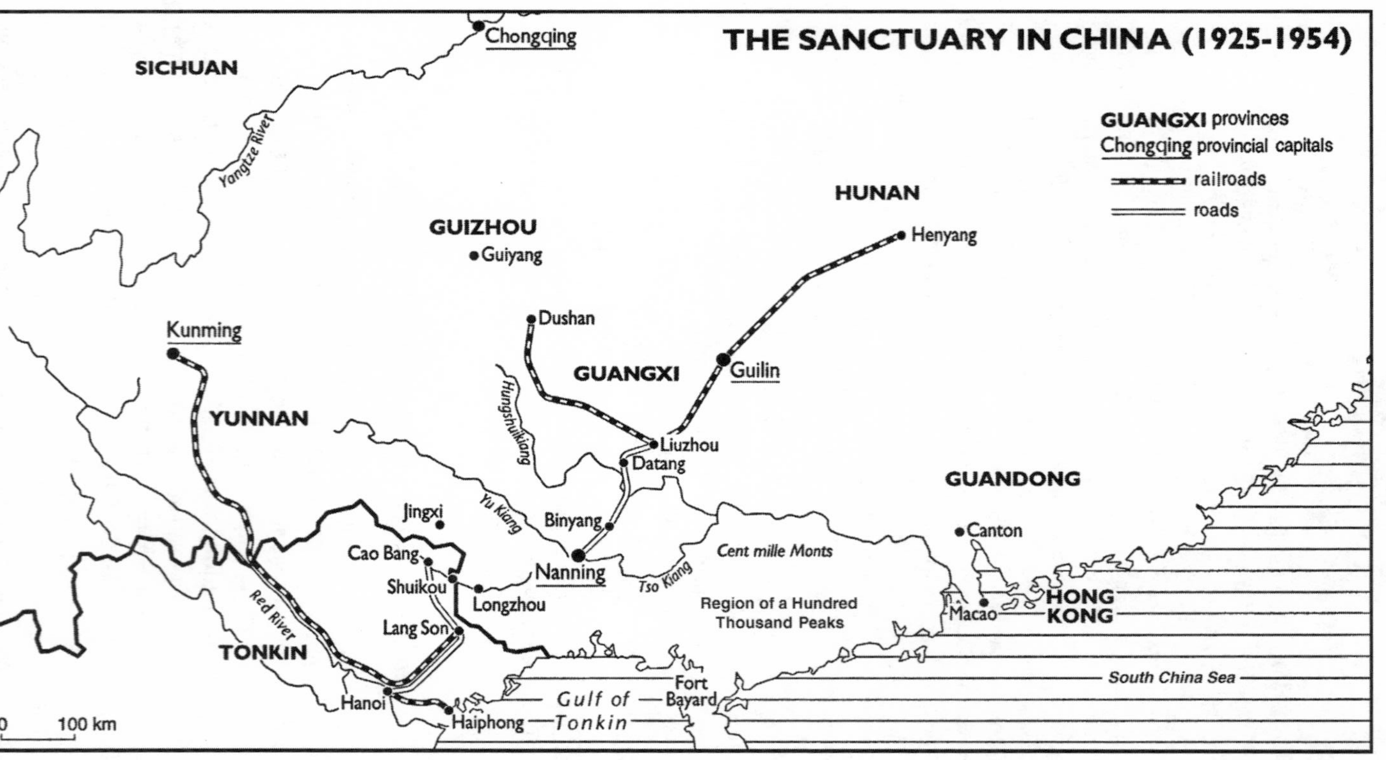

Map 1. The Sanctuary in China (1925–1954)

Phan Boi Chau lived in Hangzhou but occasionally went to Canton, where a group of his young compatriots formed an organization called the Tam Tam Xa (Association of Like Minds) in 1923, also called the Tan Viet Thanh Nien Doan (Youth of the New Vietnam). It consisted of seven men whose first concrete action was their bomb attack on Governor-General Merlin. Chau, who had just created a new nationalist party, the Viet Nam Quoc Dan Dang, placed his hopes in these young men.[33]

Ly Thuy set out to find them. He had heard that some were at the Whampoa Military Academy, and so he went there and was told by Pavel A. Plavov that two brothers, Le Hong Son and Le Hong Phong, were indeed registered at the school. Together with Ho Tung Mau, another nationalist, the four men met up at the house of the Chinese owner of an Oriental pharmacy. The man's daughter, Hue Quan, had married a Vietnamese national, Nguyen Cong Vien, better known as Lam Duc Thu.[34]

The Tam Tam Xa proposed a program to bring together as many Vietnamese patriots as possible in order to expel the French colonizers and reestablish the nation's independence and "the dignity of the Viet people." They offered no model for reshaping society, and put off the choice of a political regime until later, when the people would choose one for themselves in keeping with the "great trends sweeping through the world today." Such a project was likely to attract monarchists as well as republicans and democrats. Members of the group, as well as Phan Boi Chau himself, were receptive to the ideals and actions of the Bolshevik revolutionaries and the Soviet government, such as every nation's right to self-determination, the liberation of the colonies, and the annulment of unfair treaties imposed by the Europeans on Asian states.

It is possible that Phan Boi Chau made contact with Grigory Voitinsky or with other Soviet envoys like Maring, or, more plausibly, with the Soviet ambassador in Beijing, Adolf Joffé, through the intermediary of the rector of Peking University, Cai Yuanpei. He was familiar with Sun Yat-sen's doctrine of the Three People's Principles, which included some socialistic elements. He was certainly attracted by socialism and wrote an eighty-six page booklet on it in the 1920s. In addition, he had contact with Liu Zhifu, a Chinese anarchist from Canton, and undoubtedly was immersed in an ideological and political climate where ideas mingled freely, blending nationalism, populism, socialism, and pan-asianism, which was basically a form of regional internationalism.[35]

The young members of the Tam Tam Xa were described in a French police report as "spurning all tradition, disdainful of the old émigrés with outdated ideas, educated in revolution by agents from Moscow, and eager to play a political role."[36] They were part of the wave of Vietnamese migration into Guangdong, Guangxi, and Siam, and had set up a series of safe houses and shelters behind shop-fronts (in Kunming), in handicraft workshops (in Nanning), and in farming communities (in northeastern Siam). They, too, had arrived in China as it was reeling from civil war, and entered into a world of converging influences. Many Vietnamese who made the journey to China suffered from the difficult and risky conditions. One man traveled on a steamship that promised him passage from Saigon to Hong Kong, but was forced to hide in a narrow dinghy for five days, "folded over upon himself like a shrimp." Then he went from Hong Kong to Canton in another boat, hidden for more than one hour under the latrines, "his feet in water like a duck." And those who crossed the border overland were frequently chased by police patrols.[37]

Ly Thuy tried to draw these young men into the Comintern's orbit and the Leninist movement, and to increase their numbers by attracting more young Vietnamese and Siamese to join them. Then in June 1925, Phan Boi Chau was abducted by the French police as he was exiting the train station in Shanghai and sent immediately to Hanoi, thus clearing the way for Ly, especially since Phan's party had only a formal, inactive existence.[38]

IN JUNE 1925 IN CANTON, LY THUY FOUNDED THE VIET NAM THANH Nien Cach Menh Dong Chi Hoi, or the Revolutionary Youth League of Vietnam (also known as the Thanh Nien, or simply as the League). The original nucleus was composed of seven members of the Tam Tam Xa, two of whom became Ly's assistants: Ho Tung Mau and Le Hong Phong. He rented two adjacent buildings on Wen Ming Street, near the Peasant Institute, the Cantonese committee of the CCP, and the Pedagogy Institute of Canton (later Sun Yat-sen University and today the Canton Museum of History and the Chinese writer Lu Xun's memorial). They set up dormitories, a kitchen, and classrooms to accommodate students for a three-month training period. In total, three classes with fifty students each passed through their halls. Within the League, Ly Thuy established a core group, the Thanh Nien Cong San Doan (Communist Youth Group), as well as a group of eight children and adolescents (Thieu Nhi Doan) and a women's group (Phu Nu Doan), who were then indoctrinated with the cult of the "lost homeland" and with the spirit of sacrifice necessary to take it back.[39]

Everyone had to live frugally because Ly Thuy received no money from Moscow. He wrote to the Comintern at the beginning of this period, saying that "I only have my salary as a correspondent for ROSTA"; meanwhile he was bringing young people from Vietnam and Siam and had to provide for them.[40] He also needed money to develop teaching and propaganda materials, and to set up a network of liaisons with his country. Indeed, before his arrival, some young Vietnamese trying to reach Canton had been cheated by people who passed themselves off as smugglers. He eventually received money from Moscow, but in the meantime the Thanh Nien school was run mainly with help from the CCP. It most likely provided financial aid, but also – and perhaps most importantly – help of a more practical sort, such as dining privileges for the Vietnamese students at the Chinese Peasant Institute.

Once the students had completed their training, they climbed the hill where the patriot Pham Hong Thai was buried, next to the cemetery of the seventy-two Chinese martyrs who had attempted a putsch in 1898 against the imperial government. There they "took an oath to sacrifice themselves for the sake of the nation through self-abnegation." Only then were they admitted into the inner workings of the League.[41] Most of them returned to Vietnam, but five were sent to Moscow in 1925 to become the first Indochinese students of the Stalin School. Others, like Phung Chi Kien and Le Thiet Hung, joined the Chinese Communist guerrillas after the defeat of the Canton Commune (1927), and a few others, like Nguyen Son, rose high in the ranks of the Chinese Peoples' Army.[42]

In Canton, Ly Thuy deployed all of his organizational and pedagogical skills. He taught most of the courses at the school and was practically the sole author of the organization's journal, *Thanh Nien*. He also wrote for lesser-known propaganda sheets: *Bao Cong Nong* (Journal of Workers and Peasants), *Linh Kach Menh* (The Revolutionary Soldier), and *Viet Nam Tien Phong* (Vietnamese Vanguard). He expressed himself with the simplicity and clarity already evident in Paris and Moscow, especially since he was addressing young people with only a French-influenced primary school education; a few had been to high school, and some had had no schooling at all.[43]

The articles that Ly Thuy wrote during this period develop, clarify, and illustrate the ideas he put forth in a sixty-page booklet called *The Revolutionary Path* (Duong Cach Menh). He wanted to set himself apart from the nationalist militants of the preceding generation, including their main spokesman Phan Boi Chau, who had had no clear idea of what system to put in place after achieving independence and driving out the French. To this end, he turned to Lenin's basic principle that there is no revolutionary movement without revolutionary theory and that the latter serves no purpose if there is no party to carry it out. These words appear as an epigraph in the pamphlet.[44]

The teaching at the Thanh Nien school was not exclusively devoted to Leninism, however. Ly Thuy also discussed reformism, anarchism, Gandhiism, and the Three People's Principles of Sun Yat-sen – in order, of course, to point out their limitations. He had not forgotten his Asian cultural roots either. He went back to Confucius (which he had explained to Osip Mandelstam years before) in an article for *Thanh Nien* after the Nationalist Chinese government decided to abolish ceremonies in honor of the Chinese philosopher. He showed his mastery of paradox:

> Monarchs venerated Confucius not only because he was not a revolutionary but also because he provided strong support for their cause. They exploited Confucianism like the imperialists exploit Christianity.... Confucianism is based on three important acts of submission: of subjects to their sovereign, of a son to his father, and of a wife to her husband; and the five cardinal virtues: humanity, justice, urbanity, prudence, and sincerity.... If Confucius were still alive today and still held these views, he would be an antirevolutionary. It is more likely, however, that this great man would bend to circumstances and would soon become the worthy successor of Lenin. By doing away with ceremonies in honor of Confucius, the Chinese government has shut down an institution that was outdated and contrary to the spirit of democracy. But as far as we are concerned, we Annamites, let us perfect ourselves intellectually through the reading of Confucius, and revolutionarily through the works of Lenin.[45]

But what, then, is revolution? Nationalists, whether monarchists or republicans, believed that any violent political change is revolution. They called it *cach mang* or *cach menh*, literally translated as "changing the Mandate" (of Heaven), leading to the overthrow of a king or dynasty. Ly Thuy used the same word, but in a modern sense. He began by saying that revolution is the engine of human progress, which substitutes the good for the bad, and he used the examples of Galileo, Stephenson, Darwin, and Marx. He then defined three types of political revolution: bourgeois, national, and social. Ly illustrated his words with brief descriptions of the revolutions in America, France, and Russia. He claimed that the last finished what the first two had started by mobilizing workers and peasants to put an end to capitalist exploitation and establish an egalitarian and fraternal society. However, *The Revolutionary Path* was more than a study of semantics and political terms ("proletariat," "union," "cooperative," "International," etc.), as was the journal *Thanh Nien*. Ly added an ethical dimension to the ideological and historical ideas. This new dimension was essential, in fact, and he chose to begin his book with "the qualities of a revolutionary," qualities that one *had to* incorporate into one's moral and physical behavior, both in relations with others and in one's own activities. Consequently, the members of the League were trained in the practice of criticism and self-criticism.

It is clear that during his time in Canton, Nguyen Ai Quoc was more than the founder of an Indochinese communist movement. Indeed, he did much more than create a party apparatus and disseminate political propaganda. He also initiated his young compatriots into a political culture in which he blended an Asian ethic with modern ideas from Europe, and looked to Confucius for ideas similar to those of European socialism. He both modeled and transmitted these transcultural values.

"I Am a Normal Man"

Despite a host of demanding activities, Nguyen Ai Quoc found time to nurture friendships and make new contacts. Many of his relationships were politically motivated, of course, but he still had a sentimental side. He got along well with Zhang Tailei and his wife, who lived on the ground floor of the Borodin villa, and received a sweater knitted by the wife of Zhou Enlai, a gift fondly recalled in 1960.

The key event in his emotional life was his marriage, on 18 October 1926, to Tang Tuyet Minh, a midwife and friend of the wife of Lam Duc Thu (known as "Agent Pinot"). In a letter, Thu wrote that "Ly Thuy is getting married today to one of my wife's classmates."[46] At the time, Minh was twenty-one and Ly thirty-six. They had to overcome the opposition of Minh's mother, who knew about Ly's activities, as well as potential problems from her father's side of the family, which had been Catholic for two generations. The ceremony was held in the same place where Zhou Enlai and Deng Yingchao had been married, and Ly and Minh then went to live in the Borodin residence.

Ly had been attracted to the young woman from their first meeting at the home of Hue Quan, Lam Duc Thu's wife. With her oval face, her soft white skin, her intelligence and reserve, Minh had seduced Quoc immediately.[47] But he had to overcome strong reservations on the part of some of his comrades, such as Nguyen Hai Than and Le Hong Son ("I will get married despite your disapproval because I need a woman to teach me the language and to keep house," Ly responded.)[48] Overriding their objections, he went through with the marriage. Minh took care of day-to-day affairs, and one can imagine that after years of traveling, Quoc must have been happy to enjoy the warmth of a conjugal home. Not one to remain closed within that world, he encouraged his young wife to participate in a training program for cadres in the Chinese women's movement.

Their happiness was short-lived. In April 1927, Chiang Kai-shek put an end to the triple alliance among the Kuomintang, the USSR, and the Chinese Communists, and began a policy of severe repression against his former allies. In mid-May, Truong Van Linh, a veteran of the Whampoa Academy and an officer with the Chinese police, warned Ly Thuy of his imminent arrest. Ly bid farewell to Minh and promised to write and send for her when things calmed down.[49] He fled to Hong Kong, where he was not a welcome guest for the British, and so continued on to Shanghai, which had fallen into the hands of Chiang Kai-shek. Disguised as a rich businessman, he checked into a luxury hotel and then departed for Vladivostok and Moscow.

Later, around mid-1928, he wrote a short message to Minh, which was intercepted by the French police: "Although we have been separated now for almost a year, our feelings for each other do not need to be said in order to be felt. At present, I am taking advantage of this opportunity to send you a few words to reassure you, and also to send my greetings and good wishes to your mother."[50] These few sentences betray the practical reasons that Ly had used earlier to justify his marriage.

Friendship was also important for Ly. When he learned that Lam Duc Thu, one of his closest friends, had become an informer for the French police, he chose not to end his relationship with him. Was he just trying to keep a low profile and perhaps mislead his enemies? Or was he reluctant to end a friendship born of mutual assistance, shared memories, and trust? After the triumph of the Vietnamese revolution in 1945, when some spoke of punishing the traitor Lam Duc Thu, Ho Chi Minh reportedly requested that his former friend be left in peace. Some also say that Thu was executed behind Ho's back.

Quoc's feelings of friendship extended to comrades of the party. One day, when a discussion between Zhang Tailei and another Chinese Communist started to turn into a fight, Quoc entered the room and said, "You're both Communists, aren't you?" The two men understood and were ashamed, and they calmed down.[51]

New Departure, New Missions

The death of Sun Yat-sen, on 12 March 1925, had already aggravated the dissension within the Kuomintang, and the tensions gradually increased as the Chinese Communists made inroads in the villages and especially the countryside, matching the progress made by the Kuomintang itself. The Chinese revolution reached a turning point in 1927, leading to repercussions for the revolution in Vietnam as well. Chiang Kai-shek turned against his former allies and crushed the last Communist resistance in China, and in so doing destroyed the Thanh Nien base in Canton. From 11 to 14 December of that year, the Canton Commune was mercilessly crushed: 600 people were killed in three days of fighting, and 5,700 people were assassinated after the battle, among them the president of the commune and Quoc's friend, Zhang Tailei.[52]

The forty Vietnamese cadets at the Whampoa Academy and the Revolutionary Youth League, who had become Red Guards, either went to eastern Guangdong province to join the "soviet republic" of Hai Lu Feng (which lasted until 1928), or to the "soviet" of Paise in Guangxi (where Deng Xiaoping would later be stationed, in 1929). Still others went to Hong Kong. While the leftist government in Wuhan was reconciling with Chiang Kai-shek, now based in Nanjing, Nguyen Ai Quoc returned to Moscow with the Borodin mission.

The events in China must have helped Quoc form his own strategy for the Indochinese revolution, especially the failure of the united front with the Nationalists, who benefited from the situation. Although he left us no record of his impressions, he would have seen that the Comintern's strategy and tactics in China were weakened by a number of events: the controversy between Stalin and Trotsky (Lev Davidovich Bronstein, who founded and led the Red Army during the Bolshevik Revolution and who, after the break with Stalin, was assassinated in Mexico in 1940); the contradictory advice given by the envoys of the International; and the confusion that ensued. In the end, the Chinese Communists were the sole victims.[53]

Quoc was now convinced that Indochina needed to have an autonomous communist party. Furthermore, the Chinese experience taught him that he would have to link the national question with the social question, to ease the tension sparked by the confluence of colonialism and communism. Likewise, the Chinese revolution taught the importance of mobilizing the peasantry and its revolutionary potential in countries where urban workers were a minority (.5% of the Chinese population in the 1920s). The Communists needed to have two strings to their bow, as Nguyen Ai Quoc indicated in response to the FCP delegate at the Comintern, Jacques Doriot: "I am committed to making sure that in the future we will make the principles of Lenin and Sun Yat-sen the guiding light of the Vietnamese revolution."[54]

Quoc returned to Moscow in late 1927 and delivered a talk to the military commission of the German Communists in the city. Entitled "The Party's Military Work among the Peasants: Methods of Revolutionary Guerrilla Warfare," it basically restated what Nikolai Bukharin had written in *Inprecor* (no. 39, 21 April 1925) and he himself had written in *Bao Cong Nong* (no. 111, 27 March 1927). He claimed that the peasantry, whose cohesion and political clairvoyance were never acknowledged by Marx, represented a revolutionary potential in the colonies that absolutely had to be mobilized. Echoing what Doriot had said to members of the Revolutionary Youth League during his visit to Canton of the same year, Quoc spoke unambiguously on the subject: "The victory of the proletarian revolution is impossible in agrarian nations unless the proletariat is actively supported by the bulk of the peasant population." He even reproached the Chinese Communists for "the grave error of having joined with the Kuomintang to oppose the supposed excesses – that is, the revolutionary activities – of the peasant organizations."[55]

Back in Moscow, Nguyen Ai Quoc caught up with his compatriots from the Stalin School. Nguyen The Vinh, a Vietnamese student at the school and a graduate of the business school in Montpellier, provided a glimpse into this period through his deposition of 27 July 1931, given before the chief of the Sûreté of Hanoi. Vinh, a cousin of Nguyen The Truyen, depicted university life as well as the group of Vietnamese students, some of whom had come from Canton and others from France.[56] In 1927–28, he had met Nguyen Ai Quoc several times, describing him thus: "There is nothing particularly striking about Quoc except perhaps how thin he is. He speaks Annamite with a Tonkin accent. He wore a European suit with collar and tie. He spoke little but did not have a proud attitude like Nguyen The Truyen." In September 1927, Quoc lived in a hotel near the university that was "simply furnished and equipped with a telephone. There was a typewriter on the table."[57]

Nguyen The Vinh's account of the Stalin School is less interesting than Peng Shuzhi's, but it tallies with that of the Chinese Communist. Vinh had problems from the very beginning: While he was undergoing a medical checkup at the infirmary, all of the belongings he had brought from France were stolen, including his watch, which he had left in the dormitory. The housing was military in style, and each nationality had its own barracks leader. The day began with thirty minutes of calisthenics, and classes were held from ten to one and from three to six. Evenings were free and the students were given tickets to weekly movies and plays. In the summer of 1926, Vinh had three months of military training in Malakhovka, near Moscow, and then two months of training in July–August 1927 at Bukhov's camp. In between semesters, the students visited factories, agricultural cooperatives, and Pioneer camps. Vinh also spent time at a rest camp in Yalta.[58] He wrote that his compatriots were quite divided, but does not explain why. This is an important observation, however, because it foreshadows the internal political confrontations that surfaced later in the 1930s, implicating Nguyen Ai Quoc himself.

Quoc arranged to have Nguyen The Vinh sent to France to begin militant activities within the Vietnamese community, and to establish a solid network of relations with Indochina by recruiting liaison agents from among the personnel working on ships sailing to the Far East. In 1928, Vinh arrived in France with a Chinese passport.

Inasmuch as the Comintern could no longer look to China for sanctuary, it turned its sights back to France and the southern communication route via Singapore. The FCP was instrumental in training its Vietnamese members who, however, were divided by conflicts along social lines; since most of the workers were illiterate and did not speak French, they often felt excluded. Some of the Vietnamese had trouble with their French comrades, like Henri Lozeray, who was in charge of colonial matters and whom they accused of neglecting their training and acting like a bureaucrat. By this time, the question of founding a communist party had already been raised. Lozeray supported a party that would be created and led by the FCP, while Nguyen The Ruc, a student at the Stalin School, wanted an independent party. The problem was settled by the Vietnamese in Indochina, who decided to take matters into their own hands.[59]

Nanyang, the Southern Seas

For five years, Nguyen Ai Quoc worked for the Comintern as their representative in Europe. He went to the International Anti-Imperialism Conference in Brussels, which was organized by Willy Münzenberg, a German Communist who was very active in the international scene (he fled to Moscow in 1936 to avoid being condemned as a Trotskyite, broke with the German Communist Party in 1937, and took refuge in France, where he was assassinated in 1940 by an unknown assailant). Quoc also met the Indian Motilal Nehru, among others, but he soon turned his sights back to the Far East. He tried desperately to get the International to send him back to Asia, and on 12 April 1928 he wrote to the Far Eastern Bureau:

> Can't find work in France, useless in Germany, but needed in Indochina, so I have already requested to return there. In letters to comrades I have already provided a budget for travel and work. When Doriot passed through Berlin,

> he promised to give attention to my situation.... But up to now, I have received no direction from comrades or a reply from Doriot.[60]

Quoc awaited orders for his mission for four months. With little money to live on, he put pressure on the bureau to give him the green light. He wrote a second letter to an unknown recipient (Manuilsky?), asking for someone to intervene so that he could leave for Indochina. On 28 April 1928, V. P. Kolarov conveyed the Comintern's decision to send him to the Far East with a financial allocation of three months.[61] At the end of June, he traveled through Switzerland and Milan to Naples, where he embarked on a Japanese ship sailing via Ceylon (now Sri Lanka) to Siam. He arrived in July 1928 and remained there until November 1929, alternating visits to British Malaysia and Hong Kong. He eventually finished the work begun in Canton in 1925 by founding the Indochinese Communist Party in 1930.

Siam (which became known as Thailand in 1939) was the only independent country in Southeast Asia; that is, it had retained its political sovereignty after the West started carving up the world in the nineteenth century. Vietnamese émigrés had been going there since the seventeenth century, starting with Christians, most of whom were students at the Catholic seminary of Ayuthaya. They were joined in the eighteenth and nineteenth centuries by other Christians who had been banished by royal edict. By the end of the nineteenth century and into the twentieth, other Vietnamese had fled their country in an effort to escape French domination or else reprisals for the suppressed uprisings. Nguyen Ai Quoc estimated their number at thirty thousand.

Most Vietnamese émigrés lived in the northeast of the country along the border with Laos, where the distance between Siam and Nghe An province was at its narrowest, and where the border was porous (see Map 2). The Mekong River was fairly easy to cross in a small boat; Quoc had even crossed it himself to assess the situation in Laos. For more than a year, he wandered through this vast area delimited by Udon, Nongkhai, Sakhon, Nakhon-Phanom, and Mukdahan. He took the pseudonym "Old Chin," even though he was only thirty-eight years old. He met up with Le Manh Trinh and Hoang Van Hoan, former members of the League who had either fled or been sent there from Canton.

Quoc stayed in villages like Nachok, near the central base of Nakhon-Phanom, and in urban neighborhoods where Vietnamese families had settled. Sometimes there was already an infrastructure to welcome him, as in Ban Dong (Phitsanulok province, in the central highlands), where

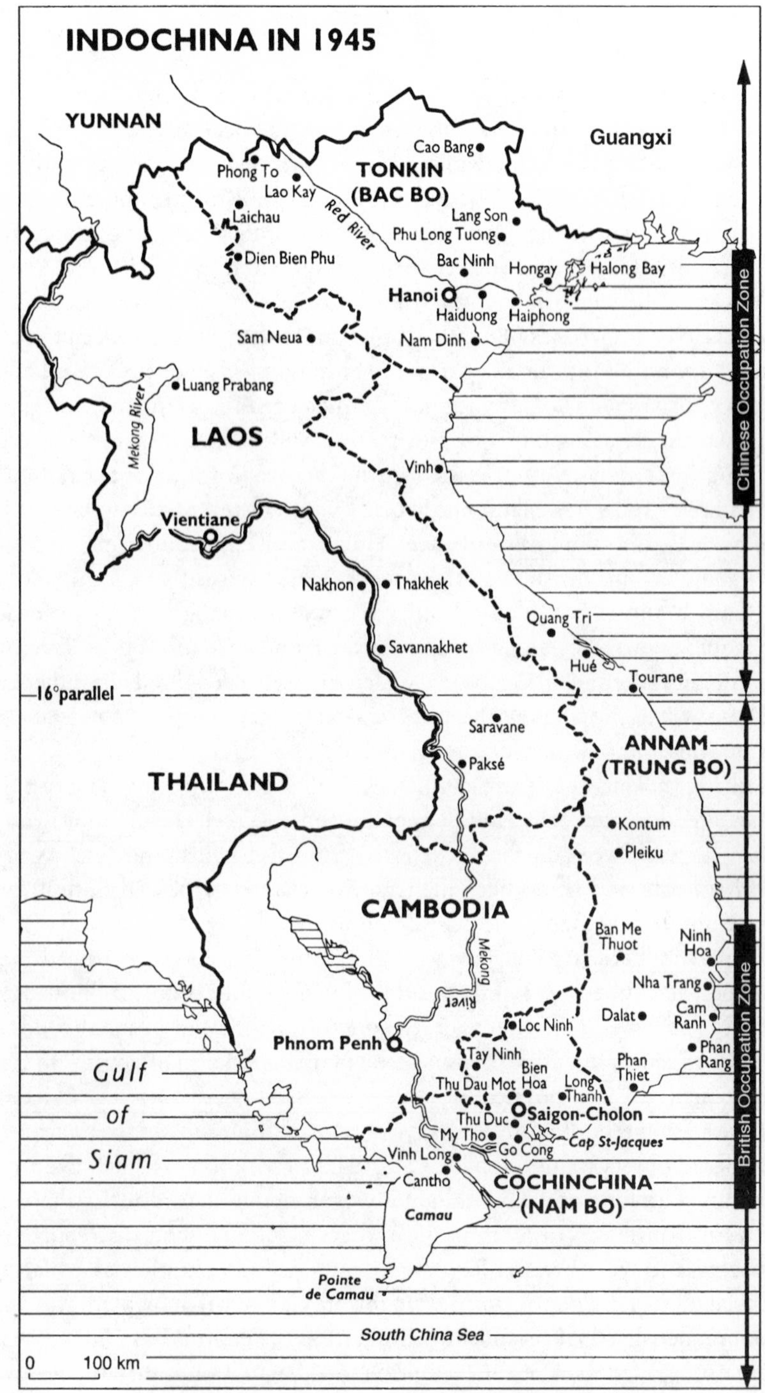

Map 2. Indochina in 1945

he made his first stop. He knew someone from "back home" there, Dang Thuc Hua, whose daughter, Dang Quynh Anh, was a friend of his sister. The family had been in the Resistance for three generations and had fled French repression against the Save the King movement. Some of them had participated in the Journey to the East and the Quang Phuc Hoi (Vietnamese Restoration Society) of Phan Boi Chau.

Wherever he went, he found a friendship association or an agricultural cooperative. Sometimes Quoc the "agitator" was well received, but other times he ran into indifference or outright hostility, as when a French missionary forbade his flock to attend meetings organized by "Old Chin."[62] He used the same methods of penetration and propaganda everywhere, inviting his compatriots to visit him in the evening to discuss the current state of their homeland and world events. After speaking, he would solicit questions from his audience. Those who knew him remember his easy manner and his talent as a teacher, which helped spread his ideas. He used a simple vocabulary and very imagistic language, incorporating popular proverbs and anecdotes inspired by such authors as Tolstoy, Anatole France, and Shakespeare, which of course delighted his audience. He also wrote short plays and historical sketches, as well as songs about the national hero Tran Hung Dao.

During the day he set himself up as a model. First thing in the morning he would do brief calisthenics, then sweep the courtyard, draw water from the well, work in the garden or in the rice fields, and fetch wood like his hosts and the other villagers. Sometimes he passed himself off as a Chinese merchant who had come to meet up with his compatriots and intermediaries from Siam. At other times he shaved his head and donned the robes of a Buddhist monk. He covered dozens of kilometers on foot, using country roads and wooded trails instead of main roads – out of prudence, but also to observe the people in their daily lives. He was sharp, mentally and physically.

Like a good ethnologist, he always practiced "participant observation," as well as "observant participation," and never forgot that a good example is better than a hundred lectures. However, he never forgot that he was on a mission from the Comintern and continued to send his reports to Moscow and write articles for *Inprecor*. It was in Siam, they say, that he translated the *ABCs of Communism*, the breviary written by Bukharin and Preobrazhensky. Five friendship associations (*Thanh Ai* in Vietnamese) were established as a result of Quoc's visit, which in reality functioned as cells of the Revolutionary Youth League and later of the Indochinese Community Party.[63]

Quoc found that in Siam, as in neighboring Malaysia under British domination, socioprofessional careers were divided along ethnic lines. Farming was done almost exclusively by the Thai and Malays, whereas the workers in the plantations, mines, and cities, as well as the merchant bourgeoisie, were Chinese nationals or of Chinese descent. This division of labor overlapped with religious affiliation: The Malays were Muslim, the Thai were Theravada Buddhist, and the Lao and Khmer were Mahayana Buddhist, while the Chinese and Vietnamese were Taoist or Confucian. All of these beliefs and cults were mixed in with the native religious substratum – in this case, that of local spirits (*phi*, *neak ta*, *nat*) – creating a variety of cultures with varying degrees of receptivity to Marxism-Leninism. Quoc saw clearly that "the class struggle does not manifest itself the way it does in the West."

During the 1930s, there was a tightening up of communist activities and recruitment in the nations of Southeast Asia, *Nanyang* in Chinese. The Comintern assigned Quoc to set up autonomous communist parties, not just sections of the CCP, as well as transethnic organizations, and to recruit essentially from the local populations (the Siamese, Lao, and Malay). He founded a communist party in Siam and one in Malaysia, but both continued to recruit their members from among Chinese or Vietnamese immigrants, or from among the Chinese themselves. This situation continued until the 1950s and 1960s, and was a stumbling block to the development of the Communist Parties of Southeast Asia.[64]

The Foundation of a Communist Party in Indochina

Nguyen Ai Quoc, now traveling as the Chinese businessman Song Man Cho, arrived in Hong Kong on 23 December 1929 to lay the foundations of a communist party.[65] The Comintern had asked him to unite the pro-communist Vietnamese groups since they had already received a request for admission by a small organization proclaiming themselves the Communist Party of Indochina on 17 June 1929.

When the Revolutionary Youth League had been dispersed by Chiang Kai-shek's anti-communist repression in 1927, most of the militants trained in Canton returned to their home provinces. Then, joined by other recruits, they organized new cells of the League, as well as workers' and farmers' unions. Faced with the stubborn refusal of the League's leadership – who had fled to Hong Kong and were now led by Lam Duc Thu – to transform their party into a communist one, militants from Tonkin founded the Communist Party of Indochina, or CPI (the Dong

Duong Cong San Dang). This new party was a product of the Tonkin wing of the League, whose members were the most radical and the most active. The majority were from a privileged background – landlords, rich peasants, government officials, or merchants – and many had gone to Franco-Annamite schools (without necessarily having finished primary or secondary education). These militants underwent a "proletarization" in order to penetrate the workers' world. They wanted to condition themselves and be in a position to denounce the Revolutionary Youth League as "petit-bourgeois opportunists" and "false revolutionaries."

This proletarian conversion met with varying degrees of success, depending on how well their members tolerated the conditions of manual labor. They found work as coolies in the mines, on large plantations, and in factories, and took jobs as porters or rickshaw drivers. Although their membership never surpassed a few hundred militants, they spread as far as Cochinchina. In 1928, they published the Comintern's program in three journals: *Co Do* (Red Flag), *Bua Liem* (Hammer and Sickle), and *Cong Hoi Do* (Red Union). The "Original Thanh Nien" followed close behind, and in the autumn of 1929 changed its name to the Annamite Communist Party (An Nam Cong San Dang) and published the journals *Do* (Red) and *Bon-se-vich* (The Bolshevik). The members also did not hesitate to denounce their former comrades as "leftist deviationists," "infantile communists," and – for want of an avian metaphor – "chickens who dress up in peacock feathers."

To add to the confusion, a small group called the Revolutionary Youth League of Annam (Tan Viet Nam Cach Mang Dang), founded in Annam in 1926 by nationalist scholars who did not want to be left out, adopted the name Indochinese Communist League (Dong Duong Cong San Lien Doan) on 1 January 1930. They offered to unite with the CPI but were systematically refused because the Tonkin-based group saw the Tan Viet as a group of nationalists, intellectuals, and petit-bourgeois. In practice, the three organizations did not run into conflict since the CPI "absorbed" the cells of the League in Cochinchina and had not yet made inroads into Annam. However, their union would have established the type of communism desired by the Third International throughout French Indochina and at practically all levels of society.

The Comintern issued a directive on 27 October 1929 ordering the formation of a communist party in Indochina. They believed that the political and social situation was ripe for the creation of a party for the proletarian masses. Quoc responded: "I was exasperated, I summoned the representatives of the three movements to Hong Kong."[66] While the people of the colony were celebrating the New Year with festivities ringing in the Year of the Horse, Quoc was playing the mediator during meetings held from 3 to 7 February 1930. Against the backdrop of noisemakers and fireworks, the delegates (except those of the League, who did not join the Vietnamese Communist Party until 24 February) clashed during four days of fierce debate, voicing their grievances and trading mutual attacks. "Comrade Vuong" (alias for Nguyen Ai Quoc) insisted on a name change, to the Vietnamese Communist Party, or VCP (Dang Cong San Viet Nam). The new party elaborated a strategy and launched its *Appeal* to the workers, farmers, soldiers, youth, students, and the exploited.

Both the discussions and the ensuing strategic platform were marked by the underlying contradiction and necessary compromise between two aims: liberating the nation and launching a social revolution. On one side, there were those who wanted to bring together all patriotic forces, including intellectuals, petits-bourgeois, midlevel peasants, and even capitalists, landlords, and rich peasants so long as "they are not avowed counterrevolutionaries." On the other side were those who wanted to take from the rich and give to the poor, ending the oppression of those in authority and restoring dignity to the meek. The new Communist Party set itself these two goals, and this dialectic remained forever present within the heart of the independence movement.

The contradictions within the Vietnamese community were similar to those that Nguyen Ai Quoc had seen among the Chinese revolutionary camp in Canton. They were even present in Moscow, deep within the Comintern and within the ranks of the Bolshevik party, where the war between Stalin and Trotsky and the Workers' Opposition had been raging since 1927. Quoc knew that these internal divisions would have to be overcome. Throughout his life he was plagued by this desire for unity: within the party, within the nation of Vietnam, and later within the socialist camp.

In 1928, the Sixth Congress of the Comintern defined a political line that came down to "class against class." It condemned the alliance between the CCP and the Kuomintang, which had been fatal to the former, and assigned tactical responsibility for the debacle to CCP Secretary General Chen Duxiu. From then on, the Comintern would not allow the newly born Vietnamese party to carry on its double strategy, where the priority was national liberation. On its injunction, the Central Committee of the VCP held a meeting in Hong Kong in October 1930, as always with the presence of "Vuong," representative of the Comintern.

At this meeting, VCP leaders denounced the purely formal nature of the unification of February 1930, which had brought together a variety of groups without providing for their ideological fusion. Their party's strategy, moreover, did not correspond to the line of "class against class." And finally, the name "Vietnamese Communist Party" expressed all too clearly a nationalist – if not chauvinist – point of view, which was a serious infraction at the time. Cambodia and Laos were under the same colonial oppression as Vietnam, and so proletarian solidarity should theoretically have come into play to form a single theater of operations for the communists of all Indochinese nations. The Central Committee decided that the party would be called the Indochinese Communist Party, or ICP (Dang Cong San Dong Duong), like the dissident group Thanh Nien, substituting, however, the French syntax for the Chinese.

The results of this Central Committee meeting ran contrary to what Nguyen Ai Quoc had written when he was in Moscow:

> The class struggle is not the same as in the West.... We are to stir up nationalism among the natives in the name of the International. These orders from Moscow strike the bourgeois as an audacious paradox, but what do they really mean? A policy that is marvelously realistic. At this point, we cannot do anything for the Annamites if we do not draw upon the great potential of their national character.[67]

Quoc's report had been read when it was published in 1924, but had evidently been shelved by the Comintern, if not listed in their "black book" of deviations. They wanted to orient all Indochinese people in the same direction, without taking into consideration the diversity of their social systems, their cultures, and the varying evolution that had been stamped upon them by French colonialism. This eventually gave rise to a number of problems among ethnic groups and among the states of the peninsula.

The Central Committee assigned Tran Phu, the first Secretary General of the ICP, to write up the *Political Theses*. Son of a low-level mandarin and himself a teacher, Tran Phu was among the first five Vietnamese to study at the Stalin School. He returned to Indochina via France, and like a good Internationalist he went to the Père-Lachaise Cemetery in Paris to pay his respects at the wall of "Les Fédérés" commemorating the Communards of 1871. The *Political Theses* laid out the strategic objectives of the ICP over the next few years. They aimed to drive out imperialism and destroy feudalism, a two-part goal corresponding to the "bourgeois democratic" phase of the revolution. In this case, the term "feudalism" designates one of the modes of production in Marxist theory, encompassing the institutions, social classes, and precolonial mentalities of the colonial regime that led to oppression and constituted an obstacle to the modernization of the country.[68]

Nguyen Ai Quoc hastened to inform the French Communist Party of the birth of the ICP, while wondering whether he was still a member of the FCP or whether he should consider himself a member of both parties. On 11 April 1931, the Executive Committee of the Comintern gave their response by recognizing the independence of the ICP from the FCP, and in 1932 they admitted the ICP into the bosom of the International as a full, separate entity. Quoc nevertheless insisted on its solidarity with the French proletariat and the necessity of reinforcing ties with the FCP.

In the years immediately following the founding of the ICP, however, Quoc complained in a letter to the Comintern that his comrades were treating him like a mailbox, as simply an intermediary with the Comintern's Far Eastern Bureau. They bypassed him and did not ask for advice and, most importantly, thought that he should not take part in any ICP decisions. In Indochina, the Communists took initiatives that placed their party at center stage, thus drawing heightened attention and making themselves vulnerable to the blows of their French adversary.

The year 1930 thus began with several important events: the birth of a communist party, a serious revolt known as the Yen Bay mutiny, and peasant demonstrations in the provinces of Nghe An, Ha Tinh, and Quang Ngai and in Cochinchina, which turned into violent clashes with the authorities, the police, and the army. These clashes came as no surprise since there had been a number of workers' strikes in Tonkin in 1928 and especially 1929. Moreover, in 1929 there were several assassinations, including that of Alfred Bazin, director of a recruiting office for Indochinese manual labor, expressing latent hostility against the colonial regime and its representatives.

The strikes were instigated by the "first" Communist Party of Indochina, whereas Bazin's assassination bore the signature of the Viet Nam Quoc Dan Dang (VNQDD), a new nationalist party created in 1925 by a group of young Vietnamese in Hanoi and modeled on the Nationalist Party of Sun Yat-sen. Dozens of its members had been arrested, which pushed them to attempt one final desperate measure. They threw in their lot with the infantry of the colonial army garrisoned at Yen Bay, among whom they had recruited several militants. They were to assassinate the French officers and petty officers, sparking a mutiny that would lead to the capture of other garrisons. But the revolt failed. The Communists who had been contacted by the VNQDD tried to dissuade them from embarking upon a venture that they deemed premature and one that did not "mobilize the masses." The plan was both adventurist and putschist, two negative qualities in the eyes of the Communists.[69]

The founding of the ICP occurred at almost the same time, in early February, while the revolt at Yen Bay was being harshly suppressed. Two months later the Communists took their turn, symbolically on the first of May, leading a mass uprising. They mobilized tens of thousands of people from the countryside in the two northern provinces, the Mekong delta, and the Center. The paroxysm of this wave of insurrection became the foundation of what was called the *xo viet* (soviets) of Nghe Tinh (among others, in Nam Dan, the district where Quoc was born). The local village authorities were dismissed, forced to submit, or assassinated; and taxes on alcohol, salt, and opium were abolished. The Communists expressed their intention to confiscate lands from the property owners and divide them up into shares, but apparently this was never put into practice.

The severity of the repression, "the white terror" as Quoc called it in his reports to the Comintern, was as vast as the insurrections themselves. The French called in the colonial infantry, the Foreign Legion, the Tho infantry, and the air force, who shot down and machine-gunned hundreds of demonstrators. A criminal commission condemned hundreds of detainees to deportation, imprisonment, and even execution.[70]

The events of Nghe Tinh clearly revealed the link between the patriotic struggle and the social war. But although the movement expressed the enthusiasm of the masses and the strength of the Communist position, it was criticized as "leftist," its opponents claiming that the class struggle had taken precedence over the national struggle through direct action, and that the proclamation of soviets was premature.

THREE

Under the Sword of Damocles

By mid-1931 the tide was turning, and the wave of nationalism and social change that had swept through Indochina, particularly in the three countries of Vietnam (Tonkin, Annam, and Cochinchina), had completely ebbed. There was a total reversal of the situation, one that was detrimental to the Indochinese Communists and to the Comintern in Asia.

THE ARREST AND ALLEGED DEATH OF NGUYEN AI QUOC

The events of Yen Bay, Nghe Tinh, and Cochinchina had been a serious blow to France's colonial domination, judging by their consequences. There were polemics in the French press; debates in the House of Deputies; a mission assigned to the new Minister of the Colonies, Paul Reynaud; news reports (R. Vanlande, A. Viollis, and Pierre Herbart); books (Do Duc Ho, Villemotier-Comberaine, Jacques Dorsenne); and demonstrations against anticolonialist repression in Indochina.[1] The situation had become critical and was exacerbated by the global economic crisis that the Communists hailed as the last gasp of world capitalism.

The confidence of French officials was shaken further by an additional element: the participation of the peasantry. They were "usually calm people with good common sense, indifferent to the flow of ideas that go beyond the scope of their immediate interests." How could they be "suddenly transformed into partisans of revolt and fanatics of upheaval?"[2] One member of the commission investigating the events in North Annam, undoubtedly a priest, took a historical perspective: "Annamite society is currently in the same state as Roman society was when the first Christian sermons brought new aspirations to people's souls, leading to the destruction of their old society."[3] French authorities were alarmed by this eruption of the "red peril," for they had originally thought that Yen Bay was a communist insurrection (in fact, the VNQDD carried a red flag but without the hammer and sickle), and also because the Chinese Communists had just created a short-lived soviet in Longzhou, a border town very close to Dong Khe and That Khe.

General Henri Claudel wrote a lucid inspection report on the Far East, entitled "Research into the Causes of the Insurrection Movement," that ended with these lines:

> A social movement does not hold itself in check, but tramples everything in its path. The army knows how to fight an armed enemy that it can see and measure itself against; it cannot change people's minds and improve society. The Sûreté can arrest men, but it can not imprison their thoughts.[4]

On the opposing side, in a report from August 1931, General Lombard called for "a merciless and immediate repression against all Communist crimes," and advocated an "agreement between the governments and the police forces of the British and Dutch Indies, who share common interests with us."[5] Doctor A. F. Legendre joined him in advocating the creation of "a federation of the great colonial powers (except Japan) with a Flying Squad to mount against the Cominternists."[6]

The Arrest of Nguyen Ai Quoc

Dr. Legendre and General Lombard got their wish in 1931, when circumstances came together in favor of the French. With the help of moles (including a student at the Stalin School), the testimony of defectors (either voluntary or rooted out by force or torture), the tenacity of the Indochinese Sûreté, a bit of luck, and the imprudence or mistakes made by Communists who forgot the rules of secrecy, the police managed to confiscate mail and identify addresses. As a result, in the early morning hours of 6 June 1931 in Hong Kong, Nguyen Ai Quoc (still using the name Song Man Cho) was caught in a trap set by the Special Branch of the police of His British Majesty. They had found his name in the address book of the Frenchman Joseph Ducroux, who did not have time to destroy it before being captured by the British police in Singapore. Ducroux, the Comintern's envoy in China from 1926 to 1928, had gone back to Singapore in 1931 under the name Serge Lefranc and opened an import-export office, which was under police surveillance without his knowledge.[7]

The address book was the starting point of a whole series of arrests, some of them netting "big game." Nguyen Ai Quoc was taken in Hong Kong, and on 15 June, the husband-and-wife team known as the Noulens were brought into custody (Hilaire Noulens, actually Paul Ruegg, who ran the Comintern's Far Eastern Bureau in Shanghai). Other militants of a lower rank, but who played a crucial role as liaison agents, were also arrested. From 1931 to 1932, the ICP was progressively decapitated: First the General Secretary Tran Phu was captured (and died shortly afterward in prison), then its Central Committee was taken in Saigon, and finally those "returning from Moscow" were plucked one by one. By 1933 the ICP was in dire straits.[8]

It was imperative that Nguyen Ai Quoc be shielded from the wrath of the colonial justice system. On 10 October 1929, the Imperial Court in Vinh (Nghe An province) had already found him responsible for the troubles in Annam and condemned him to death. Capital punishment was later commuted to forced labor in perpetuity, but in 1930 the Supreme Court of Hué deferred sentence until the accused could stand trial again to face further accusations of "plots and assassinations." Moreover, the circumstances of 1930–32 had made the colonial authorities anything but forgiving. The four leaders of the VNQDD were taken to Yen Bay and publicly beheaded. The Communists Nguyen Duc Canh and Nguyen Phong Sac, leaders of the Nghe Tinh movement, were both executed (Canh was guillotined in Haiphong and Sac's body was never found). The Indochinese government asked the governor of Hong Kong to extradite Nguyen Ai Quoc, and France's ambassador in London took steps to make His Majesty comply with the French request.

From the moment of his arrest, Quoc became the subject of fierce negotiations between the British and French authorities. Both the police and the governor of the colony agreed to send the detainee to a French jail, but Quoc was lucky, so to speak, to have been taken prisoner in a politically liberal nation with laws protecting the individual. Ho Tung Mau, a colleague from his Canton days, quickly alerted the president of the Hong Kong bar, the solicitor Frank Loseby, who enlisted the aid of his colleague in London, D. N. Pritt. In Hong Kong, Loseby passed the case on to another solicitor, F. C. Jenkin, who ended up pleading Quoc's case. The Soviet-based International Red Aid was notified and no doubt secretly organized Nguyen Ai Quoc's defense by obtaining the services of British lawyers. The same happened in Indochina, where accused Communists were defended by Charles Cancellieri from the bar in Saigon.[9]

From June 1931 to January 1933, Quoc was moved from prison to a hospital for treatment of what was thought to be tuberculosis and was eventually cleared of his charges in September 1932. From the hospital he took a room at the YMCA and then with the Losebys, but things got complicated when he was given orders to leave the British colony within three days. He tried to leave in August but was stopped in Singapore and sent back to Hong Kong because his papers were not in order. He had no choice but to disappear once again into semiclandestinity with the continued help of Loseby.

The tribulations he endured turned out to be preferable to extradition to a Vietnamese jail, since he almost certainly would have been executed – despite assurances by the French ambassador in London that the Résident Supérieur in Annam would commute the punishment set by the Imperial Court. Quoc was eventually freed, thanks to the defense tactics adopted by his lawyers, who used all of the resources available under British law. The case was brought before His Majesty's Privy Council in London where Loseby subsequently invoked habeas corpus to avoid extradition and then obtained permission for Quoc to go to Moscow via Singapore. The government of Hong Kong was represented by Stafford Cripps, later a prominent Labor Party politician, who adopted a sympathetic approach. In the end, they arrived at a settlement instead of having a public trial. These legal proceedings revealed the contradictions that existed among the Foreign Office, the Governor of Hong Kong, the British police, and the bar. They also brought out the differences between British and French law, as well as the different views and behaviors of the British and French governments, even though they were both imperialist powers.

Quoc's case received much public attention, like the Sacco-Vanzetti case and the trial of the Bulgarian Communist Georgi Dimitrov. Campaigns were orchestrated by the International Red Aid and the League Against Imperialism, among others. The Case of "Nguyen the Patriot" was on the front pages of the biggest Hong Kong newspapers, bestowing a new halo on "the country man from Nghe Tinh."

With his freedom restored, Nguyen the Patriot became a problematic guest for the British. The French, meanwhile, continued to press them for custody. It was not an ideal situation, but it was better than being in prison or confined to house arrest. As it turned out, Nguyen Ai Quoc had been well treated in prison and allowed contact with the outside world. Mrs. Loseby and her daughter Patricia visited him and brought what he needed to regain his health, as did the wife of the Vice Governor of the Colony, who was a writer and playwright. It seems that no one could resist his charm, as Loseby wrote thirty years later: "After thirty minutes with Ho, I was entirely won over; he radiated an extraordinary force of conviction."

Loseby eventually came up with a ruse to solve the problem: He announced in late 1932 that Nguyen Ai Quoc was dead. His death seemed plausible to almost everyone since he was thought to have been suffering from tuberculosis. *The Daily Worker* and *L'Humanité* published the news, in Moscow the Vietnamese students at the Stalin School organized a funeral service, and in Paris Léo Poldès wrote a heartfelt tribute to Nguyen the Patriot in a special edition of his journal *Le Faubourg*. The news was also taken seriously in the opposing camp. In an earlier article from April 1932 in the *Revue des Deux Mondes*, the journalist Jacques Dorsenne had already predicted that "the Annamite leader, even more than by human justice, has been condemned by divine justice. Tuberculosis forgives no one, and if the decision of the judges in London does not take effect soon, Nguyen Ai Quoc, the gentle enlightened one with blood-stained hands, will not be alive."

Loseby orchestrated Quoc's escape with the help – or even complicity – of the Vice Governor of Hong Kong. The steamship *An Hui*, en route from Hong Kong to Shanghai, left the port and waited briefly until a tender (the personal tender of the Vice Governor, some sources say) came alongside so that Quoc, clad in the long tunic of a Chinese scholar, his chin bristling with a real or fake goatee, could climb up the gangway.[10] On 25 January 1933, he disembarked in Amoy (now Xiamen), where the firecrackers ringing in the Year of the Rooster recalled the Tet (New Year) festivities of three years earlier when he had arrived in Hong Kong. Fortunately for him, he did not go directly to Shanghai because, paradoxically, the Hong Kong police had warned the French police that the man they were looking for was on his way there.

Quoc's goal was to reach Moscow. He went first to Shanghai in July disguised as a wealthy businessman, then checked into a fancy hotel and rode around in a rented car complete with chauffeur, a subterfuge that exempted him from an identity check by the French police. Nearly out of money, he was saved by Soong Qingling, Sun Yat-sen's widow. Through her, Quoc learned that his French friend Paul Vaillant-Couturier, a member of the FCP, was in Shanghai attending a peace congress. He met up with him and wrote two lines of poetry:

> After three years of wandering adrift
> Here I am back in the great family of workers and peasants.[11]

Some readers may find the second line a bit ironic, but the important thing is that Quoc himself believed it. Then, accompanied by his friend, he made his way back to Vladivostok in the spring of 1934.

This return to the "great socialist family" did not mean that Nguyen Ai Quoc had seen the last of his troubles. Indeed, having emerged from his trials unscathed – evading the French police and maybe even the scaffold, obtaining legal defense by liberal lawyers, and receiving the indulgence of His Majesty's Privy Council – and having regained his freedom with the complicity of the Vice Governor of Hong Kong, he now found himself under suspicion by the Soviets of having made a deal with the British secret services. This type of suspicion is dangerous in any type of revolutionary organization, especially a secret one. It was even more critical within a communist regime like the Soviet Union, where Stalin was increasing his absolute power through the use of terror: against the "Nepmen" (supporters of the New Economic Policy, 1920–28), kulaks (the rich peasant class in the Ukraine), Trotskyites, saboteurs, and, of course, foreign agents.

ON THE RAZOR'S EDGE IN MOSCOW: 1934–1938

Nguyen Ai Quoc returned to the USSR in the spring of 1934. He left us an account of those days in his second autobiographical work, entitled *Vua di duong, vua ke chuyen* (Walking and Talking), published in 1963 and signed T. Lan. In it he recalled the difficult living conditions he had experienced in the USSR in 1924 and then offered several comparisons. First, he described the difference between Germany, whose sad and despairing people were suffering economically in 1923, and the young Soviet republic, where the Russians were full of hope for a better life despite the difficulties. The second comparison noted the economic and social progress that had been made in the USSR by 1935. The success of the first Five Year Plan meant that living conditions "in all aspects" had "improved greatly," and he congratulated the Soviets for canceling the rations on food and clothing only seventeen years after revolution, civil war, foreign intervention, and famine. And most importantly, this agricultural and once backward nation was on the point of becoming a great industrial power. The children whom Quoc had met in the Pioneer camps in the 1920s were now doctors, engineers, and even military officers. They were living proof of the great effort that had been put into raising educational levels and promoting children of the peasantry and the working class to higher social positions.[12]

The achievements that Quoc saw in 1934 reinforced his belief that the Soviet regime was the model to follow. His correspondence with Moscow in the early 1930s was increasingly full of requests for informational materials to better promote the "Nation of Socialism" and its achievements.[13]

In 1930, he published a hundred-page booklet entitled *Nhat ky chim tau* (Chronicle of a shipwreck), which tells the story of three shipwrecked sailors – a European, an Asian, and an African – who are picked up by a Soviet ship. The Soviet government shows them around the country and points out the achievements of the young nation, then sends the three men back to their own countries.[14]

Quoc had no doubts about the brilliant future of the Soviet Union, but he was not blinded by his faith, as we see in a letter to Giao (Bui Cong Trung), head of the Vietnamese group at the Stalin School. In 1930, Quoc had made a number of recommendations for welcoming three Vietnamese delegates to the Workers' International. He strongly suggested that "during excursions, you must draw their attention to what is beautiful and positive, so that they can compare it with the situation in our country. When you find less appealing aspects like the *besprizorny* [vagabond children] and the *nepmen*... you will have to explain them to our comrades so they do not leave with a bad impression."[15]

He had a clear picture of the situation in the USSR, but still felt the need to explain the facts by relativizing them, as did Vaillant-Couturier. In his letter to Giao, for example, he wanted his countrymen to "compare it with the situation in our country," since people from colonized nations tended to favor the Soviet system, in contrast to visitors from parliamentary or liberal democracies, who often took a different view.

Consequently, Quoc does not seem to have written or issued a statement concerning the evolution of the Soviet Union once Stalin consolidated his power in the late 1930s, with its merciless repression and bloody purges within the Communist Party. The assassination of Sergei Kirov on 1 December 1934 unleashed a spate of arrests and trials in Moscow (1936–38), following which a large part of the Bolshevik old guard who had opposed Stalin (Zinoviev and Bukharin among others) were executed. Many lesser-known Communists and non-Communists were also imprisoned or killed. The poet Osip Mandelstam and General Blücher, to mention only those among Quoc's acquaintances, were struck down by these ruthless purges. Borodin fell victim only after World War II, during Stalin's second reign of terror and the *Beriashchina* (L. P. Beria was chief of the secret police and Minister of the Interior). Quoc kept a low profile, obviously aware that as a member of the Comintern he was at risk himself, but also because everyone kept quiet when they saw family, friends, neighbors, and colleagues disappear every day. Alexander Solzhenitzyn describes this type of situation in his exposé *The Gulag Archipelago*, wherein each new arrest is greeted with indifference.[16]

In Reserve or in Penance?

After a stay at a sanatorium in the Crimea, Nguyen Ai Quoc returned to Moscow in October 1934. Shortly thereafter he left the Lux Hotel, where he had been staying with other Comintern personnel, and entered the Lenin School as a boarder under the name of Lin. As a result, he was not at the Lux when officers of the GPU (the Soviet internal security apparatus) stormed in during the night, nor did he see the sealed-off bedroom doors the following morning.[17] At the Lenin School, he was soon transferred from the Chinese to the French language group, which was deemed "more appropriate," though this is not explained. The school trained or recycled high-level cadres from communist parties, and for some reason the International had decided that Quoc needed to be brought up-to-date. The words of Vera Vassilieva in this regard are fairly clear: "Quoc must study seriously before we send him on a mission." Were they just trying to keep him busy while he was waiting? Or was it a period of observation following the accusations of his comrades in the ICP and his suspicious "jailbreak"?

Certain facts lead us to believe that Quoc was definitely sidelined. The Seventh International Congress of the Comintern was held in Moscow on 25 July 1935, but Quoc had only an advisory position within the Vietnamese delegation, so played only a minor role. Three other delegates from Indochina were present: Le Hong Phong, Secretary General of the Overseas Executive Committee of the ICP, which had been running the party since the Central Committee was all but annihilated in 1931; a young female revolutionary from Nghe Tinh province named Nguyen Thi Minh Khai; and Hoang Van Non.[18] Phong was the first to leave for Asia in 1935, and on 25 September of the same year, Quoc confided to the writer Ilya Ehrenburg: "I only have one hope, to return to my country as soon as possible."[19]

His hopes were soon dashed after Khai and Non also left Moscow during the summer of 1936. In the meantime, the Comintern's cadre service authorized Quoc to draw up a "bio" and get his passport and travel papers in order, but then, suddenly and without explanation, they announced that his departure was postponed because "the situation has changed."[20] He had no choice but to continue his studies and devote himself to the Vietnamese students in Moscow.

Quoc, still operating under the name of Lin, enrolled in the Institute for the Study of National and Colonial Questions (the new name for the Stalin School), which became his new home in December 1936. For one year he continued his studies and prepared a thesis on *The Land*

Revolution in Southeast Asia. He also translated Marx and Engels' *The Communist Manifesto* and, significantly, Lenin's *Leftism: An Infantile Disorder*.[21] More of his compatriots had enrolled at the Institute, and he taught *quoc ngu* to those who "had no education." He also gave lectures on politics, mediated discussions that often turned bitter, and arbitrated the heated disputes that split the members of the group, urging them to remain united in their purpose. Nguyen Khanh Toan, who was in charge of the Vietnamese students at the time, remembers:

> Ho was in close contact with the Vietnamese group. He joined us regularly in the evenings to share his experiences with us, stressing revolutionary morality, especially solidarity. Some of the younger students, out of provocation or arrogance, used to quibble about minor issues. Our Uncle arbitrated the conflicts. He tried to instill in all of us certain essential principles, to combat pride, selfishness, egocentrism, lack of discipline, and anarchy, while reinforcing unity and placing the interest of the revolution above everything else. He often said: "If you cannot be united in a small group, how will you be able to unite the masses, fight the colonialists, and save our nation?"[22]

Indeed, beyond the personal dissension and friction among those from different social milieus and cultural levels, the Vietnamese community was also aware of the anti-Trotskyite campaign that was spreading throughout the Soviet Union, and by the wave of terrorism shaking the communist world.

Beyond these activities with his compatriots, Quoc also did some physical exercise every day and participated in the activities of the Francophone group at the Institute. He even played the role of flag bearer in a play commemorating the anniversary of the Paris Commune. In his free time he took advantage of Moscow's vibrant cultural scene – one of the paradoxes of this period – and went to museums and plays; he also visited cultural halls, children's gardens, and the rural communities known as kolkhozes. Vassilieva's daughters remember that he used to visit their family, sometimes accompanied by a young woman named Lan, alias for Nguyen Thi Minh Khai.

We Must Save Comrade Nguyen Ai Quoc

In 1938, while the arrests were multiplying around him, Quoc was brought before a disciplinary board of the Comintern led by Dmitri Manuilsky, Vera Vassilieva, and the Chinese Kang Sheng. We do not have a written record of the meeting that could reveal what reproaches or accusations were brought against Quoc, but we do know that Vassilieva defended him by putting his faults – whatever they were – down to inexperience. (Perhaps her leniency was due to the fact that her husband, Mark Zorkii, had been swept up by the wave of purges and was in prison, and so she wanted to help those in a similar predicament.) Kang Sheng called for severe sanctions against his Vietnamese comrade, but Manuilsky and most probably the Finn Otto Kuusinen, head of the Far Eastern Bureau of the Comintern, were more indulgent.

On 6 June, Quoc sent a letter to a comrade from the Comintern, whom he does not name but who is undoubtedly Manuilsky:

> Dear Comrade, today is the seventh anniversary of my arrest in Hong Kong and it is the beginning of my eighth year of inactivity. I am taking this occasion to write you so that you will change the sad situation in which I find myself. Send me anywhere or keep me here but give me a useful task to accomplish; do not leave me idle for too long, *as if I were cast aside and outside of the party* [Quoc's emphasis]. I would be very grateful, dear comrade, if you would agree to meet me. I think it would be good since we have not seen each other for a long time. Dear comrade, please accept my best wishes, as a communist and a friend.[23]

This letter seems to have been Quoc's last recourse for escaping the poisonous atmosphere that had hung over Moscow since the onset of the widespread purges, and probably also for avoiding imminent arrest. The Institute finally announced that "Student number 19 (Lin) is no longer enrolled in the Institute as of 29 September 1938: he is returning to his country."

One day in October, Quoc went to visit Nguyen Khanh Toan at the Institute and chatted with him, but said nothing about his imminent departure. The next evening, in the cold Moscow air, Quoc boarded a Trans-Siberian train at Yaroslavsky Station, heading east.[24] About the same time, it was decided in a secret resolution from the Politburo of the Soviet Communist Party, dated 17 October 1938, that the mass terror would come to a halt. The end of the *Yezhovshchina* (Yezhov was the head of the Soviet secret police) coincided with Quoc's departure – or perhaps even his escape.

Was Nguyen Ai Quoc a Bigamist?

It seems pretty clear that the four years in Moscow were a political "wilderness" for Quoc, but did his emotional life also suffer? Nguyen Thi Minh Khai, the twenty-four-year-old delegate at the Comintern Congress, had filled out a bio in which she claimed to be the wife of Nguyen Ai Quoc. In March 1930, she had been sent from Haiphong to Hong Kong to help Quoc in his activities at the local office of the Far Eastern Bureau. Were they more than comrades? Two documents from the Far Eastern Bureau mention a request by Quoc for permission to marry. If the request was genuine, then Quoc planned on getting remarried while his first marriage was still legally binding. Or perhaps he used the word "marriage" to avoid the term "cohabitation." All things considered, the affair was no more than a minor episode, but it intrigues historians; the "bio" was written up by Vassilieva inasmuch as Khai did not speak Russian. What is more, the words "wife of" are crossed out in the document, according to those who have seen it.[25]

If there really was a romantic liaison, one could say it ended poorly for Quoc, since Nguyen Thi Minh Khai married Le Hong Phong in a city hall in Moscow before returning to Indochina, where the couple met a tragic end.[26] The story would also lend credence to a rumor that in addition to a political rivalry between the two men – Phong having become the highest-ranking leader of the ICP – there was a personal one as well.

Although this "conjugal" imbroglio remains somewhat of a mystery, an unpublished document sheds some light on the state of mind of Nguyen Thi Minh Khai. In a letter seized by the Indochinese Sûreté, she responded to friends of a man with whom she had had a liaison in the past:

> The marriage is nonsense, a bore, trouble.... Now it's all over.... My only husband is the Communist Revolution. This is why I feel a brotherly attachment and affection for Do [Tran Dai Do was her suitor]. Do is an excellent comrade, a dear friend, a sincere and courageous patriot whom I revere deeply.... Our former relationship planted the seeds of a friendship in our hearts that is far superior to love in its purity, its strength, and its duration.[27]

This written declaration shows Nguyen Thi Minh Khai to be among the many men and women throughout history who sacrificed themselves for a religious or political cause deemed worthy of their self-abnegation. When such a sacrifice is pushed to the extreme, it resembles the phenomenon called *kamikaze*.

The Paradox of the 1930s

Although Nguyen Ai Quoc had been severely criticized by the leaders of the newly founded ICP for his rightist views, decisions made at the

Seventh Congress of the International in 1935 eventually strengthened his position within the ideological debate.

Beginning in 1931, the Central Committee of the ICP had been sending its reports directly to the Comintern, bypassing Quoc altogether, causing him to complain that he had been "reduced to nothing but a mailbox." In 1932, the attacks on Quoc became stronger. An article in the *Cahiers du Bolchevisme* denounced "opportunists" who had led the party astray and were responsible for the failures of 1930 and 1931. In 1934, Quoc was mentioned by name in an article in the *Tap Chi Bon-Se-Vik* (Bolshevik Review), which was published by the Overseas Committee. The author expressed the following grievances:

> Nguyen Ai Quoc has rendered a great service to our party; nevertheless, our comrades should not forget his nationalist tendencies and his mistaken directives regarding the fundamental issues of the bourgeois democratic revolution and his opportunistic theories which are still deeply rooted within most of our comrades . . . Nguyen Ai Quoc does not understand the directives of the Communist International. He has not unified the three organizations from top to bottom.

Quoc had furthermore advocated a tactic of reform and collaboration among the classes, suggesting "neutrality toward the bourgeoisie and rich peasantry, alliance with the middle and small property owners, etc."[28]

Until 1935, Quoc was not in step with the political line of "class against class," which had been defined by the Sixth Congress of the Comintern (1928) and espoused by the First National Congress of the ICP (held in Macao in 1935). But five months later, ICP leaders themselves were put in an awkward position vis-à-vis the Comintern, when the latter called for all Communist Parties to form a unified antifascist front. This strategy was aimed primarily at European communists, who had to unite with democrats of all stripes, but then Japan began its military expansion in Manchuria (1931) and China (1937). This posed a threat to all of Asia, as did Hitler's rise to power in Europe, and was used to justify the new strategy of the Comintern, which considered Japan a "military and fascist" power.[29]

Meanwhile, the emergence of the Popular Front in France forced the government to moderate its colonial policies. It liberated political prisoners, increased freedom of the press and of assembly, and broadened its tolerance of social movements. The ICP responded to this new turn of events by organizing an Indochinese Democratic Front – its answer to the Popular Front. This Front demanded freedom of association and political affiliation, and moderated its attacks on colonialism. Local ICP organizations called for the cessation of attacks on the indigenous bourgeois and wealthy landlords, thus heeding Nguyen Ai Quoc's recommendation to leave the door open to all of their countrymen who wanted to join the communists in order to realize a common objective. Nevertheless, the ICP was playing a double game: Militants who had been released from prison would act within the law, while the others would continue to operate in the shadows.[30]

UNDER CHINESE GUIDANCE: 1938–1941

In 1938, Quoc passed through Alma Ata (now Almaty) and Urumqi before reaching Lanzhou, in Gansu province, where he was received by the liaison office of the Chinese Communist army, which worked closely with its Soviet counterpart to guard their borders. He donned a commander's uniform and became Commander Hu Guang of the 8th Route Army. He spent two weeks in Yan'an, the primary communist base in northwestern China where Mao Zedong had established his general headquarters at the end of the Long March, and then headed south to Guangxi province, which was his main theater of operations until 1945.[31]

Quoc did not write much about Yan'an in his autobiographical account, *Walking and Talking*, but he was struck by the prevailing sense of equality that he found there. The Chinese General Zhu De, for example, wore no insignia of his rank, and so Quoc at first mistook the general for the cook. This observation confirms just how important "equality" was for him, that it was perhaps even the definitive criterion by which a society was to be judged. In the same account, he recalls an exchange six or seven years earlier with a Chinese nurse from the prison hospital in Hong Kong. She asked him, "What is communism?" Quoc replied: "No one will be exploited anymore, we will love each other and we will all be equal. Now, for example, you wear a blue collar while the chief British nurse wears a red one. Communism will abolish this hierarchical difference and you will no longer have to wear the blue collar for the rest of your life." These two observations are accompanied by a more general reflection on the Soviet kolkhozes, whose "main purpose is to ensure equality and the solidarity of the members of the collective."[32]

From Guangxi he traveled as far as the Tonkin border, then to Hunan and on to Yunnan and then Chongqing, in Sichuan province, where Chiang Kai-shek and the Nationalist Chinese government had set up their new capital after the Japanese advance. In total, Quoc spent more than four years in China, and except for several months spent not far from Cao Bang, he did not return definitively to his country until April 1945.

NGUYEN AI QUOC HAD LAST SEEN CHINA IN THE 1920S WHEN IT WAS IN the midst of a civil war; he now found it at war with Japan. In December 1936, after the "Little Marshal" Zhang Xueliang and General Yang Hucheng took Chiang Kai-shek hostage in Xian, the Nationalist generals and Communist leaders signed an accord to end the civil war – at least officially – and to unite their forces against the Japanese. Those areas of Chinese territory not occupied by the Japanese armies were then transformed into a patchwork of overlapping Nationalist and Communist zones. This "sleeping with the enemy" was not easy, and sometimes ended in violent clashes. Tensions ran high everywhere, as Quoc saw for himself during his journey from Yan'an to Guilin: While crossing a "white zone" (under Nationalist control), he and his traveling companions were stopped and allowed free passage only after intense negotiations.

A French officer, Jacques Guillermaz, who crossed the province in 1941 by motorboat on his way from Tonkin to Nanning, wrote that "there were some menacing Annamite revolutionaries [on board]. They were obviously on their way to the camp at Liuzhou where Zhang Fakui, commander of the 4th War Zone, took them in, taught them, and watched over them."[33] But Guillermaz did not stop in Guilin, so did not know that Nguyen Ai Quoc, alias Commander Hu Guang, was often in the area. In the spring of 1943, Guillermaz passed again through Guilin, where General Zhang Fakui was holding Nguyen Ai Quoc hostage. Apparently, he knew nothing about it.

The 8th Route Army, commanded by General Ye Jianying, had a liaison office in Guilin, but the troops were billeted in the village of Lo Mac, six kilometers north of town. Commander "Hu Guang," who passed for a Cantonese because of his accent, was not content merely to observe but put himself to work. He began to accompany Jianying into Hunan where, at the request of Chiang Kai-shek himself, the Communists organized and taught two courses in guerrilla training. Quoc now pretended to be the secretary of the communist cell.

Upon his return to Guilin, Quoc became leader of the "cultural club" of his unit, organizing cultural evenings (singing, music, theater, and perhaps cinema). He also ran the newspaper bulletin board, led political discussions, and was even in charge of hygiene and cleanliness, which were considered a part of culture and were a serious concern in China at the time. In his new role as political commissioner of the Red Army, however, he surprised his comrades by wielding a broom and brush himself when not busy tapping on the "French keyboard" of his Hermès typewriter, which someone had recently bought for him in Haiphong.

He wrote letters, reports, and the wall bulletins on his new machine, and he kept the Comintern up-to-date on the situation in China and Indochina and on the activities of the Trotskyites. He also wrote several articles for *Notre Voix* (Our Voice), a journal published legally in Hanoi by the ICP. For Quoc, however, nothing replaced personal interaction, the face-to-face contact with others, and so he went to Chongqing to confer with Zhou Enlai, head of CCP liaison with the Chiang Kai-shek government.[34]

In 1940, he assessed the situation in Yunnan, where Vietnamese nationals had established a sizable community of more than ten thousand people. Most of them were working in Yunnan for the French railway linking Kunming with Haiphong via Hanoi, which had 11,959 native workers in its employ in 1939. In the villages lining the tracks, the families of the railway workers had set up small shops (tailors, dressmakers, hairdressers, mechanics, etc.) and other businesses, mainly inns and vegetable stands.[35]

Quoc organized courses in political training, as he had done in Thailand, but according to accounts of this period as well as Quoc's own reports, the ICP had less of a foothold here than the VNQDD. Consequently, he had to reckon with the nationalists, who received the active (mostly financial) support of the Chinese Kuomintang. He did not try to confront them directly, but deployed his talents as a tactician to infiltrate their organization and capture the minds of the young patriots who had no political experience but were eager to take action.

During his travels, Quoc surprised his companion Vu Anh with his presence of mind and fertile imagination. Traveling the length of the railway toward the border with Tonkin, Quoc found himself in Tche Tsouen, where important railyards had been bombed by Japanese aircraft, causing a number of Vietnamese deaths. Once in town, Quoc passed himself off as a worker looking for employment, but he also masqueraded as a master of Buddhist rites. Naturally, he was asked to perform a funeral service. Phung Chi Kien (a member of the Overseas Committee), who was introduced as Quoc's assistant, wondered nervously how they were going to get out of this predicament. They went to the pagoda and Quoc winked at Kien, signaling him "to walk toward the altar, kneel down, and open the prayer book," as Quoc did himself. Then "Uncle Ho did his job with perfect ease and seriousness." Kien heard him chant some revolutionary songs and he did the same, noting that "women and men prostrated themselves and no one was the wiser." That evening, Uncle Ho and Kien circled the altar while chanting with the others, and some "party comrades who were present couldn't help but smile."[36]

"The Right Moment Only Comes Once in a Thousand Years"

In June 1940 in Kunming, Nguyen Ai Quoc learned that German troops had marched into Paris and that Hitler was now in control of France. He immediately understood the importance of this event and knew that it would mean great changes for Indochina, and that the Communists would have be ready to face them.

From that moment on, Quoc wasted no time. He had learned that the Chinese Nationalist government was planning to send armed forces into Indochina to counter the Japanese, who had attacked the French garrison at Lang Son in September 1940 and destroyed the railway line from Yunnan, leaving three airfields at their disposal. The following year on 29 July, the Darlan-Kato Accords were signed in Vichy, giving the Japanese the right to station their troops and travel throughout the peninsula.[37]

Quoc's network was made up mostly of militants and communist sympathizers from the Vietnamese diaspora, but it also included two colleagues from his Canton days: Ho Hoc Lam, a former partisan of Phan Boi Chau and a man of the old guard, and Le Thiet Hung, a graduate of the Whampoa Academy and of the Revolutionary Youth League. Lam had remained in contact with leading circles of the Kuomintang, while Hung had stayed in the Nationalist Chinese army. The two men were "moles," well placed among the Chinese Nationalists and the Vietnamese who moved in those circles.[38]

In Liuzhou, General Zhang Fakui was making preparations for the entry of Chinese troops into Indochina and appointed Truong Boi Cong in charge of organizing the Vietnamese, in order to form a front and a cohort of Vietnamese guides. Truong Boi Cong was an old Vietnamese exile who held the rank of brigadier general in the Kuomintang army; some say he had almost forgotten his native language. Cong was joined by two Vietnamese nationalists, Vu Hong Khanh and Nguyen Hai Than, who had been biding their time and taking advantage of Chinese subsidies. Their dependence on the Chinese Nationalists only invited the charges of corruption and embezzlement that were brought against them later by the ICP. Cong himself was later abandoned by the cohort of forty-two Vietnamese he had assembled, and was even arrested and incarcerated for a while under Zhang Fakui's orders, on charges of having set up a network of arms and opium trafficking.

Vo Nguyen Giap, Pham Van Dong, and other young compatriots of Quoc joined him in Guilin, but he decided not to send them to the Military Academy of Yan'an. Instead, he summoned the forty-two militants who had deserted Zhang Fakui and organized a course in political training in Jingxi district, right near the border with Tonkin. It was an interesting period because of the contacts they established with the villagers who took them in. They managed to blend in with the masses like "fish in water," something that Quoc had already done in Siam. They settled into two ethnic Zhuang-Nung villages, whose population had supported the Chinese Communists since the 1920s. To begin the training, Quoc made five recommendations to his companions: Help the local people in their daily tasks; familiarize yourselves with their customs; learn the local language; learn to sing, read, and write; and judge the right time and place to make revolutionary propaganda, and in an appropriate way – "make it so that the people consider us serious, dedicated to our work, disciplined; then they will trust us and help us."[39]

Apparently, they managed to be accepted by the local population, because the training period ended after twenty-five days without any external interference. On 27 January 1941, the first day of the Chinese Year of the Snake, Quoc and his comrades visited the inhabitants of the two villages; Quoc wore a blue jacket and scarf and brown trousers, and he carried a cane, like an old Nung. They presented New Year's greetings written on red votive paper, and handed out candy to the children before saying their farewells. Then, on 8 February, the Vietnamese group set out on mountain trails for border marker 108 – one side written in characters and pointing to China, the other side in French pointing to Tonkin. When he arrived at the border, Quoc called for a pause and spent some moments in silence. After thirty years he had finally come home.[40]

A NEW STRATEGY FOR THE ICP: THE VIET MINH

Today Pac Bo is still a Nung hamlet some thirty kilometers from Cao Bang, spread out across the rice paddies and cornfields that form clearings in the dense undergrowth of the mountain. It lies on the banks of a stream with water green "like jade," clear and cold, that Nguyen Ai Quoc named Lenin, and at the foot of an abrupt peak that he called Marx. It was a "safe" place (*an toan*), for the ICP had burrowed into Cao Bang province starting in 1930, and its influence was continuing to grow (see Map 3). In fact, though the region was sparsely populated, several thousand demonstrators went to meet the French radical-socialist Justin Godart, Secretary of State for the Popular Front, when he arrived on a research mission in 1937. Some of the villages were considered "lawless," meaning that colonial authority no longer held sway there. In 1943, three of the nine districts of the province were entirely under communist control.

Nevertheless, Quoc strictly adhered to the rules of secrecy and chose to find shelter with his comrades in a cave called Coc Bo, rather than with a sympathizer from the village in his house on stilts. The cave was located just steps from the Chinese border, and so they could quickly take refuge by running down a trail. He stayed there for about a year before establishing his new base in Lam Son in April 1942, which was still in Cao Bang province but deeper into Tonkin, a sign that the free zone was expanding.

The group lived in austere conditions, sleeping on planks of wood in darkness broken only by the light of an oil lamp, in a permanent damp cold that could not have been good for Quoc's lungs. Indeed, he had frequent attacks of fever, but he underscored his decision to stay by naming one of the stalagmites in the cave after Karl Marx because it resembled his profile. Their diet was frugal, fortified only by fish caught in the river. Some of the men wrote about their experiences and admitted that they found the living conditions very difficult, but they did not complain because Quoc was right there with them. Quoc himself described these circumstances in a humorous poem:

> Mornings by the river, nights in the cave,
> Soup of corn and bamboo shoots, that is our daily menu.
> An unsteady rock as a desk: I translate the history of the Party.
> Really, the life of the revolutionary is not lacking in charm.[41]

Apparently Quoc did calisthenics every morning, climbed the slopes of Karl Marx to sweat out his fever, and then dived into the cold waters of Lenin. To each his own way of practicing the dialectic.

The Lessons of China

Quoc finally unpacked his kit bag at Pac Bo, bringing with him his trusted Hermès typewriter and the invaluable lessons he had learned in China, like the tactic of a unified national front and the creation of "red bases." These bases established a foothold by incorporating armed forces trained

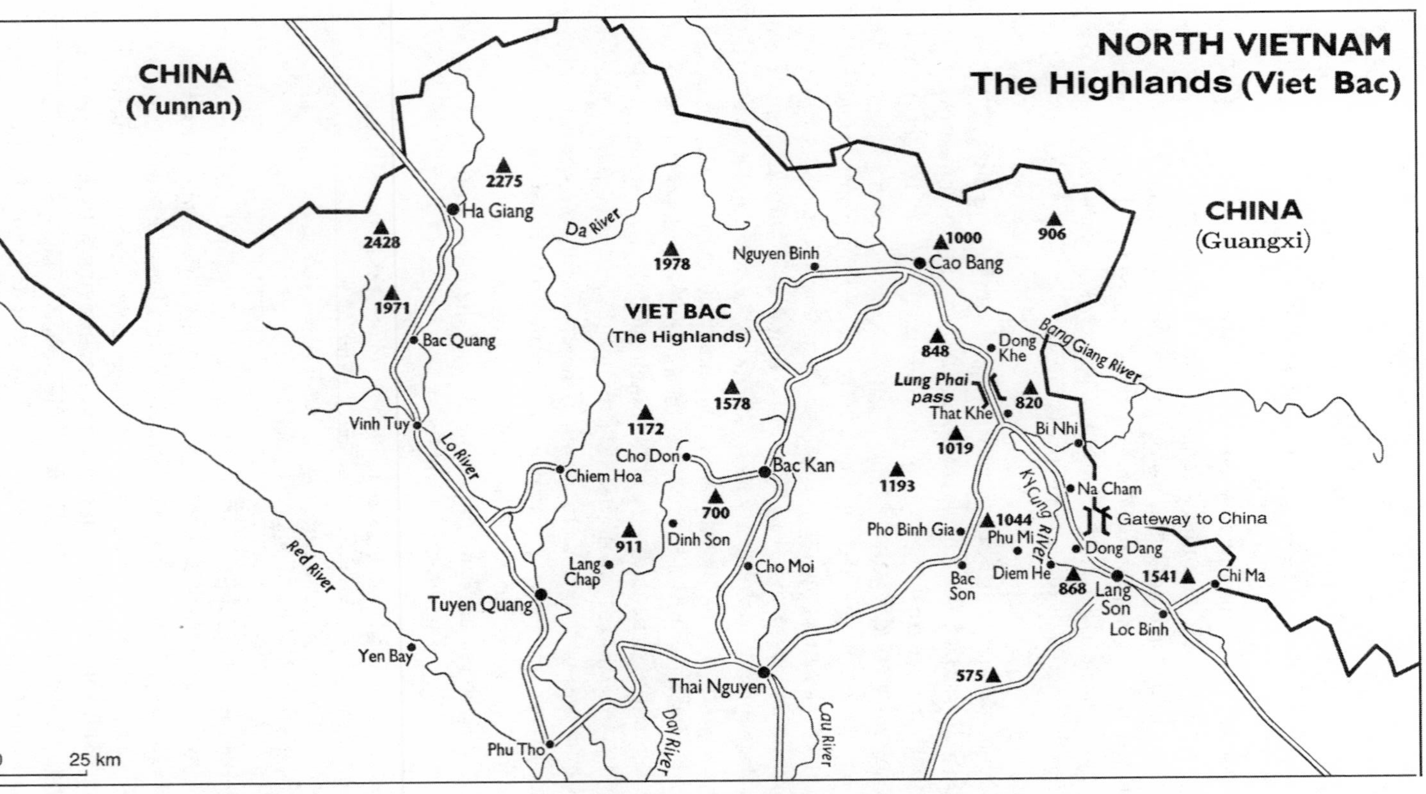

Map 3. North Vietnam

in guerrilla tactics among the local, mostly rural, population, who had had their "consciousness raised" by the Communists. All the same, the Chinese Communists, especially Mao Zedong, were still reluctant or even frankly opposed to an alliance with their sworn enemy Chiang Kai-shek. They only agreed to do so under strong pressure by the Comintern, notably during the incident in Xian, according to the correspondence between Georgi Dimitrov and Stalin between 1934 and 1943. The anti-Japanese alliance was clearly part of the strategy set forth at the Seventh Congress of the International of 1935 as it was one facet of the united antifascist front.

Quoc's experience in China provided him with a strategic goal for the early 1940s: Drive out the French and the new Japanese aggressors to establish a "new democracy," whose European version in the immediate postwar period would be called "people's democracy." However, the Chinese Communists had suffered as a result of their frontist policy and learned the lesson of the "tragedy of the Chinese revolution" (1924–27).[42] They had ended up absorbed by the Kuomintang – a "united front" over which they had no control and at the mercy of their adversaries. This time, then, the Communists were organizing their own armed forces and establishing a territorial base so that they could act independently.

They had a particular method for establishing a base among the local population, especially with the ethnic minorities from the outlying areas of China and northern Vietnam. First they made contacts; then if they came to an agreement it was consecrated by an oath of brotherhood. The following two accounts are strikingly similar, one from Le Quang Ba, a Vietnamese of Nung background, and the other from the Chinese Communist Commander Zhu De. Ba wrote:

> According to local custom, we cut off the head of a chicken and let its blood run into a bowl of alcohol, near the incense smoke. Each of us added a drop of blood from our own hand into the bowl; then we took a spoonful of the mixture with a white spoon and drank it.

All of the Communist militants, Nguyen Ai Quoc included, performed this ritual in 1941 with Zhuang villagers on the Chinese side of the border. And Zhu De wrote that during the Long March, the Chinese Communists had to cross the territory of the Lolo, aggressive warriors hostile to the Han. Liu Bocheng, one of the leaders of the Red Army, forged an alliance with the Lolo chief by an oath of brotherhood.[43] These experiences shed some light on the origin of the ethnic policies that were adopted by the People's Republic of China and then by the Democratic Republic of Vietnam, although they differ from each other, as well as from those of the Soviet Union.

At this point, it is tempting to see Nguyen Ai Quoc as a disciple of Mao, but the Chinese Communists had been forced to flee to the countryside and mobilize the peasantry after having been crushed in the cities in 1927–29. Quoc, on the other hand, was teaching about the revolutionary potential of the peasants at the Thanh Nien school back in 1927, and Jacques Doriot, during his visit to Canton, was heading in the same direction. Both the sociological conditions and the changing context had led Quoc and Doriot to pick up on the potential of the Asian masses, independent of the ideas taught in Moscow. It is true that Mao wrote his famous *Report on the Peasant Movement of Hunan* during that same period, while he was director of the Peasant Institute in Canton, but one must be careful not to consider this a theory of revolution since the Institute was a product of the Kuomintang, not the Chinese Communist Party.

The Founding of the Viet Minh

Nguyen Ai Quoc's first initiative upon arriving at Pac Bo was to convene an expanded Central Committee to define a strategy more suited to the new situation. On 28 February 1941, Quoc summoned as many of the leaders as he could reach, making sure that the meeting was held on "our nation's soil." From 10 to 19 May 1941, the meeting of the Eighth Central Committee was held in the cave of Coc Bo. Six men were present: Nguyen Ai Quoc, Truong Chinh, Hoang Quoc Viet, Hoang Van Thu (an ethnic Tay), a delegate from Annam, and one from Cochinchina. Phung Chi Kien and Vu Anh are also mentioned in some documents, but they could not have arrived in time for the conference.

The committee predicted the victory of the Soviet Union and the Allies over the fascist states, and agreed that even though the Indochinese revolution was a struggle for national liberation, it was still an integral part of the world revolution, its fate linked to that of the Soviet Union and the Chinese Revolution. To attain their goal, they would have to throw open their ranks to as many people as possible, meaning that they would have to abandon their plans for a radical agrarian revolution. They would confiscate only the land of "colonialists and landlords who are traitors to our country," and distribute it to the poor peasants and landless laborers. The revolution would be achieved through armed struggle led by the party, and all Indochinese peoples would be liberated, including the Khmer and Lao.

To lead this struggle, the Communist Party would have to broaden its influence and multiply its organizations among the urban working class and peasants. They would also have to recruit and train cadres from the proletariat. Members of the committee then named Dang Xuan Khu, alias Truong Chinh ("long march," in Vietnamese), Secretary General of the Party.

Nguyen Ai Quoc proposed the creation of a united national front called the League for the Independence of Vietnam (Viet Nam Doc Lap Dong Minh Hoi), better known as the Viet Minh. Clearly, then, it was established by the Indochinese Communist Party, and its board of directors (*tong bo*) were Communists. On 6 June, Quoc launched an appeal to the people of the nation, announcing that French colonial domination was nearing its end and calling for everyone to unite and bring about the liberation of the country, to restore its independence and set up a new democracy in which the people would be free. For Quoc, independence was the most important of all political values, a collective freedom, of course, whereby the independence of the nation would lead to the freedom of its people. Individuals do not stand apart from society, and so individual liberty comes second, or more precisely it has to be limited so that equality – of utmost importance to Quoc – can be applied to its fullest.

With these goals in mind, he published "The Ten Policies of the Viet Minh" (*Muoi chinh sach cua Viet Minh*), which sums up the objectives of the united front. He also wrote a "History of Our Country" (*Lich su Nuoc ta*) in verse to illustrate the political orientation that had just been decided, preceded by "We Must Learn the History of Our Country." These writings exalt the nation's glorious and heroic past, going back to the myth of the Dragon People (Lac Hong) and to the royal dynasties who fought against Chinese invasions. And the condensed chronology that accompanied the "History of Our Country" shows Quoc's continued pedagogical aims. He also published a journal almost single-handedly, called *Viet Nam Doc lap* (Independent Vietnam), in which he popularized his ideas, demands, and advice. More than 150 issues were distributed in the region of Cao Bang–Lang Son–Bac Son. These publications are striking in their diversity, ranging from political advice to short poems on everything from peasants and workers to women and children, from scathing attacks on Pétain and Decoux to the "Song of the Soldier," the "Song of the Guerrilla" (sung in a round), and fables.[44]

It is commonly believed that this policy of national unity exalting a nation's past was heretical to the internationalism of the Comintern. The latter did indeed denounce Great Russian or Greater Han nationalism and generally considered national struggle to be contradictory to class action, but it did not deny colonized people the right to celebrate their feelings or their national past. By founding the Viet Minh, Ho Chi Minh brought together – or at least into synergy – the dynamism of nationalism and that of international communism. As a result, in 1941 Ho was in step with the resolutions of the Seventh Congress of the Comintern (1935) and the directives issued by its president, Georgi Dimitrov: "to explain to the laboring masses in a historically objective way their nation's past, to link their current struggles with the traditions of their people," to acclimatize proletarian internationalism within each country so that it can "sink roots deep within their homeland."[45]

Quoc continued to train Communist militants and translated into *quoc ngu* Stalin's *The History of the Bolshevik Communist Party of the USSR*, which had replaced *The ABCs of Communism* as a basic manual. This replacement was in keeping with current changes within the Soviet Union, as both Bukharin and Preobrazhensky had been shot on Stalin's orders, even though Stalin's history of the Bolshevik Communist Party highlighted and magnified the role that both had played in the revolution. This does not necessarily mean that Quoc approved of the Great Terror or that he was an admirer of Stalin, but he was still on a mission for the Comintern, thus a "dumb and disciplined" militant.

Continuing with his communist activities, he wrote two booklets, *Guerrilla Tactics* and *The Instruction of Military Cadres*, to prepare for an eventual insurrection. This stress on the military dimension was inspired in part by the Chinese experience, and by the recent failures of the ICP in this regard.[46]

In 1939 and 1940, while Quoc was still in China, dramatic events were taking place in Indochina: The ICP was banned along with the FCP, France surrendered to the Germans in June 1940, the Japanese attacked Lang Son in September of the same year, and the Franco-Thai war broke out in December. All of these events led Communist leaders to believe that it was time to implement Lenin's "revolutionary defeatism" – that is, working toward the defeat of one's own nation in war as a way to destroy the status quo and spark revolution from the resulting chaos – by provoking the mutiny of newly mobilized infantrymen. The uprisings in Bac Son in the North and in Nam Bo (Cochinchina) turned out to be premature. They were cruelly suppressed and the ICP was decimated; they began to recover only in 1943. Nguyen Ai Quoc recommended that they hold themselves at the ready but act only with extreme caution.[47]

Nguyen Ai Quoc and the Trotskyites

Responsibility for the physical elimination of the Vietnamese Trotskyites is attributed to Nguyen Ai Quoc. What was his opinion of Trotskyism and the Trotskyites? Should we turn to Stalinism for an explanation?

The debate basically rests on the fact that the Ho Chi Minh–style vision of the Vietnamese revolution – as realized via the initiatives described earlier – goes against the "permanent revolution" of the urban working class, which transcends national borders and retains a total mistrust of nationalism. This opposition became more antagonistic as the conflict between Stalin and Trotsky took a dramatic turn, and could explain Quoc's position.

We must begin by understanding how those in Asia found themselves implicated in an internal affair of the Soviet Communist movement and felt compelled to take sides. The divergence of views between Stalin, on the one hand, and the Workers' Opposition and Trotsky, on the other, gradually spread to other nations, beginning with China. The defeat of the Chinese Communists at the hands of Chiang Kai-shek was blamed on Stalin, who had made them dependent on the Kuomintang, and so some of the Chinese living in Moscow in 1927 began to espouse Trotsky's position.

Since 1925, several hundred Chinese had received training at the Sun Yat-sen University, established for this purpose, and at Soviet military academies. However, as we saw in Nguyen The Vinh's account, the discussions about Trotsky began in 1927–28 among foreign students, including the Vietnamese. Wang Fanxi, a Chinese Trotskyite, remembered this period: "We didn't know the history of the Russian revolution, almost nothing about the USSR, nor of the international workers' movement. We were completely at a loss when someone asked us to take part in the controversies."[48] He discovered that Stalin was responsible for the defeat of the Chinese Communists but did not yet contest Soviet leadership. Only progressively did he learn about the ideas of the Opposition, rallying to them after having seen the film *The End of Saint Petersburg* by Pudovkin. Wang gained an admiration for Trotsky, despite the party's propaganda, which minimized the critical role he had played in determining the result of the Russian Revolution.

The campaign against Trotsky crossed international borders after those considered to be his followers were arrested, imprisoned, shot, or deported to the Soviet Union. One Vietnamese student from the Stalin School was accused of "relations with the Trotskyites" and spent some twenty years in Siberia, as did a number of Chinese.[49] Still others, according to Wang Fanxi, were expelled to China. In 1938, the Comintern sent the Chinese Wang Ming to China to purge the CCP of its "Trotskyite" elements and to cut off all relations between the Stalinists and their adversaries inasmuch as the bonds of friendship and camaraderie had not all been broken. Wang Fanxi realized in retrospect that the Chinese Trotskyites had committed the error of refusing to join the united anti-Japanese front and organize the peasantry to fight the invader. This only lent credence to accusations against them of being Japanese agents, as their European counterparts were considered "Hitlerian-Trotskyites" and the Spanish POUM (Workers' Party of Marxist Unification) were seen as Franco's fifth column.

At the time, Quoc was the Comintern's envoy in China and felt compelled to publish articles from May to August 1939 in *Our Voice*, the journal of the ICP, condemning the betrayal of the Chinese Trotskyites.[50] In so doing, he echoed Wang Ming's actions within the CCP and criticized the Vietnamese Trotskyites, who were well established in the Saigon-Cholon metropolitan area among workers, young people, and the intelligentsia. The Comintern wanted to clean up the Communist movement in Indochina, as they had in China, since the ICP had cooperated with the Trotskyites in 1936–37 in a common front known as "The Struggle."[51] This collaboration certainly was not an easy one, but it was unusual and unorthodox enough to convince the FCP to send its deputy Maurice Honel to Indochina to "advise" on the rupture between the ICP and the Trotskyites.

Quoc's report to the International on 12 July 1940 forbade any alliance of the ICP with the Trotskyites. He took specific aim at Ta Thu Thau, the most visible personality within the Indochinese Trotskyite movement, while also recognizing his influence on the people:

> Ta Thu Thau is an intellectual who studied in France; he has a good literary style and talent as a public speaker but he is a hypocrite and a pseudo-savant. Also, the young people and the workers of Saigon are largely held under the sway of this group. In the countryside of Cochinchina and elsewhere, it does not have the same influence.[52]

The Vietnamese Trotskyites, broken up more and more into splinter groups, fired back with the same, denouncing the ICP's obedience to Stalin, their rightist politics, and the Stalinist terror in the USSR. But fundamentally they condemned the "social-patriotic deviations" of the ICP.[53] After the revolution of August 1945, the conflict became even more poisonous and took a tragic turn as several Trotskyites were assassinated by the ICP. Tran Van Giau, who chaired the revolutionary committee of Cochinchina, denounced the Trotskyites as counterrevolutionaries, while the latter accused him of collusion with a French commissioner from the Indochinese Sûreté and of preparing for the return of the French. These mutual accusations were equally gratuitous and meaningless.

At His Risk and Peril

Nguyen Ai Quoc was back in Asia and seemed at ease, most likely because he was far from Moscow and had reconciled his patriotic ardor with his Leninist revolutionary zeal. He had found a way to combine the national struggle with the dream of international revolution, and had even received the approval of the Comintern. On 15 May 1943, Stalin decreed the dissolution of the Comintern, strengthening the autonomy that Quoc was already enjoying on his home turf. The communiqué from the Executive Bureau of the Comintern reads as follows: "The Communist International as the directing center of the international working class is to be dissolved, thus freeing the sections of the Communist International from their obligations arising from the statutes and resolutions of the congresses of the Communist International."[54]

Nevertheless, it would not take much for Quoc – now calling himself Ho Chi Minh (Well of Light) – to see his lifeline broken once again. On the night of 13 August 1942, Ho Chi Minh had set out for China. He wanted to go to Chongqing for a variety of reasons, most importantly to meet with Zhou Enlai (the Communist representative with the Nationalist government) and find out about the general situation there, as well as the Comintern's instructions for the current phase of the world conflict. He also knew that the provisional capital of the Chinese Nationalist government was home to an important Soviet delegation consisting of more than a hundred people, as well as the command post of U.S. operations in the China-Burma-India theater, led by General Joseph Stilwell. Ho had undoubtedly sensed that the United States would become a major force in the Asia-Pacific region, and so wanted them to become acquainted with the Viet Minh.

Ho's journey through China was no casual hike. The countryside was crawling with deserters who had become bandits, the territory was partly controlled by the Chinese Nationalists, and the Japanese army made the occasional incursion. He was dressed as a country geomancer and, as usual, he walked. Accompanied by his traveling companion, Le Quang Ba, he stopped in a village in Guangxi that harbored Vietnamese Communists.

After two days of festivities for Tet Trung Nguyen (the fifteenth day of the seventh lunar month), an important local festival, he left again with a young guide, the son of his Zhuang host.[55]

Then he had a stoke of bad luck, for on the road to the district capital of Jingxi, the local police stopped to check the papers of the two men and had them placed under arrest. Ho must have been angry at himself for breaking the cardinal rule of a clandestine revolutionary: prudence. He had the identity card of a journalist and a travel pass issued in 1940 by the Chinese 4th Military Command, both of which had expired. Since he had claimed to be going to Chongqing to meet with the Chinese government, they suspected him of being a spy or a saboteur. This was on 19 August 1942.[56]

Thus began a long and itinerant detention. Ho was carted through thirteen districts of Guangxi; he estimates that he passed through eighteen prisons until 10 September 1943, when he was put under house arrest in Liuzhou, then officially set free in March 1944. On 9 August 1944, he set out for Pac Bo, two years to the day after his arrest.

Ho Chi Minh left behind a *Prison Diary*,[57] which includes more than a hundred quatrains (134 in the *Complete Works*)[58] that he wrote to pass the time and withstand the suffering:

> I've never cared for humming verse.
> But what to do inside a jail?
> I'll hum some verse to pass long days.
> I'll hum and wait until freedom comes.

The poems are like vignettes that capture the different aspects of prison life, some miserable and despairing, others consoling and optimistic. He must have missed his "imperialist" prison of Hong Kong, which was nothing like the ones in China. First, he was led from one prison to the other on foot, usually with hands and arms tied, on an exhausting march covering dozens of miles:

> Nine days of rain, one day of sun.
> Heaven above just doesn't care.
> All tattered shoes, mud-splattered feet –
> Still I must walk and slog ahead.

When his jailers offered him transport by boat:

> The boat floats down the river towards Nanning
> Feet tied to the roof [of the junk], torture victim from another age.

And when they traveled by train, he was tied up in the tender on a pile of coal.

The prison was overrun with thieves, beggars, bandits, drug addicts, and the insane – that is, innocent people like the woman whose crime was to be married to a man who was a "draft dodger" in the army – and so the only room left was by the latrines:

> New "boarders" must, so goes the rule,
> lie down at night near the latrine.
> If they desire a good night's sleep,
> let them come up with some hard cash.

In prison, as in the outside world, inequality was the rule. Anyone with money could soften up the jailers and keep them from stealing a prisoner's tobacco or personal belongings (such as Ho Chi Minh's cane). Hard cash could buy a normal meal, if not a good one, some tobacco, alcohol, or maybe even opium. On the other hand, though poverty may lead to selfishness and disgrace, it can also spark feelings of humanity and solidarity:

> Marvelous encounter. Idle conversation.
> The good sir Quach showed much concern for me.
> Like a coal fire on a snowy night . . .
> There are still such hearts under the vaulted sky!

Ho spent time with men who had fallen into ruin and suffered both social and moral ostracism, which taught him more about mankind than he could have learned from a course in psychology. It confirmed what he already believed about human ambivalence, which was central to the philosophy of the Confucian sage Xunzi:

> All faces have a harmless look in sleep.
> Awake, men differ: good and evil show.
> No virtue and no vice exists at birth –
> of good and evil nurture sows the seeds.

The hardship of prison also strengthened his conviction that one can surmount obstacles with a goal and a strong desire to attain it:

> Fortunately
> I've borne and endured.
> I've yielded not one inch.
> The body's racked with pain.
> The spirit stays unbowed.

Ho Chi Minh remained strong-willed and defiant during his confinement, but he had not been forgotten by his comrades. The very day of his arrest, in fact, he had run into the daughter of his host; she notified Le Quang Ba, who returned immediately to Tonkin to inform ICP leaders. The alert was sounded and the "red phone" rang throughout the network of Communists, sympathizers, and other connections, as it had in 1931. First, the Chongqing government telegraphed General Zhang Fakui, head of the 4th Military Command, to open an investigation into this suspect whom the Guangxi police were leading from prison to prison. In the meantime, Zhou Enlai had stepped in and contacted the Chinese General Fen Yuxiang, who then brought the case to Li Zongren, Vice President of the Republic of China. The latter went straight to Generalissimo Chiang Kai-shek. After difficult negotiations, Ho was apparently taken to the Department of Political Affairs of the 4th Military Command in Liuzhou for interrogation.[59]

On a morning in late winter 1942, a young lieutenant of the Nationalist army was taken with compassion at the sight of the new arrival at the army's political department. But who was this "frail old man with a long beard, white hair, wearing a faded military uniform that was torn in a number of places and old worn-out shoes, trying to withstand the cold north wind" as he left his narrow cell to empty his bucket?[60] Normally, the prisoners that they brought there were "political prisoners or 'reds,'" wrote this lieutenant on duty. For his part, Ho wrote:

> They're soft as cotton, legs so long unused.
> I lurch and stagger, trying hard to walk.
> But soon enough I hear the warden shout:
> "Hey you, come back! No more loafing around!"

Through the grille of the cell, the lieutenant noticed Ho doing calisthenics to fight the cold, then pressing against the wall to shield himself from drafts. This Chinese officer also told of how he observed Ho reading newspapers, those of the Kuomintang, of course, but also *The Destiny of China*, written by Chiang Kai-shek himself.

After several months of imprisonment in conditions that were relatively better than before, Ho learned of the arrival of his quasi namesake, General Hou Zhiming, director of the political department. The Chinese lieutenant and his comrades saw an immediate change in the prisoner's status. Ho went from prisoner to guest, taking his meals in the officers' mess, first with Hou Zhiming and his colleagues, then by himself. Out of hospitality, Ho invited the young lieutenants who had shown him some kindness to have dinner with him. As in Hong Kong and elsewhere, his charm once again came into play. One lieutenant recalls that "we were so impassioned by what he told us that we forgot to eat," adding that Ho "never spoke of politics but only of the customs, culture, and people in the countries he had visited."[61]

He even impressed Zhang Fakui. One day as the general was riding by the river, he saw the "frail Annamite" bathing in the cold water. The general, who was dressed warmly in a fur coat, couldn't hide his stunned admiration: "What? You, a southerner, dare dip into these wintry waters? Brrr!!!" Once they got better acquainted, the general came to consider his "guest" a "very good man. He spoke softly while stroking his beard. He kept a cool head and worked hard."[62] Zhang Fakui was also impressed by Ho's Chinese education. In the end, he asked Ho to participate in the reorganization of the front made up of independent Vietnamese groups, called the Vietnamese Revolutionary League (Viet Nam Cach Menh Dong Minh Hoi). The other nationalist leaders paled in comparison to Ho, or at least did not seem up to the task at hand. The general beseeched Truong Boi Cong, whom he had named head of the Dong Minh Hoi, to invite Ho to become their Vice President. Truong immediately agreed.

The resulting congress was held with twenty delegates, personalities, and representatives of parties, such as the VNQDD, the Dai Viet (Great Viet), and Phuc Quoc (National Restoration). The only Communists present were Ho Chi Minh and Le Tung Son, whom Ho had placed among the leadership of the league. However, the nationalists were torn apart by rivalries and had a poor political program that only accentuated the strength and clarity of Ho's report, which also earned the approval of Zhang Fakui.

It seems that Ho had the general "in his pocket," judging by an anecdote passed on by Le Tung Son. During the final banquet at the close of the Congress (29 March 1944), Chinese soldiers stood near the guests and filled their rice bowls as soon as they were empty. Ho made the assembly laugh by grabbing the platter of rice, setting it down next to Zhang, and saying, "Let us put the rice here and serve ourselves as needed." After alcoholic drinks and then tea, Ho engaged in a verbal and poetic joust with the general's wife and other guests, and then invited them to sing. He himself sang and "spread out his arms and danced, his feet resounding softly on the wood floor, while everybody kept rhythm by clapping their hands and laughing out loud."[63] Ho's actions revealed his egalitarianism and he risked insulting the top brass present at the table, but amidst the excitement of the banquet and after a number of toasts, the joke was received with good humor.

The tide had thus turned completely, strengthening Ho's belief that nothing was permanent, that everything in this world evolves:

> Things move in cycles – such is nature's law.
> After the stormy days come days of calm.
> The world has promptly changed its rain-soaked garb.
> All hills and forests spread brocade to dry.
> Warm sun and gentle breeze – flowers flash their smiles.
> Tall trees and sparkling boughs – birds chat away.
> Men join all myriad beings and rejoice.
> The sweet follows the bitter, as a rule.

Nature has become Ho's inspiration; he never once evokes the dialectic of Marx or Mao.

Before taking leave of his "Chinese hosts," Ho Chi Minh said to Zhang Fakui, "I am a communist but what is important to me now is the independence and the freedom of my country, not communism. I personally guarantee you that communism will not become a reality in Vietnam for another fifty years."[64]

"THE RIGHT MOMENT"

> Now France is occupied
> The French have no strength left,
> they do not have enough people left to govern us
> The Japanese pirates have just arrived,
> the government is hanging by a thread
> Chinese, Americans, Dutch, English arrive together.
> War and its troubles are raging everywhere
> This presents a good occasion for us
> Let us rise up and reestablish the land of our ancestors.
>
> – Ho Chi Minh[65]

The Bastion of Cao Bang–Bac Son–Vu Nhai

Ho set out for the base that had been set up in the mountains and forests of the Cao Bang–Bac Son–Vu Nhai region, accompanied by eighteen young militants whom he had trained in Liuzhou – including a woman who would become his companion for a number of years.[66] These border regions were inhabited mostly by ethnic minorities, such as the Tay, Nung, and Dao (called Man at the time),[67] who had a clan-based social system and lived scattered throughout the territory. Their settlements straddled the China-Tonkin border where communications were difficult. Both the French officers and administrators, as well as the mandarins, who were generally Viet or Tho Ty (descendants of mixed Viet-Tay unions), had to assert their control constantly.

In fact, the border was often crossed by armed Chinese gangs, from bandits and smugglers to regular soldiers and paramilitary units from the Chinese army. Moreover, Vietnamese survivors of the Bac Son uprising had formed a sort of underground resistance, and the ICP continued to spread its influence despite French campaigns to flush them out. In the month of January 1945 alone, there were twenty-two assaults, armed robberies, and assassinations reported along the border.

The French authorities were on high alert, as the Viet Minh continued to gain in strength with a now-legendary progression: Between 1942 and 1943, three of the nine districts in Cao Bang came completely under Communist control. In Haquang, for example, the Viet Minh increased their numbers from a thousand in 1941 to three thousand in 1943, and they created fifteen self-defense militia groups (*tu ve*).

The Viet Minh, who named their bases after national heroes like Quang Trung and Hoang Hoa Tham, pushed their positions southward toward the Red River delta. By the time Ho arrived at the area delimited by Cao Bang–Bac Son–Vu Nhai in 1944, the Viet Minh had acquired even more territory and strengthened their influence. In response, the French police stepped up their "cleansing" operations. On 8 July 1944, the French found a Viet Minh base near Soc Giang equipped to house some forty men, with a cache of arms, lists, tracts, and clothing. What the Sûreté discovered was that Viet Minh propaganda had penetrated the Tonkin infantry and the Indochinese Guard, and so the decision was made to "re-establish authority, purge the Indochinese Guard, and keep an eye on the key players."[68]

In August 1944, two village chiefs were assassinated and several revolutionary hideouts were discovered, proving that "there was some voluntary support on behalf of the population."[69] Louis Arnoux, the perspicacious head of the Indochinese Sûreté (with the title Police Superintendent), had already identified the leader of the movement in a letter to Governor-General Decoux, in which he confirmed the effectiveness of "the guerrilla tactics advocated by the propaganda leaflets printed in China by the anti-French parties – whose leader now seems to be Ho Chi Minh, alias Nguyen Ai Quoc."[70]

In 1945, the situation worsened for the French. In January, rebels were present in a number of communities, and tracts were being distributed by the Viet Minh's armed propaganda wing. The tension that had spread throughout Tonkin in late 1944 had become even more acute by early 1945. A report filed in February by the Résident of Thai Nguyen province noted that everyone was extremely nervous, both the French and the Vietnamese, and stated: "The fact remains that for a few weeks now the average Annamite in the street will answer back more frankly and show less complacency than in the past. Isn't that a sign that the situation is critical?"[71]

In the months before the Japanese takeover of 9 March 1945, the Vietnamese Communists overcame the setbacks of 1944, which had put them in an extremely precarious position, and even extended their control, following the leadership of Vo Nguyen Giap, Hoang Van Hoan, Chu Van Tan, Le Thiet Hung, and Hoang Van Thai. (Trained at the Military Academy in Guilin, Thai was put in charge of the Military Academy in Tan Trao.) On Ho Chi Minh's orders, they chose members for their self-defense militia and combined them with Chu Van Tan's mobile armed group (Cuu Quoc Quan, or Army of National Salvation), creating the Armed Propaganda Brigade of the Vietnamese Liberation Army (Doi Viet Nam Tuyen Giai Phong Quan). It consisted of thirty-one men and three women divided into three platoons and placed under the leadership of Hoang Sam and a political commissioner.[72] They had a hodgepodge collection of weapons, but in December 1944 they "showed their claws" by attacking two Indochinese Guard posts in the province of Cao Bang and expanding their armory.

The American Connection

Ho Chi Minh needed a way to shore up his revolutionary base, but given his total mistrust of the Kuomintang, he must have made it a priority to contact the "Allies," represented in China primarily by the U.S. Air Force. Unit 14 was based in Kunming under the command of General Claire Chennault, who had been fighting the Japanese since the 1930s as squadron leader of the Flying Tigers. But Ho wanted to do more than protect his base; he wanted material help from the United States in the form of weapons and medicine, as well as a source of information and communication. He hoped that the Americans would relay his demands, appeals, and propaganda to the outside world.[73]

An opportunity presented itself in the person of Lieutenant Rudolph Shaw, whose plane had crashed due to mechanical damage in December 1944, about sixty kilometers from Pac Bo. He was picked up by the Viet Minh and kept out of reach of the French and Japanese, who were both looking for him. When he heard of the incident, Ho asked for the pilot to be brought to him immediately: This would be his entrée to the U.S. command in China!

It took twenty-two nights for Shaw and his escort to travel the sixty kilometers to Pac Bo. One witness recalls that the pilot did not know who was escorting him, and that no one spoke any English. As he trudged through the jungle for the first time in his life, Shaw succumbed several times to fatigue, despair, and tears. At last he was introduced to a small man with a wispy beard who didn't look like someone of consequence but who but spoke fluent English, and he broke into tears again.

With his goal in mind, Ho Chi Minh set out for Kunming with Shaw, a Tay guide, and a Vietnamese bodyguard armed with a pistol. They went first to Jingxi and returned the American pilot to his base; then Ho and his companions continued on in secrecy to avoid being detained by the Chinese. They took the road to Kunming, then the train from Yunnan to the station of Pi Sichia. Along the way, Ho and his bodyguard stopped at two towns to hold political meetings, at which Ho was confronted by Vietnamese nationalists who had come to challenge him. At one point they were stopped at a roadblock for questioning by the Chinese Nationalist Army, but they managed to pass through, thanks to the safe-conduct pass provided by Zhang Fakui.

Phung The Tai, the bodyguard, wrote about his journey with Ho Chi Minh, depicting a man who, despite extremely fragile health, was determined to accomplish his mission of establishing relations with the United States. An impulsive young man of twenty-three, Phung The Tai did not understand the behavior of his elder, who was exhausted, malnourished, and often feverish. Why, for instance, did Ho save money to buy Shaw some meat and bread while the Vietnamese had only a thin soup and a half a bowl of rice each? "It wasn't fair!" Tai later recalled. "Uncle Ho knew how I was feeling and just smiled."[74]

One day when a village chief refused to sell him a chicken, Tai finally gave in to his anger and threatened to beat the man to death. Ho learned of this incident and was "clearly unhappy, telling him frankly: 'You are acting like Chiang Kai-shek's militarists!'"[75] He wanted to train his young companion the hard way to get used to a frugal diet, and he refused to let Tai hire a horse but made him walk instead, teaching him discipline and respect for the local people – and not only the poor ones.

Throughout the voyage, Ho made up lessons for his companions and discussed political themes, carefully distinguishing between the ideas of Sun Yat-sen and those of the Vietnamese revolution, which had to be a proletarian revolution on both the social and national levels. He also told them about the October Revolution of 1917 and the creation of the Soviet Union. From time to time, he recited verses from the classic repertoire, such as "The Complaint of the Warrior's Wife," which he taught to both of his unschooled compatriots. In this case as in others, Ho acted upon his belief that men are neither "angels nor brutes" but just in need of education. For him, education was more than mere training; it entailed caring for the health and well-being of others. Those close to him were very touched by his attentiveness. Phung The Tai, for one, saw him "as neither a leader nor head of state but like a father, the head of a family."[76]

When the three men arrived in Kunming, Ho went directly to Tong Minh Phuong, a former student at the University of Hanoi who had been living in Kunming since 1943. Ho asked him to open the *Dong Duong caphe*, the Indochina Café, located in a dressmaking shop, where Communists could meet and find accommodation. Next he turned to the Communist Pham Viet Thu for help making contact with the Americans, first by trying to reach the Free French representatives in Kunming, then U.S. Ambassador Clarence Gauss, who was posted in Chongqing.

In Washington, the State Department was very reserved at the time, as its representatives in China had received the directive to do nothing that might displease the French General Charles de Gaulle (one of the paradoxes analyzed by the historian Mark Bradley). President Franklin Roosevelt knew little about Indochina but was a staunch opponent of French colonialism, and he suggested that the colony be taken away from the French and put in the hands of an international trusteeship. The responsibility for this stewardship would fall, of course, to the United States, who had already shown in the Philippines that they knew how to lead a backward people toward modern civilization. Despite this vision of future progress, the United States erred in underestimating the Indochinese people in the present. In other words, the Americans founded their policies on the same preconceptions that had plagued the French and other European imperialist nations – on prejudices born of the same racial hierarchy.[77]

The Right Moment: Act I

Although the first contacts were not very promising, the situation in Indochina changed dramatically on 9 March 1945 as developments in the war forced Japan to end its four-year "cohabitation," or shared authority, with France. The Japanese had been retreating steadily before the Allied advances, notably the retaking of the Philippines by the United States. They feared that the French in Indochina would attack them from the rear (Governor-General Decoux had transferred his allegiance from Pétain to de Gaulle, and the Japanese knew that the French Resistance had networks in Indochina), and so they attacked the colonial army, dispersed its ranks, disarmed them, and imprisoned its soldiers. The government was put in Indochinese hands, and nearly all French nationals were held in the main cities.[78]

This change of direction led to the disbanding of the anti-Japanese networks that had linked the AGAS (Air Ground Aid Services), the OSS (Office of Strategic Services), and especially the GBT (an acronym for L. L. Gordon, Harry Bernard, and Frank Tan, who worked for the Saigon branch of Texaco and had left behind a web of information). From then on, the United States had no information about Japanese activities in Indochina, and no longer had an organization that could help downed pilots in the area. As a result, the AGAS was put in charge of information and sabotage behind Japanese positions, and was open to any offer of assistance.

This was the perfect time for Ho to make the Viet Minh known to – and thus recognized by – the United States as a much-needed source of help. On 17 and 20 March 1945, Ho met with Lieutenant Charles Fenn of the AGAS at the Indochina Café. Fenn knew about Ho's Communist affiliation, but now had a green light from the U.S. command and also from his embassy. He accepted the cooperation of the Viet Minh on Vietnamese soil and agreed to an immediate demand for arms; he even agreed to provide the "American blondes," which became Ho's favorites: Lucky Strike cigarettes. Both sides resolved that in the near future, the United States would send a military team with weapons and instructions to the Viet Minh base in the Highlands. Ho then refused the offer of financial subsidies. After this meeting, Lieutenant Fenn, who had studied graphology, analyzed Ho's handwriting. His report sheds yet more light on the personality of his correspondent:

> The essential features are simplicity, desire to make everything clear, remarkable self-control. Knows how to keep a secret. Neat, orderly, unassuming,

> no interest in dress or outward show. Self-confident and dignified. Gentle but firm. Loyal, sincere and generous, would make a good friend. Outgoing, gets along with anyone. Keen analytical mind, difficult to deceive. Shows readiness to ask questions. Good judge of character. Full of enthusiasm, energy, initiative. Conscientious; painstaking attention to detail. Imaginative, interested in aesthetics, particularly literature. Good sense of humor.
>
> Faults: diplomatic to the point of contriving. Could be moody and obstinate.[79]

The Vietnamese now had their "American connection," and the Americans had made contact with the Vietnamese.

Ho Chi Minh did not stop there, however, pressing Fenn to arrange a meeting with General Chennault. He asked for a signed photo, and the general, of course, could not refuse a dedication to the man who had saved one of his pilots. Ho knew that this glossy souvenir would come in handy and held onto it as a guarantee, a legitimization, and a weapon of propaganda. For an American like Chennault, however, whom Fenn describes as a sort of celebrity who relished his popularity, the gesture meant nothing.

Thereafter, Ho was registered in Fenn's list of correspondents as "Lucius." He flew to Paise, near Jingxi, with two Chinese-Americans, Frank Tan and the radio operator Mac Shinn, accompanied as always by his bodyguard Phung The Tai. After November 1944 and the Japanese capture of Guilin and Nanning, Zhang Fakui and the headquarters of the 4th Military Command had fallen back to Paise. This was where Ho had his first meeting with Major Archimedes Patti, Chief of the OSS in Indochina; the two men met again in autumn 1945 – but this time in Hanoi.

Ho Chi Minh considered the events in Kunming the first step toward official U.S. recognition of the Viet Minh. The French, meanwhile, whose officers had arrived from Calcutta or Kandy (Sri Lanka), were divided between Gaullists (the mission of General Petchkov) or Giraudists (under Commander Meynier). Still imbued with the ideas of imperialism, they were all condescendingly defiant toward the Viet Minh, when not ignoring them outright.[80]

The Right Moment: Act II (April–August 1945)

Indochina was in an intense state of turmoil, especially the three nations of Vietnam, as nearly ninety years of French domination had come to an end in the space of twenty-four hours. In April 1945, the Japanese granted independence to the three monarchs, Bao Dai, Norodom Sihanouk, and Sisavang Vong, but their authority was contested, and the economy – beset by requisitions, destruction, and inflation – was on the brink of a general collapse, according to the government's Director of Economic Services.[81] Tonkin and North Annam suffered because of poor rice harvests in 1944–45, a situation that was exacerbated by the destruction of the roadways and other means of transport by the Allied air forces. Rice from Cochinchina could no longer reach Tonkin, and famine struck a number of provinces, causing hundreds of thousands of deaths (some say up to a million). The Viet Minh seized the occasion to blame the French and the Japanese for the catastrophe because they had requisitioned rice and forced the farmers to cultivate oil seeds and jute instead of food crops.[82] Ho Chi Minh sent Major Patti a black book of the situation in Tonkin, containing numerous photographs of the famine victims.

At the same time, the Viet Minh came out of hiding and mobilized the population to seize the rice that both the French and the Japanese had stored in case of food shortages. Indeed, after 1943, the Japanese had not been able to ship their cargo to Japan due to the destruction of most of their naval fleet by Allied air strikes and submarine torpedoes.

Since September 1944, meanwhile, the Viet Minh had been preparing for an insurrection to take power in the three provinces of Cao Bang, Lang Son, and Bac Son. Once again, Ho had to step in and tone down the ardor of his followers, for his intuition and sense of strategy led him to believe that the Japanese surrender was near. After all, why not wait until the fruit was ripe to pick? A premature uprising could turn violent, especially since the Viet Minh neither held power in every area nor were uniformly organized throughout the territory. Ho also knew that the Viet Minh had competition, that his own followers had not yet agreed to unite all anti-Japanese forces, and that they lacked the fervor of unified action – including with the French, who were fleeing the Japanese but who still bore the taint of colonialism.

In his memoirs of this period, Vo Nguyen Giap related that during an attack on a French post, he ordered his men to fire only on command. He had hardly shouted "hands up" to a French officer when one of his guerrillas shot the officer down, unable to contain his hatred. Such things happen in the heat of battle.[83] Phung The Tai recalls an act that he committed in cold blood when he ran into a group of five French citizens, including one woman, escorted by troops fleeing the Japanese advance.

He first demanded that the sergeant stop serving his "superiors," then had the five people killed because they were his enemies, eagerly taking their money, watches, and jewelry:

> When I told comrade Vu Anh about this, he became pale and worried. [Vu Anh] said: "What am I going to tell Uncle Ho? Could it be that you haven't really understood the Viet Minh's policy of unity?" I was very sorry for what I had done, and really was an idiot.... It was obvious that Uncle Ho sensed what had happened even before he was told, for when he accepted my transfer to another position he recommended that I not act rashly.[84]

After assigning a new mission to Tai, Vu Anh also reminded him that he was to spread propaganda and get a foothold within the villages, not open fire with abandon.

In fact, whenever possible, Ho dissuaded his colleagues from assassinating individuals, whether police, informers, key figures, or mandarins. He emphasized that there would always be someone to replace a fallen enemy, and that in any case, it would not further their struggle for liberation.

ON 4 MAY 1945, HO MOVED TO TAN TRAO, A VILLAGE TO THE EAST OF Tuyen Quang in the Viet Minh stronghold, less than eighty kilometers from Hanoi. From there, he pressured the United States to send liaison agents, as well as instructors, for "the one thousand guerrillas" that he claimed were present in the region of Cho Chu–Dinh Hoa. The Viet Minh were looking for a place to set up a landing strip for their airplanes, but the Americans made the first move. On 17 July, they parachuted in the Deer Team under the command of Major Allison Thomas. Thomas was immediately impressed by the warm welcome given by "Mister Hoe," who "speaks excellent English but is very weak physically.... He received us most cordially."[85] The Deer Team stayed until 9 September and got as far as Hanoi with two hundred guerrillas, trained and instructed by Thomas in the use of the latest weapons.

Among the men of the team, Ho discovered one Frenchman, Lieutenant Robert Montfort, and two Indochinese noncommissioned officers from the colonial army. He had them taken to China immediately, along with twenty other French citizens – men, women, and children – who had been captured by the Japanese in the mountain station of Tam Dao and liberated by the Viet Minh. Major Thomas later reported that the French of Tam Dao were treated well and that he was surprised by the absence of hard feelings on the part of the Viet Minh. For that matter, Ho emphasized to Thomas that he "liked the French," but that his followers hated them and he could not be responsible for their reactions, the example of Phung The Tai (and certainly others) having made him more cautious. At times mistrustful, however, Ho often interrogated Lieutenant René Desfourneaux, a Frenchman who had taken American citizenship and was an information officer in the U.S. Army and part of the Deer Team. Ho suspected him of being a French agent disguised as an American, or feared the reaction of his guerillas. It bears mentioning that these guerrillas were recruited from among the survivors of the repression recently committed by French troops, when many had lost family and friends.

During this period, Ho was laid low by a serious case of malaria. Desfourneaux conveyed his impression of Ho, whom he had heard described as a formidable person: "A bunch of bones covered by dry, yellow skin, trembling like a leaf, and staring at us with glazed eyes." Those close to Ho thought that his last hour was near, until an old Tay went into the forest and came back with a tuber that he brewed into a miraculous concoction. There are two opinions about what happened: Some say it was a magic potion drawn from the land and the knowledge of the local people; the Americans claim that Ho was saved by the quinine and sulfonamides of the Deer Team's medic.[86]

The presence of the Americans was a determining trump card in Ho's hand. By means of the team's radio, he was surely one of the first Vietnamese to hear about the atomic bombings of Hiroshima and Nagasaki on 6 and 9 August, and on the 15th he was the first to learn of the Japanese surrender. These events convinced him that he should not miss the chance "which only happens once every thousand years."[87]

The country had been turned upside down. In principle, the ruling government was under Tran Trong Kim, named by Emperor Bao Dai, and it contained some pro–Viet Minh ministers. The Japanese authorities, meanwhile, had left in place the mandarins and the entire structure of the indigenous bureaucrats, supervised by Japanese advisors where possible. Vietnam was in total upheaval from north to south. In many areas, the mandarin authorities, officials, and notables had already been won over to the cause of independence within the nationalist or communist movements, whereas other areas were contested by a variety of groups: nationalists, National Salvation (Cuu Quoc) committees sent out by the Viet Minh, "Cochinchinese" religious sects like Hoa Hao and Cao Dai, and, of course, the Catholics in areas where they had widespread representation. The country had become a mosaic of competing territories. Prison camps and jails opened their doors, allowing more than just political prisoners to regain their freedom.[88]

Although the Japanese surrender was not yet official, on 13 August the Central Committee of the ICP and the leadership of the Viet Minh founded the Committee for National Insurrection, presided over by Truong Chinh, Secretary General of the ICP. On the same day, the new committee proclaimed their prime military directive: a general uprising throughout the country.

Ho Chi Minh showed that he was able to keep pace with the "acceleration of history" taking place before his eyes. Even more, he wanted to be in the forefront of events, rather than carried along in their wake, and be prepared instead of caught off guard. He asked the Executive Committee of the Viet Minh – in fact, of the ICP – to call for a national congress. There was no question of holding elections to choose delegates since there was no time. As a result, the delegates who arrived in Tan Trao were mostly Communists or members of the Viet Minh, or sympathizers like the leader of the Vietnamese Scouts in Tonkin. The Communists of Cochinchina invited a representative of the Hoa Hao religion to join them, but they arrived at the congress after it was over.

During the congress, Ho sat on a bench like an attentive pupil before being invited to address the participants. He emerged from anonymity only gradually, as if to set up the element of surprise: Nguyen Ai Quoc was alive! Once again, he showed himself to be an expert communicator. The participants were especially impressed that some forty of their comrades had been trained and equipped by the Deer Team, whose presence alone seemed to guarantee Anglo-American support for the Viet Minh. They commented on the photo of General Chennault that Ho had displayed prominently in one of the straw huts near the *dinh* (communal house combining village hall, temple, school, etc.) where the congress was holding its meetings.

Ho made such a strong impression – even sensation – that he was able to convey the previously unacceptable idea that they absolutely had to negotiate with the French for a progressive independence, rather than engage in a frontal assault. In the midst of the excitement and euphoria, Ho kept a cool head. In order to carry out negotiations, they would need a spokesman, and so on 16 August the congress appointed a five-member Provisional National Liberation Committee, four of whom were Communist, presided over by Ho Chi Minh. The Vietnamese present at Tan Trao saw this committee as a sort of provisional government whose goal was to "win back the independence of the nation."

On 22 August, Ho left Tan Trao for Hanoi and secretly entered the city on the 26th via the old native quarter known as the "thirty-six streets," many of which bore the name of the trades that were practiced there (Street of Silk, Street of Hatters, etc.). He then formed a provisional government and wrote a declaration of independence, which he read aloud on 2 September in Place Puginier (named for a Catholic bishop who had been influential during the French conquest of Tonkin), renamed Ba Dinh Square, a stronghold of anti-French resistance. The Democratic Republic of Vietnam (DRV) was born on that day before a crowd estimated at several tens of thousands.[89] One of Ho Chi Minh's autobiographical accounts paints the following portrait:

> President Ho is dressed as always in a khaki suit and black cloth sandals. His hair is already going gray above his high, large forehead, and he has sparkling eyes and a straight nose. He has a moustache which covers his upper lip, and a thin face; his slightly darkened skin led us to believe he had been exposed to the elements of the forest and to the difficulties of life in the Resistance.[90]

In September 1945, Ho had arrived at a point in his life's journey where fate was in his favor, and the ceremony in Ba Dinh Square was the staging of a double resurrection: that of an individual who embodied the Resistance, and that of an independent nation.

Until then, Ho Chi Minh had worked far from his homeland, and often far from and outside of his party. However, he was its organizer and inspiration, and had trained its first militants and leaders. (This did not mean, of course, that he was not frequently contested by his peers, as we have already seen.) From that moment on, he became a figurehead, and we see the first outlines of an icon being drawn.

FOUR

Father of the Nation

THE HEAD OF STATE AND THE DIPLOMAT WALKING A TIGHTROPE

The new state was immediately assailed by threats from within and without.[1] During the war, the Americans and the British had sought to bring Indochina into their respective theaters of operation: the China-Burma theater under the command of U.S. General Albert Wedemeyer and that of the Southeast Asia Command (SEAC) of British Admiral Louis Mountbatten. Toward the end of the hostilities, General MacArthur brought the Dutch Indies into SEAC to better focus on the Japanese archipelago.

After the defeat of the Axis powers, the Allied nations held a conference in Potsdam in late July with the participation of Winston Churchill, Harry Truman, and Joseph Stalin. They decided that the French would not be permitted to return immediately to Indochina, and that the Indochinese peninsula would be divided into two parts along the sixteenth parallel. The Japanese would be disarmed by Chiang Kai-shek's troops in the North and by the British army in the South. On 9 September, the two armies began to arrive in Indochina: The Yunnan army under General Lu Han entered from the northwest, troops from the Guangdong army landed in Haiphong, and the 20th Indian Division led by British General Douglas Gracey was flown into Saigon. There were also some six hundred Frenchmen from the "Light Intervention Corps" (CLI) who had remained in or were parachuted into the region, mainly in Laos. In early 1946, French military units who had taken refuge in China after the Japanese coup of 9 March returned to Indochina via Thailand.

Because the large-scale demonstration of 2 September 1945 in Saigon had resulted in several police "mishaps," General Gracey rearmed French soldiers who had been imprisoned by the Japanese so as to "reestablish order." During the month of October, the 5th Colonial Infantry Regiment and elements of the 2nd Armored Division of French General Philippe Leclerc moved into Saigon as well. Regardless of their position on independence, leaders of the new republic of Vietnam, and the Vietnamese people as a whole, were justified in fearing the Chinese Nationalists' hold on their country and the French government's intention of restoring their domination. On 27 November 1945, Ho summed up the situation before the Council of Ministers:

> We are governing through a difficult period. Chinese, French, and Japanese are present on our soil, and now we have to deal with the famine. Our ministries do not communicate with each other, and our government has no common plan of action. We lack personnel, even though we have flung open our ranks.[2]

The President of All Vietnamese and the Quest for Unity

The leaders of the provisional government of the DRV had to legitimize their authority, not only to counter the foreign presence but also to solidify their power, which they had assumed by force in a takeover led by a minority. They needed to assert themselves throughout the entire country and to be recognized as the new government, but first they would have to set up a legislative and institutional framework. From September 1945 to the end of 1946, Ho Chi Minh signed 181 decrees on everything from education to justice, the army, the police, taxes, agriculture, and the forests, as well as business and industry.[3] The old colonial administrative and police bureaucracies were retained after the most zealous pro-French or pro-Japanese elements had been eliminated, often physically.

Ho devoted special attention to the nation's young people. A number of youth and sports organizations had been set up by Commander Jean Ducoroy during the Vichy regime, in keeping with the doctrine of national revolution that the French, then in support of the Pétain government, had imported to their colonies. One of their main priorities was to shape the youth along the lines of *mens sana in corpore sano* (a sound mind in a sound body), training them to go forth and serve the "Motherland," that is, France. It was especially critical in Indochina since the Japanese had already been spreading pan-Asian, anti-Western propaganda and were recruiting Indochinese for paramilitary organizations.

Ho Chi Minh had learned about the Boy Scouts when he was in England, and some say that he had even read Robert Baden Powell and gone to a scout camp. Whether or not this is true, the spirit and activities of scouting corresponded to the needs of the patriotic movement: proving one's spirit and discipline, maintaining solidarity, helping one another, serving the community, and participating in outdoor activities both athletic and military in nature. The idea of the scouts was born, in fact, while Baden Powell was in command of the stronghold of Mafeking under siege by the Boers. The scouting movement had also taken hold in China in the 1920s, and both the nominal government and the "warlords" in their fiefdoms made use of it to serve both nationalist and civic roles.

The Viet Minh leadership thus wanted to encourage the scouting movement, or even lead it directly, and so they asked their young members to practice "entryism" into the Vietnamese scouting association, the Éclaireurs. The founder of the Éclaireurs of Tonkin, Hoang Dao Thuy, went to the national convention in Tan Trao and became the first director of the Republican Army Officers' School, which opened in December 1945. On 17 November 1945, Ho commemorated the fifteenth anniversary of the birth of scouting in Vietnam, and on 18 May 1946, he accepted the honorary presidency of the Scouts of Vietnam.[4] At the time, the Minister of the Interior of the newly proclaimed Democratic Republic of Vietnam estimated that there were sixty thousand registered scouts there.

Ho managed to rally the new "bourgeoisie" (generally referred to as intellectuals) to the revolution; some came spontaneously, others more gradually. Lawyers, scientists, engineers, and doctors were carried along by a wave of enthusiasm, letting themselves be convinced that it was now or never to put their skills at the service of their newly independent country.

The phenomenon was not limited to Hanoi; the same movement swept through the South, in Cochinchina, where even the highest socioprofessional class joined the revolution, from the graduates of the Franco-Annamite school system to a handful of graduates from French schools. Some of them, like the lawyers Thai Van Lung and Pham Ngoc Thuan, had a Catholic background. In Saigon, a group called the "Avant Guard Youth" was organized by Doctor Pham Ngoc Thach, an ICP leader who was also a Freemason and married to a Frenchwoman. They were the spearhead of a revolution led by the Communists, who no longer hid their true colors. These particular circumstances in the South undoubtedly stemmed from the existence of two currents driven by the ICP of Cochinchina: the Viet Minh and the so-called new Viet Minh (who had split off from the ICP in Tonkin but rejoined shortly before 1945). Be that as it may, the ICP still had to reckon with the Trotskyites and with the members of Cao Dai and Hoa Hao, who had organized into political parties (respectively, the Party of National Restoration and the Democratic and Social Party) and into paramilitary groups. They had the support of the Japanese and controlled some areas of Cochinchina.[5]

In Central Vietnam, Ta Quang Buu, head of the Scouts of Annam and professor of mathematics, transformed the Éclaireurs into "Youth in the Front Line," which then took control in Hué and helped the Viet Minh committee take power.[6] Many young Vietnamese joined the ranks, including those from the mandarin aristocracy, while Pham Khac Hoe, cabinet director for Emperor Bao Dai, and Bui Bang Doan, the Imperial Minister of Justice, joined the reformist scholar Huynh Thuc Khang in support of the republican government.[7] Aiming for the widest possible consensus, Ho proposed another initiative that would firmly link the new state with its national past: He sent Le Van Hien to Hué to convey his respectful homage and administer some pension funds to the widows of the emperors Thanh Thai and Duy Tan.[8]

Ho Chi Minh indeed "cast his net wide." His first decree appointed the citizen Vinh Thuy – also known as Emperor Bao Dai, who abdicated on 25 August – as "supreme advisor" to the provisional government of the DRV. The former monarch agreed to go to Hanoi to sit on the government council, and was immediately won over by Ho's personality. His change of allegiance was a bitter one, however. His admiration was crushed when Ho sent him off on a mission – into exile, in fact – to China. Some years later, Thuy agreed to sign an accord with the French government and play the nationalist card to thwart the Communists, but he demanded in return that the French grant him what they had accorded to Ho Chi Minh, and even more.

We do not know whether Ho's decision regarding Vinh Thuy was approved by other Communist leaders, but we do know that he was strongly criticized for releasing the mandarin Ngo Dinh Diem from the Central Prison in Hanoi, where he had been imprisoned by the French. In fact, Diem had been particularly unforgiving during the anti-communist repression in Binh Thuan province in 1930 and 1931. After the decision was made, the Communist Bui Lam burst into Ho's office and asked him if he realized that Diem, a sworn enemy of the Communists, would not have hesitated to order Ho's execution had the roles been reversed. Ho explained his indulgence by invoking Diem's father, the great mandarin Ngo Dinh Kha, who had refused to ratify the dethronement of Emperor Thanh Thai by his "protectors."

It is interesting to note that one of Diem's brothers, Monsignor Ngo Dinh Thuc, the Catholic bishop of Vinh Long, did not answer Ho's invitation to join the national coalition. Another brother, the governor Ngo

Dinh Khoi, was shot in Quang Ngai province; the same fate befell the Trotskyite leader Ta Thu Thau, who was intercepted while returning from Saigon on 7 September 1945. The central government's directives were thus not always followed at the local level. Sometimes it was better not to fall into the hands of a people's committee or a zealous but unenlightened self-defense militia, who applied to the letter the rules of revolutionary vigilance or the standing order to "exterminate traitors." This phrase could apply to the just punishment of a torturer from the colonial police or a corrupt mandarin, but also to acts of poor judgment or simply a desire for personal vengeance.

Ho Chi Minh also took steps to appease the nationalists. First, he invited Nguyen Hai Than from the Dong Minh Hoi to participate in the provisional government; then he extended the offer to Vu Hong Khanh and Nguyen Tuong Tam of the VNQDD. In November 1945, he managed to get them to sign a joint declaration, entitled "The Spirit of Union."[9] The nationalists agreed to halt attacks on the government in their press, to unite against the French colonialists, and to help their compatriots in Nam Bo (Cochinchina) fight the French army. Ho was in a delicate position regarding these nationalist circles, for he had been present at the reorganization of the Dong Minh Hoi, and especially because these men – his adversaries – had returned to Vietnam on Chinese army trucks. Since they knew they had the support of the Kuomintang, who did not hesitate to put pressure on the provisional Vietnamese government, the nationalists demanded to hold key positions within it.

In late December, Ho's government went one step further by reserving fifty seats in the National Assembly (which would be elected in January 1946) for the VNQDD and twenty for the Dong Minh Hoi. The nationalist deputies, then, would be appointed by law, not voted in by free election. Ho thereby let the nationalists avoid a popular verdict, but he simultaneously strengthened the positions of the Communist Party and its allies, such as the Democratic Party and the Socialist Party. Both parties were the result of pure political engineering by the ICP, and were created to serve as catalysts for the aspirations of "intellectuals," to benefit from the skills of "engineers," and to shore up "the cultural front."

In March 1946, Nguyen Hai Than became Vice President of the government, Nguyen Tuong Tam Minister of Foreign Affairs, and Vu Hong Khanh Special Delegate to the Council of Ministers. Of course, Ho was careful not to give the nationalists any sensitive positions, like Minister of the Interior or of Defense, which they of course wanted. And in foreign affairs, Nguyen Tuong Tam offered no initiatives and did not even open his mouth, since Ho played the leading roles himself. According to General Vo Nguyen Giap, however, all of these nominations, especially that of Nguyen Hai Than (whom Ho had put up at a beautiful villa and given unrestricted access to his private car) continued to draw protests from Ho's comrades.

In order to bypass his adversaries, Ho addressed himself directly to the people. He had a speech for children and the youth, one for women, another for the elderly, and yet another for religious communities. He held press conferences for national and international journalists and gave special interviews to foreign (mostly French) journalists, such as Dessinges and Jean-Michel Hertrich.

Ho implored the Vietnamese to work together and put themselves in the service of their country, and he was also careful not to be like the old monarchs and mandarins who were surrounded by ceremonies that isolated them from the people. He seized every occasion to mingle with the crowd, to abolish the distance between the leaders and the population. On 5 January 1946, for example, this man who claimed to be a nonbeliever went to two of the biggest pagodas in Hanoi where he met with Buddhist monks and the faithful. He talked with them and even took part in a vegetarian banquet. On the same day, he launched his "Call for the Citizens' Vote" to elect a National Assembly.

On 14 January, Ho visited Monsignor Le Huu Tu, bishop of the Phat Diem diocese in the Red River delta. He had appointed Tu as a government advisor and addressed him as "my friend." He stressed the necessity of uniting all Vietnamese to "fight against the foreign invaders and to put an end to the famine," referring to the Christian credo "God is the unity of three beings" and the Buddha's phrase "Ten thousand beings and one common feeling." Ho also reminded the crowd who had assembled in Phat Diem for his visit, including a hundred priests, that both Christ and the Buddha taught two things: Love thy neighbor and have compassion for all living beings.[10]

Before leaving Phat Diem, Ho ordered Phung The Tai to remain there at the head of his regiment, the first regular unit of the revolutionary army. This was intended to guarantee the security of the diocese but also to show clearly that there was only one nation, the Democratic Republic of Vietnam, and that the Christian community would not benefit from any immunity that was not granted to other religious or ethnic communities.[11]

The call for national unity and the defense of independence struck a chord with most Catholics, beginning with the Vietnamese clergy; at that time there were 4 Vietnamese bishops, 1,500 native priests, and some

1.6 million practicing Catholics. A French missionary remarked bitterly that "they" (the Vietnamese Catholics) wanted religious independence as well as political independence. He continued: "How painful it was to see some of our young students cross the city of Hanoi in ranks of four, fists raised behind the red flag with the yellow star." The good father did not understand that the Vietnamese Catholics had seized this occasion to free their Christian religious affiliation from French colonial domination. In fact, certain French missionaries had ardently desired and even helped to install this domination with the cooperation of their indigenous flock.[12]

Ho Chi Minh appreciated the vital role played by some of the ethnic minorities of the mountains, having found refuge among them in the past, and so he knew that he would have to grant them a special place in the organization of the young republic. In November 1945, he received delegates from the five minority groups of the Viet Bac and urged them to reinforce unity, increase production, and fight the foreign invaders. On 3 December 1945, Ho held a conference in the municipal theater of Hanoi for the representatives of twenty ethnic minorities and renewed his calls for unity, increased production, and support for the provisional government against foreign invasion, but he also emphasized their equality with the Vietnamese majority and the government's desire to help them develop their economy and educational system.

In January 1946, he put his policy of unity into practice and appointed Vuong Chi Thanh, the Muong "king" from the border district of Dong Van (in Ha Giang province), to the Vietnamese National Assembly. Before that, he had invited him to Hanoi and bestowed upon him the status of "adopted brother" with the name Ho Chi Thanh. Later, Thanh became the president of the Committee of Resistance and Administration of Dong Van, and Ho sent him a saber, a down jacket, and some badges as symbols of their alliance.

In the same way that Colonel Joseph Gallieni had "pacified" the Tonkin Highlands, Ho used the "oil spot technique" to promote the movement among the ethnic minorities who did not normally support the Vietnamese. This area was of strategic importance since a military unit of the VNQDD, under the command of Hoang Quoc Chinh, had penetrated into the area with the Yunnan army. The latter had established their headquarters in Ha Giang in September 1945, whereas the Viet Minh had no foothold in the region. In 1947, the French in turn occupied the Song Lo valley, and they too recruited allies from among the ethnic minorities of other districts.[13]

Ho did not forget about the minorities of Vietnam's Central Highlands, where French troops had begun to recover some ground. On 19 April 1946, he addressed the congress being held in Pleiku: "Be we Viet or Tho, Muong or Man, Jarai or Rhadé, Sedang or Bahnar, we are all Vietnam's children, brothers and sisters of the same blood." He appealed to them to safeguard liberty and independence.[14] But, Ho said, what is the use of independence and what does freeedom mean if our people are dying of hunger? Desperately wanting to end the famine, he organized food drives, had goods imported from central Vietnam, and requisitioned the foodstuffs that had been stockpiled before 9 March. And while he tried to keep the French at bay – they had already begun their reconquest of the South – he allowed them to deliver rice taken from the Japanese stores in Cochinchina.

In September 1945, in a characteristic move, Ho called upon those who had enough food to give up one meal per week for those who had nothing.[15] At the headquarters of the government itself (the Bac Bo Phu), located in the former Résident Supérieur's palace, Ho imposed a Spartan diet: Each person was allowed two bowls of rice, a few thin pieces of fish, some small marinated eggplants, and a clear broth. Tran Van Giau, who had presided over the Revolutionary Committee of Nam Bo and had arrived in Hanoi in November, was unhappy with the situation and decided one day to eat at the house of a friend, a rich man who was not "tightening his belt." Ho found out the next day and made a point of whispering in Giau's ear: "You refuse the salted eggplants that are served here? Right now our people are starving and you can't share their suffering, eh?" From then on, Giau had all of his meals at the Bac Bo Phu.[16]

Ho Chi Minh worked day and night, stepping up his activities in response to the difficulties that he encountered or anticipated. But despite all of his efforts to bring the people of his nation together, he was far from achieving unanimity or the "great union." Even among his supporters, his policy of national union was neither understood nor accepted by everyone, the release of Ngo Dinh Diem being just one example.

The conflicts and dissension were not all due to the nationalists or other "uncontrolled elements"; even within the Viet Minh, hostility against the French frequently led to bloody incidents, leaving some wounded or dead. The farther one got from the capital, the worse the situation became, as the local authorities – officially in the hands of the Viet Minh – often refused to apply the government directives or interpreted them in a limited way. More and more people were being assassinated as traitors, and a long-contained hatred erupted, though it is impossible to count the victims.

There were battles between the Viet Minh and their rivals, and a civil war began to brew with the arrival of Chinese troops in Tonkin. In September 1945, the armed unit of the VNQDD established itself in Lao Cay (western Tonkin); it took down the red flag with the gold star and hoisted its own, rejecting what had become the symbol of the DRV. To the east, in Mon Cay and Lang Son, soldiers of the Dong Minh Hoi did the same, but they were immediately driven out of Lang Son by the Chinese army. The nationalists were not about to give up the fight, even when they became members of the government or sat in the National Assembly. Their press never halted its attacks on the government and even stepped up its opposition, especially after Ho signed the agreement of 6 March 1946 authorizing French troops to land in Tonkin.

Now that the French army was present, the nationalists engaged in a series of provocations, including kidnappings and assassinations, intensifying their actions after Ho left for France on 31 May. As a result, they were accused of trying to sabotage the Franco–Viet Minh accords of 6 March and even suspected of attempting a coup d'état. On 11 July 1946, following the departure of the Chinese troops in June, the government began a vast police operation against the VNQDD. This operation in Hanoi ended a series of sometimes violent skirmishes that had already driven the VNQDD from its positions outside the city. Nevertheless, the VNQDD and the Dong Minh Hoi were allowed to remain as parties, though purged, composed henceforth of militants who followed Ho Chi Minh. The others were imprisoned or fled to the Chinese border, which they were able to cross once the Chinese had finally left the country.

In September 1945 in Cochinchina, ten thousand Hoa Hao crossed the northern branch of the Mekong to take control of the city of Can Tho, considered the capital of the Mekong delta, but were repulsed by the Viet Minh militia. This armed assault led to massacres on both sides and engendered a hatred that made the 1947 assassination of Huynh Phu So, a religious prophet, impossible to forgive. In 1946, the Cao Dai (or at least the dominant faction within the sect, whose "holy seat" was in Tay Ninh), allied itself with French troops against the Viet Minh, as did the Hoa Hao in 1947. All of Ho Chi Minh's efforts to rally followers of these religions to his government came to nothing in the end.[17]

The Viet Minh also executed a number of Trotskyites in Cochinchina, including the most prominent, such as Phan Van Hum, Phan Van Chanh, and Tran Van Thach. Most of these purges took place in the province of Thu Dau Mot, some forty kilometers from Saigon. They also battled the "3rd Division" of guerrillas that the Trotskyites had established in the Plain of Reeds, west of Saigon.[18] At the same time, the majority of the Khmer Krom (Cambodians from Cochinchina) joined the French troops and provided them with an auxiliary that was more than happy to massacre Vietnamese under the guise of fighting the Viet Minh.[19] A French civil administrator working in the Mekong delta in 1946 told the following story:

> We arrived in [Soc Trang] province in January... and in June, it was almost entirely pacified. The change was quick because there were eighty thousand Cambodians, and the Vietnamese were trying to protect us from them. The Vietnamese were in trouble because they had oppressed the Cambodian minority in our absence.... In 1946, our job was to limit internecine war. Sometimes we had to use force against the Cambodians. There were also defrocked monks who pretended to be prophets and who led us into actions that we regretted immediately afterward. We later had proof that we had been fooled by the rancor of the Cambodians.[20]

In the Central Highlands, the French found allies and auxiliary troops among the Rhadé, the Jarai, and other ethnic groups. Thus, Ho Chi Minh's policy of ethnic union, the "brothers and sisters, children of Vietnam," was stymied in the South, in the Center, and in the Northwest, the land of the Thai. Ho Chi Minh had frequently expressed his desire to unite all the peoples of Vietnam and all the strata of Vietnamese society, but he was perfectly aware of the centrifugal forces pulling people away from the center due to their heterogeneity, their long history of conflict, the antagonism between the classes and ethnic groups, and the political divisions brought about by the high-stakes grab for power.

Ho addressed the international press on 21 January 1946, stressing that the exceptional nature of the situation in his country justified unity of command. Basically, he said that in a democratic country, everyone has freedom of opinion and assembly, but "because of the general situation and the responsibility [that fell to him]," they only needed "one party, the party of the Vietnamese nation, to obtain independence. All Vietnamese citizens [would] be members of this party except reactionaries and those living abroad."[21] Ho was certainly right to invoke the exceptional nature of the situation, but how close was he to installing a virtual totalitarian state or even a very real "Reign of Terror," as the Jacobins had done during the French Revolution?

The conditions of the immediate postwar period were ripe for the impulse toward union – but also toward division and anarchy. This type of historical situation opens the door wide to foreign intervention, and in 1945–46 this threat became a matter of urgency for Ho Chi Minh. While trying to hold together an internally fragile republic, he had to deal with the ambitions of the Chinese and the troops of the Nationalist government, and then with the French, who had returned to "restore the sovereignty of France" over Indochina.

Against the Chinese of Chiang Kai-shek

When Ho Chi Minh heard the results of the Potsdam Conference, that the area north of the sixteenth parallel was to be entrusted to the Chinese Nationalist government, he had every right to be worried. The American Major Patti could see that Ho was very anxious beneath his outward composure.

In late 1940, Ho had told Vo Nguyen Giap that they absolutely had to hide their Communist affiliation in southern China. When he learned that the Chinese were training an expeditionary corps to send to Vietnam, he warned his comrades that they could only trust the Red Army of the Soviets and that of the Chinese: "They are the armies of our brothers and our true allies."[22] Then Ho had the bitter experience of his captivity under Zhang Fakui. During that period, he had ample time to find out about China's designs on the north of the Indochinese peninsula, particularly North Vietnam, as well as the ambitions of his nationalist compatriots, some of whom were strictly subordinated to the Kuomintang.

In addition, Ho knew that in April 1945, Zhang's adjunct, Colonel Xiao Wen (some sources call him a general), had dissolved the Action Committee that Ho had set up in Guangxi and recreated it with a majority of Dong Minh Hoi. And now Xiao Wen was about to enter Vietnam at the head of a contingent of the Guangxi army, tasked with disarming the Japanese in cooperation with troops from Yunnan. In fact, he alone remained in Vietnam as adjunct to General Lu Han, and ended up playing a major role; as director of the political department, he was one of the main representatives of the Kuomintang.

Ho arrived in Hanoi on 26 August, and again tried to anticipate the events happening around him. He called the government together to decide how to prepare for the imminent arrival of General Lu Han's troops, who were about to cross the border in Yunnan and actually entered Vietnam on 28 August. They had to quickly proclaim themselves an independent republic (Emperor Bao Dai had just abdicated), take advantage of the U.S. presence to establish a liaison with their government, act upon the United Nations Charter (signed 26 July 1945 in San Francisco) regarding the independence of colonized nations, and profit from the fact that the United States was about to grant independence to the Philippines.

That same day, Ho invited Major Patti for a visit and presented him with the declaration of independence that he had just written and that opens with the Preamble to the American Constitution of 1776. He asked for the major's opinion, then shared with him his fears of seeing the troops arrive from Yunnan, "the most rapacious and the most undisciplined of the Chinese army," in Giap's words.[23]

As the Chinese reached the sixteenth parallel, a resident of Hué described them thus:

> Dressed in yellowish uniforms, with crumpled caps and enormous puttees, they seemed to be dragging along, visibly starving. Some of their faces were puffy from sickness. That's why we called them "the *tofus*." ... As a whole they behaved decently with us. But when we learned about the devastation they caused in the markets, all the food shops and restaurants closed.[24]

According to official Chinese statistics, 152,486 soldiers (250,000 to 300,000 according to other sources) moved into the area north of the sixteenth parallel.[25] They became a considerable burden on a country whose economy was already suffering, and which was ravaged by famine and even typhus in some areas. At the same time, the Chinese dumped their devalued currency (the gold unit) into Tonkin and fixed the rate of exchange at 1.5 piastres, five or six times higher than it was worth. This was the first incidence of "piastre trafficking," which led to inflation and higher prices, a situation that was exacerbated by currency trafficking and the black market for consumer goods, especially American cigarettes. All of the materials that once belonged to the colonial administration and then to the Japanese were seized as war booty and became subject to large-scale illicit trafficking.

The very evening of the declaration of independence, Ho sent a letter to the community of Chinese nationals in Vietnam – there were more than a hundred thousand – and reminded them that the Chinese and Vietnamese were linked by culture and history, and that both had been subjected to French imperialist domination. But, he added, China had driven out the Japanese invaders and was on the road to recovering its sovereignty from the West. Vietnam, for its part, was once again a national independent state. As a result, nothing should keep the two countries from existing with good relations and in peace in *the mutual respect of their national sovereignty*.[26]

Ho Chi Minh's concern was well founded since he was up against people like General Chen Xiuhe (Tran Tu Hoa in Vietnamese), who had published a book in 1943 in Kunming entitled *Studies on the Ancient History of Vietnam: Its People and Civilization*. Chen wrote that the Viet people were the descendants of the Yueh of southern China, and that it was in their interest to strengthen their economic and cultural ties in order to become part of "the great Chinese family." Ho was not alone in his concern; the French in Chongqing who knew about this theory were also rather worried.[27]

In his relations with the Chinese, Ho always took charge and was both flexible and firm in his diplomacy; after all, the republic's very existence was at stake. After their arrival, the Chinese army controlled the radio station and automobile traffic.

The Chinese also occupied public buildings as well as the Bank of Indochina, whose funds were not available to the government in any case. To complicate matters, Ho had abolished some of the most unpopular taxes – but also the most lucrative. The Chinese tried to ignore the fact that Vietnam was now a sovereign nation, which irked the Vietnamese, but Ho chose to play for time and multiply his gestures of appeasement. For example, when the Chinese arrived at Yen Bay, they were attacked by a group of Vietnamese. Ho quickly telegraphed Chiang Kai-shek to denounce the "bandits claiming to be Viet Minh," when in fact it was indeed the Viet Minh of Yen Bay who had opposed the arrival of the Chinese troops. Ho renamed his Liberation Army the "National Guard," had them billeted in the environs of Hanoi, and used them with discretion to avoid conflict. He called upon the Vietnamese to observe strict discipline and to avoid sparking any incidents that could aggravate the Chinese. On 10 October, to commemorate the birth of the Chinese Republic in 1911, Ho joined General Lu Han at the Confucian temple and once again seized the occasion to solemnly celebrate the birth of Sun Yat-sen. He left nothing to chance. When Lu Han and his general staff arrived in Hanoi, Ho asked his secretary to make sure that certain generals had their opium pipes each evening, for he knew "the habits of those people."[28]

To cast off suspicion of the Chinese and other foreigners, on 11 November Ho publicly announced the dissolution of the Indochinese Communist Party, which would be replaced by "Marxist study groups." In other words, the ICP went back into hiding. This subterfuge fooled nobody, but the elimination of the ICP had another, nontactical meaning, which at the time went unnoticed: It marked the end of "Indochina" as an entity, thereby preempting any charges that the Vietnamese were trying to be the dominant power on the peninsula.

In other circumstances and at another time, this act would have led to the exclusion of the Communist Party or its leadership from the Communist International. The dissolution of the Comintern (May 1943) had certainly given more freedom of action to Communist Parties, but the old reflexes remained for several years, especially with the Cominform taking its place in October 1947. Be that as it may, the pseudodissolution of the ICP offered to a few Communists (like Tran Ngoc Danh in 1949) the pretext of denouncing Ho Chi Minh's "liquidations" and petit-bourgeois nationalism. At least Ho did not suffer the same fate as Earl Browder, head of the Communist Party of the United States, who was called in for questioning by the Kremlin for having dissolved his party in 1944 and advocating an alliance between communism and capitalism. Times had changed; European Communist Parties had played upon national sentiment during the war against Germany and were now exploring "national paths" to socialism. The Yugoslavian schism called Titoism (1947) resulted from this orientation.[29] Stalin himself exalted the sacrifice and heroism of the Russian people in the "great patriotic war."

ON MANY OCCASIONS, HO GAVE IN TO THE DEMANDS OF THE CHINESE general staff. For example, in October 1945 when the French sent cargoes of rice to Cochinchina to help the people in the North, Ho demanded that two-thirds go to the Chinese troops and only one-third to the Vietnamese.[30] He did the same during "Gold Week" in mid-September, when a large part of the coins, jewelry, and gold taels – gifts from the people to the nation – were used to pay for the Chinese occupation.[31]

Until the final departure of the Chinese troops, which dragged on from April to June 1946, Ho Chi Minh and his government had to swallow many affronts to satisfy the demands of their occupiers. On 18 December 1945, General Chen Xiuhe asked Ho to postpone the legislative general elections so that his Vietnamese protégés in the VNQDD and Dong Minh Hoi could get ready to take on the Viet Minh, all the while affirming that the Chinese general command would remain "neutral regarding political parties." Ho's response was again both flexible and firm. That evening he wrote them a letter in Chinese announcing that he had postponed the elections for fifteen days per the general's request, but he ended with a clear message: The Viet Minh was not a political party but a national front for unity, founded to defend the Democratic Republic of Vietnam, which was an independent nation. Then he proceeded to set out the political, social, cultural, and diplomatic programs of the government, as well as the administrative organization of the country, and concluded with the list of ministers in the provisional government.[32]

Ho may have conceded, or even capitulated, on some of the material stakes, but on political matters he showed an iron will and drew a line that he refused to cross. One day, General Lu Han invited him to his headquarters and offered to provide Chinese advisors to each minister in the provisional government, adding that Ho himself could benefit from the counsel of a Chinese advisor. Ho found these words unacceptable but remained silent; then after the second proposal, he stood up and ended the meeting by responding: "Excellency, as far as I am concerned, the Vietnamese people are the only ones who have the right to control me, no one else."[33]

By the time the last Chinese troops reluctantly set out for home, dragging their feet, Tonkin had been bled dry. The Chinese army had made an enormous dent in the food stores, but even worse, many of the soldiers, either individually or in groups, had plundered whatever they could. With the exception of those few units who were properly uniformed, disciplined, and in good physical condition, the soldiers – whom Archimedes Patti called squatters, and whose ragged and miserable appearance had struck all who saw them – took everything they could get their hands on, from furniture to plumbing fixtures to dishes.

Ho Chi Minh's worries were not over with the withdrawal of the Chinese, however. In the meantime, French troops had landed in Tonkin.

Change of Adversaries

Until 9 March 1945, all Indochinese possessions had been administered by the French. The Japanese takeover opened a power vacuum that was only partially filled by the independence granted to Indochina's sovereigns: the Vietnamese Bao Dai, the Cambodian Norodom Sihanouk, and the Laotian Sisavang Vong. France had just been liberated, and de Gaulle thought of far-off Indochina as a "ship in distress floundering in the storms." But sending troops required a means of transport and especially the good will of the Allies, in this case, the Americans.[34]

After the humiliation of France's defeat and the subsequent German occupation, General de Gaulle's ambition – and one surely applauded by a majority of the French population at the time – had been the restoration of France's imperial power. It would serve as both foundation and instrument of the international role that the French government wanted to play after liberation. And since their victory was due in part to the resources of their colonial empire, de Gaulle certainly envisaged some sort of change in the way the colonies were administered, but any increased participation of the colonies in their own affairs would be under the leadership of France and within the terms that only France would define.

The Brazzaville Conference of August 1944 sketched out a broad outline for the evolution of the African colonies. The question of Indochina was addressed in a declaration of 24 April 1945. It took a similar tack, granting relative internal autonomy within the heart of the French Union. It specified, in particular, that the five nations of Indochina were to remain together, thus denying the reunification of Vietnam (as Cochinchina, Annam, and Tonkin). The French government would remain at the controls and would continue to have the last word.

France's view of its relationship with its colonies was stated many times. As for Indochina, de Gaulle himself made their position clear on 15 February 1945 during a brief appearance at a Tet (New Year) celebration organized by the Minister of Colonies, Paul Giacobbi, who said that "the Overseas Territories [were only] an extension of the motherland." The general was more explicit: "France plans to join the hopes of their people with its own.... In the Indochinese Union and everywhere under our protection, [France] is and will remain the sole representative."[35]

This Gaullist notion was totally out of sync with the real situation that had begun with the Japanese takeover. The gap only widened as 1945 wore on, and the August revolution in Vietnam rendered it totally obsolete. One of the first Frenchmen to realize the situation was Pierre Messmer, who was parachuted in as Commissioner of the French Republic in Tonkin in December 1945. He and two of his men were captured by the Viet Minh and held for two months in a village in Bac Ninh province, where one of the men fell ill and died. The two survivors escaped and took refuge in the Chinese garrison at Bac Ninh before continuing on to Hanoi, where they met up with Jean Sainteny, de Gaulle's delegate in Tonkin and North Annam. Messmer noted:

> In the villages we passed through, the Viet Minh was efficient and well organized, and was in charge. Out of fear or conviction, the people obey without a word. In just a few weeks they erased sixty years of French colonization, whose imprint seems to have been neither deep nor solid.... In the field one thing is sure; the government's declaration of 24 March defining the new French policy is completely out of date.[36]

The French government did not want to face what was happening, however, and ignored the signals being sent and duly received. Among these was a message from Ho Chi Minh to the French government, written from his base at Tan Trao and sent via Major Allison Thomas and the U.S. government. Emperor Bao Dai also sent letters to President Harry Truman, British Prime Minister Clement Attlee, Generalissimo Chiang Kai-shek, and the one below to General de Gaulle on 18 August 1945:

> The Vietnamese people do not want, and cannot tolerate foreign domination or administration any longer. . . . I beg of you to understand that the only way to safeguard French interests and the spiritual influence of France in Indochina is to openly recognize Vietnam's independence and to renounce any notion of reestablishing sovereignty or a French administration here in any form. We could understand each other so easily and become friends if you would stop pretending that you are still our masters.[37]

On the same day, Ho Chi Minh sent the French a second message via Jean Sainteny and Léon Pignon, at the time Administrator of the Colonies, who were both in Chongqing. The letter elaborated five demands:

1. The French government will recognize the government of the Viet Minh;
2. The Viet Minh government will recognize the authority of the French government over Vietnam during a period of five or six years, beyond which the French government will grant independence to Vietnam;
3. During this period, Vietnam will be autonomous in its internal affairs;
4. The French government will enjoy privileges in the areas of industry and commerce;
5. The French will be permitted to advise in foreign affairs.[38]

As the situation gradually evolved in late 1945 and early 1946, Ho was under constant pressure by the nationalists, who were considering a coup d'état, and by the Chinese, who pushed for their own causes. He wanted to rid himself of "these fleas on the dog's back" and appear to be receptive to the French. He knew that he could not avoid a confrontation with them, and short of playing the United States against China and even France, it was better to placate the latter to get rid of the Chinese – and the nationalists along with them.

The Chinese government, on the other hand, wanted the departure of Soviet troops from Manchuria, where they had disarmed the Japanese, but in order to do that, they would have to pull their troops out of Vietnam. Then the Chinese civil war resumed, altering the local and regional political landscape, with the Chinese Communists beginning their conquest of the country by pushing the Nationalist troops towards the south. Chiang Kai-shek needed the southern armies to fight in the north of the country – an occasion for him to get rid of the Yunnanese – and he negotiated with the French government for the withdrawal of these armies from Tonkin. In October 1945, the French army began its reoccupation of Cochinchina, then the coast and the Highlands of southern Annam.

The United States, meanwhile, had made it clear that the DRV should not count on them. On 15 October 1945, Ho Chi Minh met with the French officials Jean Sainteny and Louis Caput (head of the SFIO of Tonkin and intermediary between Sainteny and Ho), and then explained to his ministers that the Vietnamese might have some individual support but that they should not count on the official sympathy of the United States.[39] On the American side, President Roosevelt supported the idea of liberating Indochina from the French and putting it under an international trusteeship, in Sino-American hands. He died on 12 April 1945, and upon taking office, Truman abandoned this project because the Soviet Union and communism had become America's primary adversaries after the defeat of the Axis powers.[40]

The French, however, continued to believe that the United States wanted to oust them from Indochina, and found proof in the sympathy that Major Patti showed toward Ho Chi Minh and the DRV. They thought that Roosevelt, Patti, and all Americans were cut from the same cloth, whereas in reality, nothing was further from the truth. Even back in the Roosevelt era, the European Section of the State Department had agreed to privilege the alliance with France, or at least try not to displease them. This allegiance was strengthened after Roosevelt's death, as mistrust of the Chinese Nationalists grew and anticommunism clearly took priority over anticolonialism, which had become just another topic of conversation.

Patti's superior was General William Donovan, founder and head of the OSS, who thought that European colonial empires were a necessary counterweight to the Soviet peril. There were even disagreements within Patti's OSS team in Hanoi. Colonel Stephen Nordlinger, who worked for the Red Cross and was in Hanoi looking after prisoners of war, was very concerned about the fate of the French, both civilian and military. He criticized Patti for neglecting them, and many fell victim to the chaos and were attacked, robbed, and even assassinated. It was Nordlinger who freed Sainteny and his driver after they had been assaulted and detained by the Viet Minh police. Patti, on the other hand, was summoned to Chongqing by Ambassador Patrick Hurley, who accused him of having compromised himself with the "reds." He left Hanoi on 1 October 1945 after sharing one last dinner with Ho Chi Minh.[41]

Following many false starts, the French and Chinese finally signed a political and military agreement that resolved a number of issues: the French settlements in China, the Yunnan railway, the status of the Chinese in Indochina, the withdrawal of Chinese troops, and the arrival of French troops in the north of Vietnam.

The Arrival of the French in North Vietnam

In order to take over from the Chinese and avoid armed confrontation, the French found it absolutely necessary to reach an agreement with the government of Ho Chi Minh, and quickly. This task fell to Jean Sainteny and his team. De Gaulle, who had entertained the idea of involving former Emperor Duy Tan once the French returned to Vietnam, saw the situation from a distance and told the Asia specialist Paul Mus, "We will return to Indochina because we are the strongest."[42] Once on Indochinese soil, however, the situation was not so clear to those in charge. Admiral Georges Thierry d'Argenlieu, the High Commissioner, and General Leclerc, commander of French military forces, as had Jean Sainteny before them, realized just how complex and difficult the situation was, and that it varied from Vietnam to Cambodia to Laos.

Leclerc, who had already begun what should rightly be called the reconquest of Cochinchina and southern Annam, ran into fierce resistance and concluded that France did not and would not have the necessary force to take control again in the North. To justify the Franco-Vietnamese accord, he wrote on 27 March:

> To get into Tonkin, we needed an Annamite government in place in Hanoi, no matter how imperfect, not one out in the bush.... In that case, had we found (apart from the Chinese) a nation in arms against us or simply in disorder, we could have just landed in Haiphong, but – I state categorically – the retaking of Tonkin, even partially, was impossible.[43]

The general's attitude was motivated by more than his realization that France lacked military strength in the face of fierce Vietnamese resistance. In fact, even before he arrived in Indochina, he had met in Ceylon with Admiral Mountbatten, who emphasized that the political situation was changing rapidly in Asia and that the French would have to come to terms with it. Sometime later, Leclerc said to General Raoul Salan, "My plan aims for something new; there have been too many changes, it is impossible to maintain the old order."[44]

Administrator Pignon, who was part of Sainteny's team, sent a report to Admiral Thierry d'Argenlieu:

> It is clear that the Viet Minh is made up of extremely dedicated and disinterested individuals. As such, they could be considered very dangerous but also very consistent, and therefore highly likely to respect their commitments to us. Without a doubt, the only man who matters is Ho Chi Minh. If he proposes something that tallies with public opinion, the masses will certainly accept it. No other party leader is capable of this.

Jean Sainteny was also quite impressed by Ho, and he wrote: "From our first meeting on 15 October 1945, I had the conviction... that Ho Chi Minh was a person of the first order." The young Lieutenant François Missoffe was part of the Sainteny mission and also liked Ho, the "small, skinny fellow" who was "upbeat, very curious, asks about everything, makes others talk a lot. I will also be meeting frequently with him. He is very sensitive. He never gives the impression of having already made up his mind about things."[45]

General Salan, who had just taken command of the French troops that had withdrawn to China after the Japanese takeover, shared Missoffe's opinion. His meeting with Ho Chi Minh on 8 February left him "a bit troubled; I have in front of me an energetic man, sure of himself, firm in his words; will we be able to understand each other?"[46] The circumstances of this meeting are quite telling. On February 2, Ho visited the French soldiers who were being treated at De Lanessan Hospital. He played the role of head of state but also "faithful friend of France. It was the festival of Tet and I was happy, on that occasion, to show my friendship for [his] country.... Besides, believe me, most Indochinese are not anti-French." However, Ho strongly repeated that the Vietnamese wanted their freedom and that he did not want to betray his country. If the French wanted to come back he could not stop them, but then "blood will flow and it will be terrible. I do not want it to happen, but French women and children will be killed. I will not be able to hold back the masses. It is too bad but I will not be able to do anything about it. It is simply the reaction of people who do not want to be enslaved."

On 6 March 1946 after heated negotiations and a race against the clock, virtually on the eve of the French arrival in the port of Haiphong, Sainteny signed an agreement with Ho Chi Minh. The contents of the preliminary accord – so called because it was meant to be completed at a general conference at an undetermined locale – reveal Ho's penchant for buying time; he preferred to achieve his goals through gradual negotiation than by frontal attack.

With this in mind, Ho agreed that the word "independence" would not appear in the text designating Vietnam as a "Free State at the heart of the French Union." He even proposed that the fate of Cochinchina (Nam Bo) be decided by popular referendum, and agreed that French troops would replace Chinese troops and remain stationed in Vietnam for a period of five years. However, Admiral Thierry d'Argenlieu did not feel that France was bound by this "military" addendum, which was the idea of the local negotiators, a way of repudiating Sainteny and General Leclerc.[47]

The agreement was signed in the hopes of avoiding bloodshed, but it sparked great discontent within the nationalist opposition and also among Ho Chi Minh's followers. Some played on the easy irony because Ho had just created a government of Unity *and Resistance*. One Hanoi resident remarked, "Who still remembers the oath of independence: we will not serve the French, not speak to them, etc.?" The nationalists could not figure out what was happening either as Vu Hong Khanh, leader of the VNQDD, signed the agreement as Special Delegate to the Council of Ministers. As soon as the news was made public, Khanh was summoned by the students at the VNQDD's school for cadres.

Another Hanoi resident, a Viet Minh cadre, wrote:

> On 7 March, I woke up and found Mai [his wife] in a panic. Groups of people were hanging out in the streets. I ran through the city and saw that emotions were running high. People were arguing, fighting, even yelling insults. What has caused this discord? One simple poster, a proclamation signed by two names: Leclerc and Ho Chi Minh.[48]

The public notice announced the arrival of French troops and asked the people to please welcome them.

As for the Viet Minh, the editorial of 17 March 1946 in their French-language newspaper, *La République*, articulated the strong reluctance of the Vietnamese:

> The government is having a hard time making itself understood.... The obedient citizens finally accepted the government's policies more out of confidence in Ho Chi Minh than out of conviction. No matter, let us ring in the dawn of a new era.... The Vietnamese people walk through the streets brooding over their discontent. But they still have their foundation, since the

> confidence they put in the person of Ho Chi Minh taught them to do the right thing.[49]

Indeed, on 7 March, Vo Nguyen Giap and Ho had been forced to defend their decision to sign the agreement of the night before. A crowd had gathered in front of the municipal theater in Hanoi, and some people were shouting angrily. Giap invoked the Treaty of Brest-Litovsk as a historical referent (signed by the Russian Bolsheviks in 1918 to end the hostilities with Germany and save the Russian Revolution), and said that policies should be decided according to "objective conditions," adding that "sometimes one must be firm and sometimes one must be pliant." Then Ho spoke:

> We have actually been independent since August 1945 but so far no power has recognized our independence. The agreement with France opens the way to international recognition. It will lead us to an increasingly more solid international position, which is a great political achievement. There will only be fifteen thousand... French troops and they will only stay here for five years.... It is a show of political intelligence to negotiate rather than fight. Why should we sacrifice fifty or one hundred thousand men when we can attain independence through negotiation, maybe within five years?.... I, Ho Chi Minh, have always led you on the path to freedom, I have fought my whole life for the independence of our nation. You know that I would rather die than sell out my country. I swear to you that I did not sell you out![50]

Before boarding a plane for France on 31 May, he repeated the same statement in an address to resistance fighters from Cochinchina.

Ho Chi Minh in France

The accords of 6 March may have prevented a war between the French and the Vietnamese but not the spilling of blood, as there was a brief skirmish when the Chinese opposed the arrival of the French in Haiphong.[51] The situation soon became permanently tense, however, due to the incompatibility of the French and Vietnamese policies.

In a way, the preliminary agreement of 6 March was just a tactical move for both sides. The High Commissioner, Thierry d'Argenlieu, focused only on his mission to restore French sovereignty, so had the short-term goal of reestablishing a footing north of the sixteenth parallel. Ho Chi

Minh, on the other hand, saw it as one step toward his long-term goal of total independence for the three Viet nations (Bac, Trung, and Nam Bo), reunified within the bosom of the DRV. And he believed he could get there through negotiation and not through war.

The words "restoration of French sovereignty" often appeared in the speeches and remarks of Admiral Thierry d'Argenlieu, and others who were carrying out French policy took them up as well. But there was another part to his mission: He also wanted to organize the Indochinese Federation by bringing Cambodia, Laos, and the Viet nations under its leadership. The key issue for both sides was that of Cochinchina (Nam Bo) where, in fact, the hostilities had continued in a number of areas because the local Viet Minh leaders and some French officers had not respected the cease-fire.

A new conference was to be held in order to decide the future of Vietnam, and Ho Chi Minh was eager to have it in Paris. It was there that important political decisions were usually made, and where he could count on political support – and not only from the FCP, which currently held ministerial positions within the tripartite government led by Georges Bidault, founder of the People's Republican Movement. It is possible that Ho also aimed to reestablish ties with the Soviet Union via its embassy in Paris.

Admiral Thierry d'Argenlieu, understandably, did not want the conference to be held in Hanoi. And the Vietnamese did not want to return to Dalat, a mountain resort and summer holiday destination where a previous Franco-Vietnamese conference had already failed in May 1946, and which the admiral wanted to establish as the new capital of the Indochinese Federation that the Vietnamese rejected. The first conference had lasted two weeks, and delegates of both sides left without having reached an agreement, mainly due to the question of Cochinchina. The admiral had also convened a conference in Dalat concerning the Indochinese Federation, while at the same time approving preparations for the founding of an autonomous republic of Cochinchina by a small group of southern bourgeoisie. This second conference in Dalat, on 1 August 1946, was presided over by Thierry d'Argenlieu and brought together representatives of Cambodia, Laos, and the autonomous state of Cochinchina. He organized the Federation by separating Cochinchina from the rest of Vietnam, which was totally unacceptable to the leaders of the DRV and was a serious provocation. Consequently, Nguyen Binh, military leader of the resistance in Nam Bo, ordered the resumption of generalized combat against the French. At this critical moment, Ho Chi Minh was in France, where he had declared on 12 July:

> [Cochinchina] is a Vietnamese land. It is the flesh of our flesh, the blood of our blood.... Before Corsica was French, Cochinchina was already Vietnamese.... On this point, I affirm that I have confidence in the new France.[52]

The High Commissioner did not stop with Cochinchina, however. He ordered the retaking of the highlands of Pleiku and Kon Tum in central Vietnam, and went to Ban Me Thuot to accept the "Great Oath of Loyalty" to France by the mountain chieftains. General Leclerc reacted to these initiatives with a telegram to General Alphonse Juin:

> Proclamation Cochinchina government will be made 1 June. It is unfortunate that we waited until Ho Chi Minh left, since this will lead to tendentious interpretation in Hanoi. In northern Ban Me Thuot, Admiral [Thierry d'Argenlieu] gave direct orders to Colonel Bourgund constituting in fact a violation of 6 March.[53]

Thus, while Ho Chi Minh was in France and the Vietnamese and French delegations were in discussions at Fontainebleau, the High Commissioner's incendiary initiatives were constituting a clear infringement of the accords of 6 March. This was reason enough to provoke the anger and concern of the Vietnamese, and confirmed what they saw as the treachery of the French, who wanted to return to their colonial past.

During his voyage, Ho Chi Minh was informed of the admiral's actions by radio, not via diplomatic channels as would have befitted a head of state. He was angry but did not abandon his trip, having decided to step into the diplomatic breach. All the same, he said to Salan, "General, do not make Cochinchina into a new Alsace-Lorraine or we will start a hundred years' war."[54] He arrived in France just as the ministerial cabinet of Félix Gouin was being ousted, and so until Georges Bidault was invested by Parliament, Ho was put up at the Carlton Hotel, in Biarritz, where the government had made his plane land.

As usual, from the moment he arrived he made contact with the locals in order to break out of his small circle of traveling companions, Salan and Sainteny among them. He spent a day by the sea with fishermen in order "to learn" from them. He visited the region of the Pyrénées-Atlantiques, went to a Basque pelota tournament, visited Lourdes – only as an observer, of course – and asked people about their experiences during the German occupation and the resistance. He also attended the commemoration of de Gaulle's call to resistance of 18 June, held at the memorial to the dead of the Biarritz resistance, and one month later he made a pilgrimage to Mont Valérien, where the Germans had shot to death a number of resistants and hostages – both of them meaningful events. He capitalized on every occasion possible to make a symbolic gesture.

In Paris, responding to the welcoming speech of Georges Bidault, Ho referred to his image of France as a nation of diverse peoples and cultures, but united within the republic and animated by a spirit of independence. He thus justified the existence of a unified and independent Vietnam, and also foresaw a French Union that would exist only on condition that all members were voluntary participants and on an equal footing.

Ho had visitors while in Biarritz, including the French Communist Charles Tillon, serving as Minister of Aviation (the FCP held six new ministerial positions in the new government), who had been sent by his party to see that Ho Chi Minh received a proper welcome. Ho must have explained to Tillon in person his tactic of a united front as a means to national independence, as well as the supposed dissolution of the ICP, which must have caused some suspicion. Tillon would certainly have understood his Vietnamese comrade, since he had led the paramilitary troops and partisans in the national resistance against the German occupiers, and even the FCP put national unity before the class struggle or the revolution when they disarmed the "patriotic militia." Ho was also visited by some of his countrymen, such as the scientist Buu Hoi and Nguyen Manh Ha, a Catholic and founder of the Vietnamese Christian Youth Workers and son-in-law of the Communist deputy Georges Marrane.

When Ho was finally invited to Paris by the new Prime Minister, he did not attend the Fontainebleau Conference. He let Pham Van Dong defend the cause of the Democratic Republic of Vietnam, and most probably had no illusions about the outcome of the discussions. He knew that the conference would end in an impasse due to the actions of the High Commissioner, who had begun to set up an Indochinese Federation within the framework of the French Union, and who also encouraged General Jean-Étienne Valluy, Leclerc's successor, to encroach upon territory under Vietnamese sovereignty. During this period, the admiral even said that France did not have to "refrain from using the *ultima ratio*" – military force – to achieve its aims.

A short time later in Paris, in November 1946, Georges Bidault declared to the interministerial commission on Indochina, "Cochinchina is a French colony. It will remain so pending the decision by the National Assembly. It is the High Commissioner's duty to ensure that order is respected by all means possible against anyone who opposes it." Pierre Messmer remarked, "Legally this is true. Politically it is absurd."[55]

The two points of view were obviously irreconcilable, and on 1 August, Prime Minister Pham Van Dong refused to participate in the conference because of Admiral Thierry d'Argenlieu's actions, denouncing them as a violation of the accords of 6 March. The Fontainebleau Conference came to a sudden halt. The night before Ho was to return to Vietnam, Salan said to him – and Ho must have known it was true – "We are going to fight each other, and it will be very difficult." Indeed, Ho had told Sainteny and Marius Moutet, "If we have to fight, we will fight.... You will kill ten of us and we will kill one of you, but you will be the ones who grow tired."[56]

LET US GO BACK A FEW MONTHS, HOWEVER, TO 22 JUNE 1946 WHEN Ho Chi Minh had just begun his trip to Paris and was a guest of the government of the French Republic. He was initially put up at the Royal Monceau Hotel but left soon after to stay with friends in Soisy-sous-Montmorency, the Aubracs, who had been key players in the anti-German resistance.[57] He stayed on the second floor of their house, had a Vietnamese cook, and was able to receive several dozen people in their garden.

Ho was on a diplomatic mission and knew how to make a media event out of his activities, even in the days before television or the Internet. He made as many contacts as he could, got to know people, and lobbied. He sent Nguyen Manh Ha to meet Francisque Gay and Maurice Schumann (of the People's Republican Movement, also called the French Christian Democracy or MRP), and sent Hoang Minh Giam (former member of the SFIO in Tonkin) to the SFIO congress. Both were disappointed to find that Vietnam was not an urgent problem, nor even a problem at all, for the MRP and the SFIO. Giam noted sadly that he ended up making proposals and battling leaders of the SFIO but that the congress remained impervious to Vietnamese demands.

Ho was clearly engaged in large-scale diplomatic maneuvers, yet his first visits were to Léo Poldès. A police report from 17 July notes: "At 12:50, the President was driven to 79 Rue des Moines, the residence of Léo Poldès, who accompanied him to 9 Impasse Compoint... then to the Cinema Printania, on Rue Brochant, where he attended the meetings of the Club du Faubourg hosted and run by Léo Poldès."[58] Poldès then took Ho to his country house for the weekend, and on 25 July, Ho "visited his friend, the Antillean lawyer Jean-Baptiste Paul." He was trying to find his old friends and colleagues from the 1920s, former members of the Intercolonial Union, militants of *L'Humanité*, *La Vie Ouvrière*, the CGT (the major French association of trade unions), and even those who had left the Communist Party.

He also met some new arrivals, like Jacques and Raymond Rabemananjara (the former representative from Madagascar at the National Assembly), who had come to see Ho and express their sympathy for the Indochinese people. The meeting of the three men is interesting because it shows that Ho Chi Minh was not a warmonger. They said to him:

> Mister President, it has escaped no one's attention that the nature of the problem in Madagascar is identical to the one in Indochina. We asked to see you because we want your insight. We have faith but we lack experience; you have both.

Ho responded that "suffering teaches maturity" (a phrase he certainly applied to himself and his politics), then continued:

> There is salvation for all of us in the French Union, and you are lucky because it is an organization based upon the voluntary participation of its members, so you will be spared a war. However, we must clearly define what the term French Union means. We will reach an agreement at the Fontainebleau Conference, of this I am certain. We have a stake in it, France has a stake in it. *The key is to rid the French Union of all imperialist ideas, and above all to bestow upon it this character of free consent, which makes it both new and original.* ... Your task, our task, is the following: to win over the sympathy of the French people. Express your legitimate aspirations simply, without second thoughts. No one is better qualified than the French to hear cries for Liberty. Here, especially in Paris, there are plenty of impartial souls willing to listen to you, and to enlighten you.[59]

Ho was also busy in his new role as head of state, a guest of France, and so had to participate in his share of public ceremonies and social gatherings. On 14 July 1946, Bastille Day, he sat at the official podium next to Prime Minister Bidault, whose behavior prompted a journal entry from Jacques Dumaine, Director of Protocol at the Ministry of Foreign Affairs. Apparently Bidault did not want Ho's chair to be placed in line with his, but set back a bit. This was "a real headache" for Dumaine, who had a high opinion of the Vietnamese president: "Ho is playing the role of Mahatma, and his simplicity is quite genuine." Dumaine later invited Ho for lunch, and wrote: "We had an intimate lunch with Ho Chi Minh. One has to admire the mastery of this self-taught man, his language skills, his ability to make his views accessible, to make his intentions seem moderate, and his politeness. His entourage is nervous, fanatical, and reckless, while he plays the wise and insightful one."[60]

President Ho appeared at dozens of public events: placing a wreath of flowers on the Tomb of the Unknown Soldier beneath the Arc de Triomphe, going to the wall of the Fédérés in Père-Lachèse Cemetery, and praising the ballet students at the Opéra. He attended press conferences, dinners, and the famous garden party at Bagatelle's at which he offered roses to the women – he was in a rose garden, after all. (It was during this last event that he invited himself to stay at the Aubracs'.) Ho's charm seduced everyone, his prestige grew, and he continued to display the pleasing face of the independent Vietnamese nation. What better ambassador could Vietnam have found?

Some people have claimed that Ho Chi Minh went to France to try and impress the French while his followers and compatriots secretly prepared the offensive against their troops and their colony in Indochina. Of course, Ho played a special role in the negotiations with the French, that of public relations, but he never "played to the gallery" while concealing his government's demands.

Ho's sincerity shines through in his account of this trip, which reveals his thoughts and feelings about France and the French people.[61] He wrote daily about where he went, what he did, and whom he met (without personal comments about the people, however). He also noted international events that were important to him, like the declaration of independence in the Philippines in July 1946 and the U.S. atomic tests on Bikini Atoll. But was it through ignorance or courtesy that he failed to mention the French evacuation of Lebanon and Syria in 1946, when France was forced to give up its colonialist claims in the Middle East?

Amidst these impersonal notations, however, Ho wrote on 30 June that he had wanted to take a walk in Monceau Park at six o'clock in the morning but found the gate locked. When the guardian, a war veteran, learned that Ho was a foreigner and had just arrived in France, he let him in without knowing that he was in the presence of a head of state. Ho remarked: "It is just a small anecdote but it is enough to show that the French, in France, are courteous and respectful of foreigners."[62]

The most interesting part of his travel journal is undoubtedly the last section, which he called "The Beautiful Qualities of the French." He found that the French have a passion for lofty values like liberty, equality, and fraternity, for which many sacrificed their lives over the previous 150 years. They argue and lose their tempers, and fight amongst themselves, but once the affair is settled they do not hold grudges; they are once again friendly and sociable. He wrote: "In sum, the French *in France* [Ho always stresses this difference] are kind and affable. During the few months I spent in France, these virtues were obvious to me." He then added that "it was not because I was the president of a nation that they behaved that way; they just naturally showed friendship towards us."[63]

1. Poster commemorating the fiftieth anniversary of Vietnam's independence, 1995. Lithograph, © Bridgeman-Giraudon.

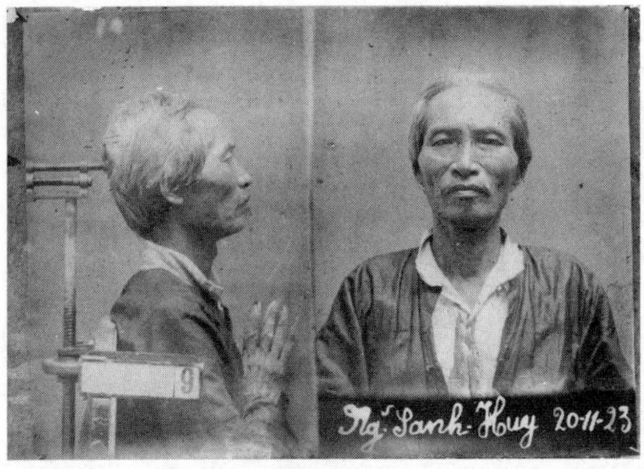

2. Nguyen Sinh Huy (Nguyen Sinh Sac), father of Nguyen Tat Thanh (photo taken by the Sûreté of Phan Thiet, 20 November 1923). © Centre des Archives d'outre-mer.

3. Nguyen Tat Thanh on the Alexandre III bridge in Paris. © Centre des Archives d'outre-mer.

4. Nguyen Ai Quoc at the Congress of the French Socialist Party in Tours, 25–30 December 1920. © Collection Viollet.

5. Ho Chi Minh, Zhu De, and Deng Xiaoping (?) in Yan'an, winter 1938–39. © Agence Vietnam Presse.

6. General Leclerc meeting with Ho Chi Minh, along with Jean Sainteny, Commissioner of the Republic, in Hanoi, 15 March 1946. © Collection Viollet.

7. Zhou Enlai and Ho Chi Minh on 10 May 1960. Archives of the magazine *Révolution*; © DR.

8. Ho Chi Minh and the Chinese General Chen Geng in Nanning, February 1950. Photo taken by Le Phat; © DR.

9. Deng Xiaoping, Ho Chi Minh, and Tong Ping Wu (in the background) in 1965. © Archives of the magazine *Révolution*; © DR.

10. Ho Chi Minh and Mao Zedong in June 1966. Archives of the magazine *Révolution*; © DR.

11. Ho Chi Minh and Kliment Voroshilov, President of the USSR, in the Presidential Palace gardens, Hanoi, 1957. © Agence Vietnam Presse.

12. Alexei Kosygin, Prime Minister of the USSR, on a visit to Vietnam in 1965, with Ho Chi Minh and Tran Duy Hung, Mayor of Hanoi. © Agence Vietnam Presse.

13. Trotsky and Nguyen Ai Quoc in Moscow in 1921 at the Third Congress of the Comintern. It is generally thought that Nguyen Ai Quoc did not visit Moscow before 1923 (according to his official biography). Private collection; © DR.

14. Ho Chi Minh surrounded by peasants from the village of Hung Son (Bac Thai province) in 1954. © Collection Viollet.

15. Ho Chi Minh, flanked by Le Duan and Truong Chinh (General Giap behind Le Duan), at the Third National Congress of the Vietnamese Workers' Party in 1960. © Collection Viollet.

16. The Ho Chi Minh Mausoleum in Hanoi, 1989. © F. De Mulder-Viollet.

17. Monument dedicated to Ho Chi Minh in Moscow, Akademicheskaya Square. © DR.

This travel journal was not meant for immediate publication and was not a tool for propaganda, and so the sentiments are probably genuine. Ho's profound sympathy toward France and the French people in general explains why, when the Fontainebleau Conference was not reconvened, he kept trying to reach a minimum accord with the French government before returning to his country. Not wanting to give up entirely and resign himself to leaving things as they were, he signed a modus vivendi with the Minister of Colonies, Marius Moutet, on the eve of his departure. Ho Chi Minh accepted the Indochinese Federation, and the French agreed to hold a referendum on Cochinchina to determine whether it would be brought under the jurisdiction of the DRV or set up as an autonomous state within the federation. The two parties decided to meet for a second conference in January 1947. In the meantime, they agreed to have joint Franco-Vietnamese commissions hammer out the concrete – and sometimes delicate – details of "cohabitation" and cooperation.

On 14 September 1946, Ho Chi Minh took the train for Toulon and then boarded the sloop *Dumont d'Urville* (the same ship that had taken the young Emperor Bai Dai home in 1932), setting sail for a one-month crossing. He was visibly nervous; in France a number of Vietnamese nationals – from Trotskyites to nationalists to supporters of an "all or nothing" philosophy – were already criticizing him for his delaying tactics and for the accords of 6 March. Some expressed their grievances personally or by petition, while others held demonstrations and shouted out angrily as his train pulled into the stations of Montélimar and Marseilles on its way to Toulon.

From this relatively brief stay in France, Ho Chi Minh returned with the modus vivendi signed in the final hours. Given the unstable and unpredictable situation, one could imagine that applying the terms of this agreement would be incredibly difficult, but Ho returned to his country as President of the Democratic Republic of Vietnam, invested with a legitimate power that extended to his government as well. Pham Duy Khiem, a moderate intellectual, openly told a French officer about the period: "At one point, the harmony between France and the Viet Minh seemed so solid that I was about to offer them my services as an Annamite and as a friend of France."[64]

French reports on the "pacification of Cochinchina" note the definitive impact of the March accords on the people. Those who had joined or moved closer to the French side between November 1945 and March–April 1946 pulled back again, or withdrew into a careful watchfulness. The Viet Minh took advantage of this détente to become stronger and squelch French efforts to create an autonomous, hence separatist, Cochinchinese state.

During this period, and specifically because of the question of Cochinchina, forces normally opposed to the Viet Minh, like the political-religious movement Hoa Hao, gave it their approval. Their journal *Quan Chung* (The Masses) "supports the central government of Vietnam to strengthen independence and cooperation with France on the basis of liberty and peace. In order to establish a democratic regime, we must fight the imperialist invaders and the camouflaged colonialists. Fight the regime of the Republic of Cochinchina."[65]

The Catholic priest Cao Van Luan had served as chaplain for the Vietnamese Catholics in Paris and knew Ho Chi Minh's position on religion. He was also aware that the government of his country was in Communist hands, but he wrote nonetheless, "I never agreed that Vietnam should become a Communist state, but I am Vietnamese and the priority at that time was to regain our independence."[66]

The monarchist Tran Trong Kim, who presided over the government after 9 March 1945 and then fled the Hanoi regime in the summer of 1946, reported on the behavior of his compatriots: "I heard many people say clearly that they did not like the Communists at all, but that they were the only ones who could resist the French. Ah well, first we will resist; then, if we win, we can do something about the Communists. But to bow our heads and become slaves again to the French as before, I would rather die!"[67]

Then, on 10 November 1946, Doctor Nguyen Van Thinh, President of the "Autonomous Republic of Cochinchina," called together his ministers. And, as if wanting to underline the nearly general consensus in favor of Ho Chi Minh, he apologized for having led them into misfortune. Later that evening he killed himself.

The Limits of Delaying Tactics

Admiral Thierry d'Argenlieu insisted that President Ho stop in Cam Ranh Bay to meet with him aboard the cruiser *Suffren*. They had first met in Halong Bay on 24 March 1946 aboard the *Émile Bertin*. The meeting was held on 18 October, and Ho wanted to bring one other person, Dr. Tran Huu Tuoc, who had decided to leave his medical practice in Paris (and a promising career) to return to Vietnam and serve his country. Tran later related an anecdote that shows yet again Ho's sense of humor and repartee. When Ho was seated between the admiral and General Louis

Morlière, the former said to him, "Mister President, look how you are flanked by the Army and the Navy." Ho replied, "But you know, Admiral, it is the painting which makes the frame valuable."[68]

Thierry d'Argenlieu wrote in his journal:

> Meeting with Ho. He is fairly calm and inclined towards the verbal accords.... This extremely disagreeable fixation of abruptly and quickly kissing both cheeks....

And he wrote to Moutet:

> I think our meeting was quite productive; the president seemed rather anxious about the situation that he will find upon his return.... I have the impression, however, that he sincerely wants, at least for a time, to seek an agreement with France to consolidate the results already acquired and continue to make new progress.[69]

Three months passed between the date of Ho's return and the start of hostilities north of the sixteenth parallel, a period rife with dramatic events that eventually led to the inevitable conclusion of 19 December 1946.

The French and Vietnamese governments had begun their dispute at Fontainebleau using only words as weapons, and despite the violence of Pham Van Dong's discourse, no one was injured. Things were different in the field. First of all, military hostilities had never totally ceased south of the sixteenth parallel, and the implementation of the 6 March accords did not go well in the North either; but it could not have been otherwise, given the state of mind of those involved and their respective interpretation (or violation) of the accords.

When the French reoccupied the palace of the Governor-General of Indochina and the head office of the Bank of Indochina, the aftershocks were quelled by the intervention of the joint Franco-Vietnamese commissions. But when French troops wanted to establish garrisons in Bac Ninh and Lang Son or reoccupy the mining area of Hong Gay, the confrontations were deadly. A report from a Captain Le Flahec in April 1946 was a sign of things to come. Le Flahec was part of a joint Franco-Sino-Vietnamese commission in charge of preparing for the withdrawal of Chinese troops, and he had to travel from Nam Dinh to Tourane (now Da Nang) via Hué. His account, though a bit impressionistic, provides an important glimpse of the situation by describing the obstacles raised by the local Vietnamese authorities, "because Viet Minh leaders did not accept without deep bitterness the need for the French to come in and move throughout the country." As a result, the authorities did everything they could to "show that the Vietnamese are the masters in their own country."[70] According to Le Flahec, the situation was extremely complex and diverse, and the government did not have authority everywhere; the accords had been signed, but either they were not communicated or they were not accepted by "the base," and so were not applied. These observations were confirmed in the course of 1946 as the continuing war south of the sixteenth parallel and the drama of Haiphong drove the conflict to a crisis point.

The High Commissioner and the French command saw – or perhaps chose to see – only proof of bad faith and betrayal on the part of the Vietnamese, while the government of the DRV and most Vietnamese denounced France's attempt to retake its colonial possessions by gradually whittling away their national sovereignty. From the Vietnamese perspective, the French were trying to catch them in a trap: They had established garrisons in key positions along the Chinese border and in the Thai area in the Northwest, and now there was pressure from their offensives in the Center, notably the reoccupation of the ancient imperial capital of Hué. After Ho's triumphant return from France, Ngo Van Chieu, a Vietnamese military officer, noted that "our politicians seem very eager to live on good terms with the French. Honestly, I have to say that this is not the case with the army and the *tu ve* groups [self-defense militia]."[71]

The grievances from both sides crystallized on 20 November 1946 around the battle of Haiphong. Indeed, the French had wanted to put an end to the rampant smuggling going on at the port, citing arms trafficking as just one pretext for taking action. (Another reason never mentioned is the depreciation of the Indochinese piastre, issued by the Bank of Indochina, due to foreign purchases.) In principle, the problem stemmed from the Vietnamese Customs Service, for by signing the modus vivendi of September, Ho Chi Minh had made a concession allowing some federal involvement in DRV affairs. In so doing, he provided the French with a certain justification, because both the customs and the printing of currency were a federal (i.e., French) responsibility. When a French ship stopped to inspect a Chinese junk laden with gasoline, the Vietnamese attacked. The battle spread to the market and then to the rest of the city, which had been completely occupied by the French army following the failure of the joint commissions to broker a peace and impose a cease-fire.

The battle of Haiphong was immediately seen as the prelude to the French army's general offensive to topple the government of Ho Chi Minh.

But the Vietnamese had captured French plans detailing possible scenarios in the event of an escalation of the conflict, in particular General Valluy's directive Number 2 to "transform a possible counterattack into a coup d'état."[72] As a result, in early December, Ho sent Nguyen Luong Bang to the stronghold in the Viet Bac to prepare for the transfer of the party and of government services.

The French command was sure that the Vietnamese were preparing a general uprising. Yet while some saw Ho Chi Minh as a friendly façade behind which he was hiding plans for aggression, others thought that he was no longer in control of the situation inasmuch as his policies were being repudiated and his opinions and directives not respected. Consequently, Ho had to distance himself from his anti-French colleagues by reshuffling his government (which he had already done upon his return from France, making it more homogeneous by keeping only the Communists and their allies). This project alarmed General Leclerc, who wrote on 7 December:

> Unfortunately it seems that an essentially different method [than the negotiations] has been employed in the last few months. We want to break the Vietnamese resistance through force, using the methods we used during the Conquest; moreover, I do not believe in the effectiveness of Ho Chi Minh and his team.[73]

On 2 December, Ho, ill and confined to bed, had a last meeting with Sainteny, who had just returned from the chaos of Hanoi. Both the Vietnamese and the French were waiting for a battle that seemed both inevitable and imminent. Truong Chinh, Secretary General of the ICP, declared to General Vuong Thua Vu, who had just been named head of the military command of the capital by the Politburo, "French aggressors are preparing feverishly and, sooner or later, they will attack us."[74]

After flying over the Red River delta between Haiphong and Hanoi, Sainteny sent a cable to Pignon: "Situation still tense. Continuation defense preparations. Very sensitive evacuation visible of local businesses, by Party decree. . . . Seems that Ho Chi Minh has been passed over by Tong Bo [directorate of the ICP] and majority of government that refuses all conciliation without return to *status quo ante*"[75] – that is, to the situation before Haiphong. But Sainteny was wrong. Ho himself continued to present this demand to Vincent Auriol, newly elected President of the French Republic, as well as to Marius Moutet, and then to the new Prime Minister Paul Ramadier, in early 1947.

The Hour of Truth

The French, starting with Jean Sainteny, refused to believe that Ho Chi Minh's position was as rigid as that of his collaborators and supporters, and it seems that they did not ask themselves just how far the President would push the concessions. However, in his negotiations with the French, Ho had never hidden the fact that he was intransigent on two issues: internal sovereignty and the unity of the three Vietnamese regions, Bac Bo, Trung Bo, and Nam Bo. At the same time, the French were trying to get the Autonomous Republic of Cochinchina on its feet by demanding the withdrawal of Vietnamese forces from the southern part of the country.

Vu Ky, Ho's personal secretary, passed through Hanoi on 18 December and witnessed the growing exodus of the civilian population as the French army was attempting to destroy the barricades set up by the *tu ve*. The French army had already occupied the seat of the Sûreté, the police stations, and then the government ministries. For two days, sporadic and localized fighting left victims on both sides, while French soldiers built barricades and fortifications in the European neighborhoods whose shutters were all closed.[76]

At dawn on 18 December, in the neighborhood of the "thirty-six streets," a clash between French parachutists and the *tu ve* led to more than twenty deaths. At eleven o'clock, Commander Jean-Julien Fonde met with Vo Nguyen Giap and asked him to raise the barricades to allow the French to pass through. Giap answered, "That depends on you. We have made our decision. We will not give in anymore."

Fonde responded, "Prevent the irreparable, Mister President."

Giap: "It is your move. After Nam Bo, the Highlands, the Thai countries [between the Red River and the Da River], Hong Gay, Tien Yen, Haiphong, Lang Son . . . this is the end. We will not give in anymore."

Vo Nguyen Giap got up, shook his hand, and it was all over.[77]

Pham Duy, a young musician and composer from the resistance in Cochinchina, wrote that he "found all of Hanoi preparing for a war that everyone saw as inevitable." He was spending the evening of 19 December at a friend's house when the Vietnamese offensive began, and later wrote: "We were not surprised at all, and neither was anyone in Hanoi for that matter, when we saw that what had to happen was happening."[78]

One could say that the irreparable had begun in Haiphong in November, and then the course of events led ineluctably to the battle of Hanoi on 19 December 1946. The Vietnamese had been preparing themselves for war ever since the events of Haiphong, and were afraid that the French would remove the "good" Ho Chi Minh to separate him from the "bad" Viet Minh. As a result, starting on 26 November, the President had left Bac Phu every night, wearing a tunic and the black turban of a village notable, and went to a refuge that had been set up in a village near the capital. On the evening of 3 December, he changed his destination, and from then on spent his nights a dozen or so kilometers from Hanoi in Van Phuc, a village famous for its silk, where the Communists had already established a "hideout" before the revolution.[79]

From there, Ho tried one last approach. On 18 December he asked Hoang Minh Giam, whom he had called back from Paris, to make contact with Sainteny. Obviously, however, he had little hope left because he had already anticipated what was about to happen. Later that evening (perhaps during the night), he wrote "in one sitting" his *Call for National Resistance* (officially dated 19 December). Vu Ky described the scene:

> The small oil lamp gave off a halo of light. Uncle Ho, sitting on his bed, meditated while staring at the piece of paper before his eyes. Near Hanoi, the gunfire was heavier than on preceding nights. With his schoolboy's penholder, Uncle Ho began to write his Call.[80]

Then he dictated a telegram to Léon Blum, who had just formed a government to succeed that of Georges Bidault, and who had never received Ho's previous letter sent on the 15th via the French authorities in Saigon. In the telegram, Ho expressed his hope that Blum's "socialist" government would look into the Indochinese problem with understanding. The cable did not reach Léon Blum until the night of the 22nd.

At the same time, Ho was awaiting the return of Hoang Minh Giam, but Sainteny had inexplicably put off the meeting asked for by Giam. After learning of General Morlière's ultimatum demanding the complete disarmament of all Vietnamese armed forces – the equivalent of a surrender – Ho was informed that the meeting with Sainteny had not taken place. He then saw clearly that a reprieve from armed confrontation was no longer possible. This is the impression that emerges from the account written by Vu Ky when, on the 19th at 12:30, he went to the room where Ho was pacing back and forth, waiting for him:

> When Uncle Ho learned that Sainteny had broken off contact with Hoang Minh Giam, he frowned, remained pensive, and took a few steps toward the table where the *Call to National Resistance* was lying, which he had to deliver to the Party's Executive Committee that afternoon; he blurted out quietly but distinctly and categorically: "All right, we will fight."

Around 2:30 that afternoon, Truong Chinh, Secretary General of the party, Le Duc Tho, and Vo Nguyen Giap – all members of the Executive Committee – met with Ho Chi Minh to discuss the *Call*. According to Ho, "the situation did not allow us to make concessions anymore." He then said to Giap, "We will solemnly read the *Call* after the battle of Hanoi begins. We will launch the battle around seven or eight o'clock tonight, by sabotaging the generators of the electric power stations of Yen Phu with the help of workers." Ky continued:

> At 3:15 the meeting ended, my comrades left, the image of this instant remains clearly etched in my mind. Truong Chinh was lost in thought. He jumped when we greeted each other and said, "Oh! Hello comrade!" – not like all the other times when he was always the first one to greet me with a calm and fresh smile. As for Le Duc Tho, always expansive, he tapped me on the shoulder and said, laughing, "In any case, we are already prepared." Van [Vo Nguyen Giap], looking secretive as usual with his felt hat stuffed onto his head, his dark glasses, and his long overcoat, followed without saying a word.... Ho Chi Minh continued to write for a moment, then finished, put his papers back into his satchel, and warned me: "Prepare to leave, we will take to the road tonight."... It was 6:45 P.M., 19 December 1946.[81]

Until 1988, Vietnamese leaders claimed that the French had unleashed the hostilities on the night of 19 December 1946, while the French have always avowed the contrary. In 1988, Vietnam officially admitted that they had launched the offensive to avert the French attack, which they were certain was imminent.[82] General Vuong Thua Vu explained:

> On 19 December at 2 P.M., I went to the Ministry of War to receive my orders. After comrade Vo Nguyen Giap had explained the unfolding of events in Haiphong and Lang Son, he said, "The enemy has sent us an insolent ultimatum demanding that we surrender our arms and that they themselves restore order in the capital. We want to take advantage of the peace to build up our nation, but if we continue to make concessions the enemy will continue their advance. We cannot stop here. The hour for battle has arrived. The Executive Committee of the Party's Central Committee just sent a telegram to all fronts and all military zones stating clearly that our government has rejected the enemy's ultimatum. Also, within the next twenty-four hours the French will attack us... make sure everything is ready!"... At 4 P.M., I returned to the HQ at the front, near the airfield of Bach Mai. All of the section leaders and cadres from the military sectors were already assembled. I verified all the preparations for action one more time. When, in the name of the ministry, I gave the order to the front to raise the signal to open fire, everyone in the office suddenly stood up. Gone in an instant were the pensive

faces, tense from so many difficult days and nights spent dealing with the provocative and contradictory moves of the enemy. Everyone was happy because we were going to fight and burn off the surplus of hate that we had repressed for so long.[83]

THE LEADER OF NATIONAL RESISTANCE: 1946–1954

The war spread rapidly throughout the entire Indochinese peninsula, spilling over into Cambodia and Laos and bringing into play the logistical networks in Thailand and then in southern China. The Vietnamese used the resources available to them through a theater of operations with numerous regional offshoots, and also benefited from the presence of the Vietnamese diaspora spread throughout Cambodia, Laos, Thailand, and southern China, a majority of whom gave their active support. The mountainous landscape, large forests, and dense network of waterways provided them with both refuges and bastions, as well as a means of travel and communication. These conditions and their lack of sophisticated weaponry favored – or even necessitated – the use of guerrilla tactics.[84]

The resistance fighters in the second half of the twentieth century benefited from what was sorely lacking in the era of their fathers and grandfathers: organization. The Communist Party was their link to an international circle of influence, and the Indochinese front was a very real part of a virtually global front against imperialism. From 1945 to 1950, the dynamism of Asian communism ensured the victory of the Chinese Communist Party and provided the Vietnamese resistance with a neighbor already won over to their cause. Their Chinese ally provided sustained military and economic aid and offered an invaluable "sanctuary." The metaphor used ironically in the 1970s, that Vietnam and China are "like teeth and lips," rang true during these crucial years.[85]

THE WAR REACHED A TURNING POINT IN 1950, AS THE VIETNAMESE Liberation Army won its first important victory over the French Expeditionary Corps of the Far East (CEFEO). After this battle, known as the RC4 (Colonial Road 4), the Cao Bang–Lang Son, or the "Battle of the Borders," the Vietnamese army underwent a complete transformation that allowed it to engage in mobile warfare and to confront the CEFEO in conventional battles (while still using guerrilla tactics). The disaster of Cao Bang–Lao Son took 4,800 French lives, and 10,000 weapons fell into the hands of the Vietnamese army, but the material situation of the French military was not seriously compromised. However, as General Yves Gras wrote:

> The disaster was mostly of a moral nature. The basic fact is that the French troops – considered to be the best – were crushed in the open countryside by an army of Vietnamese peasants whom we used to scorn. The shock waves of such an event go far beyond the physical outcome. Cao Bang was to the Franco–Viet Minh War [First Indochina War] what Bailén was for the war in Spain or Valmy for the French Revolution.[86]

Four years later, Phung The Tai wrote a report that paints a bleak portrait of the unit under his command, near Sonla, in September 1946: "We didn't have enough food, clothes, or medicine. The rate of sickness was high, mostly due to malaria."[87] Ngo Van Chieu, who participated in one of the first attacks against a French post in Laos in early 1946, described his unit: "We look more like a gang than an organized army. We have ill-assorted weapons and very little ammunition. The Japanese [a section of Japanese soldiers led by a Japanese officer who had gone over to the side of the Vietnamese revolution] seem disciplined."[88] When Chieu returned to the front in 1951, after having been seriously wounded, he noticed the contrast:

> We continue to march through the mountains and the jungle. Thousands of coolies accompany us. An amazing change has taken place within this army that I have known since its very beginning.... The roads leading in from China echo in the night with the noise of trucks bringing us weapons and ammunition. Trucks designed especially for our roads, similar to the American GMCs [Molotovas].[89]

In 1950, Ho Chi Minh went to China and then joined Mao Zedong in Moscow, shortly before the DRV received international recognition by the People's Republic of China (PRC) and then by the USSR. This trip had great political importance, since the DRV had been isolated until that point but now had the support of the PRC. The two countries were connected by a number of links, and the PRC had become the eastern buffer zone of the USSR. The alliance of all socialist countries was the order of the day, and no one would have guessed that the seeds of the Sino-Soviet schism were planted that very year.

In opposition to "U.S.-led imperialism," the DRV was now part of the "socialist camp" – the "Soviet bloc" to its adversaries – which was spreading across the globe with apparent ideological and political unity.

This raises a number of questions: Did this situation have an effect on Vietnam's internal development? Did the struggle for national independence remain the sole objective of Ho Chi Minh and his party, while local and regional conditions were in flux? Did the Resistance now enter its "socialist" phase? What was the role and the behavior of Ho Chi Minh amidst this instability? Did the old contradictions between Ho and the Communist Party resurface?

AT THE VERY BEGINNING OF THE 1950S, THE FRENCH STOKED THE "nationalist fire" by calling upon former Emperor Bao Dai to head up a new Vietnamese state. Then the North Korean government declared war, providing justification for a war against international communism. On 4 February 1950, the U.S. government officially recognized the Associated States of Indochina, Vietnam, Laos, and Cambodia. "Western" strategists constructed their "domino theory," whereby the Communists had to be stopped or else all of Asia would "go red." In the eyes of the French and their American allies, the new crusade wiped out the stigma of colonialism that had clung to earlier interventions. On 30 June 1950, the United States made its first delivery of military equipment to the French for their Indochinese theater of operations.

For their part, the Vietnamese Communists felt freer to reveal their convictions and their program. They pulled out their flags again, and during the Second Congress of the ICP (11–19 February 1951) they created the Vietnamese Workers' Party (VWP), with a membership of 776,349 (compared to 5,000 in the ICP in 1945). The new name was less restrictive than that of the Communist Party, and was designed to attract a greater number of people. At the same time, it was more in keeping with the social reality of a working class that was actually a small minority. Furthermore, the new name specified that the party was Vietnamese, showing that it did not claim to speak for all of the peoples on the peninsula, and opening the way for the foundation of communist revolutionary parties in Laos and Cambodia.

The Beginnings of War

Ho Chi Minh had left Hanoi on the afternoon of 19 December 1946 and withdrawn some twenty kilometers away; the battle would continue in the city until March 1947.[90] Ho gave his New Year's radio address from a pagoda, where the Vietnamese had installed the radio station "The Voice of Vietnam." As Hanoi burned, some people fleeing the capital on the road to Sontay may have seen their President by the side of the road, where his Ford had blown a tire.

The *tu ve* progressively evacuated the neighborhood of the "thirty-six streets," which had become a fortress, and the city's regiment withdrew to the outskirts. Meanwhile, French troops expanded their siege and progressed with the help of air support. Only then did Ho go from Hadong to Sontay, accompanied by his staff and his police escort, to the long-standing stronghold in the region of Thai Nguyen–Bac Can–Tuyen Quang.

In May 1947, the resistance government set up its capital in the Dinh Hoa district (Cho Chu, in colonial times), dividing the services and personnel among villages and caves in what is known in the nation's memory as "the zone of total security," *An Toan Khu* (ATK). In reality, the security was relative, for on 7 October, General Valluy launched Operation Léa with several thousand men, including nine hundred parachutists, attacking the hideout and nearly capturing Ho Chi Minh and his government (news of Ho's capture was sent to General Salan, but it turned out to be false). Operation Léa was followed by Operation Ceinture (Belt), neither of which led to conclusive results. Ho continued to live, work, and move about the stronghold until his return to Hanoi in 1954, though he left a few times to go to Thanh Hoa, in the border zone of Cao Bang, and to Moscow via Beijing. All meetings of the main organizations were held in the ATK: the Central Committee of the party and of the government, the Viet Minh Congress (which became a larger front, *Lien Viet* – the Vietnamese Alliance – in 1951), and so forth. The ATK was also the jumping-off point for the regular troops (which took the name People's Army of Vietnam in 1950) during the major offensives of 1951–54 into the panhandle, the Red River delta, the Da River, and lower Laos.[91]

The French Communist Léo Figuères met with Ho in 1950 in the ATK and found him to be

> smiling, offering his hand and seeming, I'll say, in quite good health.... At sixty years old, he had achieved such results by adhering to a strict personal discipline. He got up early and went to bed early, never forgetting his personal calisthenics. His daily schedule was meticulously organized and divided between conducting affairs and physical exercises. He jumped, ran, walked, swam. Near his offices there was a volleyball court where he played competitive games with the young secretaries and bodyguards. He told me about his success at catching fish, and showed me vast vegetable gardens where he worked at least one hour a day.[92]

The image provided by Figuères is inseparable from others that fill a memory album: Ho writing articles, directives, and letters; Ho walking or riding a small horse to go to a congress, a meeting, or the front when Vo Nguyen Giap's army was engaged in mobile warfare in the free zone of Thanh Hoa; Ho talking with the local people and soldiers. This album of photos-souvenirs-propaganda is extensive, but it gives us an idea of the leader of the national resistance in action, of his method and spirit.

Ho Chi Minh was playing the double role of head of state and military leader, but not like the Emperors Le Loi and Quang Trung had done, nor like Trotsky or Tito.[93] In May 1947, Paul Mus had been sent by Marius Moutet to try one last time to put an end to the fighting. His mission failed because the French government demanded the unconditional surrender of the Vietnamese. Ho's response to Mus has gone down in the annals of history: "In the French Union there is no place for cowards. If I accepted these terms, I would be one." Another of Mus's observations says even more about the role Ho played in the eyes of his people:

> Whoever found himself near the Vietnamese people in these difficult hours.... did not fail to notice, under the complexity of their reactions, an intimate note of sentimentality.... What especially struck me during those trying times was that, for the youth, the ultimate reference was not in the warrior heroes and heroines of Vietnamese history but in the benediction that Ho, the guide and doyen of the nation, bestowed upon all of them.[94]

Ho Chi Minh was not the strategist bent over geological survey maps, nor the general watching the battle from high on a hillside (even though the album of memories contains photos of this type), nor the man riding at the head of the assault (there are no photos at all of this kind). He led the war of resistance by drawing upon his philosophy of human relations, by preferring face-to-face encounters, direct dialogue, and correspondence in verse, and by reciting proverbs rather than presenting arguments based on the rules of Marxist dialectic.

Ho strove to forge links with the people and with soldiers, and asked his cadres to do the same. He took his cue from a familial framework and struck an emotional and sentimental chord: One must be with others, put oneself in the midst of others, and talk to them, show them that they are respected and taken into consideration. Whenever possible, one must set an example and put oneself on the line. Numerous anecdotes from those close to him – not necessarily sycophants or staunch believers – illustrate this behavior, whereby his actions accompany or immediately follow his words and sometimes even replace them. Ho Chi Minh was always trying to set an example. To illustrate, one day, he and his bodyguards were on the banks of a flooded river while a group of men and women remained on the other side, too scared to cross. Ho said to his companions: "Let us remove our clothes and cross; that will encourage our compatriots to do the same."[95]

One night in the ATK, Vu Dinh Huynh, who had been Ho's secretary in France, was awakened by a noise near the next hut. Alarmed, he took out his gun and shot into the darkness. At daybreak he saw that he had shot the water buffalo of one of the villagers. Ho sent Huynh to apologize immediately and pay for the damages, telling him that one must never lose an occasion to show the people that the leaders are at their service.[96] As an illustration, he borrowed an image from the Chinese writer Lu Xun whereby the party (of workers) was in charge of the country, but "the water buffalo and the horse [were] the faithful servant[s] of the people."[97] On many occasions, Ho denounced the "mandarins of the revolution," and when villagers offered him a quilted blanket – quite a luxury at the time – he refused, making do (for the time being) as they did by covering himself with tree bark for the night.

Ho behaved in the same way with soldiers (*bo doi*) and porters (*dan cong*), as well as with civilians who supplied the troops and who were indispensable once Vo Nguyen Giap's troops engaged in mobile warfare, sometimes far from their bases. (In 1951, Giap mobilized 25,719 soldiers and 30,000 porters.) Ho sometimes went unannounced to the theaters of operation. On the eve of the battle of Dong Khe, on the RC4, he dressed as a Nung peasant and walked among the columns of porters. One day, he inquired about the health and morale of the female porters, whom he had seen sleeping back-to-back in the rice fields on the dried-out terraces because there was not enough room with local families. Another time, he was concerned that everyone had a sufficient supply of food, water, and tobacco. At Tuyen Quang, he asked a soldier, "How much is your daily ration of rice?" The man replied, "Eight hundred grams, Uncle." Ho then turned to the man in charge of supplies and said, "The ration must be increased to nine hundred grams."[98]

Still other accounts relate a crucial moment in the Battle of the RC4, revealing facets of Ho Chi Minh's personality. Colonels Pierre Charton and Marcel Lepage, at the head of two columns that were to join together, were captured and kept in separate caves, along with the commander of a medical unit. Ho visited them, accompanied by Phan Phac, the Chief of Staff, and by Tran Minh Tuoc, president of the Resistance Committee of Lang Son province. We have four accounts of this episode, which are as fascinating for what they share as for what they do not. All of them, however, reveal Ho Chi Minh's sense of humor, his skill, and his penchant for role playing (hence, his talent for wearing disguises and lying), as well as his desire to convince his adversaries of the just cause of the Vietnamese resistance.

Ho asked Phan Phac to introduce him to the French officers as the "political advisor at the front." "High advisor," said Phac. "Drop the 'high,'" retorted Ho. "The ceiling of the cave is low, and if I am the high advisor I will bump my head."

After speaking with Lepage and the medic about the validity of the war, Ho went into Charton's cave. Phan Phac related their meeting as follows:

> Lieutenant-Colonel Charton, military leader of Cao Bang, was leading the retreat from the city with his battalion but they were wiped out halfway through their retreat; he and his men were captured. Charton was a real fascist. He had only just met Uncle Ho when he began complaining: "Just think, sir, for days I have not been able to shave or shine my shoes." He continued: "If Maréchal Pétain were still running France, this war would certainly not have happened, and the French army would not have been defeated." Uncle Ho did not interrupt him, and invited him to smoke a cigarette; then he gradually got him to speak more. In the end, Charton had to admit that the war of conquest was immoral, that the colonialists had lost, and that our army was victorious. Then he added: "Because of your attitude, I can talk to you, but how could your young cadres have convinced me?"[99]

In his book, Colonel Lepage said nothing about his face-to-face meeting with Ho,[100] but Colonel Charton did, providing us with this surprising version:

> The following afternoon, still within my prison of stone, I had a visitor. The sentinels brought in a small old man dressed as an Annamite, with the ever-present goatee.
>
> "You are indeed Colonel Charton?" he asked. "I am Little Louis. Do you know who I am?"
>
> I told him that I had never heard of Little Louis.
>
> "That was my name in the Resistance. I worked on the railroads in France during the Occupation and my friends called me that."
>
> "Were you with the Resistance?"
>
> "If you mean someone who fought to drive the invader from France, then yes I was indeed, because I fought in France with the 1st Army. I was with the 5th Armored Division. I was even seriously wounded at Orbey in the

Vosges mountains, in late 1944. But if you believe that a Resistant is first and foremost a combatant who seeks to impose a certain way of thinking on his countrymen, I regret to inform you that that was not my case. I have always kept my esteem for Maréchal Pétain."

"I am not a Communist," I said.

"That is too bad," he answered, quite disappointed.

He gave me some English cigarettes – the only ones the Vietnamese liked – and a packet of *Olibet* cookies. Then he left me. I never knew who he really was. This "Little Louis" must have been an important person because otherwise he would not have been able to get through the roadblock and find me in my secret prison.[101]

Tran Minh Tuoc, the third witness, makes no mention of Charton's Pétainism, but wrote:

Charton's attitude was brittle and rude, revealing a hardened legionnaire who had lived a long time in the colonies. Before leaving, the president offered Charton some cigarettes and he even gave him a pack of Philip Morris. When Ho came out of the cave he asked Phan Phac and me, "Which of these two colonels, in your opinion, is the most despicable?" Phan Phac quickly said, "Charton farts in our faces all the time and says nasty things about us. He is the most detestable." The president replied, "But Lepage is the more formidable of the two. Charton is boorish and talks without beating around the bush. He is easier to handle and convince."[102]

Similar accounts illustrate Ho Chi Minh's concern for others, as well as his nonconformist behavior. After 1951, as the Chinese Communist influence spread to every activity in the resistance zone, Ho's singularity stood in distinct contrast to the weighty backdrop of political reeducation or "brainwashing." Xuan Phuong, a former doctor and journalist, wrote of her experience:

What has especially changed now is that every month we have meetings to help us understand the meaning of our struggle. They show us that capitalism is cruel, that it exploits the proletarian class and that we have to fight it. The only thing that matters from now on is the working class. Every month new political commissioners arrive from who-knows-where. Obviously people with peasant origins, severe, coarse. The meetings last several hours. After listening to their talks, we have to take a piece of paper and write about our lives, making personal commentary. What do we think of our past? All we have to do is write a self-criticism and a criticism of our class: we are finally aware of our wrongs, while before we didn't understand a thing. They insist: "Are you sure you completely understand?" "Yes, I am sure I completely understand." This could last hours, repeating the same thing. It was during this time that we saw Ho Chi Minh for the first time. . . . Ho Chi Minh was full of concern for us, more worried about giving us practical advice than delivering a message. . . . Everyone met up again later in the kitchen. . . . Ho Chi Minh saw that we only had rice with a few extremely bitter papaya leaves for vegetables. I heard him asking my seatmate, "Is it good?" My friend was terrified. "Oh, it's extremely good. Extremely good," he repeated. "No, my son, it is not good. When I see you eating that," Ho Chi Minh said to us, "it gives me great pain. . . . We absolutely have to begin there. We have taken back our country with empty hands. . . . You do not have the right to think that all of this is good, even less to say it."[103]

Ho's concern for those who fought and died also extended to those who were trying to survive – his compatriots, both friends and enemies. His government left Hanoi in December 1946, accompanied by the ongoing exodus of the civilian population, and so Ho invoked national solidarity to make sure that the refugees had enough food and shelter. In February 1947, he asked Vu Dinh Huynh to restore the real estate holdings of Pham Le Bong, who expressed a desire to take in and house five hundred refugees on his property. It should be noted that Pham Le Bong had been a landlord, industrial entrepreneur, and owner of a newspaper, and had served in the House of Representatives of the People of Tonkin as a monarchist.[104] In March 1947, Ho criticized the Ministry of the Interior for not staying on top of the situation, for not organizing aid relief, and for not providing for the needs of the refugees. He wrote, "We must do something to show the people that the government will not let them down."[105]

In January 1947, he extended his condolences to the father of a young soldier who had fallen in one of the first battles. The father, Dr. Vu Dinh Tung, was Director of the Heath Services of Bac Bo, but he was also a Catholic. Ho wrote:

I have learned that your son gave his life for the nation. You know that I have no family and no children. Vietnam is my family. The youth of Vietnam are my children. Losing a young man is like someone ripping out my entrails. . . . Our children and our young brothers are dying so that our country may live. . . . They are the pious children of God, who have put into practice the words "God and Country." These young people make up a nation of heroes. You will undoubtedly continue to help our country by participating in the resistance and you will give happiness to the soul of your son who is in Heaven.[106]

When Minister Phan Anh announced the birth of his son, Ho sent him a poem:

You have one more child
Your other children have a younger brother
Uncle Ho has one more nephew
The State has one more citizen
Who is a future soldier.[107]

Ho monitored the conditions of the French civilian and military prisoners, assigning the responsibility to Vu Dinh Huynh in January 1947. Huynh had to make sure that the prisoners had enough to eat and drink and, if necessary, he had to raise their monthly allotment to two hundred dong.[108] Ho wanted to show the world that they could differentiate between the prisoners and the policies of their government and military leaders. In another case, in his desire to reassure Reverend Léopold Cadière, under house arrest in Vinh since 19 December 1946, Ho wrote to him: "Please feel that you are among friends, and we would be very happy to do whatever we can to help you. Please accept, Reverend Father, my apologies and my friendship, and give my best wishes to all French friends."[109]

Ho was obsessed with national unity because he knew it was fragile; he also knew that the government's directives were not always applied. Nearly every time that an incident led to clashes within the Vietnamese camp, he contacted those involved and sent representatives to the area where the union was at risk. This happened, for example, in those areas where Catholics were in the majority. He wrote a letter on 1 February 1947, responding to Monsignor Le Huu Tu:

> Religious freedom is clearly written into our constitution. Whoever violates the constitution and attacks Christianity will be punished.... It is unfortunate that minor disagreements arise between compatriots because moral education is not yet widespread, but they should not undermine our great union.[110]

One month later, Ho wrote to the bishop of Phat Diem that he had ordered the release of seven Catholics suspected of murder – as the bishop had requested – but Ho, in turn, requested that his parishioners blow up bridges to slow the progress of French troops.[111] It was probably during this period that Dong Sy Nguyen, a unit commander, was sanctioned for having attacked a Catholic village (which did not keep him from ending his career with the rank of lieutenant general).

After Operation Léa, Ho Chi Minh divided his ministers into five groups, one of which remained at the base while the others were designated "special units" to be sent out on missions. Vu Dinh Hoe, Minister of Justice, traveled three thousand kilometers in four months with his group, "observing, listening, questioning, and looking into many affairs." Two of these affairs tell us much about the situation in the free zone. The first concerns arbitrary arrests and the disappearance of prisoners, when some members and cadres of the Viet Minh (ethnic Nung and Tho) fell victim to the "excessive zeal" of Ly Ban, a high-ranking member of the Security Services, and of Chinese origin. Ly was "narrow-minded, not close to the people, and acted without proof." The Special Section investigated him, freed the prisoners, and presented the government's apologies to the people. The second affair concerned a local bandit who had joined the resistance but continued to attack and rob French convoys for personal profit along the Hanoi–Lang Son road. He organized a banquet for the delegates of the government and made them understand that those who "commanded the troops at the border did not have to obey the orders of the king." During the course of this mission, Vu Dinh Hoe paid a visit to French hostages, mostly civilians who had been brought in during the battle of Hanoi. He also went to see the magistrate, Henri Morché, former president of the Court of Appeals in Hanoi who was detained with his family, and he insisted that the camp leader treat the prisoners well.[112]

The Turning Point of the 1950s

In 1950, the Vietnamese resistance movement was no longer isolated by the French army; it had broken the siege. It now had the support of Communist China, while the French, with increased aid from the United States, tried to mobilize Vietnam's anti-communist nationalists. In 1951, General Jean-Marie de Lattre de Tassigny established the Vietnamese National Army. Most of the world was now clearly split into two antagonistic camps, though a number of nations, like Nehru's India, Tito's Yugoslavia, and Nasser's Egypt, proposed a third path of nonalignment. Although it showed much promise at the conference in Bandung (Indonesia) in 1955, it had no lasting future. In the midst of the Cold War, things were heating up on the Indochinese front, as well as in Korea, which had become a hot zone in June 1950 with the North Korean aggression against the South. In March 1953, French Prime Minister René Mayer went to Washington, accompanied by Georges Bidault and Christian Pineau, to discuss the situation in Indochina. The final outcome of the meeting affirmed the interdependence of Indochina and Korea in the defense of the free world.

Chinese Communist aid to the Viet Minh was primarily military in nature in 1950, but Beijing soon expanded its support into other areas. The leaders of both sides decided that Chinese troops would not intervene. Troops of the People's Army of Vietnam (PAVN) were equipped and trained in Yunnan and Guangxi, and a permanent mission consisting of seventy-nine Chinese advisors established its headquarters in Nanning, in southern China (Vietnamese schools and the university were also moved there). Additional advisors were divided among the units of the PAVN, their total number now increased to eight thousand from four thousand, with one thousand additional members of the medical staff.

Most important were the military advisors. Ho Chi Minh arranged to have Chen Geng, whom he had met at the Whampoa Academy, sent to Vietnam as his chief advisor. This brilliant Chinese general apparently played a key role in the 1950 "Battle of the Borders" (also called Cao Bang–Lang Son), although Vo Nguyen Giap's version of the story minimizes Chen's importance.[113] In November 1950, Chen left North Vietnam to lead the "Chinese volunteers" who were fighting the United States in Korea, and was replaced as chief military advisor by General Wei Guoqing. Wei was flanked by Lui Ribo, military adjunct and then political advisor, who became the PRC's first ambassador to Hanoi in 1954. Chinese advisors were now present in the PAVN, from the general command down to the battalions. They reorganized the army and the administration, and in 1951 they also instituted economic and financial reform, mainly on fiscal and monetary matters.[114]

DURING THE 1950S, THE MANICHAEAN STRUGGLE FOR POWER WITHIN global politics had repercussions in both China and Vietnam. In Vietnam it aroused the anti-French resistance, whose radicalism grew in size and intensity, opening and widening the rifts within the united front. In 1949, to ensure its control of the Red River delta, the French command had sent parachutists into the Catholic dioceses of Phat Diem and Bui Chu, south of Hanoi. The Christian population in the area (led by Monsignor Le Huu Tu) began to distance themselves from the government of Ho Chi Minh. At the Vatican, Pope Pius XII issued a decree on 1 July 1949 prohibiting Catholics from collaborating with Communists in any part of the world. The French air force dropped tens of thousands of leaflets proclaiming the decree over the resistance zones. The decree did not prevent a number of Vietnamese Catholics, including members of the clergy, from continuing their struggle within the ranks of the resistance, but the rift was widening, especially since the Vatican had just recognized the government of Bao Dai, which had been set up by the French to counter that of Ho Chi Minh. Ho stopped writing to his "friend" Le Huu Tu, but continued to send his yearly Christmas greetings to his Catholic compatriots.

Up to that point, the socialistic dimension had remained in the background during the war, or was at least toned down, but it began to assume a growing importance in the struggle for national liberation. At the same time, the Communists expanded their rigorous political training to include an intense ideological program to mold minds through collective psychological pressure and conditioning. This practice was common to all countries within the Soviet Communist sphere, including its closest neighbor, the People's Republic of China.

Radicalism also penetrated the realm of culture, as witnessed by the musician and composer Pham Duy. Duy remembers hearing a new official term for the first time at the Arts and Literature Congress held in Thanh Hoa (Zone IV) in the summer of 1950: "*People's* Arts and Literature." The opening speech introduced the notion of "socialist realism," and the poet To Huu – sometimes compared to the Soviet cultural tsar Andrei Zhdanov – declared that a type of traditional song known as the *vong co* had to be banned from the repertory despite protests from the southern composer Luu Huu Phuoc. According to To Huu, this melancholic song from the South was demoralizing and demobilizing.[115] Pham Duy was seeing the emergence of a political and cultural orthodoxy and realized that from then on, those who did not agree with it would have to either submit or move to the French-occupied zone, where a Vietnamese state under nationalist influence was beginning to take shape.

In 1951, the number of Vietnamese deserting from the resistance zone grew considerably (they called it *dinh te*, leaving one's homeland to take refuge in another). A French Sûreté official cautioned that he did not see this as a sign that the adversary was weakening. To the contrary, they would grow stronger because those who remained in the North would be the most dedicated and resolute, while those who participated in the *dinh te* would not necessarily join the nationalists and anti-communists. At the same time, the wave of migrants would leave behind a majority of soldiers and cadres – military, political, or from the peasantry – who had literally been reformatted by ideological reshaping, and who would now carry more weight in determining sociopolitical strategy.

Was Ho Chi Minh unaffected by the changes taking place around him? To be sure, he no longer had to answer to the Comintern, but he was still under the eyes of colleagues who shared his ideological convictions – an ideology that had now been given a totalitarian slant by Stalin. As a result, he could not escape the criticism and reservations of other Communist leaders, especially those who had dictatorial power at home, as well as a powerful and undeniable aura within the global Soviet movement. Stalin's presence, of course, was felt via the Cominform, the Information Bureau for Communist Parties that was founded in October 1947 and dissolved in 1956. (Note that the Cominform dealt with the Communist Parties of Europe, not those of Asia.) There was also Mao Zedong, whose star was now on the rise. And this second "big brother" was much closer to home.

In an effort to obtain much-needed diplomatic recognition of the DRV by the PRC and the USSR, Ho arranged a meeting with both Communist leaders in Moscow. In early January 1950, he set out for Beijing via Liuzhou and Nanning. He traveled incognito all the way to Nanning because he was afraid of an attack by the Nationalist Chinese, who had not yet been completely eliminated from Guangxi province by the Communist troops. He arrived in Beijing on 20 January and went from there to Moscow with Zhou Enlai, where he accompanied Mao to meet with Stalin. The entire voyage lasted almost three months. (He returned to Longzhou on 13 March, and on 2 April was back in Bac Kan for a meeting.) Ho's second aim in going to Moscow was to obtain as much material support as possible from "the Fatherland of Socialism," but in the end Stalin entrusted China with the provision of Ho's demands. According to Nikita Khrushchev, Stalin played the magnanimous leader with the order: "Send him five hundred kilos of quinine."[116]

We still do not know exactly what was said during that meeting of the three leaders, only what we find in Khrushchev's *Memoirs*. The latter, it seems, had great admiration for Ho Chi Minh:

> I have met many people in the course of my political career, but none has made such a particular impression on me. Believers often talk of the Apostles. Well, through his way of living and his influence over his peers, Ho Chi Minh was exactly comparable to these "holy apostles." An apostle of the Revolution. I will never forget that gleam of purity and sincerity in his eyes. His sincerity was that of an incorruptible communist and his purity that of a man totally devoted to his cause, in his principles and in his actions. Nobody could resist him, so strong was his conviction that communism was the best thing for his people and for all people. Every one of his words seemed to rest on the conviction that all communists were, by definition, brothers in class, so they would always be honest and sincere with each other. Ho Chi Minh was truly one of the "saints" of communism.[117]

Khrushchev also wrote that Stalin showed little sympathy for Ho, whom he called "a communist troglodyte." Stalin was even distrustful, and had someone steal from Ho's hotel the portrait that Ho, with "a look of almost childlike naïveté," had asked Stalin to sign.[118] And when Ho asked Stalin to orchestrate his official arrival in Moscow as the Vietnamese head of state, Stalin sarcastically refused. But according to Vo Nguyen Giap, it was not just a difference in temperament and personal incompatibilities. After his voyage to the USSR, Ho Chi Minh reported to the Central Executive Committee of the party that Stalin had not understood the VWP's strategy up until that point. In particular, Stalin explicitly criticized the Vietnamese for not having already implemented land reform. He showed two chairs to Ho and said to him, "This chair represents the peasantry and that one the landlords. Where do you sit?" The Vietnamese, he added, must now begin an agrarian revolution, taking advantage of the experience of their Chinese comrades. According to one version of this story, Ho responded that he could sit on both chairs at once. Vo Nguyen Giap did not mention the incident, but he did refer to the stolen photo, about which "Uncle Ho said nothing."[119] Ho must have had some reaction, and one can only wonder what he was thinking.

Stalin would certainly have delivered his remarks with a smile, but also a hint of challenge, and Ho Chi Minh gave in.[120] Land reform was decided upon in 1953 from the government's hideout in Thai Nguyen, with "Phase I" instituted that same year. After the Geneva Accords of July 1954, the reforms spread slowly but thoroughly and reached north of the sixteenth parallel in 1956. We shall return to this issue later.

THE CHINESE GENERAL, CHEN GENG, PRESENTED A CRITICAL REPORT of the PAVN and its command to president Ho Chi Minh. He found that the Viet Minh soldiers were brave, but poorly trained and led. Their officers, some of whom were corrupt, stayed behind the front lines and had no contact with their men. Generally, the Viet Minh cadres were unlike the Bolsheviks. They were too proud to accept criticism and to admit their mistakes or shortcomings. In particular, Vo Nguyen Giap was deemed "shifty" and not entirely trustworthy. Communications between the general command and the units were not well established, and some unit leaders did not obey orders from the commander in chief. Moreover, Chen suggested that Viet Minh leaders should take an active role in dealing with their French prisoners. Rather than just keeping them in camps, they should try to "convert" them with political propaganda.[121]

The principle tool of this reshaping was a policy called "rectification" (*cheng feng* in Chinese, or *chinh huan* in Vietnamese). This involved sessions of criticism and self-criticism, of "converting both body and soul," or in Christian terms, "stripping the old self bare."[122] The first rectification was administered to the PAVN in April 1951 after the failed campaigns of Tran Hung Dao, Hoang Hoa Tham, and Quang Trung (which followed the victory of Cao Bang–Lang Son). As in China, this introspection extended beyond the personal sphere to the political environment of Vietnam. No longer merely face-to-face or a matter of patient and analyst, it became a sociodrama. This mass operation became unbearably oppressive, degenerating into psychological terrorism and even thought control.

Whatever term one chooses – reform, straightening out, reshaping, or remodeling – this practice by Communist regimes became a form of repressive and oppressive violence because it was used as a weapon in the class struggle. It was meant to invert the usual power relations, to be employed by the exploited classes (the peasantry) against the exploiting class (landlords, rich peasants, and the urban bourgeoisie), but it only ended up increasing human duplicity to the detriment of its original intention. Ho had intended criticism and self-criticism to function as a sort of question-and-answer method for seeing oneself clearly, in order to strengthen personal convictions, group cohesion, and the desire to take action.[123] In the hands of the Communists, however, it became a way to blame others and put them at the mercy of external forces.

Ho Chi Minh was certainly aware of the risks involved when he undertook the defense of his friend Tran Huu Tuoc, who had decided to leave France and accompany Ho back to Vietnam. Tuoc had systematically refused to participate in the rectification sessions, using his medical activities as a pretext, but in reality he considered the sessions a waste of time. Responding to the repeated complaints of the cadres in charge of Zone III, Ho said placidly: "*chinh huan* is solely based on *free consent*. If someone refuses, he should not be forced into it. Uncle Tuoc is a good man."[124] Ho made other, similar comments:

> Insist on independent and free thought. Go deeper and understand a text thoroughly without having blind faith in every word or phrase; boldly discuss questions that you have not perfectly understood until you have fully grasped them. Ask "why?" every time you encounter a problem and study closely to determine whether it concerns real life and reason; in short, absolutely refrain from a blind obedience to books. One must think maturely.

He returned to this subject whenever possible. For example, in his meetings with cadres in April and June 1968, Ho had a basic message: I make propositions. If you do not agree with me, say so openly; do not keep it to yourself or you will only end up frustrated or unable to carry out your duties.

On the eve of the victory at Dien Bien Phu, the Vietnamese resistance was no longer following a politics of consensus, and some practices were harbingers of a dictatorship of the proletariat – that is, of the Communist Party. It is difficult to know how Ho Chi Minh behaved in the face of these changes. On one hand, he was not a fan of the Chinese government's model and thought that the Vietnamese should preserve national unity as well as their own methods of combat.[125] On the other hand, he was driven by revolutionary and Leninist convictions. How did he reconcile these contradictions? Did he foresee the excesses and changes of course that the class struggle would bring about? Did he accept what was going on or did he just give in and keep his opinions to himself?

In the meantime, Ho relied on the experience of the Chinese advisors, perhaps allowing them too much influence, to the point where Chinese practices continued even after the return of peace. Was he already aware of this situation in 1950–51, or did it dawn on him only with the gradual foundation of a regime led openly by the Communist Party? Hoang Tung, who attended numerous VWP Politburo meetings as head of propaganda, wrote an account much later that sheds light on Ho's behavior during this period.[126] According to Tung, Chinese political advisors tried to clean house within the Vietnamese party, and started by appointing political commissioners to oversee the army. At their instigation, Ly Ban, assistant to General Van Tien Dung, drew up a list of military cadres who were neither from the peasantry nor the proletariat, beginning with Vo Nguyen Giap. The Chinese wanted to replace them with cadres who had a proletarian background. When Ho received the list, he ordered it burned immediately. Likewise, when Ly Ban proposed the nomination of military and political cadres on the basis of their social background, Ho responded that one's social class was not a guarantee of quality nor of one's political virtues, that one had to assess each case individually. He gave Peng Pai as an example: The son of rich landlords, he was educated and cultivated, yet also founded the peasant "soviets" of Hai Lufeng (in Guangdong) in 1927–28 and was considered a communist hero. The same was true of General Chen Geng, Ho's friend and a man he held in high esteem. All the same, when a new Secretary General was to be named for the party in 1960, Le Duan was chosen over Vo Nguyen Giap, who had never been imprisoned by the French and who, moreover, had been trained in the French educational system.

Be that as it may, for the duration of the war, Ho Chi Minh had no choice but to bow under the weight of Chinese communization – commonly, though inaccurately, called Maoism. The Vietnamese Communists adopted it without critical thought, more or less completely accepting it completely as their own. In the opinion of Bui Tin, who had joined the revolution and the resistance from the beginning and later became a renegade from the regime in the 1990s:

> From 1951 onwards, the rise of Maoism in Vietnam largely contributed to our growing stupidity and harmed us in ways that are still with us today. We put an end to innocence, to enthusiasm, and to the mutual respect which had first united those in the Resistance. In its place, we sowed suspicion and discord in our ranks.[127]

As a result, Bui Tin believed that Ho – whom he clearly admired – was responsible for the misdeeds of Maoism to the extent that he did not resolutely discourage it, and even sang its praises publicly.

Only later did Ho Chi Minh and other Vietnamese Communist leaders wonder about this period, regardless of their reasons for admiring and copying the Chinese revolution. Could it be that Mao Zedong's goal in the 1950s was to remodel the Vietnamese Party, to seize command, and make it into a satellite of his own party? This situation eventually sparked distrust and then disagreement, both exacerbated by the Sino-Soviet conflict of 1960–80, culminating in the final rupture of 1979.

FIVE

The Force of Circumstance

The revolution is not a dinner between friends: it is not like writing an essay, painting a picture, or embroidering a flower. It cannot be achieved with such refinement, ease, and elegance, with such 'sweetness, calm, respect, modesty, and deference.' A revolution is an insurrection, the act of violence through which one class overturns the power of another. . . . These (excessive) actions are completely necessary.

– Mao Zedong

The revolution is a bloc.

– Georges Clemenceau

The revolution is not a bloc.
It encompasses both the excellent and the vile.

– Édouard Herriot[1]

THE REVOLUTION IS CRUEL

In 1954, after nine years of negotiations, political maneuvers, and military combat, the French government put an end to the war in Indochina as it had ceased to hold the public's interest. Back in July 1947, 37 percent of the French supported the "restoration of order" in Indochina by military means, and 37 percent were in favor of negotiations; by 1949, the numbers had shifted to 19 percent and 49 percent, respectively.[2] In 1988, the French Deputy and Mayor of Fréjus, François Léotard, recalled that he had cried when he heard about the fall of the French fortifications at Dien Bien Phu in 1954; he then went on to mention the start in the same year of off-track betting (*le tiercé*), which proved to be a more amusing distraction.

The war had become an American problem. On the eve of the Geneva Accords, the United States was providing 80 percent of the funding, up from 42 percent in 1952.[3] The government of Pierre Mendès-France took the necessary steps to extricate France from the mess in Indochina, and he hinted to U.S. officials that the French parliament would accept the European Defense Community (EDC) accords approving the rearmament of Germany. He knew that Europe was more important than Asia for current U.S. strategy. At the same time, Mendès-France tried to prevent an uprising in the French possessions in North Africa by negotiating a statute of autonomy with the Tunisian nationalists and setting up a reforms commission in Morocco. Yet in November 1954, a series of assassinations in Algeria marked the beginning of the nationalist insurrection in that region.

In the spring of 1954, an international conference was convened in Geneva to discuss the cease-fire in Korea, but in May (the day after the fall of Dien Bien Phu), it turned its attention to the conflict in Indochina.[4] An agreement was reached on 20 July consisting of a cease-fire followed by a redeployment of the armed forces of both parties on either side of the seventeenth parallel – a purely provisional line of demarcation. A general election was to be held within two years whereby the Vietnamese themselves would choose the regime that would unify the country. In the meantime, an International Control Commission (ICC) was established to oversee the enforcement of the accords. It was a tripartite commission, consisting of representatives from India, Canada, and Poland in an attempt to be fair, given the international balance of power. The United States remained reticent and did not sign either the accords or the final declaration, paving the way for future developments, which were more or less to be expected.

At the table in Geneva were delegates from the United States, the USSR, France, and Great Britain, as well as representatives from the associated states of Vietnam, Laos, and Cambodia. The United States, true to form, was represented by Walter Bedell-Smith and not by Secretary of State John Foster Dulles. The USSR was represented by Foreign Minister Vyacheslav Molotov, France by Foreign Minister Georges Bidault (before the fall of the Laniel government), and Great Britain by Foreign Secretary Anthony Eden. And finally, present for the first time among the superpowers was the People's Republic of China, represented by Zhou Enlai.

On 5 July 1954, Zhou left Geneva to confer with Ho Chi Minh and Vo Nguyen Giap in Liuzhou and then returned to the conference. We do not know what the three men said, but Zhou Enlai certainly played a determining role in making his allies accept the decision to divide Vietnamese territory into two cease-fire zones. Two decades later, when China and Vietnam were at war and the Vietnamese were arguing against the hegemonism of their neighbor and ally, they accused China of wanting to keep a bifurcated Vietnam and a politically divided Indochinese peninsula at its doorstep.[5] Indeed, the Soviet historian Ilya Gaiduk has advanced the plausible hypothesis that Zhou Enlai feared U.S. intervention on the peninsula more than anything else, and so preferred to have France maintain a presence and an influence in South Vietnam, Laos, and Cambodia. He was eventually disappointed, however, because Mendès-France decided to pass the baton to the Americans.

At that time, Ho Chi Minh was also convinced that Mendès-France genuinely wanted to put an end to the war and advocated doing nothing to hinder the French Prime Minister, who was dealing with "the obstacles and the undermining of the Americans."[6] Ho asked Hoang Tung, head of propaganda for the VWP, to glorify in the media the bravery and spirit of sacrifice of Vietnam's combatants and its people, but to avoid humiliating the French, given their defeat at Dien Bien Phu.[7]

We know that Ho was in favor of letting things evolve gradually by taking progressive action, and preferred diplomatic negotiation to direct and violent confrontation, and so it should not come as a surprise that he seized the occasion at Geneva to put an end to hostilities, even accepting a partial amputation – though defined as provisional – of the territory of the DRV.[8] This approach was similar to the one he had adopted in 1946, and Vo Nguyen Giap's reference to the Treaty of Brest-Litovsk was just as relevant in 1954. It is doubtful, then, that Ho had agreed to delay reunification because he was forced to do so by his Chinese ally. At the same time, the hypothesis is plausible that the Chinese had an ulterior motive for making the Indochinese peninsula into a geostrategic buffer zone. North Vietnam would become a Chinese "satellite," and Laos, Cambodia, and South Vietnam would adopt a position of neutrality, as Finland had done with respect to the USSR.

In the end, however, internal factors in Vietnam and China played a decisive role in bringing an end to the Franco–Viet Minh conflict. The war of resistance had lasted nine years, causing great suffering among the Vietnamese people and involving huge sacrifices. Vu Dinh Huynh claims that Ho was almost obsessively worried about the toll that the war had taken on his country. No amount of Chinese aid could compensate for the losses incurred, especially since the initial victory of Cao Bang–Lang Son was followed by massive setbacks for the PAVN and a heavy death toll, which tormented Vo Nguyen Giap. The Chinese, on the other hand, wanted to set their country on the path toward modernization, and the aid given to Vietnam, combined with their commitments in North Korea (since October 1950), had cost them a tremendous amount in material and human resources (900,000 Chinese "volunteers" fell on the battlefield in Korea).

In October 1954, Ho Chi Minh and his government returned to Hanoi, which had once again become the capital of the Democratic Republic of Vietnam. He was now faced with the difficult task of putting the war-torn economy back on its feet, as well as enacting the revolutionary transformation of North Vietnam. The "great union" of all Vietnamese that he had always desired had become a reality (though only relatively) from 1945 to 1946. It had faded from view during the First Indochina War, and now in a time of peace – or, rather, truce – it was undercut once again by the division of the country into two zones and the crystallization of ethnic, social, and political contradictions within Vietnamese society. This did not prevent Ho from launching one last appeal (in the pages of *Nhan Dan* on 7–9 July 1954) to the Catholics, who had now rejoined the opposing camp. He asked them to rally behind the DRV and follow the example of the French Catholics who had taken up a position against the war in Indochina in the pages of their journal *Témoignage Chrétien* (Christian Witness).

Land Reform and Reconstruction

In North Vietnam, land reform was now the social question par excellence. In the years preceding World War II, the agrarian situation had been particularly acute in the Red River delta, where the average population density was four hundred inhabitants per square kilometer (peaking in Nam Dinh and Ha Dong provinces with 1,500 inhabitants/km^2). The coastal plains in the center of the country also had a high density rate (300/km^2) and a relatively reduced area of arable land, which led to a "hunger for land" among the landless masses. By comparison, the Mekong delta was underpopulated (75/km^2), and so the colonial administration estimated that Cochinchina could receive one million immigrants from the North. In 1937, a survey to prepare for property tax reform in Tonkin counted 965,000 landlords, 882,000 of whom held less than five *mau* (1.8 hectares, or 4.5 acres), while another 968,000 people had no land at all.[9]

There were two opposing agrarian systems at the time: one in the North and Center, where small properties were in the majority; and one in the South, where big estates covered a large area. But both had a poor rural proletariat, the most abject of whom lived in miserable conditions. The French authorities in Indochina had been well aware of the economic and political importance of the agrarian issue, especially since the 1930s, during which Yves Henry, Director of the Agricultural Services of Indochina, the geographer Pierre Gourou, and the agronomist René Dumont had developed surveys and analyses of the rural environment. Some people advocated a limited use of migration and agrarian colonization, while others wanted a total redistribution of land confiscated from the larger estates.[10] As for the ICP, they remembered what Nguyen Ai Quoc had written in the 1920s about the revolutionary potential of the peasantry and its critical role in the triumph of the proletarian revolution, and so in 1937 they had assigned two of their militants – both of whom would achieve notoriety later on – to write *Van de dan cay* (The peasant question).[11] The millions of people who died of starvation in Tonkin and in North Annam in 1945 served as a reminder of the urgent need to put an end to the agrarian crisis.

The August revolution of 1945 called for the estates of the "French and of traitors" to be confiscated and redistributed. The total, however, was meager, even with the additional distribution of communal lands (most of them rice fields): In 1953, 184,871 hectares (456,600 acres) of rice fields, or 77 percent of the communal land of Tonkin, were divided among the inhabitants of 3,035 villages. In the free zones administered by the resistance government, the landlords and rich peasants who participated in the national struggle – by will or by force – had to reduce their farm rents or were not allowed to surpass the rate fixed by the government (20 percent instead of 50 percent and higher). It was a matter of "limiting the feudal landlords' exploitation of the peasants while at the same time proceeding with changes to the property system *so long as this measure does not impede the United National Anti-Colonialist Front.*"[12]

The war mobilized a growing number of people from the countryside and also porters (*dan cong*), and the peasants were required to increase production to keep up with the food demands of the people and the People's Army. In return for their sacrifices, the landless peasants would be compensated with land of their own. "Land to the tiller" was one of the main slogans of the Bolshevik Revolution, along with "Factories for the worker." A law of 28 June 1950 enacted the same process in China, while that same year Stalin called upon Ho Chi Minh for its implementation in Vietnam.

Land reform had been a part of the ICP's original plan since the beginning, under the heading of "antifeudal revolution" (in the Marxist sense, whereby a feudal regime is one in which all social relationships are based on land ownership); but initially it was coupled with the anticolonialist struggle and national unity, remaining in the background and moderate in scope. In the 1950s, however, feudalism became a prime target when the French reinstated former Emperor Bai Dai and created a puppet Vietnamese nationalist state stamped with the triad of capitalism-feudalism-imperialism. The Vietnamese Communists, who were inspired or even ordered by the Chinese to take action, believed that the time had come to "feed the fire" of land reform and finally "liquidate the feudal regime."

In November 1953, the fifth session of the Central Committee of the VWP articulated the aims of the reforms:

> To improve the living conditions of the peasants and mobilize all material and human resources to carry out a lengthy resistance; to conquer the American interventionists, overthrow the puppet administration, and completely liberate the country. We aim to liberate the productive forces in the countryside, intensify agricultural production, and pave the way for the development of industry and commerce which we need to run the resistance and reconstruct the country. We must abolish the system of colonial land ownership in Vietnam, abolish the system of feudal property, and establish the system of peasant land ownership and give the land to those who work on it.[13]

The first national conference of the VWP was held from 14 to 23 November 1953. Party leaders decided to undertake land reform, and President Ho Chi Minh signed the decree on 19 December 1953. It took effect progressively, from 1953 to 1961, and gradually spread from the liberated zones of North Vietnam to the rest of the territory after the retreat of French troops. In the end, the goal of rebalancing the land base and depolarizing society in order to bring about equality and freedom for the greatest number among the rural masses was essentially met. It was a giant step toward resolving the problems within an agrarian system bequeathed by the French colonial regime.

The Vietnamese Communists attained their goal not by actively enforcing the new laws but by following the Chinese model and engaging in a "mass struggle" through special "peoples' tribunals," public accusations of "class enemies," executions, and "reeducation." There was nothing spontaneous about the operation. The Chinese Communists had found that class consciousness was poorly developed, or not at all, among parts of the peasantry and depending on the region; and even when the peasants had had their "consciousness raised," acting upon that knowledge was another thing. Members of the CCP thus passed on the lessons of their experience to their Vietnamese comrades.

The central focus of the movement in Vietnam was social classification, to be spearheaded by the poor and landless peasants. They were to ally themselves with the middle peasantry, guarantee the neutrality of the rich peasants, and thus destroy the landlord as a social class. However, the country was still at war, and so the government was more lenient toward those landlords who had fought in the war or supported the resistance, or whose families had participated in the struggle for independence. These patriotic landlords would be reimbursed for the excess land that would be confiscated from them.

In reality, however, the distinction between social categories was not always clear. In many places, especially in the Red River delta where the property situation was a confusing tangle, landlords concealed their holdings behind a network of extended family, friends, and clients. This only resulted in new party cadres sent by the government to replace the old ones, who were considered to be too involved in the social fabric of local networks, hence capable of laxity or complicity with "class enemies." Ho Chi Minh himself described the reform – or better yet, revolution – as a "delicate and thorny rupturing." The excesses, relabeled "errors," were foreseeable: Middle-class and rich peasants were often denounced as landlords, and small landlords were classified as "big" ones. Such social classifications were sometimes arbitrary inasmuch as each land-reform team had to register 5 percent of every rural community as landlords, and to reach their goal they did not always consider the issue of patriotism. When the party later began its campaign of "rectifying errors," more than half of the so-called landlords were reclassified to a lower level.

These "errors" had tragic repercussions, such as the one in the village of Son Duong, in Phu Tho province. The mayor's wife, who had supported the Viet Minh throughout the war, was classified as a landlord, and she committed suicide after the confiscation of all her possessions. A Viet Minh cadre from the village tells this story:

> My father was an active militant with the Party during the war. Our house was frequently used for meetings of Party leaders and my father was named treasurer because he was rich.... I volunteered for the army in 1949 and was sent to China for military training.... I witnessed the land reform program in China, so wrote to my father and told him to sell some of his land.... I was not at home when land reform was begun, but I learned that they seized everything we had except for the water buffalo shed, which was given back to us because someone mentioned that my younger brother and I were in the

armed forces.... To survive, the family sold buffalo dung as fertilizer, but the money was confiscated because "the fertilizer belonged to the people."[14]

By 1987, the wounds of the agrarian revolution and its excesses were still not healed in Son Duong. The revolution had undermined village solidarity born during the war of resistance, ostracizing families that had already been broken. (For example, some women accused their in-laws of concealing their property holdings, and children were encouraged to denounce their parents.) On the other hand, two hundred hectares (500 acres) of land were redistributed among the poor families and landless laborers in recompense. In addition, because most ICP members were rich peasants or even landlords, the class struggle was accompanied by a purging of the party itself.

The journalist Xuan Phuong took part in the reform in Bac Ninh province (120 km from Hanoi) as part of the political education of "intellectuals," who were to be made aware of the hard realities of the countryside and of the destitution of most peasants. She left a terrifying account of the public accusation sessions and the executions of "landlords" (or those presumed to be). She then returned to Hanoi, still traumatized by the cruel scenes she had witnessed, and told how

> the loudspeakers announced progress in the land reform campaign. Soon no one would be able to escape it. My brother-in-law, the vice-minister, is from Nghe Anh, like Ho Chi Minh... where the reform raged stronger than in other places. His affiliation with the government did not stop his parents from being condemned to death. Every day we learn of new executions. We feel like we are witnessing the march toward total destruction.[15]

The land reform campaign was supposed to proceed with order and fairness, but it went horribly wrong, culminating in the massacre of fifteen thousand victims (most of them innocent – at least of what they were accused of). This is even a conservative estimate, released amidst controversy, while others claim it could be as high as fifty thousand.[16] The situation in China was similar and its agrarian revolution followed the same trajectory, but given its greater size and population, it probably had several million victims and led to at least one million deaths. In 1956 – too late according to some – the VWP leadership decided to "straighten the tiller," which, in communist jargon, had taken a turn to the "left." Truong Chinh, Secretary General of the party and in charge of the land reform commission, was relieved of his duties, including head of the party, and was provisionally replaced by Ho Chi Minh.

Vo Nguyen Giap, still basking in the glory of his victory at Dien Bien Phu, was chosen to present the government's self-criticism before several hundred cadres at a meeting in Hanoi, and on 18 August 1956, Ho Chi Minh himself spoke "to compatriots from the countryside and to cadres on the occasion of the fundamental success of land reform in North Vietnam." He praised what he later called (the following year, before the Supreme Soviet of the USSR) "the realization of a dream of millions of years," or giving the land to those who work on it. Then he continued:

> The Central Committee of the party and the government did not maintain total leadership in certain areas because there were no strict controls. This is why the land reform campaign resulted in errors and hindered our efforts toward village unity, our struggle against our enemies, our reorganization, etc. The Central Committee of the party and the government have severely rectified these errors and deviations, and have systematically moved toward reparations; their aim is to establish unity among cadres, unity among the people, the return of peace in our villages, increased production.... We must carefully reclassify those who were wrongly labeled as landlords or rich peasants. We must reestablish the party's membership, restore political rights, rehabilitate the honor of party members, cadres, and citizens who have been wrongly punished.... We must take care of landlords who participated in the Resistance, who supported the revolution, and who have children who are soldiers or cadres. Where we overestimated the capacity for production, we must redo our calculations accurately. As for the reparations, we must be firm and make a plan. We must immediately repair that which can be fixed.[17]

How were these corrections put into place? Xuan Phuong gives us a glimpse:

> I had to return to Bac Ninh with the same group to make up for the terrible offenses committed last year. Just imagine how much the peasants hated us when we entered the village. "Why did you come back here? Don't you think enough blood has been spilled?" This time the leader of the group is a teacher at a high school in Bac Ninh, a calm and reasonable man. The newly elected People's Committee is made up of reputable, honest people.... The feudal class is still under condemnation... but almost all citizens wrongly accused of being "landlords" have been rehabilitated. The unfortunate people who were "demoted in class" can now return and live in a part of their own house, get back some plots of their rice fields, and, most importantly, be officially classified as "peasants of the middle class." This will give their children better prospects for the future. But none of this is accomplished easily. Many of the houses, now occupied by several families, have been

> completely sacked, and it's even hard to find a room that the former owners can move back into.... But the tombs of the dead who were wrongly condemned bear witness to this shameful episode in our history. Gone are the days when everyone lived in harmony in a Vietnamese village. Now the people are divided and hate each other.

Some people have blamed Ho Chi Minh for these errors because he was the leader of the nation, while others reproach him for not intervening even when he was warned about the most flagrant cases of arbitrary violence. One example aroused particularly strong feelings and indignation among the Vietnamese, the case of Mrs. Nguyen Thi Nam, who was an important landlord and patriot. During the colonial era, she frequently provided shelter for Communist leaders, including some of the most prominent, who were on the run or passing through town. She supported the revolution, gave one hundred gold taels to the republic when Ho Chi Minh launched "Gold Week," and provided the Viet Minh with food and money. In addition, one of her sons was an officer in the PAVN. Despite all of this, she was condemned to death by a people's tribunal and executed; her son was recalled from China, demoted, stripped of his medals, and sentenced to twenty years in prison. According to Vu Dinh Huynh, Ho was informed but did nothing to prevent the tragedy. Hoang Tung related that Ho "bowed to the majority but still expressed his dissension," declaring that "the French say that one should never hit a woman, even with a flower, and you, you allowed her to be shot!"

What we know for sure is that on 8 February 1955, Ho stood up against the random violence that had accompanied the reform in many areas. At the summary conference for the second phase of land reform in the Thai Nguyen–Bac Giang zone, he condemned the use of torture and humiliation, and announced: "Some cadres are using the same methods to crush the masses as the imperialists, capitalists, and feudalists did. These methods are barbaric.... *It is absolutely forbidden to use physical punishment.*"[18] Later, he asked Hoang Tung: "How many thousands of people have been put to death?... Luckily we managed to end it in 1956. Otherwise it would have been a disaster."[19]

Ho Chi Minh was well aware of the situation in the Asian countryside, whether in China or in Vietnam. In 1924 he had written articles on the subject, stating that the "social conditions of small landlords with ten to one hundred *mau* are complex and unpredictable. With that amount of land, a peasant could end up being exploited, an exploiter, or neutral." He continued:

> [T]he class struggle does not take shape the way it does in the West. The workers lack consciousness, they are resigned and disorganized.... In this way, if the peasants have next to nothing, the landlord does not have a great fortune either.... The one is resigned to his fate, the other moderate in his appetites. So the clash between their interests is softened. That is undeniable.[20]

This observation must have led the empiricist in Ho to be prudent and moderate in carrying out reforms. Others, however, for whom reality had to mirror ideology, came to the conclusion that they had to organize the peasantry and provoke a collision between the classes by staging people's tribunals in dramatic fashion.

In this situation as in others, Ho Chi Minh sometimes gave the impression that he had resigned himself to extremist acts, as if he lacked the courage to go against the grain. He had shown audacity and courage on so many occasions, but perhaps he was capable of cowardice like anyone else. Besides, one wonders whether he was even able to make himself heard and obeyed, since we have seen that this was not always the case.

It is true that in 1957, 810,000 hectares (2 million acres) of land were distributed free of charge to 2,104,138 families, or some 8.3 million people. But it is equally true that in 1958, peasants were invited to establish production cooperatives, only to be forced to join them two years later. Collectivization was clearly already in the works because the land was distributed without the accompanying title deeds. The microproperties generated by the land reform program (the average plot per family was about 0.7 hectares/1.7 acres) would only have hindered the development of productive forces and increased production, but this was precisely the key to industrial development and to the feeding of a population suffering from the effects of war and the migration of approximately one million people to the South. Collectivization had its highs and lows, and a survey in 1957 found that 40 percent of the families in a cooperative wanted to pull out of the collective. The party then decreed that collectivization would be a "mass movement," and by 1960, the individual farmer – that is, the family farm – had disappeared entirely from the Vietnamese landscape. That same year, the government announced that 90 percent of farming families had joined cooperatives.

From 1958 to 1960, all businesses, craftsmen, and private industries were collectivized: 1,300 companies and 3,939 business owners were "reeducated," and those who refused to give up their property were accused of being counterrevolutionaries. In Hanoi, thirty-eight business owners were arrested and imprisoned, seventeen made a "gift" (whether they wanted to or not) of their possessions, twenty-nine only reluctantly merged into joint enterprises, and eleven committed suicide.[21] Meanwhile, the inhabitants of Hanoi and other northern cities were forced to register with the police to determine the amount of their food rations. This strict control was meant to facilitate surveillance, as well as to control the comings and goings of the residents. Surveillance was also carried out by block leaders and neighbors who shared communal housing, which had become a common practice except for the highest party leaders.

One witness wrote about her return to Hanoi:

> The building is now divided by bamboo partitions; it's as if we all live in the same house. Nobody has a private life anymore. [There was a retired woman from the Ministry of Foreign Affairs, a member of the building council, who spent her days monitoring people:] Every day she inspects a few rooms.... When I came back from the Resistance I was loaded with medals. Resistance medal, work medal, etc. But that didn't have any affect on my living conditions. Twelve kilos of rice, three hundred grams of meat, vegetables, and a half-kilo of sugar per month. My children are always hungry. My husband [a colonel in the army] is gone most of the time. When he comes back, his officers' salary is not enough to buy the food he needs. We have political meetings twice a week at the Ministry [of Health], almost exclusively about the class struggle.... Before, in the Resistance, everybody shared the same life, the same joys, the same sorrow. Now all of the important jobs, all the positions of responsibility, go to members of the party, so many people want to sign up just to have a highly placed job. Exactly the opposite of what Ho Chi Minh advocated, that we join the party not for personal gain but for the good of the people.[22]

Almost immediately after the start of land reform, the woman's husband was summoned to headquarters: "You have done your patriotic duty in the army," they said; "now you must return to civilian life.... All officers from families of feudal origin must leave the army."

Humanism and Belles-Lettres, or the Impossible Protest

For the Soviet Socialist states and for Communist Parties around the world, 1956 was a year of transition. The Twentieth Congress of the Communist Party of the USSR (CPSU) opened on 14 February 1956, and on the 24th, First Secretary Nikita Khrushchev gave a long speech in which he denounced "the crimes of Stalin," who had died three years before. The shock wave of these revelations was felt throughout the socialist world and beyond. Unfortunately, we do not know explicitly what the Vietnamese delegation took away with them as a result of Khrushchev's report, but it is safe to say that his remarks added to the malaise brought about by the "errors" of land reform.

In June 1956 in Poland, a workers' rebellion broke out in Poznan during the annual International Fair, leading to the rehabilitation of the Communist leader Wladislaw Gomulka. In October, he had to stand up to the four highest Soviet leaders who had arrived unexpectedly, accompanied by fourteen generals. For the first time, Zhou Enlai intervened in the affairs of the European Communist world – a sphere reserved for the CPSU – in favor of the Polish; Tito had been the first, and now the Chinese Communists dared challenge the hegemony of the USSR. On 23 October, the people of Budapest rose up and drove out the Stalinist Matyas Rakosi, but the insurrection was crushed by the Soviet army in November. This time, Mao Zedong commended the repression of the Hungarian Revolution, as he was undoubtedly worried that this type of outbreak could be contagious.

The same year, 1956, saw the beginning of China's "One Hundred Flowers" campaign, which was partly intended to ease the crisis within Chinese intellectual circles following the arrest of the writer Hu Feng, but also to respond to a profound social crisis. The shackles were loosened in May 1956 but clamped back on tightly in July 1957, just over one year later. It was also in 1957 that the Soviet writer Boris Pasternak was thrown out of the Soviet Writers' Union and subsequently forbidden to go to Stockholm to receive the Nobel Prize for Literature, which was awarded to him after the publication abroad of his novel *Doctor Zhivago*. The Hundred Flowers movement gave rise to a number of illusions, even though it never really meant to open up an era of free expression and critical debate. Rather, CCP leaders wanted to put an end to the excesses of the campaigns against Chinese intellectuals and scientists, and to encourage them eventually to reveal their true thoughts and opinions.[23]

The Twentieth Congress of the CPSU and its repercussions exposed a latent discontent and opposition within the Soviet world (in the largest sense), which seemed from the outside to be a monolithic bloc, and revealed the potential contradictions among the various Communist Parties, starting with those of the USSR and the PRC. But at the same time, China and North Vietnam were putting Stalinist regimes in place, with a dictatorship of the Communist Party, the collectivization of the countryside, the generalized and arbitrary use of coercion to eliminate all political opposition and suppress all intellectual and artistic divergence, and economic development based on a centralized, state-controlled plan.

The events of 1956 could not simply be coincidental; they point to an obvious cause and effect, to a certain influence, coaching, and reaction – even if Ho Chi Minh and Vo Nguyen Giap minimized or even denied it. The journalist Tibor Mende asked them the obvious question: By correcting the "errors" of land reform, "was Vietnam participating in the chaos shaking up the Communist world?" But Ho and Giap gave an incomplete answer, assuring him that their current situation was determined only by local factors. The leaders in Hanoi tried thus to differentiate themselves from the socialist camp, as if Vietnam's trajectory were independent of the context of international communism.[24]

The "Nhan Van Giai Pham" affair, commonly known as "the Hundred Flowers" by analogy with the events in China at the same time, was really two movements: The first began in 1955 with a circle of writers and artists from the People's Army, the second in 1956 with writers and artists not affiliated with the military. Tran Dan, the key figure in the first group, was subsequently condemned and imprisoned for "having taken inspiration from bourgeois liberalism." He had proposed the idea of separating literature and the arts from politics so that writers and artists would not become "soulless machines" applying the lessons of the party.[25] Meanwhile, Lu Dingyi, the Propaganda Director of the Central Committee of the CCP, wrote an article echoing Mao's "Let one Hundred Flowers Bloom" speech (2 May 1956). On 10 October 1956, Lu's article, "One Hundred Flowers Bloom, One Hundred Schools of Thought Contend," was translated into Vietnamese and 5,100 copies were distributed in Hanoi, sparking a debate that was not silenced by Tran Dan's arrest.

The main generator of this movement was Nguyen Huu Dang, who had been a Communist since the 1930s. He organized and founded the journal *Nhan Van* (Humanism) – *Nhan Dan* (The People) was the organ of the Communist Party – but it published only five issues. That autumn brought a flowering of other publications, including *Tram Hoa* (One Hundred Flowers), *Noi That* (Frankly Speaking), and *Tap san Phe binh* (Critical Review), some of which lasted only a short time. The critical spirit rubbed off on the official journals, and *Nhan Van*, for one, secured the support and collaboration of well-known writers: the scholar and romantic poet Phan Khoi, the lexicographer Dao Duy Anh, the philosopher Tran Duc Thao – who had worked with Sartre and Merleau-Ponty in the early days of *Les Temps Modernes*, moving from Husserlian phenomenology to Marxism – and the lawyer and literary historian Nguyen Manh Tuong.

The central focus of the movement was the relationship between literature and politics; the demand for creative freedom also meant a rejection of the ideological control of the Communist Party and the canons of socialist realism. By the autumn of 1956, the group's members were denouncing the lack of individual and public freedoms, police surveillance and repression, and the violation of what was called "socialist legality" (in reference to the CPSU's denunciation of Stalin's crimes). The party reacted defensively, motivated by the current situation in the Soviet world and the crisis of global communism. Party leaders claimed that the "Humanism and Belles-Lettres" movement was part of a plot against the party and the regime, supported and perhaps even funded by the government of Ngo Dinh Diem, President of the Republic of Vietnam (South Vietnam) since 1955.[26]

Influenced by the events in China in 1957 and dreading a situation like the one in Hungary (where debates within the Petöfi circle led to barricades in the streets), the Communist Party began its struggle against "saboteurs of the ideological and cultural front" in order to "break the right." The government began by withholding paper from newspapers; then the typographers were told to go on strike and refuse to print them. Those who had believed in an opening up of the regime were pressured and accused during public "rectification" sessions and attacked in the press. Some ended up standing trial and were sent to prison; others were put under house arrest, or they simply lost their jobs and had their food ration cards taken away.

The tactics were those of the trials in the USSR and other People's Democracies: relying on false accusations and digging up supposed crimes from the past. As a result, the philosopher Tran Duc Thao and the writer Truong Tuu were accused of being Trotskyites, and Nguyen Huu Dang was sentenced to twenty years in prison for espionage. Tran Dan was reminded that he had joined the resistance fairly late after having frequented a circle of poets who were opium smokers, and Nguyen Manh Tuong was criticized for his French intellectual training, his courses on "bourgeois capitalist literature," and his references to French law. Tuong left us the poignant tale of his calvary of social exclusion, as he was neither imprisoned nor tortured but lived as a pariah for some thirty years.[27]

Around the same time, the Chinese novelist Ding Ling, who won the Stalin Prize in 1952 and was known for being a Communist sympathizer and a feminist, was accused of being antisocialist, antiparty, and antipeople and condemned during the campaign against the "rightists." It was at this point that Ho Chi Minh supposedly spoke out, referring specifically to Ding Ling, and condemned the wave of dissent within the intellectual milieu. According to the historian Georges Boudarel, Ho published an article entitled "Break the Right" under the pseudonym Tran Luc in *Nhan Dan* on 16 September 1959, saying that he was pleased in particular about the arrest of Ding Ling.[28] In reality, of course, the Humanism and Belles-Lettres movement affected only a limited number of people, but their publications were being favorably received by quite a large public, mainly in Hanoi.

The fact that Ho Chi Minh referred only to a Chinese novelist in his approval of the crackdown – but no Vietnamese author nor a single mention of *Nhan Van* – could suggest that he did not totally approve of the repression against the antiestablishment intellectuals. In the absence of other texts or commentary regarding the crisis, the answer remains unclear. Some of the intellectuals involved were members of the Communist Party, while others had taken part in the struggle for independence and had withstood the difficult conditions in the mountains and forests – that is, they personified the policy of the "great union" that Ho continued to advocate. Vu Dinh Hoe, one of Ho's ministers, recognized that there were often misunderstandings, contradictions, and tensions between the political cadres and "specialists" (legal experts, engineers, doctors, etc.) and between the Communists and members of the Democratic and Socialist Parties (including the intellectuals). According to Vu Dinh Hoe, Ho Chi Minh always played the mediator amidst the disputes and conflicts, hoping to reconcile the opposing points of view or "cool down" the argument.

Off to War Again

The "Hundred Flowers" of Vietnam began to bloom just as the reunification of the country – part of the Communist agenda since July 1954 – was beginning to take shape, but under different terms than those set out in Geneva.

Indeed, the provisional nature of the partition was gradually giving way to the establishment of two independent states, led by two diametrically opposed regimes: a People's Democracy in the North and a Republic, in principle liberal and democratic, in the South. The South was ruled by a presidential-style government in the hands of a family clan, the Ngo. The mandarin Ngo Dinh Diem, whom Ho Chi Minh had freed from the Central Prison in Hanoi in 1945, now found himself confronting his "liberator" as defender of the free world against communism. He had assumed the presidency of the Republic of Vietnam in October 1955 after he drove

Bao Dai from power and ended the hopes of a monarchist restoration. Diem was assisted by his family: his brother Ngo Dinh Nhu and his spirited wife Tran Le Xuan; his brother Ngo Dinh Can, who served as Proconsul for the Center; and his third brother, Monsignor Thuc, who carried moral authority as a prelate of the Catholic Church.

In 1956, Ngo Dinh Diem, who had not signed the Geneva agreement, publicly rejected the idea of a national general election. Fueled by his desire to eradicate communism and erect a nationalist state south of the seventeenth parallel, he ruled in a dictatorial fashion, repressing the slightest impulse of his noncommunist opposition, from the traditional parties to the so-called politico-religious sects (Cao Dai and Hoa Hao) to Buddhist circles. The government resorted to exceptional measures and coercion, which in certain respects mirrored those of the Communists in the North. In the countryside, tribunals were set up to denounce the Communists (from then on called Viet Cong), and sentencing was carried out on the spot. The people themselves were first regrouped into large rural settlements, called "agrovilles," then into "strategic hamlets" (1962–63). Diem sent eight to nine hundred thousand refugees from the North to the Mekong delta and to the Central Highlands; most of them Catholic, they founded colonies that played a strategic role and changed the ethnic, political, and economic landscape of these regions.

In the cities, the government began to register families within each neighborhood, and they censored the press and imprisoned their opponents. At the same time, they tried to spread an official ideology inspired by Christian personalism, which was taught in seminars given for government employees. They organized the people through groups like the Republican Youth, which government workers were also called upon to join. What is more, Mrs. Ngo Dinh Nhu, shortly before her fall, set about policing morality. She banned dance parties and music of a "nature to serve Communist propaganda, [and those] contrary to good morals or serving loose morals, [as well as those] of a romantic nature."[29] If her brother-in-law, the President, had not been toppled in November 1963, Mrs. Nhu might well have gone on to establish a moral order.

But the Diem regime finally fell. It had entered into a test of strength with the Buddhist movement in central Vietnam, mainly in Hué, while in the countryside it faced a continuous escalation of the armed struggle led by the Communists (under cover of the National Front for the Liberation of South Vietnam, *Mat tran dan toc giai phong Mien Nam Viet Nam*). The Diem army, with U.S. approval, eventually fell to the opposition. Aside from a brief interval of civilian control, the southern generals held power until 1975; the last, Nguyen Van Thieu, was President from 1965 to 1975.

FOR ABOUT A YEAR AFTER THE SIGNING OF THE GENEVA ACCORDS IN 1954, one could still freely travel between the North and South; families were still visiting each other, and mail was even delivered across the borders. Migration, on the other hand, mainly from the North to the South, was strongly blocked, especially that of the Catholics. The Polish representative of the International Control Commission, Mieczyslaw Maneli, reported that in early 1955, government directives went unheeded and were even sabotaged at the local level. Ministers and members of the party's Central Committee were sent to meet with local authorities to make sure they let the Catholics leave – the government had authorized them to migrate to the South – but in vain. In a last attempt, the government had to send a special mission into the provinces and districts to explain that Vietnam had to respect and carry out international obligations.[30]

As the deadline for the general elections drew nearer, however, it became evident that they would not take place, and the two closed "regroupment zones" began to evolve into two opposing states, at the same time positioning themselves within one of the two opposing camps currently squaring off on the international scene. Ho Chi Minh seems to have retained his hope that the elections would be held and a war avoided. Did he really believe this or did he just say it as a matter of form? In 1963, Ho and Ngo Dinh Diem began a correspondence (through the intermediary Maneli) alluding to a plan for neutrality and coexistence between the two nations, or even a confederation – a plan that the French ambassador Roger Lalouette had suggested during conversations with Maneli. Ho, of course, would have been pleased to be able to settle the question in a diplomatic way. There was no follow-up, but this initial negotiation was enough to worry U.S. officials, and it undoubtedly helped persuade Ambassador Henry Cabot Lodge, Jr., to approve the overthrow of Ngo Dinh Diem by the South Vietnamese army.[31]

Among the leaders of the VWP, one faction advocated and was preparing for war in the South; it was led by Secretary General Le Duan and supported by Secretary of the Organization Department Le Duc Tho, as well as by General Nguyen Chi Thanh, Director of the Political Department of the PAVN. Ho Chi Minh expressed his objections to plunging his nation back into war; he dreaded massive intervention by the United States and its direct and collateral effects on the people. But Le Duan, the "eye of Hanoi," who had been in charge of the war in the South against the French as the party's representative to the Administrative Resistance Committee of Nam Bo, said to him, "Do not fear, Uncle, I have anticipated and taken care of everything." Indeed, two years after Geneva, Le Duan had not yet left his post in the Mekong delta and did not land at the airfield of Gia Lam (Hanoi) until 6 June 1957, after a brief stay in Phnom Penh and then Canton.[32]

In 1958, Le Duan made a brief secret mission to the South to assess the situation, after which he wrote a report entitled *The Path to Revolution in the South*. According to Duan, they needed to send help to their comrades in the South, who were being hunted and killed by Diem's police and armed forces. On 15 May 1959, General Vo Bam was assigned to lead "Group 559," the Politburo's mission to construct an access road to the South for sending troops and supplies. This was the birth of the Ho Chi Minh Trail; a maritime equivalent was built that same year by "Group 759," opening a sea channel for logistical communication between the North and South.[33] The following year, militants and combatants from the South, who had been regrouped in the North in accordance with the Geneva Accords, took the trail to rejoin revolutionary forces who had remained. Later on, when the United States began its massive intervention, units of the PAVN headed south along the trail.

The Geneva Accords had specified that French troops and those of Bao Dai would leave the area north of the seventeenth parallel, while those of the Viet Minh would evacuate the South. However, a certain number of Viet Minh remained in the South. Some rallied to Diem's government (some of them "moles" who were very effective at striking at the heart of the enemy fortress);[34] others only wanted to return to civilian life and live in peace. Still others had received the order to keep a low profile and wait for the "right moment" ("sleepers," as they are known in the secret service). Workshops and caches of weapons and munitions were also created in preparation for an eventual "D day."

In 1960, hostilities began when armed groups successfully attacked several important military, administrative, and economic targets. On 20 December, the VWP officially established the National Front for the Liberation of South Vietnam (NLF), just as nineteen years earlier, Ho Chi Minh had founded the League for the Independence of Vietnam (Viet Minh). (See Map 4.) The guerrilla war spread and kept the republican army in check. In 1964, the "Viet Cong" were victorious at Binh Gia, northeast of Saigon, with the result that the U.S. government was forced to adopt direct intervention instead of limiting itself to sending military advisors

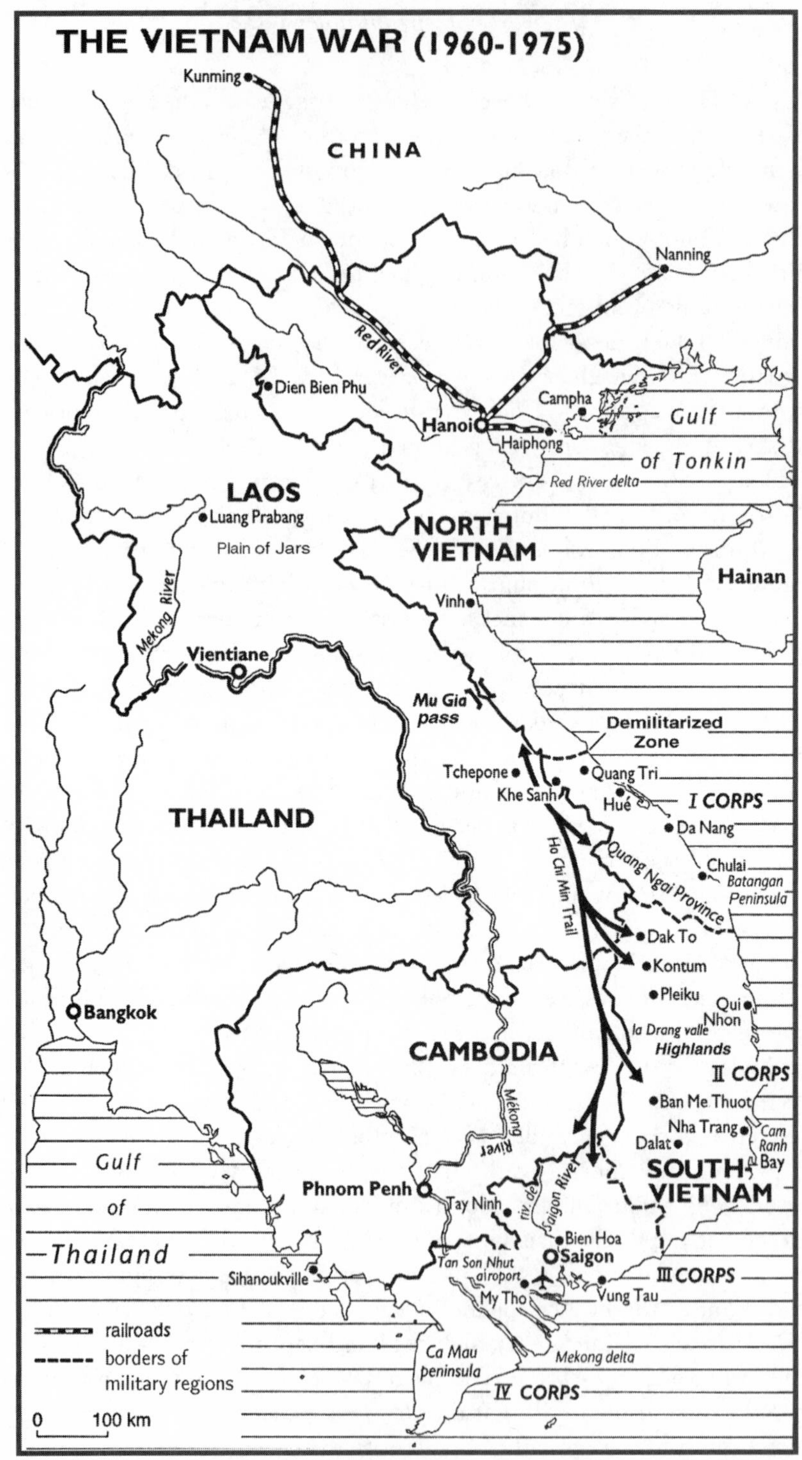

Map 4. The Vietnam War (1960–1975)

and special forces (the Green Berets). The incident at the Gulf of Tonkin, which pitted two U.S. destroyers against the North Vietnamese fleet, was undoubtedly a provocation or a test by the U.S. Navy (let us just say that the maneuver was rather ambiguous). It provided a pretext for massive and direct U.S. engagement by land, sea, and air, which is precisely what Ho Chi Minh had feared. The Americans had taken matters into their own hands, a decision that ended up demoralizing the South Vietnamese army. It also fed Communist propaganda, which called for the liberation of South Vietnam from the yoke of "American imperialism and its South Vietnamese lackeys."[35]

This war, like the one before it, spilled over into neighboring Cambodia and Laos, whose leaders (Norodom Sihanouk and Souvanna Phouma) tried in vain to practice neutrality. Consequently, what Americans call "the Vietnam War" was, in fact, a second Indochina war. North Vietnam conceived of one single theater of operations, encompassing the two Vietnams as well as the neighboring territories, and pulled to their side the Lao and Khmer pro-communist circles.[36]

When U.S. leaders realized that their strategy had failed, they went back to what they called the "Vietnamization" of the war: While continuing to aid South Vietnam, they negotiated with the North in 1968 and then pulled their troops out, following the Paris Accords of January 1973. But the Vietnamese civil war lasted until the fall of the republic in April 1975, while in that same year the Cambodian republic fell (under General Lon Nol, who had toppled Sihanouk in 1970), as well as the Laotian monarchy.

Ho Chi Minh had undoubtedly dreamt of a "red Indochina," echoing the glory days of the Comintern (the Union of Soviet Socialist Republics of Indochina?), but he died in September 1969 and so never saw it realized. He never saw his country unified and independent, but at least he was spared the last ruptures of the socialist camp in Asia, which saw Vietnam at war with the "Khmer Rouge" and with the PRC. In the end, the crowning moment of the communist project in Indochina was short-lived.

Most analysts conclude that it was during this period that Ho Chi Minh and his confidence man, General Vo Nguyen Giap, were pushed to the sidelines. The Vietnamese had expected Giap to be appointed head of the VWP, replacing Ho, who had served in the interim following the dismissal of Truong Chinh in 1956. However, as mentioned previously, Giap was criticized for never having been imprisoned by the French and especially for having studied at French schools and universities. Furthermore, he was suspected of being in league with the Soviets; he had even been nicknamed "the Soviet." In the late 1950s, to be Soviet or pro-Soviet fell under the category of neo-revisionism, that is, renouncing the revolution and taking a reformist position, hence betraying Leninism.

In 1960, the Third Congress of the VWP officially named Le Duan as First Secretary of the Party (like the Soviets, the Vietnamese had done away with the title Secretary General). Le Duan and Le Duc Tho, Chairman of the Organization Department, worked in tandem to monopolize decision-making power even beyond Ho's death. General Nguyen Chi Thanh, who held a key post as Commander of the Political Department of the PAVN, equaled Giap in rank and joined the party's Politburo. In a real sense, this troika was in control of Vietnamese policy and imposed their plans for an all-out war in the South by attacking U.S. troops head-on (in contrast to Ho, according to Maneli, who did not want to attack American troops directly at the outbreak of hostilities in the South.) From then on, the leading trio, and with it most of the Central Committee, decided that Ho Chi Minh would play only a diplomatic and symbolic role.

A COMMUNIST TORN BY CONFLICT

From 1956 onward, the "great socialist family" that Ho had so ardently praised entered a difficult period wherein "intrafamily" relationships were stretched to the breaking point. Relations between the CPSU and the CCP unleashed a conflict that permeated the socialist camp and led to a schism. Communist nations and parties around the world were forced to choose sides.

It all began with a disagreement over the final assessment of the Stalin dictatorship and of communism's global strategy that turned into a serious rupture. The Soviets, under the leadership of Nikita Khrushchev, adopted a de-Stalinization program in domestic policy and peaceful coexistence in their foreign policy. Mao, on the other hand, was instituting radical changes in China, such as the Great Leap Forward (1957–58), the People's Communes (from 1958), and the Cultural Revolution (1965–69). In foreign affairs, he supported revolutionary movements around the world and held to a policy of international tension, advocating an "uninterrupted revolution" (that some likened to, or even confused with, Trotsky's "permanent revolution"). Mao thus turned his back on the peaceful coexistence that Zhou Enlai had advocated in the name of the PRC during the Bandung Conference of 1955.[37] The Chinese accused the Soviets of "revisionism," while the Soviets denounced the "leftism" and "adventurism" of the Chinese, which were soon exacerbated by Mao's murderous utopia ("peasant messianism") – in short, the "infantile diseases of communism."

After four years of arguments and attacks, the Soviet Union broke off relations with the PRC and suspended all programs of economic, scientific, and technical aid (1960). The disagreement between the two parties had become a conflict between nations. The old historical dispute concerning their northern borders resurfaced, and the Soviets and Chinese ended up in battle on the Ussuri River and in Xinjiang province. The stakes, though not explicit, were extremely high: The leadership of the communist world would go to the ultimate leader of the socialist camp.[38]

Unfortunately for North Vietnam, this internecine war progressed alongside their war of reunification, and as the U.S. intervention escalated, so did the Vietnamese Communists' urgent need for help from their "brother nations." Ho Chi Minh's golden rule for leading the revolution and revolutionary war had always been unity – of the nation, of the Communist Party, of all Communist Parties – in order to sustain the unity of the socialist camp. And so the North Vietnamese soon called upon their "brothers" for critical support: Despite their relative success in reconstructing the country, they were still in dire need of food due to a soaring, unchecked growth in population.[39] The USSR, the PRC, the German Democratic Republic, and Czechoslovakia responded, becoming the main contributors to the modern industrialization of North Vietnam. From 1955 to 1960, hundreds of Soviet and Chinese experts (among others) worked to construct eighty electrical power stations, machine-tool works, and steel factories and to restore the mining industry with the help of extensive material aid (factories, primary materials, hydrocarbon). In conjunction with this activity, thousands of Vietnamese received professional training in China and other countries of the Eastern Bloc.[40]

Obtaining support from their brother nations in order to further the struggle against the South Vietnamese government and its powerful American master became a very delicate affair. The antagonism of the Sino-Soviet conflict was exacerbated by the reforms of Khrushchev – who was dismissed in 1964 – that were being contested in the USSR, and by the fact that Mao, the "Great Helmsman," was sailing the Chinese vessel into a storm that would not abate until 1976.

Ho Chi Minh took up his pilgrim's staff once again to play the conciliator in the meetings and congresses of the communist world, but also to obtain much-needed aid from his Chinese and Soviet comrades. Through it all, he maintained an equal balance between China and the USSR, and managed to hold this position until his death in 1969. In fact, it was only after his death that North Vietnam chose to align itself with the Soviets. During the Third Party Congress of the VWP in Hanoi in September 1960, Ho immediately asked the Soviet and Chinese delegations, in very strong words, to refrain from attacking each other during the congress. He greeted the delegations of his "brother parties," then began his speech with an ecumenical word:

> You have come from distant countries but we make up one family, proletariats from the four cardinal points, we are all brothers.... We must fill ourselves with Marxism-Leninism and... preserve the solidarity within the party, between all Communist Parties and all nations of this great Socialist family.[41]

Roughly two months later, during a conference in Moscow for eighty-one Communist Parties, the Chinese Liu Shaoqi left the room in anger, but Ho Chi Minh brought him back and pressed Khrushchev to be more conciliatory by integrating the Chinese point of view (denunciation of U.S. imperialism as well as the revisionist danger for global communism) in his final declaration. Khrushchev wrote in his *Memoirs* that Ho told him, "For us, things are twice as difficult. Do not forget, China is our neighbor."[42] Was Ho's position simply based on circumstance and proximity? It is quite possible that Ho leaned toward the Soviet policy of peaceful coexistence and a transition to socialism along multiple paths, not just through armed struggle (just as Khrushchev did not rule out armed struggle as a way to secure the triumph of socialism in any given country; it all depended on place and circumstances). According to Nguyen Van Tran, Ho began to suspect Mao "of observing the battle between two tigers from high on his mountaintop" (meaning the United States and the USSR), and he added that "Mister Ho is faithful to the Soviet Union and he agrees with its strategy of peace, but he does not agree with his own party and this is tormenting him."[43]

According to Liu Shaoqi, the Chinese were convinced that Ho had other reasons for not wanting to get involved in their quarrel with the Soviet Union, beyond tactics and ideological agreement.[44] On 25 February 1963, during a meeting of the Central Committee of the PRC, Liu severely criticized the Vietnamese party, and notably Ho Chi Minh:

> Ho Chi Minh has always been a rightist. When we implemented land reform, he resisted. He did not want to become the chairman of the VWP and preferred to stay outside the party and become a nonpartisan leader. Later, when the news went to Moscow, Stalin gave him a harsh lecture. It was only then

> that he decided to implement land reform. After the war with the French had ended, he could not decide whether to build a capitalist or a socialist republic. *It was we who decided for him.*[45]

The Sino-Soviet dispute engendered fierce debates among Vietnamese leaders and within the VWP regarding the correct attitude to adopt. The controversy produced a rift that turned the Vietnamese Communists against one another, especially in the higher echelons of the party. Until the Soviets sent military support in 1965, following a visit to Hanoi by Prime Minister Alexei Kosygin and the general staff of the Soviet armed forces, China had seemed like the only ally they could count on.

Mao, for his part, needed to maintain tension within the Chinese masses in order to see his utopian projects through to the end, and he had designated American imperialism as Public Enemy Number 1. The political and military support given to North Vietnam was, thus, intermingled with events within China itself, and the leadership of the VWP took up the combat against "neo-revisionism or modern revisionism." They made their position known openly in December 1963 during the eleventh plenary session when the Central Committee irrevocably condemned "modern revisionism" – without, however, referring to Khrushchev or even to the USSR.[46] This was an added affliction for Ho, who refused to have Vietnam dragged into the ideological polemic. According to Vu Thu Hien, Ho said, "How will we appear to weaker nations who depend on us if we criticize socialism? If dissension reigns among us, who will listen to us?"[47]

Ho Chi Minh was involved in the ninth plenum, and even presided over it. The historian Ralph Smith believes that he was ambiguous on this subject, and some think that he lacked courage. Vu Thu Hien, son of Vu Dinh Huynh, wrote that General Le Liem (political commissioner during the battle of Dien Bien Phu) went before the tribunal to defend their alliance with the Soviet Union and to contest the anti-Sovietism of the "pro-Chinese." He had spoken with Ho beforehand and Ho supposedly encouraged him, assuring him of his support. But Ho left the room to smoke a cigarette in the hallway during the antirevisionist discussions, and after Le Liem's talk he remained silent and turned his head. Vo Nguyen Giap, who had his head down during the speech, said nothing. Le Liem did not understand the behavior of "the grandfather."[48] Ho did not vote on the final resolution, claiming as an excuse that he was presiding over the meeting.

A dozen members of the Central Committee, who either did not vote on the resolution or who were suspected of being pro-Soviet, were arrested in 1967 for "antiparty activities": Vu Dinh Huynh and his son, Hoang Minh Chinh, and other generals and former ministers were incarcerated for several years (many years, in the case of Hoang Minh Chinh) without a ruling. They were eventually liberated with neither explanation nor rehabilitation.[49] The only one to escape arrest, though he was undoubtedly the main target, was Vo Nguyen Giap; but from then on, he was kept at a distance from important decisions, and his enemies spread the "filthy" rumor that he was the adopted son of Louis Marty, the chief of the French Sûreté.[50]

Ho Chi Minh became even more troubled and unhappy when he noticed that, from 1966 onward, the leaders in the "first circle" with whom he shared his evening meals had lost all feelings of conviviality; they looked at one another as if they were strangers, and nobody dared openly express his thoughts anymore. Unity, "the great union," was just a façade, an expression empty of meaning.

Ho's last trip to Moscow was in 1961, but he repeatedly said that a man must never forget the stream where he slaked his thirst, and his was Lenin and Moscow. Then, as the pendulum swung more and more toward the Soviet Union, Ho went to China nearly every year to celebrate his birthday and to undergo treatment by Chinese doctors, who used a blend of modern medicine and so-called traditional remedies. He usually went to Guangxi province, probably because it was close to Vietnam, but in May–June 1967 he went to Guangdong for treatment, and in March–April 1968 to Beijing while Wei Guoqing was harshly suppressing the Red Guards to end the chaos of the Cultural Revolution in Guangxi.

Were these trips just his way of compensating for the tightening of relations with the USSR? Or did he still feel a connection with China, given the emotional attachments and loyal bonds of friendship that he had forged there in the past? Two years before his death, he asked the Vietnamese Consul General in Canton to look up his wife Tang Tuyet Minh, but was told that they had found no trace of her. (We will see later why the answer came back negative.)

Ho probably did not have good memories of his meetings with Mao. He would certainly have remembered the discussion they had in November 1960 about the military and revolutionary situation in Vietnam and Laos. Mao applauded the brutality of counterrevolutionaries inasmuch as the Chinese revolution had benefited from the massacres carried out by Chiang Kai-shek. Ho reacted by saying that killing was not moral, and so justifying it was equally immoral. Mao responded, "He kills, I kill, it is not a question of morality." Liu Shaoqi went even further, saying that morality was not relevant when dealing with capitalist counterrevolutionaries. He added that moralists did not believe in the class struggle and so were consequently anti-Marxist. He asked, "Do you believe in morality? How can you say that Eisenhower is a rational being and that morality can safeguard peace? You should know that Eisenhower's reasoning is different from ours."[51]

In May or June 1965, Ho met Mao for the last time, but in Changsha, since in 1966 the violence of the Cultural Revolution would sweep through China, especially Beijing. This last meeting must have left a bad impression because Ho was kept waiting for several days before obtaining an audience with Mao. One of his companions, Tran Huy Lieu, alluded to the protocol of the Chinese imperial court and said, "I am a nationalist like our President Ho and I shit on the celestial Court."[52] Memories of the historical suzerain–vassal relationship between the two countries had obviously not been forgotten.

In the end, Ho Chi Minh's refusal to openly take sides in the battle paid off – North Vietnam got support from both China and the Soviet Union. From what we know, both countries were simultaneously counting on reaping the benefits of their generosity. Zhou Enlai, for example, criticized Ho for placing Chinese and Soviet aid on the same footing, and Deng Xiaoping ordered the Vietnamese not to speak of them at the same time. The Vietnamese eventually leaned more toward the Soviets, partly due to China's internal turmoil (1966–70), and even joined the ranks of the Committee of Mutual Economic Aid (COMECON) in 1978, forging a privileged alliance with the USSR until its demise in 1991. Then in 1979, Deng Xiaoping, who had been the true ruler of the PRC since 1977, decided to attack his neighbor as "punishment."

IN 1965, A CRUCIAL YEAR, THE CHINESE CREATED A "VIETNAMESE Assistance Group" led by Luo Ruiqing (chief of the General Staff and considered a "professional," he was dismissed that same year). A "Group in Charge of Support for Vietnam" was also formed by representatives of the ministries. This time, however, the Chinese did not intervene or participate directly in Vietnamese decisions, as they had during the Franco–Viet Minh conflict. The Chinese provided logistical support and antiaircraft defense in the North as far as the twenty-first parallel, allowing the Vietnamese to use their own troops to fight in the South. Chinese land forces would intervene only if the United States invaded the North. From

1965 to 1969, 80,000 Chinese soldiers from the Army Corps of Engineers (working on airfields, bridges, roads, and telecommunications) and 15,000 artillery soldiers, forming two antiaircraft divisions, encamped in North Vietnam to work in rotating numbers. These 95,000 men (some sources say 180,000) built, among other things, a giant underground airfield at Yen Bay. Then, from 1968 to 1970, the Chinese gradually pulled their troops out of North Vietnam.[53]

After the dismissal of Khrushchev, Soviet aid continued, following Prime Minister Kosygin's visit to Hanoi in February 1965.[54] The new Soviet leaders did not want the Chinese to be the sole providers of aid to Vietnam, and agreed to supply sophisticated weapons, like ground-to-air missiles with their gunners. They also furnished combat aircraft and thousands of tons of transport supplies, munitions, and medicines, which were shipped from the USSR, Poland, Czechoslovakia, and the Democratic Republic of Germany.

The aid sent from socialist countries around the world was considerable, despite Chinese attempts to thwart it. For example, from 1965 to 1969, Soviet convoys were often blocked by the Chinese government, the Red Guards, or sometimes the provincial authorities, who refused to open their ports to Soviet ships. The Chinese alleged that the Soviets were planning to use Vietnam as a base for surrounding China. As a result, some of the supplies and personnel had to be brought to Vietnam by sea from Vladivostok.

From 1969 to 1972, following negotiations between China and the USSR regarding their northern border, the Chinese were more conciliatory and facilitated the transit and even the transport of Soviet aid. They concurrently reduced their own shipments to the Vietnamese, and reproached them for secretly preferring the Soviets and for holding negotiations with the United States. On 17 October 1968, Zhou Enlai sent a brief message to Le Duc Tho, stating, "In a short time, you have accepted the compromising and capitulationist propositions of the Soviet revisionists; therefore our two parties and two governments have nothing more to say to each other."[55]

This obstacle must have given the Vietnamese pause, especially Ho Chi Minh, who advocated socialist solidarity without restriction or reserve. After Ho died on 2 September 1969, the events of the previous ten years led some of his colleagues, such as Viet Phuong, to question themselves. Phuong had joined the ranks of the revolution in 1945 and then took part in the Resistance; upon his return to Hanoi he became the personal secretary of Prime Minister Pham Van Dong. In January 1970, Viet Phuong wrote a collection of poetry entitled *Cua mo* (Open door), which questions the "delirious enthusiasm based on illusions and lies."[56] In the poems, he makes fun of partisan behavior:

> Just saying "he's a comrade" means someone cannot be wicked
> . . . .
> Moscow was more beautiful than any paradise
> We had decided that Soviet watches were better than Swiss ones
> It was our faith, our desire, and our pride
> We imagined that the moon in China was rounder than the one in America
> . . . .
> Maybe now after a quarter of a century we finally know
> What it means to love, what it means to kill

In another poem, he evokes a Communist Party like the one Ho described in 1945, as a gathering of people descended from common ancestors, not a partisan party or a party of class:

> The Party is Hung Vuong, Nguyen Trai, Quang Trung[57] crossed with Lenin
> The result was Uncle Ho
> . . . .
> We make the Party, we do not follow it
> We feed the Party with our hearts like coal feeds the fire
> The Party is not our master but it teaches us how to be masters
> . . . .
> When the Party is extinguished and exists no more
> It will leave us only a life of radiance and love[58]

The author of these poems is not only a great admirer of Ho Chi Minh; he reiterates the direction and the drive of Ho's project: a close association of the national and social, where the latter is based on populism, rather than "class-ism."

FROM THE LEGEND TO THE MYTH

Knowing that Ho Chi Minh greatly enjoyed role playing, one could suspect him of having created his own legend; after all, he himself provided us with two autobiographical accounts of his journeys and exploits.

However, other reports confirm the legend, from the police informers in his entourage to the testimonies of those who came into contact with him – intimately or from a distance – throughout his lifetime. Both friends and adversaries (from Léo Poldès to General Valluy and Major Patti) painted a seductive portrait, even if sometimes tinged with the "beauty of the Devil," as when Ngo Dinh Diem called him "the man as pure as Lucifer" in his interview with the English novelist Graham Greene.[59]

Ho's fame as a young Annamite goes back to 1919 ("he who carried his solitary revolt through the streets of Paris"), and then grew in 1932 with the official announcement of his death due to chronic tuberculosis. He may not have been the sole author of the "Demands of the Annamite People," but he alone had the audacity to present the message to Colonel Edward House, foreign affairs advisor to U.S. President Woodrow Wilson. He repeated the challenge by going into the office of Albert Sarraut, Minister of the Colonies, to demand the restoration of Vietnam's independence. He is reminiscent of Mahatma Gandhi, who had the same calm audacity to tell the Simon Commission (investigating the status of India from 1927 to 1930): "Quit India!"

In 1931, when a court from the Protectorate of Annam condemned him to death, Ho only grew in stature and was illuminated by a halo of prestige. This is to be expected when a man stands up to the authorities and then evades capture, even a violent criminal, but in this case, it was the hero in the struggle for national liberation. The incredible end to his problems with the British authorities in Hong Kong and Singapore landed him on the front pages of all the newspapers, and in the end he was transfigured by the news of his death. According to the words of the French poet Victor Hugo:

> Those who piously died for their country
> Have only their coffins, let the crowd come and pray.[60]

A leaflet was printed by Communist Party committees and the Indochinese Red Aid in France revealing that Nguyen Ai Quoc had been elevated to martyr for the national cause: "Comrade Nguyen Ai Quoc, the brilliant founder of the Indochinese Communist Party, mistreated by the British colonialists in collusion with the French imperialists, died in prison in Hong Kong, last 26 July. . . . Nguyen Ai Quoc's life was exemplary."[61] As a result, when he reappeared like a deus ex machina in Ba Dinh Square on 2 September 1945 before a crowd of tens of thousands of people to proclaim the birth of the Democratic Republic of Vietnam, one can imagine the whispers running through the crowd: "Who is it? Who is that man?" The effect of surprise – they had pronounced him dead and yet there he was, like Lazarus, resurrected – certainly made him larger in the eyes of his compatriots.

Not yet the "Father of the Nation" or the "Great Hero," he was that providential man whom every country awaits and summons mightily in a crisis. Vietnam was at such a point, as the Japanese stripped the French of their power but then surrendered to the Allies, as the Chinese moved into the North while the British and French took the South, and as both the countryside and the cities were rocked by turmoil. The future was anything but certain. In 1951, the military leader of the resistance in the South, Nguyen Binh, was summoned to Hanoi and had to pass through Cambodia. On his way he met an old Vietnamese man who asked him the name of the new emperor of Vietnam. "He is not an emperor," Binh specified." "Yes he is," said the man, "Vietnam always needed an emperor at its head." The response clearly reveals what the people expected: to be governed.

During the course of the war, the resistance movement was in need of a collective imagination, of communal myths that would strengthen cohesion, and so "heroes" (*Anh hung*) were created: "Hero of the Armed Forces" and "Hero of Work" were the two main types in Vietnam.[62] Ho continually stressed the importance of educating cadres in order to mobilize the population, but also to legitimize the power of the new government; these "new heroes" were also meant to set an example, as well as to form a link between the government and the people of the nation.

The heroes were not just a utilitarian invention; the Soviet model came naturally, so to speak, to those nations that became part of the socialist world, as happened with neighboring China as well. But Ho Chi Minh was more than a hero, or rather, he did not belong in the category of these "new heroes"; he soon became a mythical figure, the object of a veritable cult.[63] By 1945, elements of the myth of Ho Chi Minh were in place: the idealized portrait of the man, the legendary tale of his past, and the use of this representation to mobilize the people and spur them to action. This was achieved via all possible means, from graphic arts to statuary, cinema, theater, poetry, songs, nursery rhymes, and education in schools. It soon became a habit to celebrate his birthday by offering gifts and organizing festivities. In 1950, when the National Assembly presented its birthday wishes, the Reverend Father Pham Ba Truc offered this Catholic prayer to "Our God Ho Chi Minh":

> *Oremus pro domino nostro Ho Chi Minh*
> *Dominus conservet eum et*
> *Vivificet eum et Beatam*
> *Faciat eum in terra et*
> *Non tiodat eum un animan*
> *Inimicorum ejus!*[64]

The homage rendered to Ho Chi Minh while he was alive foreshadowed the cult that grew after his death, culminating in the construction of the mausoleum in Ba Dinh Square, a mecca of national reverence where pilgrims wait in line to circle the embalmed body of the "Father of the Nation."

A cult of personality is most often the work of the entourage (or should we say the court?) but can it spread without the consent or even the encouragement of the subject? The affair of Ho Chi Minh's mausoleum illustrates this problem, for we know for certain that Ho wanted neither the mausoleum nor the viewing of his body. He wanted to be cremated and his ashes put into urns, which would then be placed at the four corners of the country inside small chapels where people could go and pay their respects. (He was undoubtedly thinking of the funerary stele of Nguyen Trai or that of Confucius, where he himself had made a reverent visit.) We also know that these last wishes were expressed in his "Testament" but that they were censored from the version released to the public.[65] In other words, the Politburo used Ho Chi Minh's body to accomplish its own future plans: They would create a pilgrimage site to attract those from the South once the reunification of Vietnam was complete.

The falsification of the Testament and what became of Ho post mortem shed light on those responsible for his cult, on the function of the cult, and thus on the real status of Ho Chi Minh at the heart of the regime. On several occasions, Ho had protested against the national celebration of his birthday, and once asked why they did not celebrate the birth of the republic instead. Another time he said that one could legitimately honor the birth of Karl Marx or Lenin but not his, since he was only their disciple and should not be put on an equal footing with them. In the last years of his life, he spent his birthdays in China, claiming that he needed to seek medical treatment or therapy there (which was true). Could it also be true that he was trying to escape the festivities in his own country?

It is possible, however, that Ho had other reasons for going to China. According to a Chinese source, while Ho was in Guangdong province in 1965, he asked his friends there to find him a beautiful young Chinese girl to keep him company in Hanoi. Why would he choose a Chinese girl when there were so many beautiful girls in Vietnam? Ho answered, "Because in Hanoi everybody calls me Uncle Ho." Humor? Yes, though with an undercurrent of sadness.

If we accept the view that Ho Chi Minh was "pushed to the sidelines" in 1963, or maybe even as early as 1960, we see that the cult purposefully had a double function, or was at least ambivalent: It gave the Vietnamese a unifying figure to rally around, but it also served to isolate the man himself. The image of an exceptional being raised on a pedestal implies his separation from others.

In this regard, it is interesting to consider the fate of his wife, Tang Tuyet Minh, and the other women in his life. After circumstances had forced Nguyen Ai Quoc and Tang Tuyet Minh to separate in 1927 to flee repression, his young wife worked as a midwife, even after the Communist Chinese victory of 1949–50. When she learned that her husband had become president of the DRV, she tried in vain to renew ties with him. She wrote letters to him and to the ambassador of the DRV in Beijing. None of the letters made it to Ho, or at least Minh never got a response from him. One day she received a visit from envoys of the CCP, who asked her to stop trying to contact the man she had married in Canton thirty years earlier and to cease her correspondence. In return, the CCP would see to all of her needs. When Ho died, Tang Tuyet Minh erected an altar with his portrait and lit candles (she was a Christian, most probably Catholic). She died much later, in November 1991.[66] In the end, reasons of state had prevailed over emotion.

One woman of Tay origin, Do Thi Lac, began living with Ho in the Highlands in 1944 and gave birth to a son in 1956. She moved to Hanoi in 1954 and was put up in town, but made occasional visits to the palace. She wanted Ho to make their union official, but he responded that he would need the Politburo's authorization, which he knew he would not get. She died in 1957 in a traffic accident.[67] It was also in 1954 that a young and pretty cadre from Thanh Hoa was chosen to take care of "the psycho-physiological equilibrium and the good health of Uncle Ho." The young woman, Nguyen Thi Phuong Mai, agreed on condition of official marriage, which was refused because "it would not be of any political advantage for Uncle Ho."[68] The exaltation of the myth and the celebration of his grandeur put Ho under constraints that must have cost him dearly, and which, in the end, neutralized him, as the historian William Duiker has accurately pointed out.

At his death, Ho Chi Minh became the object of a fervent cult that was almost religious in nature, befitting a Communist leader from the Soviet circle. One immediately thinks of the cults surrounding Lenin, Stalin, Mao Zedong, and Kim Il Sung. This should not surprise anyone who sees communism as a secular religion or admits that the fertile soil of the peasant mentality in these countries favors this type of devotion.[69] However, the Vietnamese have celebrated a cult of national heroes for centuries, as well as the cult of ancestors, and so as "Father of the Nation" Ho fit into both categories. Today one finds the Ho Chi Minh cult in chapels devoted to him alone, or in conjunction with village tutelary spirits, or sometimes even with the Supreme Being of the Cao Daists (yet he has never appeared at a séance...). This fits in well with the widespread syncretism in Vietnam, where beliefs and cults thrive in combination.

EPILOGUE

A Man at the Interface between Two Worlds

Most communist regimes disappeared from the international scene at the end of the twentieth century, the USSR in the lead. But the Socialist Republic of Vietnam is still on its feet. Does it owe its survival to its founding father?

Ho Chi Minh's journey is inextricably linked with the parallel conflicts of the twentieth century: colonized nations against imperialist states, and the nations espousing Soviet socialism against those defending capitalism and liberalism. Within the century's great opposition, these two conflicts intersected or became superimposed on each other to the point where capitalism was identified with imperialism and socialism with anti-imperialism.

This identification, which is by no means an absolute, raises a question: Was Ho Chi Minh a true patriot entirely devoted to the independence of his country and the liberation of his people? Or was he the instrument of imperialist expansion in the guise of the universal emancipation of enslaved peoples? In the beginning, the young Ho was certainly driven by the idea of restoring independence to his nation, which had a thousand-year history and reached its territorial and political apogee in the mid–nineteenth century. His only question was, "How?"

The European conquests of the nineteenth century upset the world order of the scholar-officials within the Chinese cultural sphere, namely, the nations of China, Korea, and Vietnam. The Japanese quickly found a way out of the dilemma, but only because they were not fully subjected to Chinese influence. The other three countries, however, did not know how to respond to the challenge of modernity that imperialism cast their way.

Ho spent his youth under a colonial regime and witnessed the failure of local insurrections, which taught him that one must seek answers from the very nations that had subjugated a vast part of the globe. He understood the paradox of French colonialism, a system that enslaved others and yet still celebrated its humanist values, and he first tried to scale the steep face of imperialism from the European side. But he quickly ran into nearly insurmountable obstacles in the way of reform: the strength of the interests invested in colonialism, the national and international stakes for the countries involved, and the deeply rooted racist mentality that prevailed in the nineteenth century.

In 1917, the Bolshevik Revolution set ablaze the empire of the tsars and trumpeted its goal to liberate all peoples subjected to colonial domination. To Nguyen Ai Quoc, this seemed like the answer to his "How?" Later, in 1945, he opened up to the American Lieutenant Charles Fenn:

> First, you must understand that to gain independence from a great power like France is a formidable task that cannot be achieved without some outside help, not necessarily in things like arms, but in the nature of advice and contacts. One doesn't in fact gain independence by throwing bombs and such. That was the mistake the early revolutionaries all too often made. One must gain it through organization, propaganda, training and discipline. One also needs . . . a set of beliefs, a gospel, a practical analysis, you might even say a bible. Marxism-Leninism gave me that framework.[1]

This would lead one to believe that Ho's choice was pragmatic and his actions utilitarian.

If one looks closer and attentively reads his letters and articles from the 1920s, however, one sees not only that Nguyen Ai Quoc was won over by Marxist ideology but also that he discerned affinities between his Asian philosophical background and the new ideas he found in Europe. As we have seen, he never failed to underline the similarities between Confucian and European ideas, that all men are brothers across the "four oceans" and that one must ensure social order through an equitable division of the means of production (land, in this case). At the same time, he understood that it was pointless, if not impossible, to transpose into his country the principles of government based on a European model, especially since he had witnessed the economic crises and political malfunctions that shook Europe in the 1920s and 1930s. He saw with his own eyes the pauperization of the Germans in 1923, the victory of fascism in Italy, the rise of national socialism in Germany, and the Great Depression of 1929. All of these crucial events underlined the faults, or perhaps even the failure, of liberal and parliamentary democracy.

Ho Chi Minh readily adopted the posture of pedagogue, professor of morality, and if necessary even arbitrator. He described himself thus, in the third person: "The first time I met him, he struck me as being like a country schoolmaster."[2] Some fifteen years later, the British writer Graham Greene described him in these terms: "I was reminded of a Mister Chips, wise, kind, just (if one could accept the school rules as just), prepared to inflict sharp punishment without undue remorse."[3] This choice of persona grew partly out of his Confucian upbringing, which had a strong impact on him, but also stemmed from his observations of human behavior, including within the communist world. Ho acquired the conviction early on that proclaiming revolutionary principles and changing a political regime do not automatically make a man virtuous.

He liked to say, "To bring about socialism you need socialists." Living as a socialist involved working with others on a common project and disregarding oneself, not reciting Marx by heart and without hesitation. The American journalist Harold Isaacs asked him if he thought that one-party rule was a good thing. Ho responded, "It is a good thing if the party is good, otherwise it is a bad thing."[4] The duality within everyone – an idea that Ho undoubtedly got from the Chinese sage Xunzi – led him to say, one year before his death, "Everyone has good and evil in his heart. We must live in such a way that the good part blossoms like a flower in springtime and the evil part gradually disappears. This is the attitude of the revolutionary."[5]

For Uncle Ho, hell is not "other people," as the French philosopher Jean-Paul Sartre said. Rather, he urged his compatriots to combat individualism, greed, waste, and bureaucracy, reminding them that "the enemy is within our own hearts." This almost seems to echo the beliefs of the Manichaeist religion of the Persians, but the idea is also present in Xunzi, one of the main Confucian thinkers. Xunzi believed that "nature is evil and [that] whatever is good in it was manufactured." His conception of the social order follows suit:

> Hsun-Tzu (Xunzi) ardently dreams of a society in which the rules of *li*, which are the rules which can in the best of worlds be internalized by education and moral suasion, will be the primary means for creating harmony and security. But he has no prejudice against the view that these must be strongly reinforced at all times by external penal rules and institutions which rely on physical coercion.... The good order can be inaugurated and maintained only by a vanguard elite. The ongoing quality of this vanguard elite – however this quality is conceived – remains crucial from beginning to end.... Hsun-Tzu, in spite of his emphasis on an externally imposed system, is thus passionately concerned with the education or self-education of those with a vocation to rule.[6]

There is an obvious kinship between Ho Chi Minh's ideas and Xunzi's, though Ho was also steeped in the perennial Sino-Vietnamese philosophy that blended Confucianism (in its plural form incorporating Confucius, Mencius, Xunzi, and Wang Yang Ming)[7] with Buddhism and Taoism. In sum, Ho retained his original education and then closely linked it with Leninist theory, which essentially defines the strategy and tactics of revolution and the taking of political power. It was Leninism that motivated the men who took the helm of the Communist Party and the DRV in the 1960s. According to Bui Tin, Le Duan said to him in private, "I am better than Uncle Ho. He opens his mouth and follows the code of Confucian morality, speaking of human dignity, loyalty, good conduct, wisdom, and faithfulness. But what is all that? Outdated moralism. As for me, I support the collective power of the workers."[8] Basically, it seems that Ho was following in the footsteps of the first Asian reformers, both Chinese and Japanese, who had extolled the association of "the Asian spirit with Western know-how."

There is a trace of melancholy in the quatrain that Ho composed in 1965 when he traveled to the hometown of the Kong clan (Confucius is the romanization of Kong Fu Zi), in Gufu, Shandong province:

> On 15 May I visited Gufu
> The old temple is still in the shade of an old pine tree
> [But] where is Confucius's authority now?
> Only a few rays of the setting sun light up the antique stele.[9]

The many years he spent abroad did not weaken his identity. The coldly rationalist and utilitarian political apprenticeship that the Comintern made him undergo did not supplant his early training, and it even seems secondary. In Ho's terms, the Comintern phase was "transitory," while the "permanent" one, his Vietnamese-ness, formed his original cultural base.

Today – it is now 2006 – what remains of the two doctrines that guided Ho Chi Minh throughout the twentieth century? In the Socialist Republic of Vietnam, which is now independent and united, the Communist Party still holds power, at least at the top. But Marxist-Leninist catechism has been replaced with "Ho Chi Minh thought," which itself is the fruit of a sort of interbreeding (a mixed marriage, so to speak). It affirms the primacy of personal virtues in the service of one's nation and the common good. In these postsocialist times, Vietnam is pursuing its path within the market economy, and its society is being restructured according to a monetary hierarchy, leading to a growing inequality of income and social status. Perhaps the Vietnamese could use the memory of Ho Chi Minh's struggle for independence and his ethic to inspire an alternative and compensatory ideal of equality and brotherhood.

One wonders, nevertheless, whether there is a place in Ho's politico-intellectual horizon for freedom. Must one admit, with Bui Tin, that "Ho had a limited capacity – perhaps even a deficiency – for developing democracy and legality and to understand that it was necessary"?[10] Ho did not envisage human freedom and happiness outside of a familial and national community, especially not one that would undermine the interests of that collective. And, of course, those interests are defined by the party of the state.

In the end, Ho Chi Minh remained faithful to the holistic conception of the relationship between individuals and society; still, this does not prevent an individual from keeping to himself or withdrawing from his social group. His behavior was determined by the urgency and constraints imposed upon him by various situations, for Ho Chi Minh was a man of situations – those of the colonized and those of the revolutionary. However, he fully adopted the Soviet Socialist model and never repudiated it, thereby confirming and reinforcing the limits imposed on freedoms and on what we exalt today under the name of "human rights."

Behind the prism of appearances through which Ho Chi Minh revealed himself to the world, we find the tragedy of idealists who engage in political action. He tried to combine his unifying and temporizing patriotism with a revolutionary doctrine that bred antagonism and violence. The last two won out in the end, and Ho, steeped in Confucian humanism, gave in to – or rather was crushed under the weight of – an implacable system that he had helped put in place through his indisputable charisma.

Timeline

Year	France	Russia/USSR	China	Vietnam
1860	Second Empire (Napoleon III)	Abolition of feudalism by Tsar Alexander II.	Second Opium War, opening the empire to foreigners.	Beginning of the French conquest and their hold on the Indochinese peninsula.
1870–1876	Prussian War, fall of the Second Empire, establishment of the Third Republic.			Continuation of the conquest.
1883–1885	Franco-Chinese War		China recognizes the French protectorate in Tonkin.	The protectorate in Tonkin is recognized by China.
1894–1895			Sino-Japanese War	
1898–1900			Imperial China is divided into Western spheres of influence. Boxer Rebellion. The "100 days" of the Chinese reformers.	Resistance against the French conquest is more sporadic but continues to have an impact.
1902–1908		Russo-Japanese War. Founding of the Bolshevik Party. Revolution of 1905.	Sun Yat-sen founds the Kuomintang (Nationalist Party).	Paul Doumer creates the Government-General of Indochina, sets up its services and financial system. Reformist movement in Vietnam.

1911–1912			Revolution topples the Qing empire and establishes a republic.	
1914–1918	France allied with England against Germany and the Austro-Hungarian Empire.			
1917–1918	The Americans enter the war, allied with the French. The Germans surrender.	Revolution breaks out in Russia: February and October 1917. The Bolsheviks take power, overthrow the monarchy, and set up the Soviet Republic. Founding of the Third International (Comintern).		
1920	Founding of the French Communist Party (FCP).		Founding of the Chinese Communist Party (CCP) in Shanghai.	
1924–1928		Stalin eliminates his opponents. Forced collectivization of the countryside. Widespread famine in the Ukraine. Launching of the first Five-Year Plan.	"Second Chinese Revolution" and death of Sun Yat-sen. The Nationalists break with the Communists and begin harsh crackdown.	Nguyen Ai Quoc founds the Revolutionary Youth League. Nguyen Thai Hoc founds the Vietnamese Nationalist Party (VNQDD).

(*continued*)

Year	France	Russia/USSR	China	Vietnam
1930				Founding of the Indochinese Communist Party (ICP). Yen Bay Mutiny led by the VNQDD. Uprisings in North Annam and Cochinchina led by the ICP.
1931–1935			Japan conquers Manchuria. Soviet Republic of Jiangxi and beginning of "The Long March."	
1936	Era of the Popular Front.	Beginning of the "great purges."		Legal activities of the ICP tolerated.
1937	Decline of the Popular Front.	Stalin's "great purges."	Japan invades China; incident in Xian sparks the birth of the united anti-Japanese front.	Large-scale strikes and repression.
1939	France and England declare war on Germany. The FCP is outlawed.	Stalin signs a nonaggression pact with Hitler.		The ICP is outlawed.
1940–1944	France occupied by Germany and governed by the Pétain government based in Vichy.	1941: The Germans invade the USSR.	Faced with anti-Japanese resistance, a pro-Japanese government is set up, presided over by Wang Ching Wei. 1941: Japan attacks the United States.	The Vichyist governor Decoux collaborates with the Japanese.

1945	Germany surrenders, then Japan.		The Chinese civil war resumes.	In April 1945, Japan grants independence to the states of Indochina. The ICP takes power in the guise of the Viet Minh and proclaims the birth of the Democratic Republic of Vietnam.
1945–1954	France wages war in Indochina, then pulls out in 1954, passing the baton to the Americans.	Stalin dies. Beginning of the "thaw," but the USSR is engaged in the Cold War against the United States and its allies.	Communist victory. Mao Zedong proclaims the People's Republic of China in 1949. Engagement in the Korean War against the United States	Chinese and Soviet send aid. The French stoke the "nationalist fire." Vietnam is divided into two parts.
From 1960	General de Gaulle ends the Algerian War, establishes and heads the Fifth Republic. He makes a speech in Phnom Penh in 1966 advocating the withdrawal of all foreign troops from Vietnam.	Progressive de-Stalinization. Policy of peaceful coexistence. Nikita Khrushchev dismissed in 1964. Soviet military aid to Vietnam begins in 1964.	Large-scale Chinese aid to Vietnam. War with India. Beginning of the Sino-Soviet conflict. Great Leap Forward, Peoples' Communes, the "Great Proletarian Cultural Revolution."	The civil war resumes. American intervention in the war, which lasts until 1975 after having spread throughout the entire Indochinese peninsula.
1969	De Gaulle steps down from the presidency.		The CCP is reconstituted in the Ninth Congress in 1969.	Death of Ho Chi Minh.

Chronology

1890

May 19: Birth of Nguyen Sinh Cung (who later takes the name Nguyen Tat Thanh) in the village of Hoang Tru, Nam Dan district, Nghe An province (North Annam); son of Nguyen Sinh Huy (Nguyen Sinh Sac), a scholar-official, and Hoang Thi Loan, a farm worker and weaver.

1908–1909

Thanh studies in Hué, the imperial capital. He interrupts his studies and travels to South Annam and Cochinchina.

1910–1911

Nguyen Tat Thanh works as a teacher's assistant at the private school Duc Thanh, in Phan Thiet (Central Vietnam).

1911

June: Thanh embarks on the steamship *Amiral Latouche-Tréville*. He spends time in Marseilles and Le Havre.

1912

Thanh works aboard a cargo ship of the Chargeurs Réunis company and sails to Africa.

1913

He visits the United States.

1914–1918

Thanh lives in London.

1919

Thanh moves to Paris and lives at 6 Villa des Gobelins (13th arrondissement) where he adopts the name Nguyen Ai Quoc and joins the French Socialist Party

(FSP). He writes for *L'Humanité* and *Le Populaire de Paris*. He presents his *Demands of the Annamite People* at the peace conference at Versailles.

1920

Quoc takes part in the Eighteenth Congress of the FSP in Tours and votes for membership to the Third International. He works for *L'Humanité* and *La Vie Ouvrière*.

1921

July 16: Quoc moves to 9 Impasse Compoint (20th arrondissement) and founds the Intercolonial Union, he also writes for the *Revue Communiste* (issues 14 and 15).

December: He attends the First Congress of the French Communist Party (FCP)/Section Française de l'International Communiste in Marseilles.

1922

He founds the journal *Le Paria*, mouthpiece of the Intercolonial Union. He writes a theatrical work, *The Bamboo Dragon*. He joins the FCP's Committee of Colonial Affairs as delegate from Indochina.

June 18: Léo Poldès puts on a production of *The Bamboo Dragon* at the festival for *L'Humanité* in Garches.

1923

March: Quoc moves to 3 Rue du Marché des Patriarches (5th arrondissement).

June 13: He leaves for Moscow and enters (perhaps) the University of the Toilers of the East (the Stalin School), while continuing his work at *L'Humanité*. In October he joins the Executive Bureau of the Crestintern (Peasants' International).

1924

June–August: Quoc attends the Fifth Congress of the International.

November: He joins Borodin and the Soviet mission in Canton (Guangzhou).

1925

June 21: Quoc organizes the Revolutionary Youth League (Thanh Nien) and publishes the weekly of the same name. He publishes *French Colonialism on Trial* in Paris. He marries Tang Tuyet Minh, a Chinese student and midwife.

1927

May: Quoc flees Canton to escape the Chinese Nationalists.

June: He goes to Moscow.

August: He spends time in the Crimea.

October: Publication of *The Revolutionary Path*.

December: Quoc attends the conference of the Anti-Imperialist League in Brussels.

1928–1929

January: Quoc travels to Moscow, Berlin, and Paris on a mission for the International. May or June: He travels through Switzerland into Italy and sets sail from Naples aboard a Japanese ship returning to Asia via Ceylon (now Sri Lanka).

July 1928–November 1929: He visits Thailand, mainly the Northeast, where Vietnamese settlements have been established.

December 23, 1929: He arrives in Hong Kong.

1930

February 3–7: Quoc unites the various communist splinter groups into a single Vietnamese communist party, which adopts the name "Indochinese" in October.

March–April: He travels to Thailand and Malaysia.

May: He goes to Singapore, then leaves for Hong Kong.

1931

June 6: Quoc is arrested by the British police in Hong Kong and incarcerated in Victoria Prison, after which he is hospitalized.

1932

Public announcement of the death of Nguyen Ai Quoc.

1933

January 22: The Hong Kong police put Quoc on the ship *An Huy* bound for Shanghai, but he disembarks in Amoy (Xiamen).

1934

February: Quoc arrives in Moscow via Shanghai and Vladivostok.

June 14: First Congress of the Indochinese Communist Party (ICP) in Macao, without the presence of Quoc.

1935–1938

Quoc attends the Seventh Congress of the International in Moscow.

He works as researcher at the Institute for National and Colonial Questions and teaches at the Stalin School.

1936

Period of the Popular Front in France. Members of the ICP intensify their legal activities, which they had begun in 1933.

1938–1941

Quoc is active in China within the Chinese Communist Party (CCP), then returns to Vietnam. He is spotted in Singapore in 1939.

1939: The ICP returns to secrecy.

1941

February 8: Quoc goes back to the border zone and establishes his base in Pac Bo (north Vietnam). He translates *The History of the Bolshevik Communist Party of the USSR* into Vietnamese, writes *Guerrilla Tactics* and *The Instruction of Military Cadres*. He publishes the journal *Viet Nam Doc Lap* (Independent Vietnam), which is distributed in the region of Cao Bang.

May 15–19: He convenes and presides over the Eighth Conference of the Central Committee of the ICP, marking the creation of the Viet Minh (Viet Nam Doc Lap Dong Minh Hoi) in Pac Bo.

August 1: Publication of the first issue of *Viet Nam Doc Lap*, the organ of the Viet Minh, with a poem by Nguyen Ai Quoc on the cover over the red flag and gold star.

Japanese troops move into Indochina following the accords between the Vichy government and Japan, marking the beginning of the Franco-Japanese cohabitation and collaboration.

1942

Nguyen Ai Quoc adopts the name Ho Chi Minh. He sets out for Chongqing.

August 17: He is arrested in China and imprisoned by the Chinese Nationalists in Guangxi from 29 August 1942 to 10 September 1943.

1944

March: A congress is held in Liuzhou to reorganize the Dong Minh Hoi (Vietnamese Revolutionary League) under the aegis of Zhang Fakui, and an accord is established between the ICP and the Vietnamese nationalists.

August 9: Ho returns to Vietnam.

October: Ho's *Letter to the Nation* appears, signed for the first time with the name Ho Chi Minh.

December: Creation of the Propaganda and Liberation Army of Vietnam.

1945

March 9: The Japanese bring down the French colonial regime.

March 20: Ho meets with Charles Fenn at the "Indochina Café" in Kunming.

March 29: Second meeting with Fenn and Frank Tan, after which Ho meets the American Claire Chennault, Commander of the "Flying Tigers" squadron.

June: The Viet Minh establishes the "Viet Bac Free Zone."

August 15: Japanese surrender.

August 13–15 (or 16–17): The Viet Minh Front holds a national congress at Tan Trao and forms a provisional government led by Ho Chi Minh.

August 26: Ho enters Hanoi.

August 29: Emperor Bao Dai abdicates and accepts Ho's offer to serve as political advisor.

September 2: Ho Chi Minh proclaims independence in Hanoi.

Chinese troops led by General Lu Han occupy North Vietnam.

September 25: French troops arrive in Saigon and begin their reconquest of Cochinchina and South Annam, marking the beginning of the First Indochina War.

November: Dissolution of the ICP.

1946

January 6: Elections for the Vietnamese National Assembly; the Viet Minh wins 97 percent of the vote. Ho draws up the constitution.

March 2: He forms a government of "Unity and Resistance."

March 6: Agreement signed in Hanoi between the French and the Vietnamese.

French troops arrive in Tonkin.

Departure of the Chinese troops who had been brought in to disarm the Japanese.

May 30: Ho Chi Minh becomes the honorary president of the Vietnamese scouting movement.

May 31: Ho flies to France.

June 12: He arrives in Biarritz.

June 22: Ho goes to Paris, in the midst of the Franco-Vietnamese negotiations at Fontainebleau. He does not take part in the talks but travels throughout France, mostly in Normandy.

September 14: Ho reaches an accommodation with Marius Moutet, signing a modus vivendi before returning to Vietnam. He stops in Lyon, Avignon, and then Marseilles where he visits his countrymen who had been mobilized during World War II and sent to France.

September 19: Ho returns to Vietnam by ship.

October 30: He creates a new government without the pro-Chinese nationalists.

November: Battle between the French and the Vietnamese in Haiphong following other bloody incidents.

December 19: Rupture of the Franco-Vietnamese accords and beginning of hostilities. Ho appeals to the nation: "The Resistance will Win."

1947

May 12: Paul Mus meets with Ho Chi Minh.

The French government launches its "Bao Dai solution," creating a nationalist Vietnamese state to oppose the Democratic Republic of Vietnam (DRV).

1949

October: Mao Zedong proclaims the birth of the People's Republic of China (PRC).

1950

Communist Chinese troops arrive at the Vietnamese border. Beginning of active and intensified Chinese Communist aid.

January 19–March: Ho travels to China and the USSR as head of state, his first trip overseas since 1946.

October: French defeat on the Colonial Road #4 (RC 4), between Cao Bang and Lang Son.

The PRC, followed by the USSR, recognizes the DRV.

1951

February 20: Ho celebrates Tet (New Year) in Nanning.

The United States increases its military aid to the French army in Indochina.

Creation of the Vietnamese Workers' Party (Dang Lao Dong), or VWP, the new name of the Communist Party.

1952

October 28: Ho meets with Stalin and Liu Shaoqi.

1953

March: Stalin dies.

November 29: Ho tells the Swedish journal *L'Expressen* that he is ready to negotiate with the French.

December 19: Ho signs a law instituting land reform.

1954

April 1: Ho is in Moscow with Pham Van Dong and Zhou Enlai, where they meet with Khrushchev.

May: Defeat of the French Expeditionary Corps at Dien Bien Phu.

July 5: Ho and Vo Nguyen Giap meet with Zhou Enlai in Liuzhou to discuss the Geneva talks.

July 20–21: The Geneva Accords are signed, marking the end of hostilities and the splitting of Vietnam into two "provisional" zones until 1956. Ho returns to Hanoi.

1955

June 23: Ho goes by train from Nanning to Beijing via Wuhan.

July: He visits the Soviet cities of Novosibirsk, Sverdlovsk, Irkutsk, and Moscow, where he is received for the first time as head of state.

1956

The South Vietnamese government refuses to hold elections leading toward reunification.

Completion of land reform, begun in 1953 in North Vietnam, and correction of "errors."

Beginning of the "Hundred Flowers" movement (in reference to the similar movement in China), known in Vietnam as "Humanism and Belles Lettres" (Nhan Van Giai Pham*)*.

1957

May: Voroshilov meets with Ho in Hanoi.

June: Ho visits the village where he was born in Kim Lien.

July: He goes to Moscow, Beijing, and Pyongyang. The trip lasts two months, and he visits all of the "people's democracies" in Europe, including Yugoslavia.

November: meeting of Communist Parties in Moscow.

1958

February: Ho Chi Minh goes to Burma and India.

May: Completion of the wooden house on stilts that Ho had built on the grounds of the Presidential Palace for his residence.

Summer: Ho and Mao meet in Beidahe, a seaside resort on the Gulf of Liaotung.

1959

January: Ho goes to Beijing and Moscow (Twenty-first Congress of the Communist Party of the Soviet Union, the CPSU).

February 14: He returns to Hanoi.

February 27–March 10: Ho visits Indonesia and returns via Kunming.

May: During the fifteenth plenum of the Central Committee, the VWP calls for a reprise of the armed struggle to reunite the South with the North.

The Politburo assigns General Vo Bam to the command of "Group 559," tasked with building the Ho Chi Minh Trail.

August: Ho visits Xian.

Late September: He goes to Beijing for the tenth anniversary of the PRC and spends two months in Hainan.

1960

January 1: Ho signs the decree instituting the new constitution: "Organize the State to Move toward Socialism."

May: Ho celebrates his seventieth birthday in China.

September 5–10: Ho Chi Minh presides over the Third Congress of the VWP.

Le Duan becomes the party's First Secretary.

November 11–25: Ho attends the conference of eighty-one Communist Parties in Moscow.

Establishment of the National Front for the Liberation of South Vietnam.

1961

April 9: Ho Chi Minh, Pham Van Dong, and Le Duan meet with Zhou Enlai in Guangxi to focus on the question of Laos.

May: Ho celebrates his birthday in Nanning, then visits the places where Mao carried out his revolutionary activities.

October–November: Ho goes to the Twentieth Congress of the CPSU in Moscow. He visits Estonia, Lithuania, and Latvia, then spends time at a rest home in the Crimea.

November 11–19: Ho leaves for Beijing.

1962

Ho Chi Minh in Beijing.

May: He spends his birthday in Hangzhou (Zhejiang province).

1963

May: Liu Shaoqi and Chen Yi meet with Ho Chi Minh in Hanoi.

September: Ho meets with Zhou Enlai at the thermal spa in Tung Hoa, near Canton.

November: Fall of the Ngo government, assassination of Ngo Dinh Diem and Ngo Dinh Nhu.

December: Ninth plenum of the Central Committee of the VWP, condemning "modern revisionism."

1964

June: General Van Tien Dung meets with Chinese army commanders in Beijing.

Summer: Ho stays at a rest home in the Crimea.

August 2–5: The Gulf of Tonkin incident, pretext for open military intervention by the United States against North Vietnam.

Autumn: Dismissal of Khrushchev.

1965

February: Bombing of North Vietnam. Massive engagement of American forces in South Vietnam. On the 15th, Ho makes a pilgrimage to Con Son to pay homage to the national hero Nguyen Trai, who expelled Chinese troops in the fifteenth century.

February 7–10: Soviet Prime Minister Alexei Kosygin visits Hanoi. Ho is present at the discussions. The USSR sends military equipment and weapons specialists.

May–June: Ho Chi Minh meets secretly with Mao in Changsha and with other leaders in Beijing. He goes to Hoangson. On his seventy-fifth birthday, he visits Gufu, birthplace of Confucius, in Shandong province.

May 15: First version of Ho's Last Will and Testament.

1966

Ho celebrates his seventy-sixth birthday in China, then visits Beijing, Shandong province, and Manchuria.

Mao launches the Great Proletarian Cultural Revolution in China.

Jean Sainteny is sent on a mission to Hanoi. Ho Chi Minh also receives Giorgio de la Pira, winner of the Nobel Peace Prize. Ho says that no peace talks with the United States are possible without the cessation of bombing and the recognition of the National Front for the Liberation of South Vietnam.

The Supreme Soviet of the USSR awards Ho Chi Minh the Order of Lenin.

1967

Ho answers a letter from U.S. President Lyndon B. Johnson.

May–June: Ho goes to Guangdong for medical treatment and celebrates his seventy-seventh birthday.

September–December: Ho receives treatment on the outskirts of Beijing, since the capital is caught up in the turmoil of the Cultural Revolution.

1968

February: The North Vietnamese launch their Tet offensive in South Vietnam. Opening of the Paris conference.

March–April 21: Ho treated in Beijing.

May: Second version of his Testament.

1969

January: Opening of peace talks in Paris, bringing together the United States and Vietnam.

February: Ho treated by Chinese doctors in Hanoi.

May: Third version (abridged) of the Testament, which will be published after Ho's death.

September 2: Death of Ho Chi Minh.

September 3: Announcement of Ho's death, delayed one day to avoid casting a pall on the festivities commemorating the declaration of independence.

September 4: Zhou Enlai, Ye Jianying, and Wei Guoqing arrive in Hanoi.

September 9: National funeral held in the presence of Soviet Prime Minister Alexei Kosygin and Jean Sainteny, representing the French government.

1973

September 2: Construction begins on the Ho Chi Minh mausoleum.

1975

April: The final military offensive to take Saigon is called "Operation Ho Chi Minh."

The Communist military victory topples the South Vietnamese regime and leads to the unification of Vietnam.

August 29: Inauguration of the Ho Chi Minh mausoleum in Hanoi, now open to the public.

1976

The cities of Saigon and Cholon and their outskirts are formed into one urban district, officially called Ho Chi Minh City.

December: Presentation of the first theatrical work in which Ho is the main character, called "The First Citizen," during the Second Congress of the Vietnamese Communist Party (VCP).

1978

January 7: The Politburo of the VCP passes resolution number 07/NQ-TU, assigning a commission led by Truong Chinh to publish the *Complete Works* of Ho Chi Minh.

1980

May: International conference for the ninetieth anniversary of Ho's birth, followed by a commemorative ceremony in Ba Dinh Square.

Publication of the first volume of the *Complete Works*.

1981

August: First national congress bringing together delegates representing the three million "wise nephews of President Ho" in Hanoi.

1984

February 3: Inauguration of a national monument (the Pagoda of the Plum Tree) in the mountains of Ha Son Binh, where Ho stayed during the war against the French.

1989

Publication of the second version of the Testament, followed by the first version. All three versions are published in May.

1990

An international symposium, held in Hanoi (March 29–30) to commemorate the hundredth anniversary of Ho's birth, is entitled "President Ho Chi Minh – Hero of National Liberation and Eminent Personality within the Culture of Vietnam."

Along the same lines, a commemoration of Ho's birthday is held at UNESCO headquarters in Paris following a UNESCO Council resolution aiming to "make known the greatness of his ideals and his work toward national liberation."

Publication of the *Tu dien Ho Chi Minh* (Ho Chi Minh Encyclopedia) in Hanoi.

May 10: Inauguration of the Ho Chi Minh museum in Ba Dinh Square, Hanoi.

May 19: A bicycle race is scheduled to conclude on the same day as Ho's birthday.

Autumn: The Ho Chi Minh Museum is finished.

A granite bust, eight meters high (25 ft.), is erected in Ho Chi Minh City.

A bronze statue is erected in Youth Park in Vinh (Central Vietnam).

The Minister of Higher Education, in collaboration with Humboldt University in Berlin, publishes twelve essays on President Ho.

A statue of Ho Chi Minh is erected in Moscow, on Akademicheskaya Square.

1992

Reissue of the *Complete Works* in twelve volumes, Hanoi.

1993

Publication of the *Ho Chi Minh Bien nien tieu su* (A Chronological History of Ho Chi Minh) in ten volumes, Hanoi.

1997

Institutes of higher education in Vietnam adopt the teaching of "Ho Chi Minh thought" in their curricula.

Notes

PREFACE

1. Jean Lacouture, Daniel Hémery, and Pierre Brocheux have published biographies in French. William Duiker and Sophie Quinn-Judge have written biographies in English, and Yevgeny Kobelev has written one in Russian. See the bibliography.
2. In *Pacific Affairs* (Fall 2001), 452–53.
3. In the Buddhist religion, the bodhisattva is one who has attained Enlightenment but refrains from reaching nirvana in order to help others. Cao Dai is the Third Revelation of the Supreme Being, a religion founded in Cochinchina in 1919 by Ngo Van Chieu, an official in the colonial government. It is called "syncretic" because it combines elements of the main religions of the Far East, but Cao Dai is essentially a spiritistic religion.
4. English translation of the "Testament" in *Ho Chi Minh: Selected Writings* (Hanoi: Foreign Languages Press, 1977), pp. 359–62.
5. See the historical magazine *Xua va Nay* [Past and Present] 48 (1998), 86 and 101 (2001). Details also provided by my own visits to Kim Lien, Pac Bo, Cao Bang, Thai Nguyen, Nanning, and Guilin.

1. IN SEARCH OF A FUTURE

1. Tran Minh Sieu, *Zi tich chu tich Ho Chi Minh o Kim Lien* [The traces of President Ho Chi Minh in Kim Lien] (NXB Nghe An, 1998).
2. Ibid., p. 11.
3. Charles Fourniau, *Viet Nam. Domination coloniale et résistance nationale (1858–1914)* [Vietnam: Colonial domination and national resistance, 1858–1914] (Paris: Les Indes savantes, 2002).
4. There are at least four possible dates of birth, provided by Ho himself: 1890, 1893, 1900, and 1903. The official history has opted for 1890 for reasons that are well presented by Daniel Hémery. Besides, a man born in 1890 would be 55 in 1945, a suitable age to become President of the Democratic Republic of Vietnam.
5. Tran Minh Sieu, *Nhung nguoi than trong gia dinh Bac Ho* [The beloved members of Uncle Ho's family] (NXB Nghe An, 1995).

6. The French placed Thanh Thai on the throne of Annam when he was eight years old, and he was supported in that position from 1889 to 1907. Sensitive and intelligent according to some, mentally ill with a sadistic streak according to others, he ended up in exile and destitute on Reunion Island. See Nguyen The Anh, "L'abdication de Thanh Thai" [The abdication of Thanh Thai], BEFEO no. 64 (1977).
7. The imperial government was composed of five ministries; the Ministry of Rites was in charge of ceremonies, examinations, and rewarding worthy subjects. Within each ministry, officials were divided into two classes with nine levels each. Sac was named to the fifth level of the second class.
8. Phan Boi Chau (1867–1940) graduated as *pho bang* in 1900 and turned his energies to the anti-French resistance. He founded two nationalist societies and went into exile in Japan. The Japanese navy had just defeated the Russian flotilla, becoming the beacon and model of modernization for the rest of Asia. Chau encouraged young Vietnamese to come and join him in Japan for training. Expelled from Japan in 1908, he withdrew to China where he continued his revolutionary activities against the French until his capture in 1925. He was condemned to death but the sentence was commuted to house arrest in Hué, where he died in 1940. He advocated and organized direct action, such as assassinations and insurrections, in contrast to his contemporary and friend, Phan Chu Trinh, who was committed to the reformist path.
9. Tran Minh Sieu, *Nhung nguoi than*, p. 40.
10. From March to May 1908 there were demonstrations in the central provinces of Quang Ngai, Quang Nam, Binh Dinh, and Thua Thien against the tax and corvée requirements imposed on the regime by the French in 1907. They had strong popular support and turned violent after a harsh crackdown. The colonial authorities did not differentiate between reformists and revolutionaries; "scholars, Chinese language instructors, active duty soldiers, university students who had gained renown through their speeches and writings, stirring up insubordination against the authority of the Protectorate" were condemned to forced labor, and some even received the death sentence by decree of the Résident Supérieur of Tonkin, on 15 October 1908. Phan Chu Trinh was considered to be one of the instigators and was initially condemned to death, then to a term in prison. He was saved by the French League of Human Rights, which made a strong impression on the young Thanh.
11. *Nhung nguoi than*, p. 69.
12. Nguyen The Anh, "L'élite intellectuelle et le fait colonial dans les premières années du XXè siècle" [The intellectual élite and colonialism in the first years of the 20th century], *RFHOM* vol. 71, 268 (1985), 291–307. And from the same author: *Monarchie et fait colonial au Viet Nam (1875–1925). Le crépuscule d'un ordre traditionnel* [Monarchy and colonialism in Vietnam: The twilight of a traditional order] (Paris: L'Harmattan, 1992).
13. *Quoc ngu* literally means "national writing." In the seventeenth century, Jesuit missionaries needed a way to evangelize the natives, so established a transcription of the Viet language using the Latin alphabet. For many

years, credit was given to a Frenchman, Alexandre de Rhodes, but today some are admitting that *quoc ngu* was primarily the work of Portuguese Jesuits. At the imperial court, Chinese characters were used for writing official documents and literary works, but there was a type of demotic writing founded on Chinese characters called *chu nom*, which could be called the first *quoc ngu*. From the beginning of their conquest in Indochina, the French popularized the romanized version of *quoc ngu*, and it eventually prevailed around 1926 when the nationalist intelligentsia realized the advantages it offered, due to its simplicity and ease of acquisition by the public. See R. Jacques, "Le Portugal et la romanisation de la langue vietnamienne. Faut-il réécrire l'Histoire? [Portugal and the romanization of the Vietnamese language. Must we rewrite history?], *RFHOM* vol. 85, 318 (1998), 21–54.

14. *Nhung mau chuyen ve cuoc doi hoat dong cua Ho Chu tich* [Glimpses of the life of President Ho], published under the name Tran Dan Tien in 1948. There are several editions, the last one from 1999 (Ho Chi Minh City: Su That). An English translation was published in 1958 as *Glimpses of the Life of Ho Chi Minh: President of the Democratic Republic of Vietnam* (Hanoi: FLP, 1958).
15. Nguyen Dac Xuan, *Bac Ho, Thoi nien thieu o Hue* [Uncle Ho's childhood in Hué] (Ho Chi Minh City: Su That, 1999), p. 63. Thanh was sometimes teased for being a *ca go* (wooden fish) because people from Nghe An were known to be frugal and carry a wooden fish that they would suck to ward off hunger. He was also mocked for his strong accent, which revealed his provincial origins.
16. Ibid., and also Nguyen Khac Phe, *Hoa si Le Van Mien* [The painter Le Van Mien] (Hué: 1997).
17. David Schoenbrun, *As France Goes* (New York: Harper & Bros, 1957), p. 232.
18. Frédéric Mantienne, *Les relations politiques et commerciales entre la France et la péninsule indochinoise (XVIIè siècle)* [Political and commercial relations between France and the Indochinese peninsula (17th century)] (Paris: Les Indes savantes, 2001).
19. Nora Wang, *Émigration et Politique. Les étudiants-ouvriers chinois en France. 1919–1925* [Emigration and politics. Chinese student-workers in France, 1919–25] (Paris: Les Indes savantes, 2002), and A. Kriegel, "Aux origines françaises du communisme chinois" [On the French origins of Chinese communism], *Preuves* 209–10 (1968), 32–41.
20. Tran Dan Tien, *Nhung mau chuyen*. Nguyen Tat Thanh's correspondence helps track his movements abroad, most importantly the letter dated 15 September 1911 that he sent to the President of the French Republic to seek admission to the École Coloniale. In November 1915, he sent his father 15 piastres care of the Résident Supérieur of France in Annam. On 15 December 1912, he sent a postal order of 3,000 francs or piastres to his father, through the same channels. In 1913 and 1914, he sent five letters from London to Phan Chu Trinh (more precisely, five letters were intercepted by the post office censors), and he also asked the Governor-General of Indochina via

the Consul General of Great Britain in Saigon to pass on a letter to his father, whose address he did not have.

21. Daniel Hémery, *Ho Chi Minh, de l'Indochine au Vietnam* [Ho Chi Minh, from Indochina to Vietnam] (Paris: Découvertes-Gallimard, 1990), p. 40; and Nguyen The Anh and Vu Ngu Chieu, *Une autre école pour le jeune Nguyen That Thanh* [Another school for the young Nguyen That Thanh] (Paris: Duong Moi, 1983).
22. Tran Dan Tien, *Nhung mau chuyen*.
23. Phan Van Truong (1875–1933) was from the North (Tonkin), and moved to France in 1910, where he worked as a language teacher at the École des Langues Orientales in Paris while studying law. A naturalized French citizen and Doctor of Law, he passed the bar in Paris but never opened his own practice. He returned to Saigon in the 1920s to start a career in law while continuing to write for the radical nationalist circle of Nguyen An Ninh and his journal *La Cloche fêlée* [the cracked bell]. Previously, he had published the first translation in *quoc ngu* of the *Communist Manifesto* by Karl Marx and Frederick Engels in the journal *L'Annam*. He worked closely with Phan Chu Trinh and Nguyen Ai Quoc, and spoke French so well that not only did he correct what Nguyen Ai Quoc wrote, but it is also believed he was the author of certain texts signed Nguyen Ai Quoc. Quoc, for his part, let it be known that Truong prevented him from writing what he wanted and that, as a result, he found a proofreader at *L'Humanité* to read his articles. This type of conflict also arose with another compatriot, Nguyen The Truyen (1898–1969), who broke from the Communists and later refused Ho Chi Minh's offer to become Vice President of the DRV in 1946. He lived in South Vietnam until his death in 1969, the same year as Ho Chi Minh.
24. Letter signed Paul Tat Thanh, CAOM, Slotfom III, 29, in *Ho Chi Minh. Textes 1914–1969*, Alain Ruscio (ed.) (Paris: L'Harmattan, 1990), p. 21.
25. Pierre Brocheux, "De l'empereur Zuy Tan au prince Vinh San, l'Histoire peut-elle se répéter?" [From Emperor Duy Tan to Prince Vinh San: Can history repeat itself?], *Approches Asie* 10 (1989–90) (Paris: Economica), 1–25; and Peter Zinoman, *The Colonial Bastille: A History of Imprisonment in Vietnam: 1862–1940* (Berkeley and Los Angeles: University of California Press, 2001), chap. 5, pp. 158–99.
26. Commander Jules Roux served in Indochina and learned Vietnamese, which he later taught at the École Coloniale. Considered an "Annamitophile" in French colonial circles, he defended Phan Chu Trinh in 1908 when he was accused of instigating the revolt in central Vietnam and called in the League of Human Rights. He became a friend of Trinh's, and stepped in again with others like Marius Moutet when Trinh was imprisoned in 1914. Moutet was a socialist and lawyer and also defended Phan Van Truong, who was imprisoned along with Trinh. In 1946, he signed the modus vivendi with Ho Chi Minh, which came to an end on 19 December 1946 with the onset of the Franco–Viet Minh conflict.
27. *Revendications du peuple annamite* [Demands of the Annamite people], copy at the Bibliothèque Nationale de France in Paris and in *Ho Chi Minh: Selected Writings (1920–1969)* (Hanoi: FLP, 1977), pp. 22–23. Thanh was

politely received by Colonel Edward House, who worked closely with President Woodrow Wilson, but who merely said that he would pass it on.

28. The Vietnamese led a communitarian life at the apartment at the Villa des Gobelins, so much so that one of their girlfriends broke off the relationship because she had to put her salary in the communal kitty as well as do the housekeeping for all three men. CAOM, SPCE 365.
29. CAOM, coll. F07–13405, doc. 306. The meeting was held in the evening, and was attended by Nguyen Ai Quoc, Phan Chu Trinh, Khanh Ky (who had initiated Phan as a photo retoucher), a Vietnamese named Le Van Xao, and. of course, Édouard.
30. Boris Souvarine (1895–1984) was a Russian militant and journalist with the SFIO, and one of the founders of the Committee to Join the Third International. He became one of the leaders of the French Communist Party and of the International. Expelled for being a Trotskyite, he eventually broke with Trotsky and became an essayist and historian. Jean Longuet was one of the founders of the French Socialist Party and an architect of the Second International. A follower of Proudhon, he was in the minority at the Tours Congress of 1920 and remained hostile to their adherence to the Third International.
31. Claude Liauzu, *Colonisés et anticolonialistes* [The colonized and anticolonialists] (Paris: L'Harmattan, 1982).
32. Raoul Girardet, *L'idée coloniale en France. 1871–1962* [The colonial idea in France, 1871–1962] (Paris: La Table Ronde, 1972).
33. From a report by "Jean," 4 January 1920. CAOM, SPCE 365.
34. In a report from 4 January 1920, Jean wrote: "Mister Quoc complains that Indochina is still unknown to other nations, he talked about Indochina to international politicians and none of them knew that it existed, they had never heard of it or thought that it is a small border province between India and China. He said that they would have to yell quite loudly to make themselves known." He continued: "Mr. Quoc writes openly in the French press about his peaceful demands regarding Indochinese policy."
35. François Furet, *Le passé d'une illusion. Essai sur l'idée communiste au XXè siècle* [The past of an illusion. Essay on the communist idea in the 20th century] (Paris: Calmann Lévy, 1995) chap. 3. According to two historians from the Sorbonne, Alphonse Aulard (a follower of Danton) and Albert Mathiez (following Robespierre), the Russian Revolution "has become a worthy successor to the French Revolution, like a younger sister or daughter; both dramatic and universal, like her elder sister," p. 91.
36. "Speech at the Tours Congress," in *Ho Chi Minh: Selected Writings*, pp. 15–17.
37. In *Avec l'Oncle Ho* [With Uncle Ho] (Hanoi: ÉLÉ, 1972), p. 47.
38. *Le Congrès de Tours* [The Tours Congress], complete text with preface, annotations, and appendices, by Jean Charles et al. (Paris: Éd. Sociales, 1980). Nguyen Ai Quoc's speech of 26 December 1920, pp. 326–27. His opinion on the Internationals in Tran Dan Tien, *Nhung mau chuyen*, p. 12. On the five Chinese, see Nora Wang, *Émigration et politique*, pp. 170 and 207.

39. Others were the West Indians Henri Charles Sarrotte, Jules Monnerville (not to be confused with Gaston Monnerville, President of the French Senate from 1958 to 1969), the Algerian Hadj Ali, the Malagasys Jean Ralaimongo and Samuel Stéphany, and the Vietnamese Nguyen The Truyen. For more on Ralaimongo, see Ho's interview with Jacques Rabemananjara in 1946 in Jacques Tronchon, *L'insurrection malgache de 1947* [The Malagasy insurrection of 1947] (Paris: Karthala, 1974). For Nguyen The Truyen, see Dang Huu Thu, *Than The va su nghiep cua Nguyen The Truyen* [The person and the activities of the revolutionary Nguyen The Truyen] (Melun: self-published, 1993).
40. See Jean Maitron, *Dictionnaire biographique du mouvement ouvrier français* [Biographical dictionary of the French workers' movement] (Paris: Éd. Ouvrières, 1987).
41. Interview with Jacques and Raymond Rabemananjara cited in Jacques Rabemananjara's deposition of 21 April 1947. See Tronchon, *L'insurrection malgache*, pp. 335–36.
42. "Contribution indochinoise à l'effort de guerre de la Métropole, 1920" [Indochinese contribution to the war effort in France, 1920], Agence FOM 271, CAOM.
43. Agathe Larcher-Goscha, "La légitimation française en Indochine: mythes et réalités de la 'collaboration franco-vietnamienne' et du réformisme colonial (1905–1945)" [French legitimization in Indochina: Myths and realities of "Franco-Vietnamese collaboration" and colonial reformism (1905–1945)], unpublished doctoral thesis, Université Paris VII (2000).
44. Stanley Karnow, "This Tiny Annamite," in *Paris in the Fifties* (New York: Three Rivers Press, 1997), p. 217.
45. Quoc even wrote for *Le Libertaire* (issues 141 and 142). But, as the historian Jean Maitron rightly observes, Quoc used all means at his disposal for voicing his opinions, sometimes regardless of political affinity or even shared beliefs. He even became a Freemason (Jacques Dalloz, "Les Vietnamiens dans la Franc-maçonnerie coloniale" [Vietnamese in the French Masonic order], *RFHOM* 320 (1998), 105. Dalloz claims to have found a membership card in the name of Nguyen Ai Quoc in the archives of the Grand Orient de France, dated 1922. I have only found a request for information on admission to a lodge, for which there was no follow-up. And in January 1923, Quoc stated in three meetings that he approved of and followed the International's ban on Communists joining the Freemasons, the League of Human Rights, and especially the anarchists (Notes de Désiré, CAOM, SLOTFOM II, 14).
46. "Indochine," published in *La Revue communiste* 15 (May 1921), in Ruscio, *Ho Chi Minh. Textes*, pp. 34–35.
47. Karnow, *Paris in the Fifties*, pp. 216–17.
48. Quoted in ibid., p. 219.
49. Letter from Jacques Sternel of 10 January 1951 to *La Révolution prolétarienne* (February 1951), p. 24. Sternel is the alias of a journalist who wrote for *L'Humanité*; his real name has not been identified.

50. "Le Calligraphe," *Planète-Action* 15 (1970).
51. The entire text of the letter is in Thu Trang, *Nhung Hoat dong cua Phan Chu Trinh* [The activities of Phan Chu Trinh] (Paris: Sudest, 1980), p. 140.
52. Tran Dan Tien, *Nhung mau chuyen*.

2. A MISSIONARY OF REVOLUTION

1. Text of Quoc's speech reproduced in *Le Paria* (1 November 1922). Dmitri Zakharovitch Manuilsky (1883–1959), a Ukrainian, was one of the key leaders of the Comintern, then of the Cominform (Information Bureau of the Communist Parties), and was trusted by Stalin. He was entrusted with overseeing the Communist parties of Europe and France, where he had done part of his university studies. He befriended Nguyen Ai Quoc and protected him during the Great Purges.
2. Tran Dan Tien, *Nhung mau chuyen*; also see the depositions of other Vietnamese who studied in Moscow, in SLOTFOM III, CAOM.
3. *Pravda* (23 January 1924), in *Ho Chi Minh Toan Tap* [The complete writings of Ho Chi Minh], vol. 1 (1919–24), p. 237. All references to *Toan Tap* are from the 2d ed., 12 vols. (Hanoi: NXB CTQG, 1995–96). There is also a first edition, in 10 volumes, published between 1980 and 1989 by Su That Publishing House.
4. From an account by the Italian Communist Giovanni Germanetto, "A Spring Morning 1924," in a collection of reminiscences about Ho Chi Minh entitled *Ngon Duoc* [The Torch] (Hanoi: Van hoa, 1980), pp. 98–100.
5. *L'envol du communisme en Chine. Mémoires de Peng Shuzhi* [The rise of communism in China: Memoirs of Peng Shuzhi], Claude Cadart and Cheng Yingxiang (eds.) (Paris: Gallimard, 1982), chaps. 4 and 5. Converted to Trotskyism, Peng Shuzhi became one of the key leaders of the Trotskyite movement in China. Peng described the university in these terms: "Its huge buildings rise up at the corner of Tverskaia Street and Pushkin Boulevard, across from the bronze statue of that eternal Russian poet. The Stalin School really is in the best possible place, inside the city. For what is Tverskaia Street if not the Champs Élysées of Moscow? When one leaves the Stalin School it is hard to resist the temptation to take a stroll down that marvelous avenue," pp. 263–64. The three to four hundred students enrolled in the first trimester of 1921–22 were housed in a former bank located on the other side of Tverskaia Street; the refectory and infirmary were in the former Stranoïe convent.
6. The Crestintern was founded during the peasant phase of the Bolshevik Communist Party when the Bolsheviks envisaged an alliance with the "peasant parties" of the Balkans and when Bukharin aimed for socialist development relying on the peasantry. Founded in 1922, it was dissolved in 1935 and its president, the Pole Thomas Dombal, was assassinated on Stalin's orders. Nguyen Ai Quoc was a member of the presidium from 1923 to 1925. He had to fight those who refused to grant any revolutionary potential to the peasantry.

7. From *Soviet Russia Masters the Comintern*, Helmut Gruber (ed.) (Garden City, N.Y.: Anchor/Doubleday, 1974), pp. 308–9. The text cited is in *Toan Tap*, 1, pp. 273–75.
8. "Lettre adressée au Comité central du PCF" [Letter to the Central Committee of the FCP], in Ruscio, *Ho Chi Minh. Textes*, pp. 50–53.
9. Letter to Comrade Zinoviev, *Toan Tap*, 1, p. 242.
10. See for example, "De la façon de poser la question nationale" [Ways of posing the national question], in *Pravda* (8 May 1921), in Ruscio, *Ho Chi Minh. Textes*, p. 34, fn. 1. This approach was often defended by those with whom Quoc spoke in Moscow.
11. Letter from 19 September 1924 in *Toan Tap*, 1, p. 305.
12. SLOTFOM III, 44. Anatoli Sokolov estimates their numbers at sixty, from 1925 to 1938; see *The Comintern and Vietnam* (in Russian) (Moscow: 1998), translated and published in *quoc ngu* in Hanoi. He knew of five others enrolled in the International Motorized Brigade, which fell defending Moscow from assaults by the Wehrmacht, including Nguyen Sinh Than, one of Quoc's uncles. These five men are not mentioned in the registers or files of the Stalin School. Most probably they were from Quoc's Revolutionary Youth League (Thanh Nien), who were welcomed for further training in the USSR after the anti-Communist repression in Canton.
13. M. N. Roy, *Men I Met* (New Delhi: Lalvani Publishing House, 1968), pp. 137–46. The Indian Manabendra Nath Roy (1887–1954) was an important figure in the Third International, from which he was expelled in 1928 for being a "rightist." He had a poor opinion of Nguyen Ai Quoc, but also of Sun Yat-sen.
14. See Cadart, *Mémoires de Peng Shuzhi*; and Hong Ha, *Bac Ho tren dat nuoc Le-nin* [Uncle Ho in the land of Lenin] (Hanoi: Thanh Nien, 1980): "Nguyen Ai Quoc was quite drawn to and interested by this school," p. 101.
15. Sokolov, *The Comintern and Vietnam*. Additional information from my own interviews and correspondence with Sokolov.
16. *Mémoires de Peng Shuzhi*, p. 272.
17. "Rapport sur le Tonkin, l'Annam et la Cochinchine" [Report on Tonkin, Annam, and Cochinchina], in Ruscio, *Ho Chi Minh. Textes*, pp. 69–74.
18. "Réponse à notre amie l'étudiante X" [Answer to our friend, Student X], in Ruscio, *Ho Chi Minh. Textes*, pp. 82–84.
19. "Entretien avec Ossip Mandelstam," in Ruscio, *Ho Chi Minh. Textes*, pp. 54–57.
20. *Toan Tap*, 1, p. 263.
21. *Ho Chi Minh. Nhung su kien* [Ho Chi Minh: Historical events] (Hanoi: 1987), p. 41; and *Ho Chi Minh bien nien tieu su* [A chronological history of Ho Chi Minh], vol. 1, p. 178 (hereafter *BNTS*). See also Hong Ha, *Bac Ho tren* for a different version.
22. Osip Mandelstam, interview published in the Moscow journal *Ogonyok* (23 December 1923).
23. Paul Mus, *Ho Chi Minh, le Vietnam et l'Asie* [Ho Chi Minh, Vietnam, and Asia] (Paris: Seuil, 1971), pp. 42–43. The Buddhist monk Hiuang-Tsang, or Xuanzang (602–664) was a pilgrim and translator of Buddhist texts, from

Sanskrit to Chinese. He traveled in search of the sources, places, and texts of Buddhism, and produced an immense body of translation work. One of his disciples published an account of his six-year journey, which took him as far as Central Asia and Afghanistan, as *Datang xiyu ji* [Records of the western regions of the great Tang dynasty]. His voyage inspired a popular novel that became famous in the sixteenth century, *Xiyouji* [Journey to the west] in which the monk undertakes his journey with a monkey-pilgrim.

24. Phan Boi Chau, *Mémoires*, translation and commentary by Georges Boudarel in *France-Asie/Asia* 194–95, vol. 22, 3–4 (1968), 191, fn. 188; and see Boudarel's *Phan Boi Chau et la société vietnamienne de son temps* [Phan Boi Chau and the Vietnamese society of his time] in *France-Asie* 199 (1969). Pham Hong Thai drowned in the Pearl River while trying to escape from the police.
25. Marie-Claire Bergère, *Sun Yat-sen* (Paris: Fayard, 1994), 3d section.
26. Hélène Carrère d'Encausse and Stuart Schram, *Le Marxisme et l'Asie, 1853–1964* [Marxism and Asia, 1853–1964] (Paris: A. Colin, 1965), and Pierre Broué, *La Question chinoise dans l'Internationale communiste: 1926–1927* [The Chinese question within the Communist International: 1926–1927] (Paris: EDI, 1976).
27. Jean-Marie Bouissou, *Seigneurs de la guerre et officiers rouges, 1924–1927* [Warlords and red officers, 1924–1927] (Paris: Mame, 1974). Mikhail Gruzenberg, known as Borodin, led the group of Soviets sent to help Sun Yat-sen and the Kuomintang, and was their political advisor. Pavel A. Plavov, A. I. Cherepanov, and V. K. Blücher (who inspired the character of Galin in André Malraux's *La Voie Royale*) were high-ranking officers of the Red Army, veterans of the October Revolution and the civil war, on temporary assignment as military advisors to the Kuomintang army.
28. Ibid.
29. Vera Vichniakova-Akimova, *Two Years in Revolutionary China (1925–1927)* (Cambridge, Mass.: Harvard University Press, 1971), originally published in Russian in 1965, cited in Thanh Dam, *Nguyen Ai Quoc tren duong ve nuoc* [Nguyen Ai Quoc's return to his country] (NXB Nghe An, 1998), pp. 95–96.
30. Thanh Dam, *Bac Ho tren duong*, and Hong Ha, *Bac Ho tren dat*. Zhou Enlai, Li Fuchun, and Chen Yannian had spent time in France as student workers and organized the Chinese Communist group there.
31. Correspondence with the Far Eastern Secretary of the Comintern in *Toan Tap*, vol. 2 (1924–30). In the book *As-tu vu Crémet?* [Have you seen Crémet?] (Paris: Fayard, 1991), authors Roger Faligot and Rémi Kauffer ignored this facet of Quoc's activities and considered him a "factotum of Jean Crémet," an opinion born of condescension and ignorance. Jean-Louis Crémet was one of the first leaders of the FCP, and then worked for the Comintern in the Far East. He eventually broke with Stalin and lived in exile in Belgium until his death in 1973. As it turns out, both Crémet and Joseph Ducroux were working as secret agents, and both were members of the OMS (the international liaison department of the Comintern,

under Alexander L. Abramov). We do not know whether Quoc was also a member.

32. From Vichniakova-Akimova, in Bouissou, *Seigneurs de la guerre*, p. 228.
33. Georges Boudarel, "Extrême gauche et nationalisme vietnamien" [The extreme left and Vietnamese nationalism], in *L'Histoire de l'Asie du Sud-est. Révoltes, réformes, et révolutions* [Revolts, reforms, and revolutions in Southeast Asia] Pierre Brocheux (ed.) (Lille: P.U.L., 1981), and Phan Boi Chau, *Mémoires*; see also David Marr, *Vietnamese Anticolonialism* (Berkeley and Los Angeles: University of California Press, 1971). Phan's "Viet Nam Quoc Dan Dang" was not related to the one created in December 1925 near Hanoi, which attempted the mutiny at Yen Bay in 1930.
34. Hoang Tranh, *Ho Chi Minh voi Trung Quoc* [Ho Chi Minh and China] (Nanning: Sao Moi, 1990) and from the same author, "Ho Chi Minh voi vo Trung Quoc Tang Tuyet Minh" [Ho Chi Minh and his Chinese wife, Tang Tuyet Minh], in *Dong Nam A Tung hoanh* (November 2001), a journal on Southeast Asia published in Nanning by the Academy of Social Sciences of Guangxi.
35. Georges Boudarel, "Extrême gauche." For more on the Three People's Principles (i.e., Sun Yat-sen's political doctrine based on the triad of nationalism, democracy, and socialism), see Marie-Claire Bergère, *Sun Yat-Sen*, chap. 10.
36. CAOM, SLOTFOM III, 131.
37. *Ngon Duoc*, includes accounts of clandestine shipboard travel, pp. 112–13 and 272–73.
38. In 1925, Phan Boi Chau took a train to Shanghai and planned to continue on to Canton by ship. While leaving the station, he was abducted by the French police and sent to Hanoi. He was tried and received a death sentence, but it was commuted to house arrest in Hué, where he died in 1940. Who betrayed him? Anti-Communists accused Nguyen Ai Quoc, who allegedly wanted to eliminate a rival and needed money for his organization (in fact, there was a substantial reward). Prince Cuong De (pretender to the throne of Annam, in exile in Japan) named Lam Duc Thu as the guilty party, unbeknownst to Ho. Phan Boi Chau, for his part, was convinced that the culprit was Nguyen Thuong Huyen, nephew of Ho Hoc Lam and living with him at the same time as Chau, so he knew about his travel plans and train times. In fact, Phan Boi Chau and Nguyen Ai Quoc never met in China; see Vinh Sinh's article in *Xua va nay* 38 (1997), 5–7.
39. See the works by Hoang Tranh, Thanh Dam, and Hong Ha.
40. Correspondence with the Comintern in *Toan Tap*, 2, pp. 8–9.
41. Nguyen Luong Bang, "Nhung lan gap Bac" [My meetings with Uncle Ho], in *Dau nguon* [The Spring] (Hanoi: Van Hoc, 1977).
42. See the account of his wife, Tran Kiem Qua, *Hoang Ha nho Hong Ha Thuong* [Memories of the beloved Hong Ha Thuong] (Hanoi: Van Hoc, 2001).
43. Huynh Kim Khanh, *Vietnamese Communism, 1925–1945* (Ithaca, N.Y.: Cornell University Press, 1982). *Thanh Nien* was published weekly from June 1925 to May 1926; *Bao Cong Nong* published 500 weekly issues from December 1925 to early 1926; *Linh Kach Menh* was published for roughly

a year (1927–28); and there were only four issues of *Viet Nam Tien Phong* in 1927.

44. *Toan Tap*, 2, pp. 257–318.
45. Article in *Thanh Nien* 80 (20 February 1927), French translation in Ruscio, *Ho Chi Minh. Textes*, pp. 91–92.
46. Letter from Canton, "Mission Noël," CAOM, HCI/SPCE 368/1116.
47. On their meeting, marriage, and the fate of Tang Tuyet Minh, see Hoang Tranh, *Ho Chi Minh voi Trung Quoc*.
48. "Mission Noël."
49. *BNTS*, 1 (1890–1930), p. 246. Two authors refer to women in Ho's life but we do not know to whom they refer. Tran Ngoc Danh writes, "the President is a widower" (*Chu tich goa vo*), and Harold Isaacs quotes Ho as saying, "'I am alone… no family, nothing.… I did have a wife once.… ' but he left it at that." See Tran Ngoc Danh's *Biography of President Ho Chi Minh*, published in France in 1949 by the Union of Viet Kieu and written in *quoc ngu*; and Isaacs, *No Peace for Asia* (New York: Macmillan, 1947), p. 164. Danh had been deputy of Can Tho and took refuge in Prague after the dissolution of the DRV's delegation in Paris. He denounced Ho's "liquidation of the ICP" to the Soviets and was then excluded from the party for "Trotskyism." This last information comes from Christopher Goscha.
50. Hémery, *Ho Chi Minh, de l'Indochine au Vietnam*, p. 145.
51. Hoang Tranh, *Ho Chi Minh voi Trung Quoc*, p. 41.
52. J. Chesneaux and F. Barbier, *La Chine. La marche à la révolution. 1921–1949* [China: The March toward the revolution], vol. 3 of *Histoire contemporaine de la Chine* [Contemporary history of China] (Paris: Hatier, 1975), p. 9.
53. See Broué, *La question chinoise*.
54. In 1927, Jacques Doriot (1898–1945), a rising star among young Communists, was the FCP's delegate to the Comintern. During a conference in Canton with the Revolutionary Youth League, he urged the group to educate and organize the peasantry for revolution. CAOM, File "Les communistes et les colonies," SLOTFOM III, 55. Later, Doriot was expelled from the FCP and founded the French People's Party (PPF) in 1934. He collaborated with the Germans and died wearing the uniform of the Legion of French Volunteers against Bolshevism (LVF).
55. The speeches at the conference were included in a volume edited by A. Neuberg (Franz Neumann) in 1928 in German, entitled *Armed Insurrection*. It was published in French as *L'Insurrection armée* (Paris: Maspéro, 1970). Nguyen Ai Quoc's words are on pages 255–59 of this French edition.
56. SLOTFOM III, 44
57. Ibid.
58. Ibid.
59. Ibid.
60. *BNTS* 1, p. 257.
61. Ibid., p. 260. Vasili P. Kolarov was a Bulgarian economist and Communist leader, and also a member of the Comintern's presidium until its dissolution in 1943.

62. *Bac Ho o Thai lan* [Uncle Ho in Thailand], a collection of accounts edited by Tran Ngoc Danh (Ho Chi Minh City: Tre, 1999). In English, see Christopher Goscha, *Thailand and the Southeast Asian Networks of the Vietnamese Revolution, 1885–1954* (Richmond, UK: Curzon Press, 1999), chap. 2.
63. Ibid., and on the Communist organizations in Siam, see: Indo NF 1036 and 39 783, CAOM. See also Dennis Duncanson, "Ho Chi Minh in Hong Kong, 1931–1932," *China Quarterly* 57 (1974).
64. Pierre Brocheux, "Libération nationale et communisme en Asie du Sud-est" [National liberation and communism in Southeast Asia], in *Le siècle des communismes* [The century of communisms], Michel Dreyfus et al. (eds.) (Paris: Éd. de l'Atelier, 2000), pp. 273–85.
65. For more on this section, see Huynh Kim Khanh, *Vietnamese Communism.*
66. T. Lan's autobiographical account, *Vua di duong, vua ke chuyen* [Walking and talking] (Hanoi: Su that, 1976), pp. 37–38.
67. From "Rapport sur le Tonkin, l'Annam, et la Cochinchine," in Ruscio, *Ho Chi Minh. Textes*, p. 72.
68. In Marxist theory, humanity evolves from primitive communism to communism via different modes of production: slavery, feudalism, capitalism, then socialism. Marxists debated, however, about the existence of an "Asian mode of production" distinct from the others. See the *Dictionnaire critique du Marxisme* [Critical dictionary of Marxism], G. Labica and G. Bensussan (eds.) (Paris: PUF, 1982).
69. The Communist view of Yen Bay in *Co Vo San* [The flag of the proletariat] 3 (February 1931), in SLOTFOM III, 48, CAOM.
70. Pierre Brocheux, "L'implantation du communisme en Indochine française. Le cas du Nghe Tinh, 1930–1931" [The establishment of communism in French Indochina: The case of Nghe Tinh, 1930–1931], in *RHMC* 24 (1977), 50–77.

3. UNDER THE SWORD OF DAMOCLES

1. Andrée Viollis, *Indochine SOS* (Paris: Gallimard, "NRF," 1935). Viollis, a French journalist, accompanied Paul Reynaud on his voyage to Indochina; and *Conclusions d'ensemble du voyage ministériel* [General conclusions of the ministerial voyage], edited by Gaston Joseph, Director of Political Affairs at the Ministry of Colonies, dated August 1931, in Indo NF 635, CAOM.
2. Governor-General R. Robin, confidential report dated 11 November 1930, Indo NF 2328, CAOM.
3. The Morché Report, from the name of the president of the Appeals Court in Hanoi who presided over the Investigation Commission regarding the events in North Annam. Indo NF 1597, CAOM.
4. General Henri Edmond Claudel (1871–1956), "Recherche des causes du mouvement insurrectionnel" [Research into the causes of the insurrectional movement], Far East inspection report, May–September 1931, Indo NF 2328, CAOM.
5. General Lombard, "Note sur l'Indochine," August 1931, Indo NF 2328, CAOM.

6. Doctor A. F. Legendre was the former director of the Imperial School of Medicine in Chengdu (Sichuan province). Without mentioning the "shock of civilizations," he entitled his book *La Crise mondiale. Asie contre Europe* [The global crisis: Asia against Europe] (Paris: Plon, 1932), p. 341, et seq.
7. Joseph Ducroux was part of the Comintern's Foreign Liaison Department (Russian acronym OMS), which played the role of a secret service. See *Komintern: l'histoire et les hommes. Dictionnaire biographique de l'Internationale communiste* [Comintern: Hhistory and men. Biographical dictionary of the Communist International], Serge Wolikow (ed.) (Paris: Les Éditions de l'Atelier, 2001), pp. 269–70.
8. See Huynh Kim Khanh, *Vietnamese Communism*.
9. Frank Loseby wrote about his role in this affair in the *New York Times* of 14 September 1969. See also Dennis Duncanson, "Ho Chi Minh in Hong Kong," *China Quarterly* 57 (January–March 1974).
10. Ibid.
11. T. Lan, *Vua di duong vua*, pp. 50–63. The death of Paul Vaillant-Couturier in 1937 deeply saddened Nguyen Ai Quoc (letter to André Marty, 12 October 1937, in *Toan Tap*, vol. 3 (1930–45), pp. 88–89).
12. Ibid. His recollections of the USSR in 1924 are on pp. 18–22, and those of 1934 on pp. 27–29. Quoc used the same argument as Paul Vaillant-Couturier; see Rachel Mazuy's *Croire plutôt que voir? Voyages en Russie soviétique* (1919–1939) [Believing instead of seeing? Travels in Soviet Russia] (Paris: Odile Jacob, 2002), pp. 222–25.
13. Letter from 28 February 1930 in *Toan Tap*, 3, pp. 27–29.
14. No copies of this book have been found, only the cover; its description in *BNTS* 2, p. 28.
15. Letter to Giao, 5 April 1930, in *Toan Tap*, 3, p. 39.
16. Nicolas Werth, *Histoire de l'Union soviétique* [History of the Soviet Union] (Paris: PUF, 2001, 5th ed.), and from the same author, "La Grande Terreur" [The great terror], in the *Livre noir du communism* [The black book of communism], Stéphane Courtois and Jean-Louis Panné (eds.) (Paris: Laffont, 2000), pp. 206–25. Werth believes that the Great Terror began with the destruction of the kulaks – the rich peasant class – (1929) and continued through the great famine in the Ukraine of 1932–33; it extended beyond the large-scale trials in Moscow and became a "police control of society."
17. For more on the repression of the Comintern personnel at the Lux Hotel, see Elena Bonner, *De mères en filles. Un siècle russe* [From mother to daughter: A Russian century] (Paris: Gallimard, 2002).
18. Le Hong Phong, known as Litvinov, was one of the first militants from the Revolutionary Youth League. He was a cadet at the Whampoa Military Academy, a student at the Stalin School, the Aviation School in Leningrad, and then the Pilot School in Borisoglebsk, near Moscow. When the Central Committee of the ICP was dismantled by the police, Phong led the party as de facto Secretary of the Overseas Executive Committee (Ban Hai Ngoai) based in Hong Kong, then in Shanghai and later in southern China. He led the delegation at the Seventh International Congress and became member of

the Executive Committee. He returned home with a Chinese passport and was captured in 1939, but not identified. He was released in January 1940 but arrested again and died on 6 September 1942 in Poulo Condor Prison from dysentery exacerbated by the poor treatment he received in prison, despite the French doctors' efforts to save him.

19. *BNTS* 2, p. 53.
20. Ibid., p. 55.
21. Ibid., pp. 55–59.
22. *Avec l'Oncle Ho*, p. 145.
23. Letter of 6 August 1938 in *Toan Tap*, 3, p. 90.
24. *BNTS* 2, p. 61.
25. This information regarding the famous *bio*(graphy) of Nguyen Thi Minh Khai comes from my interviews with the historians Anatoli Sokolov and Do Quang Hung; also see Sophie Quinn-Judge, *Ho Chi Minh: The Missing Years* (Berkeley and Los Angeles: University of California Press, 2003).
26. Nguyen Thi Minh Khai was arrested in July 1940 and shot in August 1941, even though Rear Admiral Platon, Secretary of State for the Colonies in the Vichy government, had asked Governor-General Decoux to commute her sentence because she was a woman (CAOM, Indo NF 1096). Her father, who worked at the train station in Vinh, wrote a moving letter to Maréchal Pétain asking him to give his daughter a reprieve (CAOM, SPCE 385, 3). As if to reject allusions that Nguyen Ai Quoc and Nguyen Thi Minh Khai were romantically involved, Le Quoc Su, in *Chuyen ke Le Hong Phong va Nguyen Thi Minh Khai* [The history of Le Hong Phong and Nguyen Thi Minh Khai] (Ho Chi Minh City: 2001), compares Le Hong Phong and Nguyen Thi Minh Khai with the exemplary couple of Lenin and Nadezhda Kroupskaya. Undoubtedly, he didn't know that Lenin had a mistress, Inès Armand.
27. Letter from Nguyen Thi Minh Khai sent from Hong Kong to Bui Hai Thieu in Nanjing, dated 31 March 1933, in *SPCE* 385/3, doc. 171, CAOM. In this carton, there is a list of names of Communists drawn up by an agent of the Indochinese Sûreté operating in Yunnan in 1937. Jacket cover 2890 mentions: "Nguyen Ai Quoc's wife *could be* Nguyen Thi Minh Khai, called Co Duy." Nguyen Ai Quoc was definitely very fond of her, if not more, since it was clearly in remembrance of her that he signed his second autobiographical account T. Lan – Tran Thai Lan or Tran Lan being the principle alias of Nguyen Thi Minh Khai.
28. Huynh Kim Khanh, *Vietnamese Communism*. The journals *Cahiers du Bolchevisme* and *Tap Chi Bon Se Vik* are in SLOTFOM III, 48, CAOM.
29. Pierre Renouvin, *La Question d'Extrême-Orient, 1840–1940* [The Far East question: 1840–1940] (Paris: Hachette, 1946).
30. Daniel Hémery, *Révolutionnaires vietnamiens et pouvoir colonial en Indochine* [Vietnamese revolutionaries and colonial power in Indochina] (Paris: F. Maspéro, 1975).
31. *BNTS* 2, and Hoang Tranh, *Ho Chi Minh voi Trung Quoc*.
32. T. Lan, *Vua di duong*.

33. Jacques Guillermaz, *Une vie pour la Chine, 1937–1989* [A life for China, 1937–1989] (Paris: Hachette Littérature, 1994), chaps. 7 and 8. The quotation is on p. 76.
34. *BNTS* 2; Hoang Tranh, *Ho Chi Minh voi Trung Quoc*, and T. Lan, *Vua di duong*.
35. Ibid.
36. *Dau nguon*, pp. 240–41.
37. Fabienne Mercier, *Vichy face à Chiang Kai-shek. Histoire diplomatique* [Vichy and Chiang Kai-shek: A diplomatic history] (Paris: L'Harmattan, 1995).
38. For more on the period 1940–45 in China and in the Viet Bac (Highlands of Tonkin), see the accounts of eleven men who were there, including Vo Nguyen Giap and Le Quang Ba, collected in *Uong nuoc nho nguon* [We remember the spring where we drank] (Hanoi: Quan Doi Nhan Dan, 1978) and *Dau nguon*. The standard reference in Western scholarship is still King C. Chen's *Vietnam and China 1938–1954* (Princeton, N. J.: Princeton University Press, 1969).
39. *Dau nguon*, p. 198.
40. See *Uong nuoc nho nguon* and *Dau nguon*.
41. *Toan Tap*, 3, p. 196.
42. Harold Isaacs, *La tragédie de la Révolution chinoise, 1925–1927* [The tragedy of the Chinese Revolution, 1925–1927] (Paris: Gallimard, 1967), and for a good analysis of Maoist strategy see Roland Lew, *1949, Mao prend le pouvoir* [1949, Mao takes power] (Brussels: Éd. Complexe, 1999).
43. *Dau nguon*, pp. 189–90, and *La Longue Marche: Mémoires du maréchal Zhu De* [The Long March: memoirs of General Zhu De], Agnès Smedley (ed.), 2 vols. (Paris: Presses de l'Imprimerie nationale, 1969), vol. 2, p. 116.
44. *Toan Tap*, 3, pp. 195–245.
45. In Wolikow, *Komintern: l'histoire et les hommes. Dictionnaire biographique de l'Internationale communiste*, pp. 15–92.
46. Ibid., pp. 247–62. The Japanese invasion of China in 1937 greatly worried the Indochinese; both the Vietnamese and the Chinese diaspora kept abreast of events and organized campaigns of solidarity with the Chinese people. Vo Nguyen Giap wrote several articles on the Chinese resistance in *Notre voix* [Our voice], *Dan Chung* [The people], and *Le Travail* [Work].
47. There was also a mutiny of the Garde Indigène in Do Luong (North Annam). The Communists were not involved and it was quickly aborted. On this period, see Pierre Brocheux, "L'occasion favorable. 1940–1945. Les forces politiques vietnamiennes pendant la Seconde guerre mondiale" [The right moment, 1940–1945: Vietnamese political forces during the Second World War], pp. 132–78 in *L'Indochine française. 1940–1945* [French Indochina, 1940–1945], Paul Isoart (ed.) (Paris: PUF, 1982).
48. Wang Fanxi, *Mémoires d'un révolutionnaire chinois* [Memoirs of a Chinese revolutionary] (Montreuil: Éd. La Brèche, 1987), p. 71 and following.
49. In *The Comintern and Vietnam*, Sokolov mentions the case of Dang Dinh Chuc, called Léo, who was arrested in 1938 and sent to Siberia. He was freed

in 1946 and rehabilitated in 1972; see pp. 252–53 of the version in *quoc ngu*. Bui Ai, very close to the Trotskyite leader Ta Thu Thau in Paris, was expelled from the Stalin School in April 1930 "for special reasons," p. 261. Two other students from the Stalin School were sent away for reeducation in factories, but it is not clear whether this was for political reasons.

50. *Toan Tap*, 3, pp. 125–29, and pp. 134–37.
51. Hémery, *Révolutionnaires vietnamiens*, chap. 3.
52. *Toan Tap*, 3; also, he wrote that there should be no cooperation with the Trotskyites, "we must eliminate them *politically*"; directive of 1939 (pp. 138–39), in "Trotsky, instrument du fascisme," p. 156. The comments about Ta Thu Thau are on p. 170.
53. *Luttes des classes* [Class struggle] 39 (15 June 1932). After the rupture of the coalition "The Struggle" in 1937, the journal remained in Trotskyite hands and the polemic raged between the two camps: Articles in the press and pamphlets proliferated on the Popular Front, the Soviet Union, the trials in Moscow, André Gide's *Retour d'URSS* [Return from the USSR], etc. The discussions and arguments penetrated all the way to the jails and prison camps. For more on this, see the interesting recollections of Ngo Van (author of *Vu An Moscou* [The Moscow trial], Saigon, 1937) entitled *Au pays de la cloche fêlée. Les tribulations d'un Cochinchinois à l'époque coloniale* (In the land of *La Cloche Fêlée*: The tribulations of a Cochinchinese in the colonial era) (Paris: l'Insomniaque, 2000).
54. Excerpt from the Resolution of the Presidium of the Executive Committee of the International, dated 15 May 1943, in Jane Degras, *The Communist International: 1919–1943. Documents*, vol. 3 (Oxford: Oxford University Press, 1965).
55. *BNTS* 2, p. 165, and King C. Chen, *Vietnam and China*.
56. Ibid.
57. Poems in *Reflections from Captivity: Phan Boi Chau's Prison Notes and Ho Chi Minh's Prison Diary*, David Marr (ed.), Christopher Jenkins, Tran Khanh Tuyet, and Huynh Sanh Thong (trans.) (Athens: Ohio University Press, 1978). Poems 3 and 5 have been altered slightly from this published translation.
58. *Toan Tap*, 3, "Nhat ky trong tu," pp. 263–427. A book entitled *Ho Chi Minh khong phai la tac gia* [Ho Chi Minh is not the author of the prison diaries], published in Toronto in 1990, asserts that Ho Chi Minh probably wrote only a dozen of the poems and that the others were written by an old Chinese prisoner. Part of the work, then, was borrowed from someone else. In its final form, the *Diary* was supposedly assembled by an editorial committee created for this purpose by Communist Party leaders in 1960. The man who blew the whistle was a Catholic priest who taught Chinese at the university in Hué and was imprisoned and subjected to reeducation after 1975. His opinion is based essentially on a semantic analysis, the accuracy of which can only be evaluated by someone who knows Chinese characters. I cannot say if this is true since I do not speak Chinese, but it seems to me that the freshness, the spontaneity, and the humor reflect what we have already seen in Ho's work.

59. *BNTS* 2.
60. Lieutenant Banh Duc's recollections in *Xua va Nay* 28 (June 1996), 11–12.
61. Ibid.
62. Zhang Fakui, *Oral History*, in Columbia University Library, New York.
63. Le Tung Son, *Nhat ky mot chan duong* [Journal of one stage] (Hanoi: Van Hoc, 1978), p. 129.
64. "Souvenirs de Zhang Fakui," *Revue hebdomadaire l'Union* (Hong Kong, 1962), cited in *BNTS* 2, p. 205.
65. For the period 1944–45, see *BNTS* 2 and *Toan Tap*, 3. There are a number of accounts: See Vo Nguyen Giap's memoirs, entitled *Nhung chan duong lich su* [Stages of history]; the French translation unfortunately does not contain the chapters on the composition or workings of the resistance groups. See also *Dau nguon*; Chu Van Tan, *Ky niem ve Cuu Quoc Quan* [Reminiscences on the Army for National Salvation], English translation by Mai Elliott (Ithaca, N. Y.: Cornell University Southeast Asia Program, 1974); and *Lich su Quan doi Nhan Zan* [History of the People's Army of Vietnam], vol. 1 (1930–54), edited by the Army Historical Research Committee (Hanoi: People's Army Publishing House, 1977) .
66. Quoted in Phan Ngoc Lien, *Nghien cuu Lich su* [Historical research] 149 (1973), 17.
67. For more on the Man peoples and Bac Kan province, see annual reports in CAOM, RST 6726, 2957, 7017.
68. CAOM, RST 7017.
69. Ibid., 5968.
70. Note no. 3072/SG, CAOM, GGI, CM 633. This is the same Louis Arnoux (often misnamed as Paul) who introduced Nguyen Ai Quoc and Albert Sarraut in Paris in 1922.
71. CAOM, RST NF 7017.
72. Vo Nguyen Giap, *Nhung chan duong lich su*, and Chu Van Tan, *Ky niem ve Cuu Quoc Quan* .
73. For this period, see the memoirs of Jean Sainteny, *Histoire d'une paix manquée: Indochine 1945–1947* [History of a failed peace: Indochina 1945–1947] (Paris: Fayard, 1954); Archimedes Patti, *Why Viet Nam? Prelude to America's Albatross* (Berkeley and Los Angeles: University of California Press, 1980); Charles Fenn, *Ho Chi Minh: A Biographical Introduction* (New York: Scribner's Sons, 1973). Also see David Marr, *Vietnam 1945: The Quest for Power* (Berkeley and Los Angeles: University of California Press, 1995); Mark Phillip Bradley, *Imagining Vietnam and America: The Making of Postcolonial Vietnam, 1919–1950* (Chapel Hill: University of North Carolina Press, 2000); and Stein Tønnesson, *The Vietnamese Revolution of 1945: Roosevelt, Ho Chi Minh, and de Gaulle in a World at War* (London: Sage Publications, 1991).
74. Phung The Tai, *Bac Ho, nhung ky niem khong quen* [Uncle Ho, unforgettable memories] (Hanoi: QDNZ, 2001), p. 61. Phung The Tai attained the rank of General of Army Corps, commanding Vietnam's antiaircraft defense.
75. Ibid., p. 70.
76. Ibid., p. 78.

77. Fenn, *Ho Chi Minh*, and Bradley, *Imagining Vietnam*, chap. 3.
78. Jacques Valette, *Indochine 1940–1945. Français contre Japonais* [Indochina 1940–1945. France against Japan] (Paris: Sedes, 1993).
79. Fenn, *Ho Chi Minh*; the handwriting analysis is in Appendix C, p. 132; Patti, *Why Vietnam?*.
80. Sainteny, *Histoire d'une paix manquée*; Guillermaz, *Une vie pour la Chine*; Jean-Marie de Beaucorps, *Soldats de jade* [Jade soldiers] (Paris: Kergour, 1998). See also the documents in the appendix in Valette, *Indochine*.
81. J. Martin, "Rapport au Conseil du gouvernement général" [Report to the Council of the General Government], 3 February 1945, in RHSGM 139 (1985).
82. *Nan doi 1945 o Viet Nam. Nhung chung tich Lich su* [Historical accounts of the famine of 1945 in Vietnam], Van Tao and Furuta Moto (eds.) (Hanoi: 1995).
83. Vo Nguyen Giap, *Nhung chan duong lich su*, p. 152.
84. Phung The Tai, *Bac Ho*, pp. 98–99.
85. Thomas's remarks in "U. S. Senate Committee on Foreign Relations, The United States and Vietnam, 1944–1947, 92nd Congress, 2nd sess., Staff Study no. 2, April 3, 1972," pp. 285–87.
86. René Desfourneaux, "A Secret Encounter with Ho Chi Minh," *Look Magazine* (9 August 1966). And for American-Vietnamese cooperation, see the "Report on OSS Deer Mission by Major Allison Thomas, 17 September 1945," in *Vietnam: the Definitive Documentation of Human Decisions*, Gareth Porter (ed.), vol. 1 (New York: Coleman Enterprises, 1979). Also see the memoirs of Archimedes Patti, written thirty-five years later and, according to Mark Bradley, quite different from his reports of 1945.
87. *BNTS* 2.
88. Marr, *Vietnam 1945*, is the best history of this crucial period.
89. *BNTS* 2.
90. Tran Dan Tien, *Nhung mau chuyen*, p. 8.

4. FATHER OF THE NATION

1. This subchapter is based on information from the following: *BNTS* 3 (1945–46) and *Toan Tap*, vol. 4 (1945–46); the memoirs of Vo Nguyen Giap, Archimedes Patti, and Jean Sainteny, *Histoire d'une paix manquée*; the memoirs of Pierre Messmer, *Après tant de batailles* [After so many battles] (Paris: Albin Michel, 1998); the works already cited by David Marr, Stein Tønnesson, and Mark Bradley; Lin Hua, *Chiang Kai-shek, de Gaulle contre Ho Chi Minh. Vietnam 1945–1946* [Chiang Kai-shek, de Gaulle against Ho Chi Minh: Vietnam 1945–1946] (Paris: L'Harmattan, 1994); *Leclerc et l'Indochine, 1945–1947. Quand se noua le destin d'un empire* [Leclerc and Indochina, 1945–1947: The destiny of an empire in the making], Philippe Duplay and Guy Pedroncini (eds.) (Paris: Albin Michel, 1992); Yves Gras, *Histoire de la guerre d'Indochine* [History of the Indochinese War] (Paris: Denoël, 1992); Peter Dunn, *The First Vietnam War* (London: Hurst & Co.,

1985); and Bernard Fall, *Le Viet Minh. La République démocratique du Viet-Nam. 1945–1960* [The Viet Minh: The Democratic Republic of Vietnam, 1945–1960] (Paris: A. Colin, 1960).

2. *BNTS* 3, pp. 76–77.
3. List in *Toan Tap*, 4, pp. 501–14.
4. Recollections of Hoang Dao Thuy in *Xua va Nay* 27 (1996), pp. 12–14. He writes that the leadership of the ICP began to practice "entryism" to infiltrate its militants into the scouting organizations in 1943. He also writes that at the closing of the convention in Tan Trao, the participants started singing the (Scottish) song known by scouts of all nations, "It is but a good-bye, my brothers." Le Duy Thuoc also provided his account in *Xua va Nay* 39 (1997).
5. Pierre Brocheux, *The Mekong Delta: Ecology, Economy and Revolution (1860–1960)* (Madison: University of Wisconsin: Center for Southeast Asian Studies, 1995).
6. Ta Quang Buu, *Nha tri thuc giu Nuoc va cach mang* [An intellectual defender of the country and the revolution], a book of his recollections. Comments on the scouts, pp. 255–71 and 287–97. I thank Emmanuel Poisson for having brought this book to my attention.
7. Pham Khac Hoe, *Tu Trieu dinh Hue den Chien khu Viet Bac* [From the court in Hué to the Resistance Zone of the Viet Bac) (Hué: 1987). And see the account by one of Bui Bang Doan's sons, Bui Tin, *1945–1999. La face cachée du régime* [1945–1999: The hidden face of the regime] (Paris: Kergour, 1999), pp. 19–45. This French edition is a translation and updated version of *Following Ho Chi Minh: Memoirs of a North Vietnamese Colonel* (Honolulu: University of Hawaii Press, 1995). See also Xuan Phuong, *Ao Dai, du Couvent des oiseaux à la jungle du Viet Minh* [Ao Dai: From the Couvent des Oiseaux to the Viet Minh jungle] (Paris: Plon, 2001). Translated into English as *Ao Dai: My War, My Country, My Vietnam* (Great Neck, N.Y.: Emquad International, 2004).
8. Phan Thi Minh Le, "A Vietnamese Scholar on a Different Path: Huynh Thuc Khang," in *Viet Nam Exposé: French Scholarship on Twentieth Century Vietnamese Society*, Gisèle Bousquet and Pierre Brocheux (eds.) (Ann Arbor: University of Michigan Press, 2002); and Le Van Hien, *Chuyen cong can dac biet* [Account of a special mission] (NXB Danang, 1986), pp. 36–37.
9. *BNTS* 3, pp. 74–75.
10. *Cuu Quoc* [National salvation] 141–42 (14–15 January 1946), the organ of the Viet Minh.
11. Phung The Tai, *Bac Ho*, pp. 117–20.
12. Monsignors Jean-Baptiste Tong, Ho Ngoc Can, Ngo Dinh Thuc, and Le Huu Tu wrote a message to the Pope on 23 September 1945, then another on 4 November to Christians throughout the world and to the people of the United States and Great Britain. Archives of the Missions étrangères de Paris (hereafter, MEP), DH 300. The first was published in *Témoignage chrétien* [Christian witness] on 30 November 1945 and distributed to churches in Paris on 25 November 1945. The French missionaries' notes are in the *Bulletin des MEP* 1 (July 1948), 54.

13. *Cuu Quoc* 107 (3 December 1945), and on the "Muong king," see the article in *Xua va Nay* 38 (April 1997). The ethnic groups of the Highlands of North Vietnam provided a large number of soldiers and porters to the great battles of the 1950s. At Dien Bien Phu, two of the four divisions of the People's Army were made up of Tay (called Tho in the colonial era). Ho knew that the victory was due to the sacrifices of these men and women. After 1954, two autonomous zones were created: the Tay Bac and the Viet Bac. Their autonomy was quickly suppressed, or ignored, which sheds light on another contradiction of the political strategy of the Vietnamese Communists (beyond the opposition of the national and social): The desire for unity entails centralization, while multiethnicity requires a more federated state. Three factors impeded the federation of autonomous nationalist regions, which would still have been under the hegemony of the Viet majority (called *kinh*): the necessity for unity in wartime; regional strategy – ethnic minorities who lived on both sides of the borders with China, Laos, and Cambodia could be drawn toward autonomist tendencies; and finally, reception by the Highlands of a large part of the *kinh* migration from the delta and the overpopulated plains. Above all, there was a definite Vietnamese ethnocentrism, and many Vietnamese considered their culture to be the "most advanced" and the engine of modernization. These circumstances led to the establishment of a centralized state.
14. *Toan Tap*, vol. 6 (1950–52), pp. 217–18.
15. *BNTS* 3, p. 25.
16. Tran Van Giau in *Xua va Nay* 99 (September 2000), p. 12.
17. On the Hoa Hao, see Hue Tam Ho Tai, *Millenarianism and Peasant Politics in Vietnam* (Cambridge, Mass.: Harvard University Press, 1982). On Cao Dai, see Jayne Werner, *Peasants, Politics, and Religious Sectarianism: Peasant and Priest in the Cao Dai in Vietnam* (New Haven, Conn.: Yale University Southeast Asian Studies, Monograph 23, 1981). In the end, only the Cao Dai sect of Cao Trieu Phat – whose headquarters were in Bac Lieu – joined the Viet Minh.
18. Testimony of Ngo Van, who survived the persecution of the Trotskyites in Cochinchina, in *Au pays de la cloche fêlée*, pp. 165–203.
19. Pierre Brocheux, *The Mekong Delta*, pp. 188–98.
20. Nguyen Hien Le, *Hoi Ky* [Memoirs], vol. 1 (Ho Chi Minh City: 1993). He writes about the anarchy in Cochinchina, the murderous behavior of the Cambodians, the execution of the Hoa Hao by the Viet Minh in Can Tho in December 1945, the blind zeal of the Viet Minh militants (who detained the author because he was traveling with a manual on agricultural hydraulics written in French), and the crimes committed by bandits and French soldiers.
21. *Cuu Quoc* 147 (21 January 1946).
22. *BNTS* 3, p. 103.
23. Patti, *Why Vietnam?* p. 220, et seq.
24. Xuan Phuong, *Ao Dai*, pp. 58–59.
25. Lin Hua, *Chiang Kai-Shek*, p. 47.
26. *BNTS* 3, pp. 274–75.
27. Cited in Lin Hua, *Chiang Kai-Shek*, pp. 66–67.

28. Message of 8 September 1945 published in *Cuu Quoc* (10 September 1945); and Vu Thu Hien, *Dem giua ban ngay* [Darkness at noon] (Stanton, Calif.: Van Nghe, 1997).
29. Josip Broz, known as Tito, was a member of the Comintern and leader of the Communist Party of Yugoslavia. He led the armed resistance against the Germans in Yugoslavia and later was President of the Federal Socialist Republic of Yugoslavia until his death in 1980.
30. *BNTS* 3, pp. 47–48. The account of the redistribution of rice by the Chinese is in Sainteny, *Histoire d'une paix manquée*.
31. Patti, *Why Vietnam?* pp. 337–39.
32. Text of the letter in *Xua va Nay* 8 (1995), 6–7.
33. Le Van Hien, *Chuyen cong*, p. 26.
34. This section is based on information from *BNTS* 3, *Toan Tap* 4, and *Paris-Saigon-Hanoi. Les archives de la guerre 1944–1947* [Paris-Saigon-Hanoi: The war archives, 1944–1947] (Paris: Gallimard-Julliard, 1988), a good anthology of archival documents and eyewitness accounts, edited by Philippe Devillers.
35. Archives of the Paris Police headquarters, BA 2153/ "colonie indochinoise de Paris" I[1], A6193.
36. Messmer, *Après tant de batailles*, chap. 8, "Mission Impossible."
37. Presented by Philippe Devillers in *De Gaulle et l'Indochine. 1940–1946* [De Gaulle and Indochina, 1940–1946], Gilbert Pilleul (ed.) (Paris: Institut Charles de Gaulle, Plon, 1982), p. 193.
38. In *BNTS* 3, pp. 263–64. See also Chen, *Vietnam and China*, p. 107.
39. *BNTS* 3, p. 44. Jean Sainteny took advantage of Major Patti's mission to go to Hanoi in August 1945. He formed a rather privileged relationship with Ho Chi Minh that became a lasting friendship, and it shows through in his two books, *Histoire d'une paix manquée* and *Face à Ho Chi Minh* [Confronting Ho Chi Minh] (Paris: Seghers, 1970).
40. Tønnesson, *The Vietnamese Revolution*, and Bradley, *Imagining Vietnam*. Bradley stressed that the Americans had a very poor opinion of the Vietnamese – Ho Chi Minh excepted – and even of Ho's government. Patti himself described the Vietnamese in one of his cables as "politically immature," at the mercy of Japanese or Communist *agents provocateurs*, and he claimed that they harbored an "inferiority complex with regard to the French." The American general Philip Gallagher, advisor to the Chinese troops in Indochina, deemed Ho's government lacking in "executive capabilities." He believed that the Vietnamese were militarily "overly enthusiastic and naïve" and would be massacred by the French in the event of war (p. 136). They all noted the leading role played by the Communists at the heart of the Viet Minh and of the government.
41. Patti, *Why Vietnam?*
42. Devillers, *Paris-Saigon-Hanoi*, p. 119. Emperor Duy Tan was left destitute by the French in 1916 because he had agreed to lead an uprising and was then exiled to Reunion Island. He later joined the forces of the Free French. He had been contacted by de Gaulle to go on an exploratory mission in Indochina but died in an airplane accident on 28 December 1945 in

Ubangi-chari. Perhaps de Gaulle secretly wished to reseat Duy Tan on the throne in place of Bao Dai?

43. See Salan's *Mémoires*, p. 192.
44. Devillers, *Paris-Saigon-Hanoi*, p. 155; François Missoffe, *Duel rouge* [Red duel] (Paris: Ramsey, 1977), p. 25.
45. Devillers, *Paris-Saigon-Hanoi*, p. 112, and Sainteny, *Face à Ho Chi Minh*, p. 65.
46. Raoul Salan, *Mémoires, tome 1: Fin d'un empire, le sens d'un engagement, juin 1899–septembre 1946* [Memoirs, volume 1: End of an empire, the meaning of an engagement, June 1899–September 1946] (Paris: Presses de la Cité, 1970), pp. 288–92.
47. Devillers, *Paris-Saigon-Hanoi*.
48. Ngo Van Chieu, *Journal d'un combattant Viet-Minh* [Journal of a Viet Minh combatant] (Paris: Seuil, 1955), p. 100.
49. Pierre Brocheux, "Déceptions et méfiances vietnamiennes" [Vietnamese deceptions and mistrust], in *Leclerc et l'Indochine*, pp. 228–42. The quotation is on p. 236.
50. *BNTS* 3. Excerpts of the speech translated into French in Devillers, *Paris-Saigon-Hanoi*, p. 152.
51. Lin Hua, in *Chiang Kai-Shek*, suggests that it was due to a misunderstanding.
52. *Le Monde* of 14–15 July 1946, in Devillers, *Paris-Saigon-Hanoi*, p. 199.
53. Cited by Colonel Bodinier, "Le Général Leclerc et la négociation vietnamienne" [General Leclerc and Vietnamese negotiation], *Revue Historique des Armées* 2 (2002), 72.
54. Salan, *Mémoires*, vol. 1, p. 389.
55. Messmer, *Après tant de batailles*, p. 178. Jean-Julien Fonde, who cochaired the joint commission in Tonkin, wrote about the widespread malaise that permeated their relations with the Vietnamese over the problem of Cochinchina in *Traitez à tout prix... Leclerc et le Viet Nam* [Negotiate at any cost... Leclerc and Vietnam] (Paris: Laffont, 1971).
56. Salan, *Mémoires*, vol. 1, p. 404, and Jean Sainteny, *Histoire d'une paix manquée*, p. 231.
57. The Aubracs had been in the Resistance since its inception and became famous when Raymond broke out of prison with the help of his wife Lucie. Raymond Aubrac was also part of the National Resistance Council; see his *Où la mémoire s'attarde* [Where memory lingers] (Paris: O. Jacob, 1996), pp. 181–92.
58. APP (Archives de la Préfecture de Police de Paris), carton BA 2436.
59. Interview at the Royal Monceau Hotel based on the deposition of Jacques Rabemananjara, 12 April 1947, during his trial in Antananarivo (author's emphasis); see *L'Insurrection malgache*, pp. 335–36.
60. Jacques Dumaine, *Quai d'Orsay: 1945–1951* (Paris: Julliard, 1955), p. 103. When Georges Bidault was accused of having received Ho with all honors, he responded that he had placed the Vietnamese President in the second row. See Bidault's *D'une résistance à l'autre* [From one resistance to another] (Paris: Les Presses du Siècle, 1965).

61. "Nhat Ky Hanh Trinh cua Ho Chu tich. Bon thang sang Phap" [Travel notebook of President Ho: Four months in France] in *Toan Tap*, 4, pp. 323–411. "Nhung duc tinh cua nguoi Phap" [The beautiful qualities of the French], pp. 410–11. This *Notebook* is not in the first edition of *Toan Tap* from the 1980s.
62. *Toan Tap*, 4, p. 450.
63. Ibid., pp. 410–11.
64. Letter from Captain Duprat to General Valluy dated 8 January 1947, SHAT (Services Historiques de l'Armée de Terre), 10H 164, Dossier 1. Pham Duy Khiem, brother of the musician Pham Duy, graduated from the prestigious École Normale with a degree in grammar, and was a fellow student and friend of Georges Pompidou at the École Normale Supérieure.
65. *Quan Chung*, collection of the CAOM, Aix-en-Provence. Huynh Phu So, founder and prophet of the religion, had meanwhile agreed to participate in the Resistance and Administration Committee of Nam Bo. He wrote a similar article in *Quan Chung* (13 November 1946).
66. Cao Van Luan, *Ben giong Lich su. Hoi ky 1945–1965* [In the course of History: Recollections 1945–1965] (Glendale, Calif.: Dai Nam, c.1976), p. 86. Luan became rector of the University of Hué during the Ngo Dinh Diem presidency.
67. Tran Trong Kim, *Mot con gio bui* [In the tempest] (Saigon: Vinh Son, 1969), p. 171.
68. *Chuyen ke ve Bac Ho* [Anecdotes about Uncle Ho], Thai Kim Dinh (ed.) (NXB Nghe An, 2000), vol. 2, pp. 34–37.
69. Georges Thierry d'Argenlieu, *Chronique d'Indochine. 1945–1947* [Chronicle of Indochina, 1945–1947] (Paris: Albin Michel, 1985), p. 335. The Admiral is referring here to the first meeting, during which Ho said that relations between France and Vietnam should be not only of friendship but of fraternity, and then he suddenly kissed the Admiral on both cheeks, which caught him off guard.
70. Le Flahec, "Quelques missions en pays Viet Minh (souvenirs)" [Some missions in Viet Minh country (recollections)], in *Cahiers CHEAM* vol. 43, no. 1221. Another interesting testimony is from the Administrator René Moreau, who served in the countryside in Vinh: *8 ans otage chez les Viets, 1946–1954* [Held hostage for eight years by the Vietnamese, 1946–1954] (Paris: Pygmalion-Gérard Watelet, 1982). On the worsening of the situation and events after Ho Chi Minh's return from France, see Fonde, *Traitez à tout prix*. Jean-Julien Fonde was a French officer who served during some of the bloody clashes, like the one at Bac Ninh.
71. Devillers, *Paris-Saigon-Hanoi*, p. 189.
72. Ngo Van Chieu, *Journal d'un combattant*, p. 100.
73. Ibid., p. 271.
74. Vuong Thua Vu, *Truong thanh trong Chien dau* [Forged in battle] (Hanoi: 1979), p. 76. He was trained at a Chinese military academy (undoubtedly Whampoa), and was considered by the CEFEO command to be the top Vietnamese tactician.
75. Cited by Devillers, *Paris-Saigon-Hanoi*, pp. 267–68.

76. Vu Ky, excerpt from his *Memoirs* in *Tap chi Lich su Quan su* [Military History Review], 12/37 (1988), p. 78.
77. Fonde, *Traitez à tout prix*, p. 312.
78. Pham Duy, *Hoi Ky Thoi Cach Mang Khang Chien* [Recollections of the revolution and the resistance], vol. 1 (of 3) (California: PDC, 1989), p. 83. In 1951, Pham Duy left Interzone IV of the Resistance for the zone occupied by the French. He later moved to South Vietnam and then fled to the United States in 1975, where he lives today.
79. Vu Ky, *Memoirs*, pp. 74–75.
80. Ibid., p. 79.
81. Ibid., pp. 81–82.
82. Pierre Sergent, *Un étrange Monsieur Frey* [The strange Mr. Frey] (Paris: Fayard, 1982). Recollections of Ernst Frey, an Austrian Communist who joined the Foreign Legion after having fled Nazism. A member of the ICP, he joined the Vietnamese revolution and became a military cadre with the Viet Minh. He claims never to have understood why Vietnamese leaders denied unleashing the offensive of 19 December 1946 (the book was published in 1982). Paradoxically, his reminiscences were taken down by Sergent, a former member of the OAS.
83. Vuong Thua Vu, *Truong thanh trong*, pp. 105–6.
84. The standard French-language reference work on the war is Gras's *Histoire de la guerre d'Indochine*.
85. On China and Vietnam during the two Indochinese wars, see two articles by Chen Jian: "China and the First Indochina War: 1950–1954," *China Quarterly* 133 (March 1993), and "China's Involvement in the Vietnam War: 1954–1969," *China Quarterly* 142 (June 1995). See also Qiang Zhai, *China and the Vietnam Wars, 1950–1975* (Chapel Hill: University of North Carolina Press, 2000).
86. Y. Gras, *Histoire de la guerre d'Indochine*, p. 354.
87. Phung The Tai, *Bac Ho*, p. 121.
88. Ngo Van Chieu, *Journal d'un combattant*, p. 60.
89. Ibid., p. 186.
90. On this period, see *BNTS* 4 and 5.
91. Ibid.
92. Léo Figuères, *Je reviens du Viet-Nam libre* [I am returning from free Vietnam] (Paris: Éditions sociales, 1950).
93. In 1418, Le Loi rallied the Vietnamese people to fight Chinese domination and founded the Le dynasty, which ruled until 1788. It was supplanted by Emperor Quang Trung, who had repulsed another Chinese invasion in the eighteenth century. In 1802, Gia Long defeated the brothers of Quang Trung and founded the Nguyen dynasty, which held the throne until 1945. Both Trotsky and Tito had broken with Stalin in an attempt to forge their own brand of communism, leading to a radical schism (and even death, in the case of Trotsky).
94. Paul Mus, *Ho Chi Minh, le Vietnam et l'Asie*, pp. 79–81.
95. General Le Trong Tan, *Tu Dong Quan den Dien Bien Phu* [From Dong Quan to Dien Bien Phu] (Hanoi: QDNZ, 2002), p. 199.

96. *Xua va Nay* 91 (May 2001), 7.
97. Speech at the Second Congress of the Vietnamese Workers' Party in *Toan Tap*, 6, p. 184.
98. Vo Nguyen Giap, *Duong toi Dien Bien Phu. Hoi uc* [The road toward Dien Bien Phu. Reminiscenses], pp. 46 and 173.
99. T. Lan, *Vua di duong*, pp. 11–12. Phan Phac relates this episode in two articles in *Tap chi Lich su Quan su* [Military history review] 22 (October 1987), 32–39 and 94; and *Tap chi Lich su Quan su* 23 (November 1987), 34–43 and 62.
100. Marcel Lepage, *La Tragique Épopée de la colonne Lepage* [The tragic epic of the Lepage formation] (Paris: NEL, 1981).
101. Pierre Charton, *RC4. Indochine 1950. La tragédie de l'évacuation de Caobang* [RC4: Indochina 1950: The tragedy of the retreat from Caobang] (Paris: SPL, 1975), p. 83. The exchange between Ho and his officers is from Dang Van Viet, *La RC4. Campagne des frontières (1947–1950)* [The RC4: Border campaign (1947–1950)] (Hanoi: ÉLÉ, 1990), p. 132. Charton's claim not to have recognized Ho Chi Minh is surprising, for even though Ho was dressed as a Nung peasant, he was still recognizable. Had Charton only seen Ho in photos? Or was the Colonel too "groggy" from his ordeal? Ho's words may seem a bit surreal, but they are plausible since we know that while he was in France, he saw the movie *La Bataille du Rail* by René Clément and asked people to tell him about the anti-German resistance. And he was certainly capable of inventing a new role for himself. As for the opinions on Pétain, this was Ho's way of hooking Charton, revealing his manipulative side. Apparently, there was also a French military doctor at these meetings who, according to Vietnamese officers, understood the legitimacy of the Vietnamese struggle, and was then disciplined after the war. He is mentioned only by the initials R.D.
102. Excerpt from Dang Van Viet, *La RC4*, p. 132. Another French edition was published by Éditions du Petit Capuchin in 2000.
103. Xuan Phuong, *Ao Dai*, pp. 131–33.
104. Letter of 19 February 1947 in *Toan Tap*, vol. 5 (1947–49), p. 53. At the time, Vu Dinh Huynh was presiding over the Administrative Resistance Committee of Ninh Binh.
105. Ibid., p. 90.
106. Ibid., p. 40.
107. *Xua Va Nay* 97 (August 2001), p. F.
108. The salary of a soldier (*bo doi*) was 150 dong. Le Van Hien, *Nhat ky cua mot Bo truong, t. 1* [Journal of a minister, vol. 1] (NXB Danang: 1995), pp. 6–7. Hien was the Minister of Finances in the DRV government.
109. Cadière 2034 (05), "Correspondence avec Ho (1946–1953)," DH 430-1, Archives MEP. I thank Gérard Moussay for granting me access to this correspondence. Cadière was one of the founders of Vietnamese studies and was eighty-two years old when put under house arrest in Vinh. He claims to have been treated well, but he was not liberated until 1954, after a number of requests.
110. Letter of 1 February 1947 in *Toan Tap*, 5, p. 44.

111. Ibid., pp. 88–89, letter of 10 March 1947.
112. Vu Dinh Hoe, *Phap Quyen–Nhan Nghia. Ho Chi Minh* [The Law–The Humanity; Ho Chi Minh] (Hanoi: 2000), pp. 130–33. According to Vu Dinh Hoe, the man named Ly Ban had been Chief of Security Services for the CCP in the Sino-Vietnamese border zone in the 1930s–1940s.
113. We have two diametrically opposed points of view: The Chinese advisor Chen Geng (in his *Journal* and in his cables to Mao Zedong) claims to be responsible for the victory on the RC4, while the Vietnamese General Vo Nguyen Giap writes that it was he who planned the campaign, which Chen Geng approved (see *Duong toi Dien Bien Phu*). Wei Guoqing (1906–94), an ethnic Zhuang from Guangxi, was on the Long March and then served in the anti-Japanese resistance. Later, he became the strongman of Guangxi and Guangdong during the Cultural Revolution and defeated the Red Guards. In Vietnam, and after Chen Geng left for Korea, Wei Guoqing "decided that the Vietnamese army would lead an offensive in Thai territory, northwest of Tonkin," according to Chinese documents.
114. On Chinese aid, see Qiang Zhai, "Les conseillers militaires chinois en 1950" [Chinese military advisors in 1950], *Revue historique des Armées* 3 (2000), 3–14; and Christopher Goscha, "L'aide militaire chinoise au Viet Minh (1949–1954)" [Chinese military aid to the Viet Minh, (1949–1954)], ibid., 15–24. Qiang Zhai has dealt more generally with this subject in *China and the Vietnam Wars*. Chen Jian also published two articles on the subject in *China Quarterly* in 1993 and 1995.
115. Pham Duy, *Hoi ky*, pp. 275–95. The congress in question was held in the presence of Chinese and Soviet delegations, as well as Léo Figuères representing the Central Committee of the FCP. The Vietnamese Communists wanted to show that they were in step with the other Communist Parties. Indeed, in 1948 and 1949, two Vietnamese from the DRV delegations in Bangkok and Prague had personally – but undoubtedly in concert – denounced Ho Chi Minh's nationalist policies to the Soviet government (see the articles by Benoît de Tréglodé and Christopher Goscha in *Approches-Asie* 16 (1999).
116. Nikita Khrushchev, *Souvenirs* (Paris: Robert Laffont, 1970), p. 456. While the PRC and the USSR officially recognized the DRV, the Thai government of Phibun Songkhram recognized the Associated State of Vietnam, established by the French and led by the former emperor Bao Dai – a significant political choice.
117. Ibid., p. 455.
118. Ibid., p. 456.
119. Vo Nguyen Giap, *Chien dau trong vong vay*, pp. 350–51.
120. "Dear cherished and respected comrade. I am returning today to my country. I thank you for everything you have done for me. I promise to be diligent in carrying out the agrarian program and the patriotic war. I hope I will be able to return here in two or three years to update you on how my work has progressed. I wish you health and long life. Warm regards." Message from Ho to Stalin, 19 November 1952, in Ilya Gaiduk, *Confronting Vietnam: Soviet Policy toward the Indochina Conflict, 1954–1963* (Stanford: Stanford University Press, 2003), p. 11.

121. From Chen Geng's *Journal* (in Chinese); I thank Christopher Goscha for showing me these excerpts, translated into English. The text was published in Beijing in 1987 and used by Chinese researchers.
122. Article by Georges Boudarel on *Chinh Huan* in *La Bureaucratie au Viet Nam*, Asie-débats 1. For this practice in China, see Theodore H. E. Chen, *Thought Reform of the Chinese Intellectuals* (New York: Hyperion Press, 1983).
123. Bui Tin, *La face cachée du régime*, pp. 48–49.
124. Vu Dinh Hoe, *Phap Quyen*, p. 308. For Dr. Tuoc and others of his generation, Ho Chi Minh used the term *Chu* (uncle, the father's younger brother); the term *Bac* (uncle, father's older brother) designated Ho, but not exclusively.
125. According to Vo Nguyen Giap (see *Chien dau trong vong vay*, p. 351), Ho Chi Minh told him that in Korea, the Chinese army had prevailed over the Americans thanks to the "human wave" tactic, but added that the Chinese could use it because of their population, while the Vietnamese had to fight according to their own methods. Ho distanced himself from the Chinese model, and ironically told a foreign journalist that he didn't feel he had to write his theory down because "Mao Zedong has already said it all."
126. Hoang Tung, *Nhung Ky niem ve Bac Ho* [Memories of Uncle Ho], published in 2002 by the State Political Publishing House but immediately pulled from circulation and burned. Hoang Tung was the editor of *Nhan Dan* from 1951 to 1982.
127. Bui Tin, *La face cachée du régime*, p. 48.

5. THE FORCE OF CIRCUMSTANCE

1. Mao Zedong, excerpt from his *Report on an Investigation into the Peasant Movement in Hunan*, February 1927. Georges Clemenceau, Deputy and Prime Minister of the Third Republic in France, from a debate in the House of Deputies, 1891. Édouard Herriot was a Member of Parliament and Minister in the Third Republic, from his book *Lyon Révolutionnaire*, 1937.
2. Alain Ruscio, *Dien Bien Phu, la fin d'une illusion* [Dien Bien Phu, the end of an illusion] (Paris: L'Harmattan, 1987), pp. 97–98.
3. On the war in Indochina, see Jacques Dalloz, *The War in Indochina, 1945–54* (New York: Barnes & Noble, 1990); the works by Devillers; and Ruscio (ed.), *Ho Chi Minh. Textes*.
4. Denise Artaud and Lawrence Kaplan (eds.), *Dien Bien Phu, l'alliance atlantique et la défense du sud-est asiatique* [Dien Bien Phu, the Atlantic alliance and the defense of Southeast Asia] (Lyon: La Manufacture, 1989); Philippe Devillers and Jean Lacouture, *De la guerre française à la guerre américaine* [From the French war to the American war] (Paris: Seuil, 1969); Irving Wall, *L'influence américaine sur la politique française. 1945–1954* [American influence on French policy, 1945–1954] (Paris: Balland, 1989); Hughes Tertrais, *La Piastre et le fusil. Le coût de la guerre d'Indochine. 194—1954*, [The Piastre and the gun: The cost of the war in Indochina, 1945–1954] (Paris: CHÉFF, 2002).

5. François Joyaux, *La Chine et le réglement du premier conflit d'Indochine. Genève 1954* [China and the settling of the first Indochinese conflict: Geneva 1954] (Paris: Publications de la Sorbonne, 1979).
6. *Toan Tap*, vol. 7 (1953–55), pp. 305–6.
7. Hoang Tung, *Nhung Ky niem*. Tung adds that Ho later suggested the same for the Americans. And on a later occasion, in 1968, Party Secretary To Huu took advantage of Ho's absence and paraded the American pilots who had been taken prisoner through the streets of Hanoi. He wanted to humiliate them by submitting them to trial by the masses. When Ho returned, he summoned Hoang Tung and criticized the Central Committee for being responsible for the "stupid" initiative.
8. *Toan Tap*, 7, pp. 321–23. On 22 July 1954, in his "Appeal to compatriots, the army, and cadres following the Geneva Conference," Ho Chi Minh stressed that the cease-fire marked an important step in the struggle for national liberation because the French army would leave Indochina. The nations of Indochina would be independent, the partition of Vietnam would only be provisional, and reunification would be achieved.
9. G. Khérian in the *Revue indochinoise juridique et économique* [Indochinese law and economics review] (1938), 488.
10. Pierre Brocheux, "Communistes et paysans au Viet Nam" [Communists and peasants in Vietnam], in *Révoltes, réformes et révolutions*, pp. 247–76.
11. The two men were Vo Nguyen Giap, future Commander in Chief of the PAVN, and Truong Chinh, Secretary of the VWP from 1951 to 1956. They took the pseudonyms of Van Dinh and Qua Ninh, respectively.
12. Central Committee of the Communist Party, January 1948; author's emphasis. See Nguyen Xuan Lai, "Politique économique et guerre de libération nationale" [Economic policy and war of national liberation], in *Études Vietnamiennes* 44.
13. Cited by Nguyen Xuan Lai in "Politique économique et guerre de libération nationale."
14. See the study by the anthropologist Hy Van Luong in *Revolution in the Village: Tradition and Transformations in North Vietnam, 1925–1988* (Honolulu: Hawaii University Press, 1992), chap. 5; the quotation is on p. 190.
15. Xuan Phuong, *Ao Dai*, p. 164, et seq. Her friend's father, Colonel Dang Van Viet, a hero of the RC4, was shot "or else they just let him starve to death." The antiestablishment writer Duong Thu Huong wrote a novel about these years, translated into English as *The Paradise of the Blind* (New York: Penguin, 1994).
16. The land reform campaign in China has been well chronicled by the American historian William Hinton in *Fanshen: A Documentary of Revolution in a Chinese Village* (Berkeley and Los Angeles: University of California Press, 1997). From 1945 to 1948 he accompanied a land reform group in China. Unfortunately, there is no equivalent study regarding Vietnam. See Le Chau, *Le Viet Nam socialiste* [Socialist Vietnam] (Paris: Maspéro, 1966), and Bernard Fall, *Le Viet Minh*; the first anti-Communist account is by Hoang Van Chi, *Du colonialisme au communisme. L'expérience du*

Nord Viet Nam [From colonialism to communism: The experience of North Vietnam] (Tours: Éditions Mame, 1964).

17. *Toan Tap*, vol. 8 (1955–57), pp. 235–37.
18. Ibid., vol. 7, p. 467; author's emphasis.
19. Hoang Tung, *Nhung Ky niem*.
20. In the journal *La Vie ouvrière* of 4 July 1924, and "Rapport sur le Tonkin," in Ruscio, *Ho Chi Minh. Textes*, pp. 69–70.
21. *La réforme de l'industrie et du commerce (1958–1960)* [Reforms in industry and commerce (1958–1960)], a study by Nguyen Thi Ngoc Thanh (Hanoi Institute of Economics, 1999, photocopied version). For more on the agricultural cooperatives, see Chu Van Lam, *Hop tac xa nong ghiep Viet Nam. Lich su, to chuc va lien vong* [Agricultural cooperatives in Vietnam: History, organization, and perspectives] (Hanoi: Su That, 1992).
22. Xuan Phuong, *Ao Dai*, p. 176.
23. In 1954, a second wave of "thought reform" in China, in conjunction with the first Five-Year Plan, sparked a crisis in the relations between intellectuals and the CCP. In 1954 and 1955, three "affairs" drove renowned intellectuals into conflict with Zhou Yang, who was compared to Andrei Zhdanov for his role as cultural tsar. The writer Hu Feng had been "a fellow traveler" since the 1920s; he had supported the Communist regime but did not hold back his criticism. He was arrested as an "agent of the Kuomintang" and condemned to life in prison. He was rehabilitated in 1980. See Chen, *Thought Reform*, pp. 85–90.
24. The economist and journalist Tibor Mende went to Hanoi during this period and was told that "it was an independent phenomenon, justified by the transition from transitory to permanent." See "Les deux Viet Nam" [The two Vietnams], *Esprit* (June 1957), 943. In a way, events during this period in the communist world seem like reflections in a hall of mirrors. Plus, North Vietnam was in a phase of reconstruction, trying to establish the base for a transition to socialism, and so it relied entirely on the help of socialist countries, beginning with China. Its economic and cultural relations with the capitalist world were reduced to a strict minimum.
25. Georges Boudarel, *Cent fleurs écloses dans la nuit du Vietnam* [One hundred flowers bloom in the night of Vietnam] (Paris: Jacques Bertoin, 1991). Tran Dan's *Ghi. 1954–1960* [Notes, 1954–60] (Stanton, Calif.: Van Nghe, 2000) had not yet been translated into French or in English when I wrote this book.
26. See the report entitled "A Look Back at the Three Years of Sabotage by the Group Humanism and Belles-Lettres," presented by the poet To Huu before the Committee of the Union of Cultural and Arts Associations, on 4 June 1958 in Hanoi, in Tran Dan, *Ghi*, appendix, pp. 423–32.
27. Nguyen Manh Tuong, *Un excommunié. Hanoi 1954–1991: Procès d'un intellectuel* [An excommunicated man, Hanoi 1954–1991: The trial of an intellectual] (Paris: Que Me, 1992).
28. According to *BNTS* 7, p. 149, this article by Ho Chi Minh was published in *Nhan Dan* 1647 (16 October 1958), but is not in the 1994 edition of *Toan Tap*, 8. Is this due to a retraction by the editors of the *Complete Works* or an error by the editors of the *BNTS*? If it was the former, then Ho denied his

attack against the rightists, or else his devoted followers wanted to remove the blame from of him for having instigated the repression against the "One Hundred Flowers."

29. According to cables from Roger Lalouette, the French Ambassador in Saigon, to Couve de Murville, Minister of Foreign Affairs in 1960: "One is copying Hanoi, a bit behind the times and with doubtful efficiency. . . . One needs to create political commissioners in the Army. . . . The regime is authoritarian but not strong." Telegram 257/62, series 32, 553, Dossier 7, Archives du Quai d'Orsay, series C-L-V/Sud Vietnam, 1956–1964, vol. 27–28.
30. Mieczyslaw Maneli, *War of the Vanquished* (New York: Harper & Row, 1971), p. 41.
31. Ibid., Ho Chi Minh supposedly alluded to the patriotism of Ngo Dinh Diem and thus to the possibility of negotiating with him. When Ambassador Lodge learned of the successful putsch by the South Vietnamese generals, he exclaimed: "It's marvelous! It's great!" The brothers Diem and Nhu were executed – shot and then stabbed – by the officers who were escorting them to army headquarters after their arrest. A spokesman for the General Staff claimed that they were both victims of an "accidental suicide." See Nguyen Phu Duc, *Viet-Nam. Pourquoi les États Unis ont-ils perdu la guerre?* [Vietnam: Why did the United States lose the war?] (Paris: Godefroy de Bouillon, 1996), p. 78.
32. Recollections of Ho An and Nguyen Van Thanh in *Le Duan. Mot nha lanh dao loi lac mot tu duy sang tao lon cua cach mang Viet Nam* [Le Duan, an eminent leader and a great thinker of the Vietnamese revolution] (Hanoi: NXB CTQG, 2002). Ho's fears were well founded, however, since the number of Americans engaged in South Vietnam jumped from 184,314 in 1965 to eventually 525,000 by June 1968. The United States dropped a total of 6,300,000 tons of bombs over Vietnam (four times more than in Europe during World War II). In 1967, 80 percent of the one hundred thousand victims in North Vietnam were civilians. In the South, the spraying of toxic chemicals resulted in long-term damage to the environment and had serious consequences on the human population, with tragic effects on embryonic development.
33. "Mo duong Ho Chi Minh" [Building the Ho Chi Minh Trail], recollections of General Vo Bam in *Duong Ho Chi Minh. Hoi ky Truong son* [The Ho Chi Minh Trail: Memories of the Annamite cordillera] (Hanoi: Tac Pham Moi, 1982), pp. 9–45.
34. One of the most well-known figures of this secret cohort was Pham Ngoc Thao. From a bourgeois Catholic family from Cochinchina, he fought with the resistance, then changed sides (under orders) to the Republic of Vietnam. He held the rank of Colonel and was head of the province of Ben Tre, then head of the Services of Psychological Warfare. After the fall of Diem's regime, he was named military attaché to the Vietnamese Embassy in Washington. He then returned clandestinely to Vietnam and was later assassinated by the police of General Nguyen Van Thieu. Both Thieu and Diem had a political advisor named Vu Ngoc Nha. Nha was a Catholic who left the North after

the Geneva Conference with the mission of infiltrating the state apparatus in the South; he was also a Communist "mole."

35. On this second war in Indochina, see Ralph B. Smith, *An International History of the Vietnam War*. 3 vols. (New York: St. Martin's Press, 1983, 1985, 1986); George McTurnan Kahin, *Intervention: How America Became Involved in Vietnam* (New York: Anchor/Doubleday, 1987); Gabriel Kolko, *Anatomy of a War: Vietnam, the United States, and the Modern Historical Experience* (New York: Pantheon Books, 1985); Marilyn Young, *The Vietnam Wars: 1945–1990*, New York, Harper Collins Publishers 1991; Lt. Gen. Phillip B. Davidson, *Vietnam at War: The History, 1946–1975* (Novato, Calif.: Presidio Press, 1988); Robert McNamara, *In Retrospect: The Tragedy and Lessons of Vietnam* (New York: Times Books, 1995).
36. The Ho Chi Minh Trail passed through Laos, and its "access roads" led just south of the sixteenth parallel in Vietnam but also in Cambodia. The headquarters of the NLF was on Cambodian territory, with five North Vietnamese divisions stationed there in 1975. Chinese supplies arrived via the port of Sihanoukville. Maneli reports being told by a North Vietnamese leader that "Indochina was just one single entity" (*War of the Vanquished*, pp. 190–91), exactly what Truong Chinh and Vo Nguyen Giap had told Major Patti some fifteen years before (Patti, *Why Vietnam?* p. 568).
37. The Great Leap Forward, the People's Communes, and the Cultural Revolution are closely linked to the Sino-Soviet conflict, which had worsened in 1956. They were Mao's attempt to lay out a Chinese path separate from the Soviet one, a path strongly marked by utopianism and voluntarism. The Great Leap Forward was an attempt to speed up economic development by mobilizing the masses and motivating them ideologically. Economic common sense and technical know-how took a back seat, while "politics took command," and "being red beat out expertise." The People's Communes went hand in hand with the Great Leap Forward, and were conceived as a shortcut to the advance of communism. Mao Zedong launched the Cultural Revolution to recapture the authority that he had lost within the party. Under the pretext of fighting the bureaucracy, he mobilized the youth "against the General Staff," but the movement ended up destroying the CCP (which was reconstituted only in 1969 at the Ninth Congress) and plunging China into civil war. These undertakings cost the lives of millions of Chinese, slowed the country's modernization, and in the end brought the bureaucracy back to power.
38. See Mario Bettati, *Le conflit sino-soviétique, t. 1: Le conflit entre partis* [The Sino-Soviet conflict, vol. 1: The conflict between parties] (Paris: A. Colin, 1971); Jacques Lévesque, *Le conflit sino-soviétique* [The Sino-Soviet conflict] (Paris: PUF, 1979); François Joyaux, *La nouvelle question d'Extrême-orient* [The new Far East question] (Paris: Fayard, 1985); François Fejto, *Chine-URSS: La fin d'une hégémonie. Les origines du grand schisme communiste. 1950–1957* [China-USSR: The end of a hegemony: The origins of communism's Great Schism, 1950–1957] (Paris: Plon, 1964).
39. During his research missions in North Vietnam in 1964, the French agronomist René Dumont noted the considerable progress that had been

made in the countryside by the 1960s in production and in the general condition of the population, but stressed that they urgently had to "break the iron law of demography." See "Problèmes agricoles au Nord Viet Nam" [Agricultural problems in North Vietnam], in *France-Asie/Asia* 183 (1965), 41–60.

40. *Kinh te Viet Nam 1945–1960* [The economy of Vietnam] (Hanoi: Su That, 1960), pp. 237–55. Published under the aegis of the Vien Kinh Te (Institute of Economics).
41. Opening speech at the Third Congress of the VWP in *Toan Tap*, vol. 9 (1958–59), pp. 194–202.
42. Khrushchev, *Souvenirs*, p. 459.
43. *Viet Cho Me va Quoc Hoi* [Written for my mother and for the National Assembly] (Stanton, Calif.: Van Nghe, 1995), p. 325. Nguyen Van Tran was from a rich Catholic family from the South. He studied in France and in Moscow (under the alias Prigorny or Axinovitch), worked as an ICP organizer in Cochinchina beginning in 1933, and was arrested and imprisoned in Poulo Condor. He was liberated in 1936, elected deputy to the National Assembly of the DRV in 1946, and joined the anti-French resistance. He returned to the Catholic faith in the 1990s. He admired and respected Ho Chi Minh but addressed him as *Ong* (Sir) to avoid flattery and, by refusal to kowtow.
44. Liu Shaoqi (1898–1969) was one of the first Chinese Communists (1922). In 1945 he was the second highest person in the party behind Mao Zedong and considered his presumptive heir. He was President of the PRC in 1959, but clashed with Mao during the Cultural Revolution. He was excluded from the party, stripped of his duties, and imprisoned. He died in 1969 from ill-treatment, but his death was not announced until 1979; he was rehabilitated in 1980.
45. From "Report by Liu Shaoqi on the Struggle against the Revisionists (February 25, 1963)," cited by Yang Kuisong in "Mao Zedong and the War in Indochina," in *New Evidence on China, Southeast Asia, and the Vietnam War* (Working papers of the International Workshop held at the University of Hong Kong, 11–12 January 2000, in conjunction with the Cold War International History Project [Washington, D.C.]). The emphasis is this author's.
46. According to Hoang Van Hoan, a member of the Politburo who fled to China in 1979, it was First Secretary Le Duan who had Khrushchev's name removed from the resolution of the ninth plenum. Did Le Duan want to keep the door open to the USSR, or was he deceiving the Chinese? Hoang Van Hoan believes it was the latter, since Le Duan was an antirevisionist in theory but anti-Chinese in practice. See Hoang Van Hoan, *Giot nuoc trong bien ca* [A drop of water in the ocean] (Beijing: FLP, 1982). Published in English as *A Drop in the Ocean: Revolutionary Reminiscences* (Beijing: FLP, 1988).
47. See Smith's, *An International History*, chap. 13. The quotation is from Vu Thu Hien, *Dem giua ban ngay*, p. 229.
48. Vu Thu Hien, *Dem giua ban ngay*, p. 363.

49. Hoang Minh Chinh, a long-standing Communist militant and Director of the Institute of Philosophy, was arrested in July 1967 along with a number of other leading figures (about thirty in total). Among them were General Dong Kim Giang, who was in charge of logistics at Dien Bien Phu, and Colonel Le Trong Nghia, Chief of the Office of Military Information, suspected of having ties with the Soviet or Czech secret services. Several other officers and civilian cadres studying in the USSR asked for and were granted political asylum by the Soviet government. The party spread word of a plot by Vietnamese revisionists led by Vo Nguyen Giap, in collusion with the Soviets.
50. See Hoang Tung, *Nhung Ky niem.*
51. From *Minutes des rencontres Ho-Mao, 10 août et 2 novembre 1960* [Minutes from the Ho-Mao meetings, August 10 and November 2, 1960], cited by Yang Kuisong in "Mao Zedong."
52. From Vu Thu Hien, *Dem giua ban ngay*, pp. 108–9.
53. Chen Jian, "China's Involvement in the Vietnam War: 1954–1969," in *China Quarterly* 142 (June 1995), 356–87.
54. Ilya Gaiduk, relying on information from the archives of the ex-Soviet Union, shows that while Khrushchev was not hostile and defiant toward Ho Chi Minh, as Stalin was, he still considered the Indochinese question of secondary importance, particularly the events in Vietnam, because Europe and détente with the United States took precedence. On the other hand, the Soviet government was not happy about the resumption of armed conflict in South Vietnam, the involvement of Laos in the Vietnamese theater of operations (which violated the Geneva Accords), and the threat to détente and peaceful coexistence. While Khrushchev was grappling with the Chinese, the "Cuban missile crisis" strengthened his resolve not to get involved in far-off and risky endeavors. See Gaiduk, *Confronting Vietnam*.
55. Li Danhui, "The Sino-Soviet Dispute over Vietnam's Anti-United States War," in *New Evidence on China*. The quotation is from "The meeting of 17 October 1968" in *77 Conversations Between Chinese and Foreign Leaders on the Wars in Indochina, 1964–1977*, archival material published by the Cold War International History Project (Washington, D.C.), 1998, p. 61.
56. The first excerpt of *Cua mo* is from the poem "Life as beloved as my wife," p. 53; the second is from "The Party," pp. 88–90 (Hanoi: Van Hoc, July 1989). Phuong was dismissed from his duties and put "out of play" for several years but was not imprisoned. The book was destroyed and then reissued after the beginning of the policy of openness called *Doi moi* (Renovation) in 1986.
57. The Hung kings were a semilegendary lineage of monarchs who ruled over the kingdom of Van Lang in the Red River delta during the prehistoric age (roughly 2000 B.C.). Nguyen Trai was a fifteenth-century scholar who refused to collaborate with the Chinese occupiers (from the Ming dynasty) and joined up with Le Loi, who hoisted the banner of national insurrection. He became the king's advisor and strategist and conquered the Chinese in 1428, but was accused of a criminal plot against Le Loi's successor and

executed along with his entire family. He was the epitome of the upstanding Confucian scholar, loyal and faithful, and is considered one of the greatest figures in Vietnamese history. At the end of the eighteenth century, Emperor Quang Trung (reign name of Nguyen Hue) founded the Tay Son dynasty by putting an end to the rule of the Le and defeating the Chinese in 1788. His son was driven out by Nguyen Phuoc Anh who, under the name Gia Long, founded the Nguyen dynasty in 1802. Quang Trung is considered a great general in Vietnam and one of the architects of military strategy. See Le Huu Khoa, "La visée de l'effet dans l'art militaire vietnamien" [Aiming for results in the military art of Vietnam], in Thierry Marchaisse et al. (eds.), *Dépayser la pensée. Dialogues hétérotopiques avec François Jullien sur son usage philosophique de la China* [Heterotopic dialogues with François Jullien on his philosophical use of China] (Paris: Les Empêcheurs de Penser en Rond, 2003).

58. According to one of Marx's theories, all nations would fade away once societies reached the stage of communism.
59. Graham Greene, *Collected Essays* (London: Bodley Head, 1969), pp. 402–4.
60. Victor Hugo, *Les Chants du crépuscule 3, Hymne.*
61. In Carton 368 of coll. HCI/SPCE, CAOM.
62. For an excellent analysis of the institution, see Benoît de Tréglodé, *Héros et Révolution au Viet Nam* [Heroes and revolution in Vietnam] (Paris: L'Harmattan, 2001).
63. *Anh hung*, "the hero," is a word frequently used in an emphatic language with a predilection for passionate speech. In a cursory analysis, I found that the term *anh hung* is not used often in reference to Ho. When it is used, it is accompanied by the epithet *Vi dai* (the great). Most often Ho is referred to as Uncle or Father.
64. *Chuyen ke ve Bac Ho*, vol. 2, p. 71.
65. The three versions of the "Testament" are in Ruscio, pp. 207–17. The original version was locked in a safe by Tran Quoc Hoan, Minister of Security and the Interior, who did not have a very clean reputation.
66. Hoang Tranh, "Tang Tuyet Minh, l'épouse chinoise de Nguyen Ai Quoc" [Tang Tuyet Minh, the Chinese wife of Nguyen Ai Quoc], in *Autour de l'Asie du Sud-Est* [Around Southeast Asia] (Nanning: Guangxi Academy of Social Sciences, November, 2001).
67. This accident gave birth to a sordid rumor. Some claim that Tran Quoc Hoan, Minister of Security and responsible for Do Thi Lac's surveillance, had evil intentions and was guilty of abuses of power. He supposedly raped Lac and then had her killed so that she would not talk. According to the rumor, he made the crime seem like an accident and then had Do Thi Lac's younger sister drowned, since she also knew about his transgressions. See Vu Thu Hien, *Dem giua ban ngay*, pp. 605–9. Of course, this horrible story is questionable and is rejected by a number of Hanoi residents.
68. Tran Gia Phuong, "Combien de femmes Monsieur Ho a-t-il eu"? [How many women did Mister Ho have?], in *The Ky 21* [21st century] (November 1998), 40–46, a journal published in the United States by the Vietnamese diaspora.

69. See Nina Tumarkin, "Religion, Bolshevism, and the Origins of Lenin's Cult," in *The Russian Review* 40 (January 1981), 35–54.

EPILOGUE: A MAN AT THE INTERFACE BETWEEN TWO WORLDS

1. Charles Fenn, *Trial Run to Doomsday*, pp. 238–39, unpublished text cited by William Duiker in *Ho Chi Minh: A Life* (New York: Hyperion Press, 2000).
2. Tran Dan Tien, *Nhung mau chuyen*, p. 8.
3. Greene, *Collected Essays*, pp. 402–4. Mister Chips was an English schoolteacher portrayed by Robert Donat in the American filmmaker Sam Wood's movie, *Goodbye, Mr. Chips* (1939).
4. *Newsweek* (25 April 1959), 44. A short version of this interview is in *Toan Tap*, 9, but the phrase cited here is absent.
5. Excerpt from an informal talk entitled "Bonne personne, bon travail" [Good person, good work], 7 June 1958. The text was published in *Cuu Quoc* [National Salvation] on 22 February and 1 March 1970.
6. Benjamin Schwartz, *The World of Thought in Ancient China* (Cambridge, Mass.: Harvard University: Belknap Press, 1989), pp. 295–96.
7. Xunzi (Tuan Tu in Vietnamese), third or fourth century B.C., was one of the three great Confucian sages along with Confucius and Mencius. Considered a realist in comparison with Mencius, the idealist, Xunzi served as master to the royal advisors Han Fei Tzu and Li Si. The latter advocated the interests of the prince and the state based on "three sister ideas: the law, position of force, and techniques of control" – the foundation of a totalitarian theory, according to Anne Cheng, see *Histoire de la pensée chinoise* [History of Chinese thought] (Paris: Seuil, 1997). Wang Yang Ming (1472–1529) was a neo-Confucian for whom moral knowledge is innate (contrary to Xunzi), but also for whom knowledge and action are related. Xunzi is almost never cited in Vietnamese texts, but is certainly known by the Vietnamese people because Phan Boi Chau mentions him in a dozen pages of his "Treatise on Confucianism." See *Phan Boi Chau Toan Tap* [Complete writings of Phan Boi Chau] (Hué: 1990), vol. 10, pp. 287–99. Tran Trong Kim also devotes an important chapter to him in his reference work, *Nho Giao* [Confucian doctrine]. Do not confuse Xunzi with Sun Tzu (722–681 B.C.), the author of *The Art of War*, nor with the Taoist thinker Zhuangzi (369–286 B.C.).
8. Bui Tin, *Following Ho Chi Minh*, p. 66.
9. Cited by Vu Ky, *Cang nho Bac Ho* [We must remember Uncle Ho] (Hanoi: Thanh Nien, 1999), p. 178.
10. Bui Tin, *Following Ho Chi Minh*, p. 66.

Bibliography

I. WORKS BY HO CHI MINH

1. *Ho Chi Minh Toan Tap* [Complete Writings of Ho Chi Minh]. This collection also includes his correspondence, reports to the Comintern and Communist Party authorities, essays on theory and politics, and poetry.

A first edition in ten volumes was published in the 1980s. Hanoi: Su That, 1980–89. A second edition in twelve volumes was published a decade later. The chronology of the volumes is different from the first edition. Hanoi: CTQG, 1995–96. In this work, I have referred exclusively to this second edition.

In English, see also *Ho Chi Minh: Selected Writings*. Hanoi: FLP, 1977.

2. The State Political Publishing House (Nha xuat ban Chinh tri Quoc gia) in Hanoi released a CD-ROM of the *Selected Works* of Ho Chi Minh in 2000. It includes 8,000 selected pages, 1,000 photographs, 220 minutes of audio recordings, a 30-minute documentary, and hundreds of revolutionary songs.

3. Anthologies and works in French:

Ho Chi Minh. Oeuvres choisies. 2 vols. Hanoi: ÉLÉ, 1960.

Ho Chi Minh. Écrits (1920–1969). Hanoi: ÉLÉ, 1971.

Ho Chi Minh. Oeuvres choisies, 1922–1967. Paris: Petite collection Maspéro, 1967.

Capitan-Peter, Colette (ed.). *Action et Révolution (1920–1957)*. Paris: UGE, 1968.

Carnet de prison. Translated by Phan Nhuan. Paris: P. Seghers, 1963. It was published in Hanoi by ÉLÉ in 1965, and then reissued by Éditions The Gioi in 1983.

Fall, Bernard (ed.). *Ho Chi Minh. De la Révolution. 1920–1966*. Paris: Plon, 1967.

Journal de Prison. Translated by Dang The Binh et al. Hanoi: ÉLÉ 1960.

Ruscio, Alain (ed.). *Ho Chi Minh. Textes 1914–1969*. Paris: L'Harmattan, 1990.

(ed.). *Le procès de la colonisation française*. Paris: Le temps des cerises, 1999.

4. Two autobiographical accounts written under different pseudonyms:

Tran Dan Tien. *Nhung mau chuyen ve cuoc doi hoat dong cua Ho Chu tich* [Glimpses of the Life of Ho Chi Minh: President of the Democratic Republic of Vietnam]. Hanoi: 1948.

An abridged English translation was published in Hanoi by the Foreign Languages Press in 1958. The French translation is *Avec le Président Ho*. Hanoi: ÉLÉ, 1970.

There is also a Chinese translation: *Hu Chi Minh Zhuang* [A Biography of Ho Chi Minh]. Shanghai: Ba Ywe Publishing House, 1949. Another biography is sometimes mentioned, published in Shanghai in 1950 by In Chu Kouan, but this is undoubtedly a reissue of the work cited here.

T. Lan. *Vua di duong, vua ke chuyen* [Walking and talking]. Hanoi: Su that, 1963; reissue 1976.

Both of these autobiographical works are in *Tac pham van cua Chu tich Ho Chi Minh* [Literary works of President Ho Chi Minh]. Ha Minh Duc (ed.). Hanoi: 1985.

Three other works provide a useful context and are indispensable for reading the works of Ho Chi Minh:

Ho Chi Minh bien nien tieu su [A chronological history of Ho Chi Minh]. 10 vols. Hanoi: NXB CTQG, 1993.

Ho Chi Minh. Nhung su kien [Ho Chi Minh: Historical events]. Hanoi: 1987.

Tu dien Ho Chi Minh. So Gian [Summary encyclopedia of Ho Chi Minh]. Mac Duong (ed.). Ho Chi Minh City: 1990.

II. WORKS ABOUT HO CHI MINH

In French and English

Brocheux, Pierre. *Ho Chi Minh*. Paris: Presses de Sciences Po, Coll. Références/Facettes, 2000.

Bui Lam, Nguyen Luong Bang, et al. *Souvenirs sur Ho Chi Minh*. Hanoi: ÉLÉ, 1965.

Bui Tin. *Following Ho Chi Minh: Memoirs of a North Vietnamese Colonel*. University of Hawaii Press, 1995.

Burchett, Wilfred. *Ho Chi Minh: An Appreciation*. New York: W. Burchett Fund/*The Guardian*, 1972.

Duiker, William. *Ho Chi Minh: A Life*. New York: Hyperion Press, 2000.

Duncanson, Dennis. "Ho Chi Minh in Hong Kong, 1931–1932." *China Quarterly* 57 (January–March 1974).

"The Legacy of Ho Chi Minh." *Asian Affairs* (Journal of the Royal Society for Asian Affairs) 23, 1 (February 1992).

Fenn, Charles. *Ho Chi Minh: A Biographical Introduction*. New York: Scribner's Sons, 1973.

Figuères, Léo, and Fourniau, Charles (eds.). *Ho Chi Minh, notre camarade*. Paris: Éd. Sociales, 1970.

Gaspard, Thu Trang. *Ho Chi Minh à Paris, 1917–1923*. Paris: L'Harmattan, 1992.

Halberstam, David. *Ho*. New York: Random House, 1971.

Handache, Gilbert (ed.). *Ho Chi Minh, L'homme et son message*. Paris: Special issue of *Planète-Action* 15, 1970.

Hémery, Daniel. *Ho Chi Minh, de l'Indochine au Vietnam*. Paris: Découvertes-Gallimard, 1990.

Huy Phong and Yen Anh. *Nhan Dien Ho Chi Minh. Thuc chat gian manh cua huyen thoai Anh hung/Exploding the Myth of Ho Chi Minh* (bilingual edition). San José, Calif.: 1989.

Kobelev, Yevgeny. *Ho Chi Minh* (in English). Moscow: Progress Publishers, 1989.

Lacouture, Jean. *Ho Chi Minh*. Paris: Seuil, 1969.

Le Manh Trinh, Nguyen Khanh Toan, et al. *Avec l'Oncle Ho*. Hanoi: ÉLÉ, 1972.

Memories of Ho Chi Minh (in Russian). Moscow: Political Press, 1990.

Mus, Paul. *Ho Chi Minh, le Vietnam and l'Asie*. Paris: Seuil, 1971.

Neumann-Hoditz, Reinhold. *Portrait of Ho Chi Minh, an Illustrated Biography*. Translated from the German by John Hargreaves. New York: Herder & Herder, 1972.

New Evidence on China, Southeast Asia, and the Vietnam War. Working papers of the International Workshop held at the University of Hong Kong, 11–12 January 2000.

Nguyen Khac Huyen. *Vision Accomplished? The Enigma of Ho Chi Minh*. New York: Colliers Books, 1971.

Nguyen The Anh (ed.). *Ho Chi Minh, l'homme et son héritage*. Paris: Éd. Duong Moi/La Voie nouvelle, 1990.

Pasquel-Rageau, Christiane. *Ho Chi Minh*. Paris: Éd. Universitaires, 1970.

Quinn-Judge, Sophie. *Ho Chi Minh: The Missing Years. 1919–1941*. Berkeley and Los Angeles: University of California Press, 2003.

Rabemananjara, Jacques. "Conversation avec Ho Chi Minh en 1946, à Paris," in Jacques Tronchon, *L'insurrection malgache de 1947*. Paris: Karthala, 1986, pp. 335–36.

Sainteny, Jean. *Face à Ho Chi Minh*. Paris: Seghers, 1970.

Salan, Raoul. *Indochine rouge: Le message d'Ho Chi Minh*. Paris: Presses de la Cité, 1975.

Souvarine, Boris. "De Nguyen Ai Quoc en Ho Chi Minh." *Est et Ouest* 568 (March 1976).

Thomas, C. David, and Lady Borton. *Ho Chi Minh: A Portrait*. Hanoi: Youth Publishing House, 2003.

Videlier, Philippe. "Ho Chi Minh aimait les blondes américaines." A comedic tale, in *Le jardin de Bakounine and autres nouvelles de l'histoire*. Paris: Gallimard, 2001, pp. 213–26.

Warbey, William. *Ho Chi Minh and the Struggle for an Independent Vietnam*. London: Merlin Press, 1972.

In quoc ngu

Bui Thiet (ed). *Dia Zanh Ho Chi Minh* [Toponymy of the activities of Ho Chi Minh]. Hanoi: TN, 1999.

Cao The Dung. *Chan tuong Ho Chi Minh và Cong san Viet Nam*. [The real face of Ho Chi Minh and the Vietnamese communists]. USA: 1989.

Chiang Yun Ching. *Hu Chi Ming tsai Chung Kuo* [Ho Chi Minh in China]. Taipei, Taiwan: 1972. A translation in *quoc ngu* from the Chinese was published in California in 1999 under the name Tuong Vinh Kinh.

Chinh Dao. *Ho Chi Minh, Con Nguoi va Huyen thoai* [Ho Chi Minh: The man and the legend]. 3 vols: 1892–1924, 1925–45, 1945–69. Houston: Van Hoa, 1993.

Dao Phan. *Ho Chi Minh zanh nhan van hoa* [Ho Chi Minh, man of culture]. Hanoi: 1991.

Do Quang Hung. *Them Nhung hieu biet ve Ho Chi Minh* [Supplementary information about Ho Chi Minh]. Hanoi: LD, 1999.

Ho Si Khue. *Ho Chi Minh, Ngo Dinh Ziem va Mat tran Giai phong* [Ho Chi Minh, Ngo Dinh Diem, and the Liberation Front]. Stanton, Calif.: Van Nghe, 1992.

Hoang Tranh (Huang Zheng). *Ho Chi Minh voi Trung Quoc* [Ho Chi Minh and China]. Translated from the Chinese. Nanning, China: Sao Moi, 1990.

Hoang Tung. *Nhung Ky Niem ve Bac Ho* [Memories of Uncle Ho]. Hanoi: NXB CTQG, 2002.

Hong Ha. *Bac Ho tren dat nuoc Le-nin* [Uncle Ho in the land of Lenin]. Hanoi: Thanh Nien, 1980.

Le Huu Muc. *Ho Chi Minh khong phai la tac gia Nguc Trung Nhat Ky* [Ho Chi Minh is not the author of the prison diaries]. Toronto: 1990.

Mai Van Bo. *Con duong van dam Ho Chi Minh* [The ten thousand leagues of Ho Chi Minh]. Ho Chi Minh City: 1998. The biography goes up to 1946.

Nguyen Ai Quoc–Ho Chi Minh. 2 vols. Ho Chi Minh City: NXB VN, 1999. Commentary and literary essays on Ho Chi Minh.

Nguyen Ai Quoc o Quang Chau (1924–1927) [Nguyen Ai Quoc in Guangzhou]. Hanoi: Institut Ho Chi Minh, NXB CTQG, 1998.

Nguyen Dac Xuan. *Bac Ho, thoi nien thieu o Hue* [Uncle Ho's childhood in Hué]. Ho Chi Minh City: Su That, 1999.

Nguyen Phan Quang. *Them mot so tu lieu ve hoat dong cua Nguyen Ai Quoc thoi gian o Phap, 1917–1923* [Some supplementary documents on the activities of Nguyen Ai Quoc in France, 1917–1923]. Ho Chi Minh City: 1988.

Nguyen The Anh and Vu Ngu Chieu, *Une autre école pour le jeune Nguyen That Thanh* [Another school for the young Nguyen That Thanh]. Paris: Duong Moi, 1983.

Phung The Tai. *Bac Ho, nhung ky niem khong quen* [Uncle Ho, unforgettable memories]. Hanoi: NXB QDNZ, 2001.

Thai Kim Dinh (ed.). *Chuyen ke ve Bac Ho* [Anecdotes about Uncle Ho]. 5 vols. NXB Nghe An, 2000.

Thanh Dam. *Nguyen Ai Quoc tren duong ve nuoc* [Nguyen Ai Quoc's return to his country]. NXB Nghe An, 1998.

Thanh Duy. *Co so khoa hoc va nen tang van hoa cua tu tuong Ho Chi Minh* [The scientific and cultural foundations of Ho Chi Minh thought]. Hanoi: KH, 1998.

Tran Minh Sieu. *Nhung nguoi than trong gia dinh Bac Ho*. [The beloved members of Uncle Ho's family]. NXB Nghe An, 1995.

Zi tich chu tich Ho Chi Minh o Kim Lien [The traces of President Ho Chi Minh in Kim Lien]. NXB Nghe An, 1998.

Tran Ngoc Danh. *Biography of President Ho Chi Minh*. In *quoc ngu*, published in France in 1949 by the Union of Viet Kieu in France.

(ed.). *Bac Ho o Thai lan* [Uncle Ho in Thailand]. Ho Chi Minh City: Tre, 1999.

Truong Chinh. *Ho chu tich, lanh tu kinh yeu cua giai cap cong nhan va nhan zan Viet Nam* [President Ho, well-loved leader of the working class and of the Vietnamese people]. Hanoi: ST, 1970 (4th edition).

Vu Dinh Hoe. *Phap Quyen – Nhan Nghia. Ho Chi Minh* [The law – the humanity: Ho Chi Minh]. Hanoi: 2000.

Vu Ky. *Bac Ho viet zi chuc* [Uncle Ho writes his Testament]. Hanoi: CTQG, 1999.

Cang nho Bac Ho [We must remember Uncle Ho]. Hanoi: Thanh Nien, 1999.

III. RELATED WORKS

In French and English

Abuza, Zachary. *Renovating Politics in Contemporary Vietnam*. Boulder and London: Lynne Rienner Publishers, 2001.

Arne Westad, Odd, et al. (eds.). *77 Conversations Between Chinese and Foreign Leaders on the Wars in Indochina, 1964–1977*. Washington, D.C.: Woodrow Wilson Center Press, 1998.

Artaud, Denise, and Lawrence Kaplan (eds.). *Dien Bien Phu, l'alliance atlantique et la défense du sud-est asiatique*. Lyon: La Manufacture, 1989.

Astier de la Vigerie, Emmanuel (d'). *Portraits*. Paris: Gallimard, 1969.

Aubrac, Raymond. *Où la mémoire s'attarde*. Paris: O. Jacob, 1996.

Azeau, Henri. *Ho Chi Minh, dernière chance: La conférence vietnamienne de Fontainebleau 1946*. Paris: Flammarion, 1968.

Bao Dai. *Le Dragon d'Annam*. Paris: Plon, 1976.

Beaucorps, Jean-Marie de. *Soldats de jade*. Paris: Kergour, 1998.

Bergère, Marie-Claire. *Sun Yat-Sen*. Paris: Fayard, 1994.

Bettati, Mario. *Le conflit sino-soviétique, t. 1: Le conflit entre partis*. Paris: A. Colin, 1971.

Bidault, Georges. *D'une résistance à l'autre*. Paris: Les Presses du Siècle, 1965.

Bodinier, Gilbert. *1945–1946. Le retour de la France en Indochine. Textes and documents*. Fort de Vincennes: SHAT, 1987.

Indochine 1947. Règlement politique ou solution militaire. Textes and documents. SHAT, 1989.

Bonner, Elena. *De mères en filles. Un siècle russe*. Paris: Témoins Gallimard, 2002.

Bousquet, Gisèle, and Pierre Brocheux (eds.). *Viet Nam Exposé: French Scholarship on Twentieth Century Vietnamese Society*. Ann Arbor: University of Michigan Press, 2002.

Boudarel, George. *Autobiographie*. Paris: Jean Bertoin, 1991.

Cent fleurs écloses dans la nuit du Vietnam. Paris: Jean Bertoin, 1991.

Giap. Paris: Éd. Atlas, 1977.

and Nguyen Van Ky. *Hanoi 1936–1996. Du drapeau rouge au billet vert*. Paris: Autrement, coll. Mémoires, 48. Translated into English by Claire Duiker. *Hanoi: City of the Rising Dragon*. Boulder, Colo.: Roman and Littlefield, 2002.

Bouissou, Jean-Marie. *Seigneurs de la guerre et officiers rouges, 1924–1927. La Révolution chinoise*. Paris: Mame, 1974.

Bradley, Mark Phillip. *Imagining Vietnam and America: The Making of Postcolonial Vietnam, 1919–1950*. Chapel Hill: University of North Carolina Press, 2000.

Brocheux, Pierre. *The Mekong Delta: Ecology, Economy and Revolution (1860–1960)*. Madison: University of Wisconsin, Center for Southeast Asian Studies, 1995.

(ed.). *L'Histoire de l'Asie du Sud-est: Révoltes, réformes, révolutions*. Lille: P.U.L., 1981.

and Hémery, Daniel. *Indochine française, la colonisation ambiguë*. 2d ed. Paris: La Découverte, 2001.

Broué, Pierre. *La question chinoise dans l'Internationale communiste: 1926–1927*. Paris: EDI, 1976.

Histoire de l'Internationale communiste (1919–1943). Paris: Fayard, 1997.

Cadart, Claude, and Cheng Yingxiang (eds.). *L'envol du communisme en Chine. Mémoires de Peng Shuzhi*. Paris: Gallimard, 1982.

Cantier, Jacques, and Eric Jennings (eds.). *L'Empire colonial sous Vichy*. Paris: Odile Jacob, 2004.

Carrère d'Encausse, Hélène, and Stuart Schramm. *Le Marxisme and l'Asie, 1863–1964*. Paris: A. Colin 1965.

Césari, Laurent. *L'Indochine en guerres, 1945–1993*. Paris: Belin, 1995.

Chaffard, Georges. *Les carnets secrets de la décolonisation*. Paris: Calmann-Lévy, 1965.

Charbonneau, René, and José Maigre. *Les Parias de la victoire. Indochine-Chine 1945*. Paris: Éd. France-Empire, 1980.

Charles, Jean, and J. Girault, J.-L. Robert, D. Tartakovsky, et al. (eds.) *Le Congrès de Tours*. Paris: Éd. Sociales, 1980.

Charton, Pierre. *RC4. Indochine 1950. La tragédie de l'évacuation de Caobang*. Paris: SPL, 1975.

Chen Jian. "China and the First Indochina War: 1950–1954." *China Quarterly* 133 (March 1993).

"China's Involvement in the Vietnam War. 1954–1969." *China Quarterly* 142 (June 1995).

Mao's China and the Cold War. Chapel Hill: North Carolina University Press, 2001.

Chen, King C. *Vietnam and China 1938–1954*. Princeton, N.J.: Princeton University Press, 1969.

Cheng, Anne. *Histoire de la pensée chinoise*. Paris: Seuil, 1997.

Chesneaux, J., and F. Barbier. *La Chine. La marche à la révolution. 1921–1949. Vol. 3 of Histoire contemporaine de la Chine*. 4 vols. Paris: Hatier, 1975.

Christie, Clive. *Ideology and Revolution in Southeast Asia, 1900–1975: Political Ideas of the Anti-colonial Era*. Richmond, Surrey: Curzon Press, 2001.

Colotti-Pischel, Enrica, and Chiara Robertazzi. *L'Internationale communiste and les problèmes coloniaux. 1919–1935*. Paris-La Haye: Mouton, 1968.

Courtois, Stéphane, and Jean-Louis Panné (eds). *Livre noir du communisme*. Paris: Laffont, 2000.

Currey, Cecil B. *Vo Nguyen Giap. Vienam 1940–1975. La Victoire à tout prix.* Paris: Phébus, 2003.

Dallin, A., and F. I. Firsov (eds.). *Dimitrov and Stalin, 1934–1943, Letters from the Soviet Archives.* New Haven, Conn.: Yale University Press, 2000.

Dalloz, Jacques. *La guerre d'Indochine, 1945–1954.* Paris: Points-Seuil, 1987. Translated into English as *The War in Indochina, 1945–54.* New York: Barnes & Noble, 1990.

Dang Van Viet. *La RC4. Campagne des frontières (1947–1950).* Hanoi: ÉLÉ, 1990.

Davidson, Phillip. *Vietnam at War: The History, 1946–1975.* Novato, Calif.: Presidio Press, 1988.

DeCaro, Peter A. *Rhetoric of Revolt – Ho Chi Minh's Discourse for Revolution.* Westport and London: Praeger, 2003.

Degras, Jane. *The Communist International: 1919–1943. Documents.* 3 vols. Oxford: Oxford University Press, 1965.

Devillers, Philippe. *Histoire du Vietnam de 1940 à 1952.* Paris: Seuil, 1952.

(ed.). *Paris-Saigon-Hanoi. Les archives de la guerre 1944–1947.* Paris: Gallimard-Julliard, 1988.

and Jean Lacouture. *De la guerre française à la guerre américaine.* Paris: Seuil, 1969.

Dreyfus, Michel, et al. (eds). *Le siècle des communismes.* Paris: Éd. de l'Atelier, 2000.

Dubs, Homer. *Hsun Tze, the Moulder of Ancient Confucianism.* London: Probsthain, 1927.

The Works of Hsun Tze. London: Probsthain, 1928.

Duiker, William. *Sacred War. Nationalism and Revolution in a Divided Vietnam.* New York: McGraw-Hill, 1995.

The Comintern and Vietnamese Communism. Athens: Ohio University Press, 1975.

Dulong, Claude. *La dernière pagode.* Paris: Plon, 1989.

Dumaine, Jacques. *Quai d'Orsay. 1945–1951.* Paris: Julliard, 1955.

Dunn, Peter. *The First Vietnam War.* London: Hurst & Co., 1985.

Duong Thu Huong. *The Paradise of the Blind.* New York: Penguin, 1994.

Duong Van Mai, Elliott. *The Sacred Willow: Four Generations in the Life of a Vietnamese Family.* New York: Oxford University Press, 1999.

Duplay, Philippe, and Guy Pedroncini (eds.). *Leclerc and Indochina, 1945–1947. Quand se noua le destin d'un empire.* Paris: Albin Michel, 1992.

Faligot, Roger, and Rémi Kauffer. *As-tu vu Crémet?* Paris, Fayard, 1991.

Fall, Bernard. *Le Viet Minh. La République démocratique du Viet-Nam, 1945–1960.* Paris: A. Colin, 1960.

Les deux Vietnams. Paris: Payot, 1967.

Fejto, François. *Chine-URSS: La fin d'une hégémonie. Les origines du grand schisme communiste. 1950–1957.* Paris: Plon, 1964.

Fenn, Charles. *At the Dragon's Gate: With the OSS in the Far East.* Annapolis, Md: Naval Institute Press, 2004.

Figuères, Léo. *Je reviens du Viet-Nam libre.* Paris: Éditions sociales, 1950

Fonde, Jean-Julien. *Traitez à tout prix ... Leclerc and le Viet-Nam*. Paris: Laffont, 1971.

Fourniau, Charles. *Viet Nam. Domination coloniale et résistance nationale (1858–1914)*. Paris: Les Indes savantes, 2002.

Franchini, Philippe. *Les guerres d'Indochine*. 2 vols. Paris: Pygmalion/Gérard Watelet, 1988.

Froment-Meurice, Henri. *Vu du Quai. Mémoires, 1945–1983*. Paris: Fayard, 1998.

Furet, François. *Le passé d'une illusion. Essai sur l'idée communiste au XXè siècle*. Calmann Lévy, 1995.

Gaiduk, Ilya. *The Soviet Union and the Vietnam War: 1964–1975*. Chicago: Ivan R. Dee, 1996.

Confronting Vietnam: Soviet Policy Toward the Indochina Conflict, 1954–1963. Stanford: Stanford University Press, 2003.

Girardet, Raoul. *L'idée coloniale en France. 1871–1962*. Paris: La Table Ronde, 1972.

Goscha, Christopher. *Thailand and the Southest Asian Networks of the Vietnamese Revolution, 1885–1954*. Richmond, UK: Curzon Press, 1999.

and Tréglodé, Benoît (eds.). *Naissance d'un État-Parti. Le Viêt Nam depuis 1945*. Paris: Les Indes savantes, 2004.

Gras, Yves. *Histoire de la guerre d'Indochine*. 2d ed. Paris: Denoël, 1992.

Greene, Graham. *Collected Essays*. London: Bodley Head, 1969.

Gruber, Helmut (ed.). *Soviet Russia Masters the Comintern*. Garden City, N.Y.: Anchor/Doubleday, 1974.

Guillermaz, Jacques. *Une vie pour la Chine, 1937–1989*. Paris: Hachette Littérature, 1994.

Harrison, James P. *The Endless War: Fifty Years of Struggle in Vietnam*. New York: Free Press, 1982.

Hartingh, Bertrand de. *Entre le peuple and la nation. La République démocratique du Viet Nam de 1953 à 1957*. Monographies 189. Paris: École française d'Extrême-Orient, 2003.

Hémery, Daniel. *Révolutionnaires vietnamiens et pouvoir colonial en Indochine*. Paris: Maspéro, 1975.

Hinton, William. *Fanshen: A Documentary of Revolution in a Chinese Village*. Berkeley and Los Angeles: University of California Press, 1997.

Hoang Van Chi. *Du colonialisme au communisme. L'expérience du Nord Viet Nam*. Tours: Éditions Mame, 1964.

Hue Tam Ho Tai. *Millenarianism and Peasant Politics in Vietnam*. Cambridge, Mass.: Harvard University Press, 1982.

"Monumental Ambiguity: The State Commemoration of Ho Chi Minh," in Keith W. Taylor and John K. Whitmore (eds.), *Essays into Vietnamese Pasts*. Ithaca, N.Y.: Cornell University Press, 1995.

(ed.). *The Country of Memory: Remaking the Past in Late Socialist Vietnam*. Berkeley and Los Angeles: University of California Press, 2001.

Huynh Kim Khanh. *Vietnamese Communism, 1925–1945*. Ithaca, N.Y.: Cornell University Press, 1982.

Hy Van Luong. *Revolution in the Village: Tradition and Transformations in North Vietnam, 1925–1988.* Honolulu: Hawaii University Press, 1992.

Isaacs, Harold R. *No Peace for Asia.* New York: Macmillan, 1947.

La tragédie de la Révolution chinoise, 1925–1927. Paris: Gallimard, 1967.

Isoart, Paul (ed.). *L'Indochine française. 1940–1945.* Paris: PUF, 1982.

Jacobs, Daniel Norman. *Borodin: Stalin's Man in China.* Cambridge, Mass.: Harvard University Press, 1981.

Joyaux, François. *La Chine and le réglement du premier conflit indochinois. Genève 1954.* Paris: Publications de la Sorbonne, 1979.

La nouvelle question d'Extrême-orient. Paris: Fayard, 1985.

Kahin, George McTurnan. *Intervention: How America Became Involved in Vietnam.* New York: Anchor/Doubleday, 1987.

Kamenarovic, Ivan (trans.). *Oeuvres de Hsun tze.* Paris: Éd. du Cerf, 1987.

Karnow, Stanley. *Paris in the Fifties.* New York: Three Rivers Press, 1997.

Kolko, Gabriel. *Anatomy of a War: Vietnam, the United States, and the Modern Historical Experience.* New York: Pantheon Books, 1985.

Khrushchev, Nikita. *Souvenirs.* Paris: Robert Laffont, 1970. Published in English as *Memoirs of Nikita Khrushchev: Commissar (1918–1945)*, Sergei Khrushchev (ed.), translated by George Shriver and Stephen Shenfield. University Park: Pennsylvania State University Press, 2005.

Labica, G., and G. Bensussan (eds.). *Dictionnaire critique du Marxisme.* Paris: PUF, 1982.

Lacouture, Jean, and Philippe Devillers. *La fin d'une guerre. Indochine 1954.* Paris: Seuil, 1960.

Lansdale, Edward G. *In the Midst of Wars: An American Mission in Southeast Asia.* New York: Harper & Row, 1972.

Larcher-Goscha, Agathe. "La légitimation française en Indochine: mythes et réalités de la 'collaboration franco-vietnamienne' et du réformisme colonial (1905–1945)." Unpublished doctoral thesis, Université Paris VII (2000).

Le Chau. *Le Viet Nam socialiste.* Paris: Maspéro, 1966.

Le Thanh Khoi. *Le Vietnam. Histoire and civilisation.* Paris: Éd. de Minuit, 1955.

Legendre, A. F. *La Crise mondiale. Asie contre Europe.* Paris: Plon, 1932.

Lepage, Marcel. *La Tragique Épopée de la colonne Lepage.* Paris: NEL, 1981.

Lévesque, Jacques. *Le conflit sino-soviétique.* PUF, 1979.

Lew, Roland. *1949, Mao prend le pouvoir.* Brussels: Éd. Complexe, 1999.

Liauzu, Claude. *Colonisés and anticolonialistes.* Paris: L'Harmattan, 1982.

Lin Hua. *Chiang Kai-Shek, de Gaulle contre Ho Chi Minh. Vietnam 1945–1946.* Paris: L'Harmattan, 1994.

Maitron, Jean. *Dictionnaire biographique du mouvement ouvrier français.* Paris: Éd. Ouvrières, 1987.

Maneli, Mieczyslaw. *War of the Vanquished.* New York: Harper & Row, 1971

Mantienne, Frédéric. *Les relations politiques et commerciales entre la France et la péninsule indochinoise (XVIIè siècle).* Paris: Les Indes savantes, 2001.

Marchaisse, Thierry et al. (eds.). *Dépayser la pensée. Dialogues hétérotopiques avec François Jullien sur son usage philosophique de la China.* Paris: Les Empêcheurs de Penser en Rond, 2003.

Marr, David. *Vietnamese Anticolonialism*. Berkeley and Los Angeles: University of California Press, 1971.

Vietnam 1945: The Quest for Power. Berkeley and Los Angeles: University of California Press, 1995.

Mazuy, Rachel. *Croire plutôt que voir? Voyages en Russie soviétique 1919–1939*. Paris: Odile Jacob, 2002.

McLane, Charles B. *Soviet Strategies in South East Asia*. Princeton, N.J.: Princeton University Press, 1966.

McNamara, Robert. *In Retrospect: The Tragedy and Lessons of Vietnam*. New York: Times Books, 1995.

Mercier, Fabienne. *Vichy face à Chiang Kai-shek. Histoire diplomatique*. Paris: L'Harmattan, 1995.

Merle, Marcel (ed.). *L'anticolonialisme européen de Las Casas à Marx*. Paris: A. Colin, 1969.

Messmer, Pierre. *Après tant de batailles*. Paris: Albin Michel, 1998.

Missoffe, François. *Duel rouge*. Paris: Ramsay, 1977

Moreau, René. *8 ans otage chez les Viets, 1946–1954*. Paris: Pygmalion-Gérard Watelet, 1982.

Morlat, Patrice. *La répression coloniale au Vietnam*. Paris: L'Harmattan, 1990.

Les Affaires politiques de l'Indochine (1898–1922). Les grand commis du savoir au pouvoir. Paris: L'Harmattan, 1996.

Indochine années vingt: Le balcon de la France sur le Pacifique. Paris: Les Indes savantes, 2002.

Mus, Paul. *Viet-Nam sociologie d'une guerre*. Paris: Seuil, 1952.

Neuberg, A. (ed.). *L'Insurrection Armée*. Paris: Maspéro, 1970.

Ngo Van. *Au pays de la cloche fêlée. Les tribulations d'un Cochinchinois à l'époque coloniale*. Paris: l'Insomniaque, 2000.

Le joueur de flûte et l'Oncle Hô. Paris: Éds. Paris-Mediterranée, 2005.

Ngo Van Chieu. *Journal d'un combattant Viet-Minh*. Paris: Seuil, 1955

Nguyen Manh Tuong. *Un excommunié. Hanoi 1954–1991: Procès d'un intellectuel*. Paris: Que Me, 1992.

Nguyen Phu Duc. *Viet-Nam. Pourquoi les États-Unis ont-ils perdu la guerre?* Paris: Godefroy de Bouillon, 1996.

Nguyen The Anh. *Monarchie et fait colonial au Viet Nam (1875–1925). Le crépuscule d'un ordre traditionnel*. Paris: L'Harmattan, 1992.

Patti, Archimedes L. A. *Why Vietnam? Prelude to America's Albatross*. Berkeley and Los Angeles: University of California Press, 1980.

Phan Thien Chau. *Vietnamese Communism. A Research Bibliography*. London: Greenwood Press, 1975.

Pike, Douglas. *History of Vietnamese Communism, 1925–1976*. Stanford: Stanford University Press, 1978.

Vietnam and the Soviet Union: Anatomy of an Alliance. Boulder, Colo.: Westview Press, 1987.

Pilleul, Gilbert (ed.). *De Gaulle et l'Indochine. 1940–1946*. Paris: Institut Charles de Gaulle, Plon, 1982.

Porter, Gareth (ed.). *Vietnam: The Definitive Documentation of Human Decisions*. New York: Coleman Enterprises, 1979.

Qiang Zhai. *China and the Vietnam Wars, 1950–1975*. Chapel Hill: University of North Carolina Press, 2000.

Renouvin, Pierre. *La Question d'Extrême-Orient, 1840–1940*. Paris: Hachette, 1946.

Roussel, Marine. "Le Culte de Ho Chi Minh à Hanoi et ses environs. Entre instrumentalisation politique et ferveur populaire. Acteurs, Modalité, Enjeux."

Mimeographed Master's thesis in Anthropology. Université Paris X-Nanterre, 2005.

Roy, M. N. *Men I Met*. New Delhi: Lalvani Publishing House, 1968.

Ruscio, Alain. *Les communistes français and la guerre d'Indochine, 1944–1954*. Paris: L'Harmattan, 1985.

Dien Bien Phu, la fin d'une illusion. Paris: L'Harmattan, 1987.

La guerre française d'Indochine. Brussels: Éd. Complexe, 1992.

(ed.). *La guerre française d'Indochine (1945–1954). Les sources de la connaissance. Bibliographie, filmographie, documents divers*. Paris: Les Indes savantes, 2002.

Sacks, Isaac Milton. "Marxism in Vietnam," in *Marxism in South East Asia: A Study of Four Countries*. Frank Trager (ed.). Stanford, Calif.: Stanford University Press, 1959.

Sainteny, Jean. *Histoire d'une paix manquée: Indochine 1945–1947*. Paris: Fayard, 1954.

Salan, Raoul. *Mémoires, t. 1: Fin d'un empire, le sens d'un engagement, juin 1899–septembre 1946*. Paris: Presses de la Cité, 1970.

Mémoires, t. 2: Fin d'un empire, Le Viet Minh, mon adversaire, octobre 1946–octobre 1954. Paris: Presses de la Cité, 1971.

Schoenbrun, David. *As France Goes*. New York: Harper & Bros, 1957.

Schwartz, Benjamin. *The World of Thought in Ancient China*. Cambridge, Mass.: Harvard University, Belknap Press, 1989.

Sergent, Pierre. *Un étrange Monsieur Frey*. Paris: Fayard, 1982.

Shipway, Martin. *The Road to War. France and Vietnam. 1944–1947*. Oxford: Berghahn Books, 1997.

Shultz, Richard H., Jr. *The Secret War Against Hanoi: The Untold Story of Spies, Saboteurs and Covert Warriors in North Vietnam*. New York: Perennial, Harper Collins, 2000.

Smedley, Agnès (ed.). *La Longue Marche: Mémoires du maréchal Zhu De*. 2 vols. Paris: Presses de l'Imprimerie nationale, 1969.

Smith, Ralph B. *An International History of the Vietnam War*. vols. New York: St. Martin's Press, 1983, 1985, 1986.

Sokolov, Anatoli. *The Communist International and Vietnam* (in Russian). Moscow: 1998. Translated into Vietnamese and published as *Quoc te cong san va Viet Nam*. Hanoi: CTQG, 1999.

Tarling, Nicholas. *Britain, Southeast Asia and the Onset of the Cold War, 1945–1950*. Cambridge: Cambridge University Press, 1998.

Tertrais, Hughes. *La Piastre et le fusil. Le coût de la guerre d'Indochine. 1945–1954*. Paris: CHÉFF, 2002.

Thai Quang Trung. *Collective Leadership and Factionalism: An Essay on Ho Chi Minh's Legacy*. Singapore: ISEAS, 1985.

Thayer, Carlyle A. *War by Other Means: National Liberation and Revolution in Vietnam 1954–1960*. Sydney: Allen & Unwin, 1989.

Thierry d'Argenlieu, Georges. *Chronique d'Indochine. 1945–1947*. Paris: Albin Michel, 1985.

Ton That Thien. *The Foreign Politics of the Communist Party of Vietnam: A Study of Communist Tactics*. New York: Crane Russak, 1989.

Tønnesson, Stein. *The Vietnamese Revolution of 1945: Roosevelt, Ho Chi Minh, and de Gaulle in a World at War*. London: Sage Publications, 1991.

Tréglodé, Benoît de. *Héros and Révolution au Viet Nam*. Paris: L'Harmattan, 2001.

Trinh Van Thao. *Vietnam, du Confucianisme au Marxisme. Un essai d'itinéraire intellectuel*. Paris: L'Harmattan, 1990.

Les compagnons de route de Ho Chi Minh. Histoire d'un engagement intellectuel au Viet-Nam. Paris: Karthala, 2003.

Turner, Robert. *Vietnamese Communism: Its origins and Development*. Stanford: Stanford University Press, 1975.

Turpin, Frederic. *De Gaulle, les gaullistes et l'Indochine, 1940–1956*. Paris: Les Indes savantes, 2005.

Valette, Jacques. *Indochine 1940–1945. Français contre Japonais*. Paris: Sedes, 1993.

La guerre d'Indochine 1945–1954. Paris: A. Colin, 1994.

Vichniakova-Akimova, Vera. *Two Years in Revolutionary China (1925–1927)*. Cambridge, Mass.: Harvard University Press, 1971.

Viollis, Andrée. *Indochine SOS*. Paris: Gallimard, "NRF," 1935; 2d ed. Paris: Les Éditeurs Français Réunis, 1949.

Wall, Irving. *L'influence américaine sur la politique française. 1945–1954*. Paris: Balland, 1989.

Wang Fanxi. *Mémoires d'un révolutionnaire chinois*. Montreuil: Éd. La Brèche, 1987.

Wang, Nora. *Émigration and politique. Les étudiants-ouvriers chinois en France 1919–1925*. Paris: Les Indes savantes, 2002.

Werner, Jayne. *Peasants, Politics, and Religious Sectarianism: Peasant and Priest in the Cao Dai in Vietnam*. New Haven, Conn.: Yale University Southeast Asian Studies, Monograph 23, 1981.

and Luu Doan Huynh (eds). *The Vietnam War: Vietnamese and American Perspectives*. New York and London: M. E. Sharpe, 1993.

Werth, Nicolas. *Histoire de l'Union soviétique*. 5th ed. Paris: PUF, 2001.

Wolikow, Serge (ed.). *Komintern: L'histoire et les hommes. Dictionnaire biographique de l'Internationale communiste*. Paris: Les Éditions de l'Atelier, 2001.

Woodside, Alexander B. *Community and Revolution in Modern Vietnam*. Boston: Houghton Mifflin, 1976.

Xuan Phuong, *Ao Dai, du Couvent des oiseaux à la jungle du Viet Minh*. Paris: Plon, 2001. Translated into English as *Ao Dai: My War, My Country, My Vietnam*. Great Neck, N.Y.: Emquad International, 2004.

Yacine, Kateb. *L'homme aux sandales de caoutchouc*. Paris: Seuil, 1970. A play about the grand scope of Vietnamese history, not the history of Ho Chi Minh himself.

Yang Kuisong in "Mao Zedong and the War in Indochina," in *New Evidence on China, Southeast Asia, and the Vietnam War*. Working papers of the International Workshop held at the University of Hong Kong, 11–12 January 2000, in conjunction with the Cold War International History Project (Washington, D.C.).

Young, Marilyn. *The Vietnam Wars: 1945–1990*. New York: Harper Collins, 1991.

Zasloff, Joseph J., and Brown MacAlister. *Communism in Indochina*. Lexington, Mass.: Lexington Books, 1975.

Zhang Fakui. *Oral History*. In Columbia University Library, New York.

Zinoman, Peter. *The Colonial Bastille: A History of Imprisonment in Vietnam. 1862–1940*. Berkeley and Los Angeles: University of California Press, 2001.

In quoc ngu

Army Historical Research Committee, eds. *Lich su Quan doi Nhan Zan* [History of the People's Army of Vietnam]. Vol. 1. Hanoi: NXB QDNZ/People's Army Publishing House, 1977.

Bich Tung Ly Dao. *Nho Nguon, Hoi ky cach mang cua mot so dong chi hoat dong o Van Nam va Quang Tay, Trung Quoc, 1930–1945* [Recollections of the beginnings, revolutionary recollections of some comrades in Yunnan and Guangxi, China]. Hanoi: VZT, 1992.

Cao Van Luan. *Ben giong Lich su. Hoi Ky 1940–1965* [In the course of history: Recollections 1945–1965]. Glendale, Calif.: Dai Nam, 1976.

Chu Van Lam, *Hop tac xa nong ghiep Viet Nam. Lich su, to chuc va lien vong* [Agricultural cooperatives in Vietnam: History, organization, and perspectives]. Hanoi: Su That, 1992.

Chu Van Tan. *Ky niem ve Cuu Quoc Quan* [Reminiscences on the Army for National Salvation]. Hanoi: 1971. English translation by Mai Elliott, *Reminiscences on the Army for National Salvation: Memoir of General Chu Van Tan*. Ithaca, N.Y.: Cornell University Southeast Asia Program, 1974.

Dang Huu Thu. *Than The va su nghiep nha cach mang Nguyen The Truyen* [The person and activities of the revolutionary Nguyen The Truyen]. Melun: Self-published, 1993.

Dau nguon [The spring]. Recollections by several authors. Hanoi: Van Hoc, 1977.

Doan Them. *Nhung ngay chua quen* [Memorable days]. Glendale, Calif.: Dai Nam, 1976.

Duong Ho Chi Minh. Hoi ky Truong son [The Ho Chi Minh Trail: Memories of the Annamite cordillera]. Hanoi: Tac Pham Moi, 1982.

Ho An and Nguyen Van Thanh. *Le Duan. Mot nha lanh dao loi lac mot tu duy sang tao lon cua cach mang Viet Nam* [Le Duan, an eminent leader and a great thinker of the Vietnamese revolution]. Hanoi: NXB CTQG, 2002.

Ho Huu Tuong. *41 nam lam bao* [41 years of journalism]. Saigon: 1972.

Hoang Cam. *Chang duong Muoi nghin ngay* [A journey of a thousand days]. Hanoi: QDNZ, 2001.

Hoang Van Hoan. *Giot nuoc trong bien ca* [A drop of water in the ocean]. Beijing: FLP, 1986. Published in English as *A Drop in the Ocean: Revolutionary Reminiscences*. Beijing: FLP, 1988.

Le Quoc Su. *Chuyen ke Le Hong Phong va Nguyen Thi Minh Khai*. [The history of Le Hong Phong and Nguyen Thi Minh Khai]. Ho Chi Minh City: 2001.

Le Trong Tan. *Tu Dong Quan den Dien Bien Phu* [From Dong Quan to Dien Bien Phu]. Hanoi: NXB QDNZ, 2002.

Le Tung Son. *Nhat ky mot chang duong* [Journal of one stage]. Hanoi: Van Hoc, 1978.

Le Van Hien. *Chuyen cong can dac biet* [Account of a special mission]. NXB Danang, 1986.

Nhat ky cua mot Bo truong [Journal of a minister]. 2 vols. (1947–48, 1949–51). NXB Danang, 1995.

Ngon Duoc [The torch]. Hanoi: Van hoa, 1980.

Nguyen Hien Le. *Hoi Ky* [Memoirs]. Ho Chi Minh City: 1993.

Nguyen Khac Phe. *Hoa si Le Van Mien* [The painter Le Van Mien]. Hue: 1997.

Nguyen Van Khoan (ed.). *Viet Minh Hoang Zieu* [The Vietminh and Hanoi]. Ho Chi Minh City: 2001.

Nguyen Van Tran. *Viet cho Me va Quoc Hoi* [Written for my mother and for the National Assembly]. Stanton, Calif.: Van Nghe, 1995.

Nguyen Vy. *Tuan, chang trai nuoc Viet* [Tuan, a Vietnamese boy]. Glendale, Calif.: Dai Nam, 1976.

Pham Duy. *Hoi Ky Thoi Cach Mang Khang Chien* [Recollections of the revolution and the resistance]. 3 vols. California: PDC, 1989.

Pham Khac Hoe. *Tu Trieu dinh Hue den Chien khu Viet Bac* [From the court in Hué to the Resistance Zone of the Viet Bac]. Hue: 1987.

Phan Boi Chau. *Mémoires*. Translation and commentary by Georges Boudarel in *France-Asie* 194–95 (1968) and *Phan Boi Chau et la société vietnamienne de son temps in France-Asie* 199 (1969).

Phan Boi Chau Toan Tap [Complete writings of Phan Boi Chau]. 12 vols. Hue: 1990.

Son Nam. *Hoi Ky 2. O Chien khu 9* [Reminiscences 2: In Zone 9 of the resistance]. Ho Chi Minh City: 2002.

Ta Quang Buu. *Nha tri thuc giu Nuoc va cach mang* [An intellectual defender of the country and the revolution].

Thu Trang. *Nhung Hoat dong cua Phan Chu Trinh* [The activities of Phan Chu Trinh]. Paris: Sudest Asie, 1980.

To Hoai. *Cat bui chan ai*. [Dusts of sand, at one's feet] Hanoi: Hoi Nha Van, 1992.

Tran Dan. *Ghi. 1954–1960* [Notes, 1954–1960]. Stanton, Calif.: Van Nghe, 2000.

Tran Do. *Ben song don sung* [Receiving arms on the river bank]. First published in 1945. Hanoi: Thanh Nien, reissued 1976.

Tran Huy Lieu. *Hoi Ky* [Memoirs]. Hanoi: 1991.

Tran Kiem Qua. *Hoang Ha nho Hong Ha Thuong* [Memories of the beloved Hong Ha Thuong]. Hanoi: Van Hoc, 2001.

Tran Trong Kim. *Mot con gio bui* [In the tempest]. Saigon: Vinh Son, 1969.

Uong nuoc nho nguon [We remember the spring where we drank]. Hanoi: Quan Doi Nhan Zan, 1978.

Van Tao and Furuta Moto (eds.). *Nan doi 1945 o Viet Nam. Nhung chung tich Lich su* [Historical accounts of the famine of 1945 in Vietnam]. Hanoi: 1995.

Vien Kinh Te [Institute of Economics in Hanoi]. *Kinh te Viet Nam 1945–1960* [The economy of Vietnam]. Hanoi: Su That, 1960.

Viet Phuong, *Cua mo*. Hanoi: Van Hoc, July 1989.

Vo Nguyen Giap. *Nhung chang duong lich su* [Stages of history]. Hanoi: Van hoc, 1977.

Duong toi Dien Bien Phu. Hoi uc [The road towards Dien Bien Phu. Reminiscences]. Hanoi: NXB QDNZ, 1999.

Nhung Nam thang khong the nao quen [Five unforgettable months]. Hanoi: NXB QDNZ, 2001.

Chien dau trong Vong vay [Fighting against the siege]. Hanoi: NXB QDNZ, 2001. A French translation of this work was published in 2003 as *Mémoires de Vo Nguyen Giap, t. 1: la résistance encerclée*. Paris: Anako, 2003.

Vu Thu Hien. *Dem giua ban ngay. Hoi ky chinh tri cua mot nguoi khong lam chinh tri* [Darkness at noon]. Stanton, Calif.: Van Nghe, 1997.

Vuong Hong Sen. *Hon nua doi hu* [Half of a ruined life]. Ho Chi Minh City: 1992.

Vuong Thua Vu. *Truong thanh trong chien dau* [Forged in battle]. Hanoi: 1979.

Index